RD PIPES

A Concise History of

the Russian Revolution

Richard Pipes, Baird Professor of History at Harvard University, is the author of numerous books and essays on Russia, past and present. His most recent book is *Russia under the Bolshevik Regime* (1994). In 1981–82 he served as President Reagan's National Security Council adviser on Soviet and East European affairs, and he has twice received a Guggenheim fellowship. He lives in Cambridge, Massachusetts.

*A Concise History of
the Russian Revolution*

1. Lenin, March 1919.

A CONCISE
HISTORY
OF THE
RUSSIAN
REVOLUTION

Richard Pipes

Vintage Books
A Division of Random House, Inc.
New York

FIRST VINTAGE BOOKS EDITION, DECEMBER 1996

Copyright © 1995 by Richard Pipes
Maps copyright © 1990, 1995 by Bernhard H. Wagner

All rights reserved under International and Pan-American
Copyright Conventions. Published in the United States by
Vintage Books, a division of Random House, Inc., New York, and
simultaneously in Canada by Random House of Canada Limited,
Toronto. Originally published in hardcover by Alfred A. Knopf,
Inc., New York, in 1995.

This work is a condensation of two volumes published originally
by Alfred A. Knopf, Inc., as: *The Russian Revolution*, copyright
© 1990 by Richard Pipes, and *Russia under the Bolshevik Regime*,
copyright © 1994 by Richard Pipes

The Library of Congress has cataloged the Knopf edition as follows:
  Pipes, Richard.
    A concise history of the Russian Revolution / Richard Pipes.
  — 1st ed.
    p.   cm.
    Abridged version of *The Russian Revolution* and of *Russia
  under the Bolshevik Regime*.
    Includes bibliographical references and index.
    ISBN 0-679-42277-3
      1. Soviet Union—History—Revolution, 1917–1921.
    2. Russia—History—Nicholas II, 1894–1917. I. Pipes,
  Richard. Russian Revolution. II. Title.
    DK265.P4742   1995
    947.084'1—dc20   95-3127   CIP
Vintage ISBN: 0-679-74544-0

Book design by Anthea Lingeman

Random House Web address: http://www.randomhouse.com/

Printed in the United States of America
10 9 8 7 6 5 4 3 2 1

To Mark, Sarah, and Anna

Contents

Illustrations

MAPS

Introduction

The word "revolution" has an interesting etymology. When asked by Soviet sociologists what it meant to them, Russian peasants responded "*samovol'shchina*," or, roughly, "doing what you want." In modern advertising, "revolutionary" has come to mean "radically new," and hence, by implication, "improved." When used in everyday speech, it is another way of saying "drastically different." From such usage one would hardly suspect that the word had its origins in astronomy and astrology.

"Revolution" derives from the Latin verb *revolvere*, "to revolve." It was originally applied to the motions of the planets. Copernicus called his great treatise which displaced the earth from the center of the universe, *On the Revolutions of Celestial Bodies*. From astronomy, the word passed into the vocabulary of astrologers, who claimed the ability to predict the future from the study of the heavens. Sixteenth-century astrologers serving princes and generals spoke of "revolution" to designate abrupt and unforeseen events determined by the conjunction of planets—that is, by forces beyond human control. Thus the original scientific meaning of the word, conveying regularity and repetitiveness, came, when referring to human affairs, to signify the very opposite, namely, the sudden and unpredictable.

The word was first applied to politics in England in 1688–89, to describe the overthrow of James II in favor of William III and Mary. As the price for his crown, the new king had to sign a Declaration of Rights by which he committed himself not to suspend laws or levy taxes without parliamentary approval, thus inaugurating a process that would end in the triumph of popular sovereignty in England. This was "the Glorious Revolution." It affected only the country's political constitution.

The American Revolution a century later had broader implications, in that it both asserted the country's independence and altered the relationship between the individual and the state. It combined the principles of popular sovereignty and personal liberty with what came to be known as the right to national self-determination. But even so, it confined itself to politics. The culture of the United States, its judiciary system, its guarantees of life and property—all inherited from Great Britain—remained unaffected by the Revolution.

The first modern revolution was the French. In its initial phase it was largely spontaneous and unconscious: In June 1789, when the representatives of the three estates swore the Tennis Court Oath, an act of defiance that launched the Revolution, they spoke not of revolution but of "national regeneration." But in time, the leadership of rebellious France passed into the hands of ideologues who saw in the collapse of the monarchy a unique opportunity to realize the ideals of the Enlightenment—ideals that went far beyond the limited political scope of the English and American revolutions, aspiring to nothing less than the creation of a new social order and even a new breed of human beings. During the reign of the Jacobins, measures were conceived and sometimes enacted that in their boldness of conception and brutality of execution anticipated the Communist regime in Russia. "Revolution" henceforth began to refer to grandiose plans to transform the world—no longer to changes that happened but to changes that were made.

Nineteenth-century Europe witnessed the emergence of professional revolutionaries, intellectuals who devoted themselves full-time to studying the history of past upheavals in quest of tactical guidelines, analyzing their own time for signs of coming upheavals, and, once they occurred, stepping in to direct spontaneous rebellion into conscious revolution. Such radical intellectuals saw the future as marked by violent disturbances, and progress as requiring the destruction of the traditional system of human relations. Their objective was to set free the "true" human nature suppressed by private property and the institutions to which it gave rise. Radical communists and anarchists imagined the coming revolution as thoroughly transforming not only every political and socioeconomic order previously known, but human existence itself. Its aim, in the words of Leon Trotsky, was "overturning the world."

This trend reached its culmination in the Russian Revolution of 1917. Although the breakdown of the Russian monarchy was due to domestic causes, the Bolsheviks, who emerged the winners of the post-tsarist struggle for power, were internationalists consumed by ideas common to radical intellectuals in the West. They seized power to change not Russia but the world. They regarded their own country, the "weakest link in the chain of imperialism," as nothing more than a springboard for a global upheaval that would completely alter the human condition and, as it were, reenact the sixth day of Creation.

The causes of post-1789 revolutions have been many and complex. The impulse of twentieth-century observers, influenced as they are by socialist and sociological ways of thinking, is to attribute them to grievances of the population at large. The assumption is that they were acts of desperation and as such beyond judgment. This view exerts strong attraction in Anglo-Saxon countries, where ideologies have never played a prominent role. But the notion that every revolution that happens is inevitable and therefore justified holds true only in a limited sense. Obviously, in a country whose government accurately reflects the wishes of the majority of the people, peacefully yielding office when it loses the people's confidence, and where the people live in reasonable prosperity, violent revolutions are unnecessary and hence unlikely; every election is a peaceful revolution of sorts. But this obvious truth does not imply its opposite: that where violent upheavals do occur, the population desires a complete change of the political and economic system—that is, a "revolution" in the Jacobin and Bolshevik sense of the word. Historians have noted that popular rebellions are conservative, their objective being a restitution of traditional rights of which the population feels itself unjustly deprived. Rebellions look backward. They are also specific and limited in scope. The *cahiers des doléances* (lists of complaints) submitted by French peasants in 1789 and, under a different name, by Russian peasants in 1905, dealt exclusively with concrete grievances, all of them capable of being satisfied within the existing system.

It is radical intellectuals who translate these concrete complaints into an all-consuming destructive force. They desire not reforms but a complete obliteration of the present in order to create a world order that has never existed except in a mythical Golden Age. Professional revolutionaries, mostly of middle-class background, scorn the modest demands of the "masses," whose true interests they alone claim to understand. It is they who transform popular rebellions into revolutions by insisting that nothing can be changed for the better unless everything is changed. This philosophy, in which idealism inextricably blends with a lust for power, opens the floodgates to permanent turmoil. And since ordinary people require for their survival a stable and predictable environment, all post-1789 revolutions have ended in failure.

The existence of popular grievances is thus a necessary but not sufficient explanation of revolutions, which require the infusion of radical ideas. The upheavals that shook Russia after February 1917 were made possible by the breakdown of public order under the strains of a world war with which the existing government could not cope. What drove the country into the uncharted waters of extreme utopianism was the fanaticism of intellectuals who in October 1917 took advantage of the spreading anarchy to seize power in the name of the "people" without daring even once, either then or during the next seventy years, to secure a popular mandate.

The Russian Revolution was arguably the most important event of the century now drawing to a close. It not only played a major part in preventing the restoration of peace after World War I, it had a direct bearing on the rise in Germany of National-Socialism and the outbreak of World War II, which the triumph of Nazism made inevitable. In the half century that followed Allied victory in World War II, the Communist regime that had emerged from the Revolution kept the world in a state of permanent tension that at times threatened to result in yet another global conflict. All this now seems safely relegated to the past. Yet to prevent it from recurring, it is essential to know how such things happened; for implicit in the history of all modern revolutions, but especially the Russian, is the momentous question of whether human reason is capable of leading humanity from its known imperfections to an imagined perfectibility. The incontrovertible failure of the Russian Revolution in 1991, when the Soviet Union fell apart and its Communist Party was outlawed, can be interpreted as conclusive proof that utopianism inevitably leads to its very opposite, that the quest for paradise on earth ends in hell; but it can also be seen as merely a temporary setback in mankind's quest for an ideal existence.

To the author of these lines, who has studied the subject for most of his life, the Russian Revolution appears as the unfolding of a tragedy in which events follow with inexorable force from the mentality and character of the protagonists. It may offer comfort to some to think of it as the result of grand economic or social forces and hence "inevitable." But "objective" conditions are an abstraction; they do not act. They merely provide the background to subjective decisions made by a relatively small number of men professionally active in politics and war. Events appear "inevitable" only in retrospect. The documents on which the story that follows is based show only human individuals pursuing their own interests and aspirations, incapable or unwilling to make allowances for the interests and aspirations of others. There were many times when the author felt tempted to admonish the protagonists to stop and think as they rushed before his eyes headlong toward a catastrophe that in the end would engulf them all, victors and vanquished alike. One emerges humbler from the experience, and less sanguine about humanity's capacity to change itself.

The present book is a précis of my *Russian Revolution* (1990) and *Russia under the Bolshevik Regime* (1994). These two books describe in detail and with full documentation the history of Russia's "Time of Troubles" between 1899 and 1924. Granted that the interest of history lies in details, many readers concerned with the subject cannot find the time to read two volumes totaling 1,300 pages supported by 4,500 references. It is with them in mind that I wrote *The Concise History*. The book follows closely the pattern of the two volumes, omitting what can be omitted, condensing the rest, and limiting references to the barest minimum.* All the information in this volume can be verified with reference to the two books from which it is derived. In the few instances where new information is introduced, I have indicated the sources.

Richard Pipes

---

* The sequence of the first four chapters of *The Russian Revolution* has been altered, and Chapter 5 of *Russia under the Bolshevik Regime* ("Communism, Fascism, National-Socialism") has been omitted. The concluding section of *The Russian Revolution*, "Reflections on the Russian Revolution," has been reproduced with almost no changes.

RUSSIAN EMPIRE CIRCA 1900

Franz-Josef-Land

GERMAN EMPIRE

SWEDEN

NORWAY

A R C

Berlin

BALTIC SEA

Gulf of Bothnia

BARENTS SEA

Vienna

AUSTRIA-HUNGARY
Budapest

Warsaw

Poland

Revel

Riga

Finland

Helsingfors (Helsinki)

St. Petersburg (Petrograd)

Murmansk

Novaia Zemlia

Vilno

Brest-Litovsk

Pskov

Novgorod

WHITE SEA

Archangel

KARA SEA

SERBIA

Minsk

Smolensk

Northern Dvina

Sofia

BULGARIA

ROMANIA
Bucharest

Kiev

Dnieper

Briansk

Moscow

Vologda

Arctic Circle

Odessa

Poltava

Riazan

Nizhnii Novgorod

U r a l   M o u n t a i n s

Ob

West

Constantinople (Istanbul)

Kharkov

Lipetsk

Volga

Perm

Gallipoli

Sevastopol

Crimea

Donetsk

Penza

Kazan

Siberia

BLACK SEA

SEA OF AZOV

Saratov

Simbirsk

Samara

Ekaterinburg (Sverdlovsk)

Tobolsk

Ob

O T T O M A N   E M P I R E

Stavropol

Don

Tsaritsyn (Volgograd)

Ufa

R U S S I A

Ural

Orenburg

Orsk

Irtysh

Ishim

Transiberian Railroad

Omsk

Tomsk

Caucasus Mts.

Astrakhan

Tiflis (Tblisi)

Erivan

CASPIAN SEA

Baku

Novonikolaevsk (Novosibirsk)

Baghdad

ARAL SEA

Turkestan

Barnaul

Semipalatinsk

Tehran

Askhabad

Amu Daria

Syr Daria

Bukhara

Lake Balkhash

PERSIA

Samarkand

Tashkent

Vernyi

Ili

Fergana

AFGHANISTAN

Kabul

BRITISH INDIA

0   200   400   600   800   1000 Miles

PART ONE

The Agony of the Old Regime

RUSSIA IN 1900

A t the turn of the twentieth century, Russia exhibited striking contrasts. A French scholar of the time, Anatole Leroy-Beaulieu, compared her to "one of those castles, constructed at different epochs, where the most discordant styles are seen side by side, or else those houses, built piecemeal and at intervals, which never have either the unity or convenience of dwellings erected on one plan and at one rush." Eighty percent of the population consisted of peasants who in the Great Russian provinces led lives not significantly different from those of their ancestors in the Middle Ages. At the other extreme were writers, artists, composers, and scientists fully at home in the West. A vigorous capitalist economy—Russia at the time led the world in the production of petroleum and the export of grain—coexisted with a regime of political censorship and arbitrary police rule. Russia claimed the status of a great world power, an ally of democratic France, and yet she maintained an autocratic regime that granted the population no voice in government and severely punished any expressions of discontent with the status quo. Alone of the great powers, she had neither constitution nor parliament. These contradictions gave the impression of impermanence—the sense, at any rate among the educated, that things could not possibly go on like this much longer and that with the advent of the new century, Russia would leap into modernity, catching up with western

Europe and perhaps even outstripping her. For reasons that will be spelled out below, the peasants also expected great changes, although of an economic rather than a political nature. The feeling, voiced by another French visitor, Jules Legras, that Russia seemed somehow "unfinished" reflected the expectations of change which filled some with excitement and others with apprehension.

The Peasantry

A griculture provided the economic and social basis of late-tsarist Russia. Approximately four-fifths of her population consisted of peasants who tilled the land and, in the northern provinces, also pursued industrial side occupations. A balloonist flying over central Russia would have seen an endless landscape of cultivated fields, divided into narrow strips, interspersed with forests and meadows, scattered among which, every five to ten kilometers, lay villages of wooden huts. Cities were small and far between.

To an extent inconceivable in the West, Russia's rural population was a world unto itself. It was integrated neither into society at large nor into the administrative machinery. Its relationship to the officialdom and the educated class resembled that of the natives of Africa or Asia to their colonial rulers. The peasantry remained loyal to the culture of old Muscovy and lived untouched by the Westernization to which Peter the Great had subjected the country's elite. Russian peasants wore beards, spoke their own idiom, followed their own logic, pursued their own interests, and felt nothing in common with the beardless agents of authority or landed gentry who exacted from them taxes, rents, and recruits, giving nothing in return. They owed loyalty exclusively to their village, or, at most, to its canton (*volost'*).

Until 1861, about one-half of the Russian peasants were serfs, subject to the arbitrary authority of their landlords. (The other half consisted of state and crown peasants, administered by government officials.) Although serfs lacked civil rights, they were not slaves. For one, they were not supposed to be publicly traded. Also, they worked not on plantations but on individual allotments, a portion of which they tilled for the landlord as their rent payment (if they did not pay it in cash or produce) and the rest for themselves; what they grew on their own allotments was theirs to consume or sell. Essentially, they were tied to the soil and met their obligations to the landlord either by performing labor

2. Russian peasants, late nineteenth century.

(customarily, three days a week) or by paying him rent. Although not protected by the courts, they enjoyed safeguards provided by customary law which neither landlords nor officials felt free to ignore.

In February 1861, Tsar Alexander II signed a decree that instantly liberated the serfs, giving them land and providing them with the equivalent of forty-nine-year mortgages with which to compensate their onetime landlords for the acreage they had lost. The principal legacy of serfdom, which had lasted for over 250 years, was to estrange the peasant from society at large and imbue him with the feeling that the world was a lawless place in which one survived by force and cunning. This mentality made it very difficult to mold him into a citizen.

The life of the Russian peasantry revolved around three institutions: the household (*dvor*), the village (*derevnia* or *selo*), and the commune (*mir* or *obshchina*).

The household, the basic unit of Russian rural life, was a joint family: father and mother, unmarried daughters, and married sons with their wives and children. It typically had between six and ten members. Under the climatic conditions prevailing in Russia, with a short growing season that called for extremely intensive but brief bursts of work in the spring and fall, large households fared better than small ones. The household was organized in a strictly autocratic manner, with its head—called the *bol'shak*—enjoying complete authority over its members and their belongings. On his death, the *dvor* usually dissolved, the individuals dividing the common property and moving out to set up their own households. This practice made for a lack of continuity in Russian rural life. In sharp contrast to their counterparts in Western Europe and Japan, Russian villages were in constant flux.

Two features of the household require emphasis because they explain a great deal of the Russian peasant's social behavior. The individual member of a household had no private property (except for his personal effects), since all its belongings were at the disposal of the *bol'shak*. He also had no personal rights, his interests being subordinated to those of the joint family. Thus the Great Russian peasant had no opportunity to acquire a sense either of individual rights or of private ownership—qualities indispensable for modern citizenship. He was accustomed to living under the arbitrary authority of the *bol'shak* and to collective ownership of the means of production.

The Russian village was an agglomeration of log cabins lining both sides of a road running through it. It had no formal organs of self-government. The village headman (*starosta*) was appointed, often against his will, by government officials, and could be removed by them. In that sense, again in sharp contrast to the situation in Western Europe and Japan, the Russian village was fluid and unstructured.

The commune was not unique to Russia—similar institutions have been identified at earlier periods of history in other parts of the world. But by 1900, for all practical purposes, it could be found only in Russia. It was a system of organizing the holding and cultivation of land starkly different from modern conceptions of ownership.

The commune was an association of peasants entitled to a share of the land at the commune's disposal. Although it coincided in many respects with the village, it was not identical with it because villagers who did not have access to the communal land, such as rural teachers and priests, did not belong. In some regions a large village might have more than one commune. The commune subdivided the acreage at its disposal into many narrow strips. At various intervals, dictated by local custom, usually between ten and fifteen years, it "repartitioned" the strips among households to allow for the changes in their size brought about through deaths, births, and departures. The purpose of such reallotments was to

3. Village assembly.

ensure that every household had enough arable land to feed its members and meet its tax obligations. The strips were assigned on the basis of soil quality and distance from the village.

In 1900, in the central provinces of Russia, virtually all peasant households were organized into communes. In the borderlands of the empire—in what had been the Polish-Lithuanian Commonwealth, in the Ukraine, and the Cossack regions of the southeast—individual farms prevailed. Membership in a commune did not prevent its members, individually or in association, from buying noncommunal land in outright ownership from landlords or other private owners. On the eve of the Revolution, these peasant-proprietors held as much land as did landlords and merchants.

All affairs of the commune were settled by the village assembly, an all-male body composed of the heads of households. Decisions, reached unanimously, were binding on all. They dealt with such matters as the schedule of agricultural work, the allocation of taxes, and disputes between households. They also decided religious allegiances, and later, after Russia was given a parliament, political affiliations that committed all members to vote for the same party.

The commune had many drawbacks. The system of strip-farming wasted a great deal of the peasant's time by forcing him to move, with his draft animals and equipment, from strip to strip. Repartitions encouraged him to invest the least and extract the most out of the land, contributing

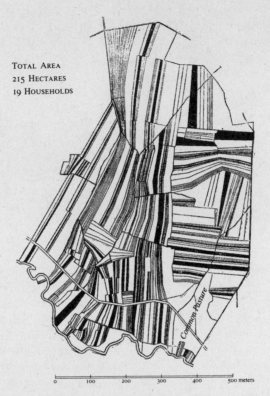

TOTAL AREA
215 HECTARES
19 HOUSEHOLDS

Common Pasture

0   100   200   300   400   500 meters

4. Strip-farming as practiced in central Russia, c. 1900.

to soil exhaustion. Finally, it maintained on the land unproductive peasant elements, inhibiting the growth of a vigorous yeomanry. Its egalitarianism leveled downward.

Nevertheless, the commune survived all challenges because it had the backing of both government officials and the peasants themselves. The government liked the commune, and passed laws that made withdrawal from it all but impossible, because it ensured the accurate payment of taxes and other state obligations, and promised (at any rate, in theory) to save Russia from massive rural unemployment. The peasant cleaved to it even more strongly. He held it as an article of religious faith that God had created land, like air and water, for the benefit of all mankind, for which reason it could be cultivated but not owned. The communal system ensured (again, in theory) that every peasant had access to an allotment of land. In his view, it was both fair and inevitable that all the land in Russia should be taken away from private owners and turned over to the communes. Russian peasants at the turn of the century confidently expected the Tsar any day to carry out such a grand national "repartition," and distribute to the communes all the land in private hands. It was this anticipation based on a retrospective belief in an age long past, when land had been available in unlimited quantities, that made the Russian peasant a potential recruit of revolutionary intellectuals.

There was general agreement at the turn of the century that Russia faced a grave and intensifying agrarian crisis due mainly to rural over-population. With an annual excess of fifteen to eighteen live births over deaths per 1,000 inhabitants, she had the highest population growth in Europe. An allotment of land which at the time of Emancipation in the 1860s had fed two mouths, forty years later had to feed three; the result was the emergence of a landless or land-poor rural class that the commune was meant to forestall. In the past, the Crown had provided fresh lands to its growing population by conquest. This it could no longer do, as the Empire had reached the utmost limits of easy enlargement and could continue to expand only at the risk of unleashing a general war. The peasant was too poor and too set in his ways to shift from extensive to intensive agriculture, which would have increased yields and enabled him to manage with less land. Industry, while expanding rapidly, could absorb only a fraction of the excess rural population. And overseas emigration, which had saved Europe from a similar predicament, was not a solution, in part because the Russian could not conceive of living in a country that did not profess the Orthodox faith and in part because, being used to communal life, he could not pull up his stakes and leave to seek his fortune abroad. So the population pressures intensified with each year, and with it the danger of a rural explosion.

Russia's industrial working class grew out of the peasantry. The majority of Russians classified as workers were part-time employees of railroads and textile firms hired seasonally, when they were not needed to help out with plowing or harvesting. The majority of Russian factories, for this reason, located not in the cities but in the countryside, to be near the labor force. Only in mining and the technologically advanced industries, such as metallurgy and machine-building, centered in the Urals, the Ukraine and St. Petersburg, did there develop a class of full-time skilled workers, separated from the village both economically and psychologically. In all, Russia at the turn of the century probably had no more than 1 million full-time factory workers, compared with some 100 million peasants. Tsarist legislation forbade the workers to organize into unions, and even modest efforts to form educational circles or mutual help associations met with severe punishment.

The mind of the Russian peasant, crucial as it was for the history of modern Russia, has not been seriously studied: intellectuals seem to have regarded the peasant as a backward creature, deliberately kept in ignorance by his masters, and therefore unworthy of serious attention. But what urban intellectuals took for ignorance was, in fact, a kind of intelligence adapted to the conditions under which the peasant had to live—namely, a harsh climate and a government that treated him exclusively as an object of exploitation. He was entirely self-reliant and counted on no one, not even fellow peasants. Of his patriotism, Leo Tolstoy had this to say:

> I have never heard any expressions of patriotic sentiments from the people, but I have, on the contrary, frequently heard the most serious and respectable men from among the masses give utterance to the most absolute indifference or even contempt for all kinds of manifestations of patriotism.

The peasant's religious sentiments and inborn xenophobia made it possible to arouse him against foreign invaders. But it provided no grounds for an appeal for sacrifices on behalf of the nation. During the Revolution and Civil War, Russian generals met with nothing but disappointment when they attempted to rally the peasants against the Communists with patriotic slogans; Communist appeals to class resentment and greed proved much more effective.

As late as the eighteenth century, the Western European peasant did not much differ from his Russian counterpart at the beginning of the twentieth. But a number of innovations introduced in the nineteenth century transformed Europe's passive rural subjects into active citizens: universal education, the creation of a national market, political parties. All were missing in the Russia of 1900. As a result, the Russian peasant was neither socialized nor politicized. He remained an outsider.

Official Russia

The government of Russia at the turn of the century displayed the same contradictions as the country at large. On top, a cumbersome bureaucratic machine claiming unlimited power; below, a population left largely to its own devices. Paradoxically, the average Russian, living under an autocratic regime, had less contact with government and felt less the impact of politics than did the citizen of democratic England, France, or the United States. This became evident during World War I, when tsarism had greater difficulty mobilizing the population for the war effort than did the Western democracies.

Until 1905, Russia was ruled by an unlimited monarchy. All power emanated from the Emperor. The Criminal Code made it a felony to question his authority or to express a desire for a change of government. All proposals, including those originating in official circles, to bring representatives of the population into the decision-making process, if only in an advisory capacity, were rejected. Political authority was regarded as the property of the dynasty, which each tsar held in trust and was duty-bound to pass on, undiluted, to his heir.

Absolutism had been, of course, the prevalent form of government in the rest of continental Europe until the nineteenth century, at which time it gave way to popular sovereignty. In Russia it outlasted the nineteenth century. It also assumed here more extreme forms. Even at the height of absolutism, Western kings respected the private property of their subjects, violations of property rights being regarded as a hallmark of tyranny. A fifteenth-century Spanish jurist articulated the principle underlying the Western political system when he wrote that "to the King is confided solely the administration of the kingdom, and not dominion over things, for the property and rights of the State are public, and cannot be the private patrimony of anyone."[1] Ownership provided an effective limitation to royal authority, even that which acknowledged no formal limitations. In Muscovite Russia, by contrast, as in the so-called "Oriental despotisms," the Tsar both ruled and owned his realm. He claimed all the land and natural resources, he monopolized wholesale and foreign trade, and, as if this were not enough, laid claim to the lifelong services of his subjects. The upper class served him directly, in the army or bureaucracy, while commoners tilled either his land or that of his servitors. This kind of "patrimonial" regime represented the most extreme type of autocracy.

The patrimonial regime in Russia began to dissolve in the middle of the eighteenth century. In 1762, the Crown exempted nobles from compulsory state service and not long afterward gave them title to the land which until then they had held conditionally. The notion of private property struck root during the nineteenth century, gaining greater respect from the authorities than did the personal rights of its owners. The abolition of serfdom in 1861 destroyed the remaining vestiges of the patrimonial social structure. In one respect, however, patrimonialism survived, and that was in the realm of political authority. The Tsar con-

5. Nicholas II and family shortly before the outbreak of World War I.

tinued to treat sovereignty as his private asset, and the state officialdom as well as the armed forces owed him personal loyalty: civil servants and officers swore allegiance not to the state or the nation but to the person of the Tsar. Government officials, too, continued to be regarded as the Tsar's private servants.

An autocratic system required an autocrat not only in name but in personality, someone who enjoyed the prerogatives of power and knew how to use them. As chance would have it, Russia in 1900 was governed by a man who lacked every quality required of an effective autocrat except the sense of duty. Nicholas II had limited intelligence and a weak will, shortcomings for which he tried to compensate with occasional outbursts of stubbornness. He enjoyed neither power nor its perquisites. He once confided to a minister that he insisted on the autocratic system not because it afforded him personal pleasure but because the country needed it. Apart from his wife and children, he cared only for Russia and the army; he found his keenest pleasure in outdoor exercise. All else left him cold. Witnesses agree that he had never appeared as happy as he did after abdicating.

His wife, Alexandra Fedorovna, was made of different stuff. A native of Germany and a granddaughter of Queen Victoria, she very quickly assimilated the patrimonial traditions of her adopted country. Aware of her husband's weakness, she constantly badgered him to act the true autocrat, to be another Peter the Great. "You and Russia are one and the same," she would tell him; or "Russia loves to feel the whip." Without her influence, Nicholas might have yielded to public pressures and agreed to play the role of a ceremonial monarch, which could have averted the Revolution.

The question arises: Why did Nicholas—and not he alone but many thoughtful Russians as well—insist on preserving an outdated political regime in the face of mounting opposition from the country's educated elite? Liberals and radicals of the time dismissed as self-serving the claims made for autocracy. But in view of what ultimately happened, these claims deserve at least a hearing.

The monarchist case against replacing autocracy with a constitutional monarchy rested on two arguments.

One held that Russia was too vast and ethnically too diverse to have an effective parliamentary regime. Her population was not integrated, but lived in scattered, self-contained communities lacking in a sense of common nationhood or even statehood. The peasantry adhered to a primitive anarchism that was incompatible with responsible citizenship; it was likely to interpret parliamentary opposition to the Crown as a sign that government was weak and that it could seize with impunity private (i.e., noncommunal) land. Only strong personal authority, standing aloof from ethnic and partisan strife, unrestrained by constitutional formalities, could hold such a country together.

Secondly, it was argued that parliamentary institutions would almost certainly be dominated by liberals and socialists who would not cooperate with a constitutional monarch. Amateur politicians, their heads filled with utopian ideas learned from Western literature, they would be satisfied with nothing less than the abolition of the monarchy and its replacement with a republic in which they would exercise full power. The result would be anarchy and civil war.

Although events proved many of their worries justified, the monarchists had no prescription for solving the political crisis other than repression.

To this end, the Crown employed five instruments: the civil service, the security police, the landed gentry, the army, and the Orthodox Church.

The Russian bureaucracy was in many respects unique. Descended from the domestic staffs of medieval princes, it continued to act as the personal staff of the monarch rather than as the civil service of the nation. A Russian official served entirely at the pleasure of the monarch and his own immediate superiors. He could be dismissed without cause and without the right of appeal. He could not resign without permission. Such practices made for servility. Totally dependent on his superiors, the Russian civil servant was virtually untouchable in his dealings with ordinary people. In tsarist Russia, a government official, as a representative of the autocrat, could not be brought to trial except by the consent of his superiors. That consent was rarely forthcoming, since an employee's misbehavior reflected badly on those who had appointed him and, ultimately, on the judgment of the Tsar himself. This situation encouraged browbeating and corruption. The obverse of servility was bullying.

Although the ministries in St. Petersburg included many qualified and honest public servants, the rank and file of the civil service was filled with unscrupulous careerists. One of the peculiarities of the Russian system was that admission into the civil service required neither a school diploma nor the passing of a qualifying examination: a candidate merely had to demonstrate the ability to read and write and to perform elementary mathematical calculations. In effect, unquestioning obedience and loyalty were the main qualifications for admission and promotion.

Perhaps the most striking feature of the Russian civil service was the system of "ranking" introduced by Peter the Great in 1722. Every member of the service had to have a rank, or *chin*, of which there were fourteen. One began at the lowest, fourteenth rank and worked his way up the career ladder. Originally, attainment of the eighth rank bestowed hereditary nobility, but by 1900 a civil servant had to reach the very elevated fourth rank to be so honored. It had been Peter's intention that each advance in responsibility be accompanied by an advance in rank. But Peter's successors perverted the system. Catherine the Great, having come to the throne by a coup that resulted in the death of her husband, Tsar Peter III, sought to make her position more secure by buying off the nobility and the bureaucracy. During her reign, advancement in rank came to depend not on the assumption of greater responsibility but simply on seniority: after serving in one rank for a specified period of time, usually three or four years, the holder was automatically promoted to the next higher rank. And since it was also the custom that only holders of *chin* could perform administrative functions, the Russian civil service turned into a closed caste. Except in the highest posts, to which appointments were made directly by the Tsar, no one could hold a governmental position without *chin*. This practice had two consequences: It isolated the civil service from society at large, and deprived it of the talents of those who were not career bureaucrats.

Russia's principal executive organs, the ministries, did not substantially differ from their Western analogues, although they did display some peculiar features. Until 1906 there was, in effect, no cabinet and no prime minister. Each minister reported directly to the Tsar and acted on his instructions without consulting fellow ministers. This practice was motivated by the fear that cabinet discussions of Imperial directives would encroach on the Crown's prerogatives. The resulting lack of a coordinated policy caused considerable disarray in administration.

The provincial administration suffered from understaffing. Although tsarist Russia has the reputation of a tyranny, and tyranny conveys the image of a heavy hand of arbitrary authority, the vast majority of Russians rarely came in contact with the state. The number of administrators, whether measured in proportion to territory or population, was only a fraction of what it was in contemporary France or Germany. The explanation lay in fiscal constraints. The Russian Treasury lacked the resources required properly to administer the immense realm and relied instead on a combination of arbitrary authority vested in provincial governors and the self-government institutionalized in the peasant commune.

Thus, while tsarist authority was unlimited, its scope was narrow. For all practical purposes, the authority of the Imperial government ended at the eighty-nine provincial capitals where resided the governors and their staffs; below this level yawned an administrative vacuum. The provincial subdivisions had no permanent government representatives: such officials as they saw came on flying visits, often to collect tax arrears, and then vanished from sight. The representatives of the ministries posted to the provincial capitals owed responsibility to their home offices and did not cooperate with one another.

The most important ministry was that of the Interior, which had charge of administering the country and ensuring domestic security. The Minister of the Interior nominated the governors, who in their discretionary powers resembled Oriental satraps. One of these powers was a Governor's right to request the Minister of the Interior to place his province under Reinforced or Extraordinary Safeguard, a kind of martial law that authorized him to suspend civil rights and shut down private institutions. The

Minister of the Interior also supervised non-Orthodox subjects, including the Jews, as well as the dissenting branches of Orthodox Christianity. In addition, he enforced censorship and managed prisons.

But the greatest source of the Minister's power lay in the administration of the political police. The Department of Police, established in 1880 following a nearly successful terrorist attempt on the life of Alexander II, was unique in that Russia alone had two distinct branches of the police—one to maintain law and order among the people, another to protect the state from them. The Police Department concerned itself exclusively with enforcing political conformity, to which end it could engage in open or secret surveillance, search and arrest, imprisonment, and, by administrative fiat—that is, without a trial—exile for periods of up to five years. Through a network of agents it penetrated every facet of the country's life; its foreign branches even tracked émigrés. Such measures were considered necessary to counteract an unprecedented wave of political terrorism by radical extremists, which in the decade preceding World War I claimed the lives of thousands of government officials. They made late tsarist Russia in many respects the prototype of a modern police state.*

To the outside world, the Imperial bureaucracy presented the image of perfect unanimity; it never aired its disagreements in public. The secrecy under which it operated much of the time reinforced this impression. In reality it was divided into two contending factions, one liberal-conservative, the other reactionary. Liberal-conservative officials, concentrated in the Ministries of Justice and Finance, while conceding that Russia required a strong central government, saw the existing system as hopelessly outdated. They wanted Russia to be governed by laws—laws, to be sure, issued by the autocrat who was accountable to nobody, but who should still be obliged to observe his own ordinances. They also believed that the government would be strengthened by the involvement of conservative elements of society, if only in a consultative capacity. They further wanted to end the isolation of the peasants by abolishing laws that kept them in the commune and subject to special rural courts. Through such measures they believed Russians would gradually be weaned to more modern forms of government.

Their reactionary opponents viewed the population at large as the property of the monarch, and any sign of public initiative as "insubordi-

---

* Other countries, too, had their security police. But, as in the case of the FBI, their powers were restricted to investigating potential subversion. They had no authority to punish.

nation." The government, in their view, could not submit to the rule of law because that would fatally weaken it, opening the floodgates to popular unrest. In the words of one Minister of the Interior:

> The sparse population of Russia, scattered over an immense territory, the unavoidable remoteness from courts which results from this fact, the low economic level of the people and the patriarchal customs of the agrarian class, all create conditions demanding the establishment of an authority which in its activities is *not restrained by excessive formalism*, an authority promptly able to restore order and as quickly as possible to correct violations of the population's rights and interests.[2]

Russians of this persuasion did not oppose changes but insisted that they be initiated and implemented from above, by the government.

Behind this attitude lay the conviction that "society"—that is, everyone not in government service—was in a very real sense an enemy of the state. This perception prevailed in the Department of the Police, the most reactionary wing of the reactionary faction. According to its one-time chief, the outlook of the tsarist security police rested on the following propositions: "that there are the people and there is state authority, that the latter is under constant threat from the former . . . Hence, any public occurrence assumes the character of a threat to state authority. As a result, the protection of the state . . . turns into a war against all society. . . ."[3] This attitude, dominant in the Ministry of the Interior and its branches, impeded reforms. Unfortunately for Russia, radical intellectuals, especially radical terrorists, played into the hands of the reactionaries.

Even so, it should have been obvious that over the long run the position of the reactionaries could not be maintained. For one thing, Russia's ambitions to be a great power forced her to encourage higher education, which was incompatible with a regime that treated its people as if they were disobedient children. Alexander Herzen, a political writer of the mid-nineteenth century, expressed this contradiction as follows:

> They give us a comprehensive education, they inculcate in us the desires, the strivings, the sufferings of the contemporary world, and then they cry, "Stay slaves, dumb and passive, or else you will perish."[4]

The other development that militated against the survival of the bureaucratic police state occurred in the Russian economy: the emergence at the end of the nineteenth century of capitalist industry. Tsarist Russia took the path of capitalism reluctantly, fearful of upsetting the largely natural, agrarian order which it favored for its promise of stability. It so dreaded the destabilizing effects of industrialization that thirty years after their invention, railroads were still virtually nonexistent in Russia. In the end, however, tsarism had no choice but to emulate the Western world. In the second half of the nineteenth century, the Russian Treasury was running a consistent deficit, which it covered by borrowing abroad. Farsighted statesmen realized that Russia could not remain a great power unless she developed native industries and generated assets that would make her independent of foreign capital. Sergei Witte, Russia's Minister of Finance and the driving force behind industrialization, argued fervently that unless Russia developed an industrial base she could not achieve economic independence, and without such independence she could not aspire to the status of a great power.

In 1897, on Witte's initiative, Russia adopted the gold standard. Henceforth all banknotes had to be backed by gold deposited in the Treasury and could be converted into gold coins. The reform gave the country one of the stablest currencies in the world, and encouraged foreign investment. Between 1892 and 1914, foreigners placed in Russian enterprises over 1 billion dollars U.S. (equivalent in 1995, in gold terms, to $20 billion). Russia experienced a sudden spurt of industrial development that, small as it was in terms of the national economy as a whole, combined with her agriculture and mining, earned her fifth place among the world's economies.

As the reactionaries had warned, the policy favoring industrial development affected adversely Russia's autocratic regime. Foreign holders of Russian bonds pressured the government to act in a lawful manner, punishing excesses by depreciating her obligations, which had the effect of forcing Russia to pay higher interest rates for loans. Equally important was the fact that both Russian and foreign businessmen took independent actions affecting employment, transport, and capital investment which made a mockery of the monarchy's claim to be the sole authority in the country. The incompatibility of capitalism and autocracy struck all who gave thought to the matter, and this awareness enhanced people's sense of the precariousness of the status quo.

Next to the bureaucracy and the police, the regime's principal support came from the armed forces.

With 1.4 million men under arms, Russia had the largest standing army in the world, larger than the combined armies of her two likely enemies, Germany and Austria-Hungary. The maintenance of such a vast and costly force can be attributed to three factors. First, great distances and a poor railway network made for slow mobilization: it was estimated that whereas Germany could mobilize fully within 15 days, Russia required 105 days. Since the conventional wisdom of the time held that the next war would be decided in a matter of weeks, speed of mobilization was of critical importance. Second, partly for lack of money, partly out of contempt for civilians, Russian professional officers failed to develop an effective system of reserves that a major national army needed, in case of emergency, to bring its forces quickly to full strength. And, finally, the Russian army was traditionally used to quell internal disturbances: in 1903, one-third of the infantry and two-thirds of the cavalry in European Russia took part in repressive operations. Neither the 1905 nor the 1917 Revolution would have been likely to occur if the army had not been fighting far away from the center of the country.

The Russian military tradition demanded that the army stay clear of politics. The officer corps regarded politics and politicians as beneath its professional dignity and served loyally whoever happened to be in power: traditionally, the monarchy, and, after its fall, first the Provisional Government and then the Bolsheviks.

The fourth pillar of tsarist authority, the gentry, was an eroding asset. During the heyday of patrimonial autocracy, the sixteenth and seventeenth centuries, the gentry (*dvorianstvo*) served as the principal arm of the Crown. The tsars granted them landed estates worked by bonded peasants and in return exacted from them lifelong service, mainly in the armed forces. But the gentry gradually succeeded in emancipating themselves from the heavy hand of the state. Over the course of the eighteenth century, taking advantage of a succession of weak monarchs, the *dvoriane* first eased the terms of service and finally, in 1762, escaped them altogether. The landed estates which they had originally received on condition of service, they now received in outright property. Although poverty forced many *dvoriane* to stay on active service, the affluent among them became a parasitic class enjoying virtually Western rights and privileges without corresponding responsibilities. The more prosperous turned to culture; the first creators and the earliest audiences of Russian literature and art came almost entirely from this class.

In the early nineteenth century, many youths among the gentry fell under the influence of Western liberal and abolitionist ideas. In December 1825, officers from some of the best families mutinied with the intention of abolishing the autocracy and replacing it with either a constitutional monarchy or a republic. The so-called Decembrist Revolt was quickly suppressed; but it began the nobility's decline because the monarchy, shocked by the betrayal of its pampered class, no longer fully trusted it and came increasingly to rely on a professional bureaucracy. The 1861 edict emancipating the serfs dealt the gentry the fatal blow. Unable profitably to exploit their estates without bonded labor and unaccustomed to living within their means, they ran into debt and had to dispose of their estates. Politically the group split, one part turning reactionary, the other joining the liberal intelligentsia. The whole drift of late Imperial legislation tended toward the abolition of estate privileges in favor of egalitarian citizenship. By 1900, *dvorianstvo* status brought no meaningful rewards and implied no political allegiance: suffice it to say that Lenin was a hereditary noble.

And, finally, there was the Orthodox Church, the established ecclesiastical body of the realm, representing approximately 55 percent of its population.* Since the reign of Peter the Great, the Russian church had lost its independence and was administered by appointed lay officials; subsequently, under Catherine the Great, it also lost its rich possessions, which were sequestered. The church never rebelled against these measures: faithful to its Byzantine heritage, it loyally supported the monarchy and stayed clear of politics. It also stayed clear of the social conflicts and ideological disputes agitating the country. It conceived its mission as being confined to the salvation of souls. The church preached submission to the powers that be and in that sense served as a dependable prop of the regime. The state rewarded it by entrusting to the clergy much of the nation's elementary education, by paying it subsidies, and by outlawing conversion from Orthodoxy.

But even in this loyal body fissures began to appear at the century's turn, in the form of a liberal clergy that wanted the church to liberate itself from dependence on the state and to take a more active part in the country's political and social life.

No one doubts that the majority of Russians, especially the peasants, faithfully observed the rites of their religion with its sacraments, fasts, and holidays. How deep this commitment was, however, is a matter of dispute: as events were to show, the devotion of Russians to their faith was not as strong as that of the Empire's Catholics, Jews, or Muslims. Russian Orthodox religiosity seems to have rested more on observance of rituals than on commitment to Christianity's ethical teachings.

---

* Nominally, some 75 percent of Russia's inhabitants were Orthodox Christians, but of that number many belonged to the Old Believers, who had split off from the official church in the seventeenth century, while others joined dissenting sects. Contemporaries estimated that approximately one out of four officially Orthodox Christians worshipped outside the Orthodox Church.

The Intelligentsia

W hy use the foreign-sounding "intelligentsia" when the English language has the word "intellectuals"? The answer is that one needs different terms to designate different phenomena—in this case, to distinguish those who passively contemplate life from activists who are determined to reshape it. Marx succinctly stated the latter position when he wrote: "The philosophers have only interpreted the world in various ways; the point, however, is to change it." The term "intelligentsia" describes intellectuals who want power in order to change the world. It is a word of Latin origin, which passed in the middle of the nineteenth century from German into Russian and from there, after the 1917 Revolution, into English.

Whether the conflicts and resentments that exist in every society are peacefully resolved or explode in revolution is largely determined by the presence or absence of democratic institutions capable of redressing grievances through legislation, and the presence or absence of an intelligentsia determined to fan the flames of popular discontent for the purpose of gaining power. For it is the radical intelligentsia that transforms specific, and therefore remediable, grievances into an uncompromising rejection of the status quo. Rebellions happen; revolutions are made. And they are made by bodies of professional "managers of the revolution," namely the radical intelligentsia.

For an intelligentsia to emerge, two conditions must be met. One is a materialistic ideology that regards human beings not as unique creatures endowed with an immortal soul but as exclusively physical entities shaped by their environment. This ideology makes it possible to argue that a rational reordering of man's environment can produce a new breed of perfectly virtuous creatures. This belief elevates members of the intelligentsia to the status of social engineers and justifies their political ambitions.

Second, the intelligentsia requires economic opportunities to secure independence: The dissolution of traditional social estates and the emergence of free professions (such as journalism and university teaching) along with an industrial economy in need of experts and an educated reading public, which, all taken together, emancipate intellectuals from subjection to the Establishment. These opportunities, accompanied by guarantees of free speech and association, enable the intelligentsia to secure a hold on public opinion, its principal means of political leverage.

Intellectuals first appeared in Europe as a distinct group in the six-teenth century in connection with the emergence of secular society and the progress of science. They were lay thinkers who approached tradi-tional philosophical questions outside the framework of theology and the church, which in the postclassical world had enjoyed a monopoly on such speculation. Like the philosophers of ancient Greece and Rome, they saw their mission as one of teaching virtue and wisdom—educating men to curb their passions and to accept life with all its dark sides, including the inevitability of death.

Then a different kind of intellectual made his appearance. Impressed by the advances of science and the seemingly limitless possibilities inher-ent in the scientific method, he saw no reason he should not apply the insights into nature that science had made possible in order to master nature. It was a notion with very wide applications. The scientific (empirical) method posited that only that existed which could be observed and measured. It raised the question whether man could be said to possess an immortal soul or ideas planted in him at birth, as taught by religion and metaphysics, for neither this soul nor these ideas could be identified by scientific observation.

The full philosophical implications of this empirical approach were first drawn by John Locke in his seminal *Essay Concerning Human Under-standing* (1690). In his political writings Locke laid down the foundations of the liberal constitutions of Great Britain and the United States. But his philosophical treatise inadvertently fed a very different, illiberal cur-rent of political thought. The *Essay* challenged the axiom of Western philosophy and theology that human beings were born with "innate ideas," including knowledge of God and a sense of right and wrong. This notion had made for a conservative theory of politics because, by postu-lating that man comes into the world spiritually and intellectually formed, it also postulated that he was immutable. From this it followed that the principles of government were the same for all nations and ages. According to Locke, however, man is born a blank slate on which physi-cal sensations and experiences write the messages that make him what he is. There is no such thing as free will: man can no more reject the ideas that the senses inscribe on his mind than a mirror can "refuse, alter, or obliterate the images or ideas which objects set before it" produce.

The implications of Locke's theory of knowledge, ignored in his own country, were seized upon and developed in France by radical thinkers, notably Claude Helvétius. In *De l'esprit* (1758), Helvétius drew on Locke's epistemology to argue that insofar as man is totally molded by his environment, a perfect environment will inevitably produce perfect human beings. The means toward this end are education and legislation. The task of the political and social order, therefore, is not to create optimal conditions in which mankind can realize its potential but rather to render mankind "virtuous." Good government not only ensures "the greatest happiness of the greatest number" (a formula attributed to Helvétius) but literally refashions man. This unprecedented proposition constitutes the premise of both liberal and radical ideologies of modern times. It justifies the government's far-reaching intervention in the lives of its citizens.

This idea holds an irresistible attraction for intellectuals because it elevates them from the position of passive observers of life into its shapers. Their superior knowledge of what is rational and virtuous permits them to aspire to the status of mankind's "educators." While ordinary people, in pursuit of a living, acquire specific knowledge relevant to their particular occupation, intellectuals—and they alone—claim to know things "in general." By creating "sciences" of human affairs—economic science, political science, sociology—they feel at liberty to dismiss as irrelevant practices and institutions created over millennia by trial and error. It is this philosophical revolution that has transformed some intellectuals into an intelligentsia, actively involved in politics. And, of course, involvement in politics makes them politicians, and, like others of the breed, prone to pursue their private interests in the guise of working for the common good.

The premises underlying the ideas of Locke and Helvétius can be applied in two ways. In countries with democratic institutions and guarantees of free speech, members of the intelligentsia pursue their objective by influencing public opinion and, through it, legislation. Where such institutions and guarantees are missing, they coalesce into a caste that tirelessly assails the existing order in order to discredit it and pave the way for revolutionary change. The latter situation prevailed in pre-1789 France and in tsarist Russia prior to 1905.

The mental and social preconditions for the emergence of a revolutionary intelligentsia first emerged in France in the 1760s and 1770s in literary associations and "patriotic" clubs. These clubs had as their immediate purpose the forging of an ideological consensus in which ideas were judged by their relationship not to living reality but to *a priori* theoretical principles defining rationality and virtue. To members of such clubs, politics was not simply a matter of better or worse, to be tested by experience, but of good or bad, to be decided on principle.

Public issues became highly personalized, and the holder of opinions judged incorrect was not merely wrong but, because the truth was self-evident and could be ignored only from bad will, also evil.

Although exclusive and inspired by ideas of its own making, the French intelligentsia of the late eighteenth century claimed to be acting on behalf of the "people"—not people of flesh and blood but an abstraction conceived in their minds; not people as they actually were but as they could and should be. One of the defining qualities of all modern radicalism is the belief that humanity as constituted is a defective product, a misshapen exemplar of the real thing. The radical intellectual claims to know better what the people need than they themselves do because he alone understands their "true," or ideal, self.

It is this group, first in France, then in other countries of continental Europe—Russia included—that transformed rebellions into revolutions: popular protests against specific grievances into a blanket rejection of the entire sociopolitical order. Nothing in early-twentieth-century Russia inexorably pushed the country toward revolution, except the presence of an unusually large and fanatical body of professional revolutionaries. No document has come to light, reflecting the wishes of the peasants or the workers themselves, that called for the abolition of tsarism and a wholesale transformation of Russia. It is the intelligentsia that with its orchestrated agitational campaigns of 1917 transformed a local fire—the mutiny of the Petrograd's military garrison—into a nationwide conflagration. A class in permanent opposition, hostile to all reforms and compromises, it prevented the peaceful resolution of Russia's ills in order to level to the ground the existing system of human relations and build on its ruins a world of its own design.

The theory and practice of socialism, and its offshoot, communism, postulate that all the existing ways of humanity are irrational and that it is the mission of those in the know to make out of them something radically different: mankind's entire past is but a long detour on the road to its true destiny. Robert Owen, an early English socialist, expressed this yearning when he spoke of wanting to change "this lunatic asylum into a Rational World."[5]

Marx, at the age of twenty-one, grasped the implications of the theories of Locke and Helvétius. "The whole development of man . . . depends on *education* and *environment*," he wrote, from which it followed that

> if man draws all his knowledge, sensations, etc., from the world of the senses and the experience gained in it, [then] the empirical world must be arranged

so that in it man experiences and gets used to what is really human . . . If man is shaped by his surroundings, his surroundings must be made human.

This, of course, was a prescription for the most drastic changes in the human condition—changes made not *by* ordinary people, since they are blind, but *for* them.

Just how boundless were the ambitions of radical socialists may be gleaned from the ruminations of Leon Trotsky. Writing in 1924, he thus depicted the new man bound to emerge from the revolutionary order:

> Man will, at last, begin to harmonize himself in earnest . . . He will want to master first the semi-conscious and then also the unconscious processes of his own organism: breathing, the circulation of blood, digestion, reproduction, and, within the necessary limits, subordinate them to the control of reason and will . . . Man will make it his goal to master his own emotions, to elevate his instincts to the heights of consciousness, to make them transparent . . . to create a higher sociobiological type, a superman . . . Man will become incomparably stronger, wiser, subtler. His body will become more harmonious, his movements more rhythmic, his voice more melodious. The forms of life will acquire a dynamic theatricality. The average human type will rise to the heights of an Aristotle, Goethe, Marx. And beyond this ridge, other peaks will emerge.

These reflections, not of an adolescent daydreamer but of Lenin's comrade-in-arms and one of the leading organizers of the Bolshevik triumph in 1917–20, provide an insight into the psyche of those who carried out the greatest revolution of modern times. They aimed at nothing less than reenacting the sixth day of Creation in order to perfect its flawed product: man's mission was nothing less than remaking himself. We can now understand what an influential Russian radical of the 1860s meant when he wrote that "man is god to man."*

The conditions in Russia around 1900 resembled those in pre-1789 France in that the country also lacked freedom of speech and representative institutions. The intelligentsia which emerged in the 1860s

---

* Such deprecation of mankind was not confined to radicals: it spilled also into the ranks of liberals. H. G. Wells, a scientific utopian, predicted in his 1933 book, *The Shape of Things to Come*, that education and social discipline would totally transform the human individual: "He will become generation by generation a new species, differing more widely from that weedy, tragic, pathetic, cruel, fantastic, absurd, and sometimes sheerly horrible being who christened himself in a mood of oafish arrogance *Homo sapiens*." (New York, 1933, 426.) Compare this with the vision of Michel de Montaigne, writing in the sixteenth century, before science had overwhelmed both religion and the philosophy of humanism: "There is nothing so beautiful and legitimate as to play the man well and properly . . . the most barbarous of our maladies is to despise our being."

recalled in many ways the French *philosophes* of a century earlier. Like its predecessor, the Russian intelligentsia constituted a closed caste, admission to which required commitment to materialism, socialism, and utilitarianism (the belief that the morality of human actions is determined by the extent of pain and pleasure they produce, and that the test of good government is its ability to assure the greatest happiness of the greatest number). No one who believed in God and the immortality of the soul, in the limits to human reason and the advantages of compromise, in the value of traditions and love of one's country, no matter how otherwise enlightened, could aspire to membership in the intelligentsia or gain access to its publications.

Contact with common Russians had no effect on these beliefs. In the 1870s, hundreds of students abandoned university classrooms to "go to the people" in order to inculcate in them such ideas. They found the people entirely unreceptive: the peasant believed resolutely in God and the Tsar, and saw nothing wrong with exploiting his fellow men as long as it was he who did it. But this evidence did not move committed radicals to alter their views. Rather, it drove them to violence. In 1879 some thirty intellectuals (in a nation of 100 million), dubbing themselves the "People's Will," formed a clandestine terrorist organization with the declared intention of murdering Tsar Alexander II. It was the first organization in history specifically dedicated to political terror, and the prototype of numerous terrorist parties that would spring up in Europe, the Middle East, and elsewhere in the second half of the twentieth century. Russian terrorists acted on the premise that antigovernment violence would demoralize the authorities and, at the same time, shatter the awe in which the masses of Russians held the Tsar. After several failures, they eventually succeeded in assassinating Alexander, but the consequences were the opposite of what they had expected. The masses did not stir; educated society, revolted by the murder, turned its back on radicalism; and the government, instead of surrendering, intensified its repression.

One consequence of the failure of terrorism was the emergence in Russia in the 1890s of a Social-Democratic movement. The Social-Democrats (SDs for short), drawing on the theories of Marx, disparaged terrorism as futile. For them, political and social change resulted from fundamental changes in economic relations. It could not be rushed. Even if the terrorists succeeded in bringing down tsarism they would not be able to establish on its ruins a democratic, socialist regime because the economic foundations for it were missing. Russia, still in the formative phase of capitalist development, was bound in time to progress to full-scale capitalism. A by-product of such an economy would be, initially, "bourgeois" democracy, and eventually, with the unfolding of its inherent contradictions, a socialist revolution. The process required patience and a careful adaptation of tactics to socioeconomic reality rather than foolhardy heroism.

The Social-Democratic strategy called for a two-stage revolution. Initially, the socialists would help the emerging Russian bourgeoisie topple tsarism and introduce into the country a Western-type regime with guarantees of civil and political liberties. Then, taking advantage of these freedoms, they would organize the working class, which they regarded as more suitable material for revolution than the peasantry, for the inevitable day when, driven to desperation by impoverishment, the "proletariat" would rise up in arms against its exploiters.

Like the peasant-oriented radicals of the 1870s, the Social-Democrats of the 1890s were soon disappointed with the attitude of those whom they claimed to represent. Closer contact with industrial workers revealed that they were not in the least radical and that their main interest lay in organizing trade unions (outlawed in Russia at the time), which, to revolutionaries, spelled accommodation with the status quo. The majority of socialists accepted this fact and dedicated themselves to helping labor struggle for economic improvement. From their ranks emerged at the beginning of the twentieth century the Menshevik faction. A minority, led by Lenin, the founder of the Bolshevik faction, concluded from this evidence that if the workers, left to themselves, were reformist rather than revolutionary, then they required a body of full-time, professional tutors to infuse them with revolutionary zeal. This latter idea, at the time known only to small circles of initiates, was destined to have the most profound effects on the entire history of the twentieth century.

Although still outlawed, Russian political parties began to take shape around the turn of the century.

The most radical was the Socialist-Revolutionary Party, a direct descendant of the People's Will, which organized formally in 1902. The Socialists-Revolutionaries (SRs) differed from the Social-Democrats in several important respects. First, they did not distinguish sharply, as did the SDs, peasants from workers, regarding both as revolutionary material. (To the SDs, the peasants, except for landless farmhands, were fundamentally a reactionary "petty-bourgeois" class and, as such, the enemy of labor.) They carried out active propaganda and agitation in the village, calling for the abolition of private property in land and the transfer of all land into the hands of communes ("land socialization"). Because this program met the wishes of the peasantry, the SRs enjoyed unrivaled popularity among them, and inasmuch as peasants were the largest social group, they had the greatest political following in the country. Much of it, however, would prove ephemeral because, unlike the SDs, the SRs were loosely organized.

The principal activity of the SRs was political terror. Like their forerunners twenty years earlier, they believed that the tsarist regime was rotten to the core and that determined assaults on its officials would bring it down. They had only contempt for the patient strategy of their Social-Democratic rivals and attracted into their ranks many intrepid youths, men and women, ready to sacrifice their lives for the cause. These actions, which had the effect of brutalizing Russian political life still further, exuded a romantic aura, representing for some youths a ritual of passage into adulthood. The main decisions concerning terror were made by an ultrasecret "Combat Organization," but many local SR cells acted on their own initiative. The first act of political terror perpetrated by the SRs was the murder in 1902 of the Minister of Education. Subsequently, until crushed in 1908–9, SR terrorists engaged the forces of law and order in constant battle.

We shall deal with the Social-Democratic Party elsewhere (Chapter V). Here, suffice it to say that unlike the SRs, who divided society into "exploiters" and "exploited," the Social-Democrats defined classes by their relation to the means of production and regarded industrial workers (the "proletariat") as the only truly revolutionary class, because, unlike the independent peasant-cultivator, a good part of their earnings was appropriated by the employer. The SDs wanted first to nationalize the agricultural land and then collectivize it in order to transform the peasant into a state employee. Unlike the SRs, they saw the "bourgeoisie" as a temporary ally in the first stage of the Revolution. And, as stated, they disparaged terrorism, believing that the time for terror was *after* they came to power and had at their disposal the entire repressive apparatus of the state.

The active membership of both these radical parties was similar: whether one joined the one or the other was largely a matter of temperament, the bolder and more adventurous generally showing a preference for the SRs. In both, the membership consisted primarily of university students and university dropouts. According to one Social-Democrat:

Essentially, the activity of the local SR groups differed little from that of the SDs. The organizations of both parties usually consisted of small groups of *intelligenty*, formed into committees, who had little connection with the masses and viewed them mainly as material for political agitation.

The principal liberal organization, which in 1905 would coalesce into the Constitutional-Democratic Party, differed in both composition and program from the radical organizations. Its leadership consisted of gentry and intellectuals, some of the latter being disenchanted socialists. The majority of Russia's professional people—academics, lawyers, physicians—affiliated themselves with it. Because of the eminence of their leaders, some of whom belonged to well-known aristocratic families, the police did not dare to treat liberals with the same ruthlessness with which it persecuted socialist youths. The liberals got around the prohibition against political activity by holding meetings disguised as professional conferences and social functions. Initially, they intended to work within the system, hoping gradually to improve Russia by raising the cultural and economic standards of the population. The government's repressive policies, however, which intensified during the reign of Alexander III, son and successor of the assassinated Alexander II, pushed them steadily deeper into the oppositional camp. Russian liberals boasted, with some justice, that they were the most radical liberal group in Europe.

The movement took organized form with the founding in 1902 in Germany of the journal *Liberation*. Its editor, Peter Struve, once a leading Marxist theoretician, set himself the mission of uniting all oppositional groups in Russia, from the conservative right to the radical left, under the slogan "Down with the Autocracy!" Two years later, on this platform, there emerged the Union of Liberation, a loose association of antiautocratic groups which would play a decisive role in unleashing Russia's first revolution in 1905.

At the beginning of the twentieth century, Russia was home to thousands of men and women committed to fundamental change. A good number of them were professional revolutionaries, a novel breed whose life's goal was overthrowing by violence all existing institutions. They and their followers might disagree over strategy and tactics—whether to engage in terror, whether to "socialize" or "nationalize" the land, whether to treat the peasant as an ally or enemy of the worker—but they were at one on the central issue: that there was to be no compromise with the existing social, economic, and political regime; that it had to be destroyed, root and branch, not only in their own country but throughout the world.

The existence of such an intelligentsia created, in itself, a high risk of social upheaval. For just as lawyers make for litigation and bureaucrats for paperwork, so revolutionaries make for revolution. In each case a profession emerges with an interest in promoting situations that demand its particular skill. The fact that the intelligentsia rejected any accommodation with those who governed Russia, that it exacerbated discontent and opposed reform, made it unlikely that Russia's problems would be resolved peacefully.

THE CONSTITUTIONAL EXPERIMENT

The Revolution of 1905

Historical events have no clear beginning or end: they fade in and out imperceptibly, and historians can never quite agree on how to date them.

It is possible to trace the beginning of the Russian Revolution to the Decembrist uprising of 1825. Or else to the 1870s, when university students, defying the authorities, "went to the people." Or to 1879–81, when the People's Will launched its campaign of political terror. More conservatively, one can date it from the years 1902 to 1904, when the three principal political movements committed to the overthrow of the autocracy—the Socialist-Revolutionary, the Social-Democratic, and the Liberational—organized as parties.

But a case can also be made for tracing its outbreak to February 1899, when major disturbances broke out at Russian universities: ebbing and flowing, the turmoil did not subside until 1905–6, when the monarchy, facing a general strike, had to yield and grant the country a constitution. Many contemporaries, police officials included, regarded these disturbances as qualitatively different from any that had occurred earlier.

The immediate cause of the 1899 university troubles could not have been more trivial; and the fact that they had such grave consequences attests to the gulf that separated Russia's rulers from the educated elite.

EUROPEAN RUSSIA

BARENTS SEA

NORWAY

SWEDEN

Gulf of Bothnia

Finland

Murmansk

WHITE SEA

Archangel

Stockholm

Helsingfors
(Helsinki)
Vyborg

Lake
Ladoga

Lake
Onega

*Northern
Dvina*

Kotlas

Pechora

Ob

Ob

U
r
a
l

M
o
u
n
t
a
i
n
s

Dagö I.
Ösel I.
*Gulf of
Riga*

Revel
(Tallinn)

Petrograd (Leningrad)

Novgorod

Vologda

Iaroslavl

Viatka

Perm

Tobolsk

Irtysh

BALTIC SEA

Riga

Pskov

Velikie Luki

Nizhnii
Novgorod

Kazan

Alapaevsk

Ekaterinburg

Tiumen

Omsk

Königsberg
East Prussia
GERMANY

Vilno

Minsk

Vitebsk

Moscow

Volga

Murom

Kama

Ufa

Ufa

Cheliabinsk

Silesia

Warsaw

Mogilev

Smolensk

Tula

Simbirsk

Samara

Orenburg

Ishim

Poland

Brest-Litovsk

Gomel

Orel

Tambov

Cracow
Galicia

Lwow
(Lemberg)

Kiev

Chernigov

Voronezh

Saratov

R U S S I A N   E M P I R E

AUSTRIA-
HUNGARY

Bug

Kishinev

Dnieper

Poltava

Kharkov

Donets

Tsaritsyn (Volgograd)

Don

Volga

Emba

Syr Daria

SERBIA

ROMANIA

Odessa

Bucharest

Crimea

*SEA OF
AZOV*

Rostov

Astrakhan

ARAL
SEA

Sofia
BULGARIA

BLACK SEA

Sevastopol

Stavropol

Caucasus Mts.

C
A
S
P
I
A
N

S
E
A

Amu Daria (Oxus)

Constantinople

Tiflis

Baku

O T T O M A N

E M P I R E

P E R S I A

0   100 200 300 400   500 Miles

At the University of St. Petersburg, it was the annual custom on February 8, the anniversary of its founding, for students—after the formal celebrations—to rush en masse into the center of the city; there they sang, cheered, and invaded cafés and restaurants.* The police had long looked upon this merrymaking with displeasure; for although it had not the slightest political overtones, it was unauthorized, and therefore in their eyes an act of "insubordination." In early 1899, the police requested the university's rector to warn the students that such revelry would no longer be tolerated; violators would be liable to imprisonment as well as substantial fines. Notices to this effect were posted at the university. In protest, the students disrupted the formal anniversary ceremonies. Then they poured into the streets and, chanting the "Marseillaise," headed for the city center. But the mounted police were ready for them and barred the bridges they had to cross. In the ensuing melee, the students pelted the police with snowballs and chunks of ice, and the police responded with whips.

Under a less insecure regime, a minor disturbance of this kind would have been resolved quickly and painlessly. In tsarist Russia, where government and the educated class treated each other as mortal enemies, it instantly escalated into a major crisis.

The agitated students held rallies, leadership of which was assumed by militants organized in an illegal Mutual Assistance Fund. Eager to exploit the incident to radicalize the student body, they appealed to the nation's universities to strike in support of their St. Petersburg colleagues. The police beating, they asserted, was not an isolated incident but another manifestation of the lawlessness that pervaded autocratic Russia: it could be remedied only by the regime's overthrow. Some 25,000 students (of the 35,000 enrolled at institutions of higher learning) responded to the appeal by boycotting classes. The authorities arrested the strike leaders, but they also appointed a commission to investigate the causes of the disturbance. Mollified by the latter move, the students returned to their classrooms.

The episode was a microcosm of the tragedy that beset late Imperial Russia: it illustrated to what extent the Revolution was the result not of

---

* Unless otherwise noted, all dates in this book prior to February 1918 are given "Old Style" (OS)—that is, according to the Julian calendar, which in the nineteenth century was twelve days behind the Western, Gregorian calendar, and in the twentieth century, thirteen days. From February 1918, all dates are given "New Style" (NS)—that is, according to the Gregorian calendar, which the Soviet government adopted at that time. When two dates must be provided to describe Russia's dealings with the West (e.g., June 10/23), the first is Old Style, the second New Style.

insufferable conditions but of irreconcilable attitudes. The government chose to treat a harmless expression of youthful spirits as an act of sedition. Radical intellectuals, for their part, escalated student complaints of mistreatment at the hands of the police into a wholesale rejection of the "system." It was, of course, absurd to insinuate that the student grievances that produced the February 1899 strike could not be satisfied short of overthrowing the absolute monarchy. The technique of translating specific complaints into general political demands became standard operating strategy for both radicals and liberals in Russia. It thwarted compromises and reforms, for it assumed that nothing whatever could be improved as long as the existing regime remained in place, which meant that revolution was a necessary precondition of any progress.

In July 1899, the government announced that henceforth students guilty of grave misconduct would lose their military deferments. When, in December 1900, fresh university disorders broke out, this time at Kiev, the Minister of Education ordered 183 students inducted into the army. In retaliation, a student terrorist shot and killed him. More university strikes followed. Henceforth, Russian universities became the fulcrum of permanent opposition: in this atmosphere of pervasive politicization, research and teaching became virtually impossible.

In April 1902, SR terror escalated further with the assassination of the Minister of the Interior. Nicholas chose as his successor Viacheslav Plehve, an uncompromising reactionary who had spent his professional life in the Ministry of the Interior and its Department of the Police. During his two-year tenure, Russia came closer than any country until that time to a police state in the modern totalitarian sense of the term. Plehve not only nipped in the bud any manifestation of public initiative but infiltrated society with police agents. His greatest triumph was placing one of his agents in the SR "Combat Organization," which directed major terrorist actions. This coup enabled him to frustrate many assassination attempts.

How pervasive the police mentality was in Russia at this time may be seen in the example of police-run trade unions. One of the ablest operatives of the Okhrana—a branch of the security police charged with protecting high government officials—a man by the name of S. V. Zubatov, conceived an original scheme of having the police take over and in this manner neutralize politically the incipient trade-union movement. Zubatov argued that labor was essentially apolitical and that by treating as seditious every manifestation of worker initiative, whether economic or even cultural, the government needlessly radicalized it and pushed it into the arms of revolutionaries. With the blessing of influential Court figures, he proceeded to organize police-sponsored trade unions. They attracted many workers. Zubatov's scheme had its drawbacks, however, for in the event of labor disturbances the authorities would find themselves in the awkward position of having to back their unions' illegal strikes against the employers. Plehve realized this danger, but, bowing to pressures from above, felt compelled to endorse the plan.

The tsarist government had considerable experience in coping with internal discontent, and it undoubtedly would have contained it this time as well, were it not for its bad judgment in becoming embroiled in a war with Japan. War carried for it two risks. One was that defeat would lower still further its prestige in the eyes of the Russian population. The other was that with the army away in the Far East, the government would lack the forces with which to crush disorders. In the eyes of some monarchists, however, these risks were counterbalanced by the prospect that a quick and decisive victory would both win tsarism popular support and isolate its opponents.

The opening of archives after 1917 left no doubt that responsibility for the war rested with Russia.

In pursuit of his grand design for industrialization, Witte had persuaded Alexander III to construct a railroad across Siberia, linking central Russia with the Pacific Ocean and China. Begun in 1891 and completed only twenty-five years later, the Trans-Siberian remains to this day the longest continuous railway line in the world (9,441 kilometers, or 5,867 miles). Witte believed that the railway would replace the Suez Canal as the preferred carrier of goods from Europe to the Far East, as well as enable Russia to establish her dominion over Far Eastern markets. To shorten the route between Lake Baikal and the line's terminal, the port city of Vladivostok, Witte obtained from Beijing permission to run this final segment across Chinese Manchuria. The Chinese stipulated that Russia must scrupulously observe their sovereignty over this region.

The Russians, however, immediately violated the terms of the accords by introducing numerous military and police units into Manchuria, ostensibly to ensure the security of the railroad but in reality to establish a strong presence preliminary to annexation. In January 1903, after long deliberations, Nicholas II yielded to his advisers who urged that Manchuria be annexed. The Japanese, who had their own designs on the area, proposed to divide it into spheres of influence, conceding Manchuria to Russia in return for Russia's recognition of their claim to Korea. The Russians rejected these approaches. They held the Japanese in utter contempt as "monkeys": common people joked that they would smother the little apes with their caps.

On February 8, 1904, without declaring war, Japan attacked and laid siege to the naval base of Port Arthur which Russia had leased from China. Sinking some Russian ships and bottling up the rest, they neutralized Russia's Pacific fleet and secured mastery of the China Sea. The land campaigns that followed took place in Manchuria, thousands of miles from the center of Russia, which caused serious logistical problems, aggravated by the fact that the Trans-Siberian Railway was not yet complete.

Six months after the outbreak of the Russo-Japanese War, the SRs succeeded in one of their main objectives: assassinating Plehve. The murder presented Nicholas with the difficult choice of selecting as Plehve's successor another reactionary or yielding to mounting popular pressure and replacing him with a liberal. The bad news from Manchuria, where the Japanese continued to press the Russians back, persuaded him to take the path of conciliation. His choice fell on Prince P. D. Sviatopolk-Mirskii, a career bureaucrat whose views were very different from his predecessor's. Mirskii concluded that Russia could no longer be governed exclusively by police methods; the monarchy had to gain the confidence of its subjects in order to isolate the radical left. The concept of political crime, in his view, should apply not to expressions of opinion but exclusively to terrorism and incitement to violence. His favorite word was "trust," and he at once set himself to win public support by abandoning some of the more odious features of Plehve's administration.

The liberals welcomed Mirskii's appointment. The most active among them belonged to local self-rule boards called zemstva. Introduced in 1864, in the era of reforms, to give the population an opportunity to improve its economic and cultural conditions, zemstva were elected by the rural gentry as well as by local peasants. They attracted intellectuals who believed that Russia needed not violent change at the top but patient, gradual improvement below; not political revolution but cultural and economic evolution. But although the zemstva had no administrative powers, the bureaucrats from the Ministry of the Interior treated them as a nuisance which interfered with their chain of command. In the 1880s and 1890s, these bureaucrats steadily restricted the boards' functions and harassed their more outspoken leaders. The result was politicization of the zemstva, as increasing numbers of their officials reluctantly concluded that law-abiding work within the system was not feasible. In the early years of the twentieth century, zemstvo deputies provided the main support of the nascent liberal movement.

Fearing that they could become the nucleus of a political party, the government from the beginning restricted zemstvo activity to the provincial level, forbidding their representatives to hold national conferences. These prohibitions were subverted in the 1890s by the device of private and professional meetings at which personal contacts were made and a common program of action formulated.

The appointment of Mirskii and his expressions of trust in society persuaded zemstvo leaders that the time had come to convene an open national conference. Mirskii, whom they approached for permission, gave a confusing response which they interpreted as a signal to proceed in the guise of an open but private gathering. At the beginning of November 1904, zemstvo representatives from all parts of Russia converged in St. Petersburg to meet in the residences of prominent liberals. The police did not interfere. The participants split into two factions, conservative-liberal and liberal. The former, maintaining that parliaments were alien to the Russian tradition, wanted constitutional change to be limited to the introduction of a representative body that would offer the Tsar nonbinding advice. The liberals would settle for nothing less than a parliament with legislative authority. In the voting, the liberals won by a margin of nearly two to one. The event may be compared in its consequences with the French Estates-General of 1789. It was the first time in Russian history that an assembly openly discussed changes in the constitution and expressed itself in favor of limits on the Tsar's authority.

In the weeks that followed, the Union of Liberation, which worked in close contact with the zemstva, organized a nationwide campaign of "banquets." Modeled on similar gatherings in France during the 1848 revolution, these ostensibly private gatherings passed resolutions calling for a constitution and a parliament and, in some cases, demanding the convocation of a Constituent Assembly. The local authorities, confused by contradictory instructions from the center, observed these happenings without taking action.

Buffeted by mounting defiance, the government sought to mollify opinion with halfhearted concessions that satisfied no one. The Crown procrastinated in the hope that a sudden reversal of fortunes on the Far Eastern front would bolster its standing at home. In October 1904, it dispatched the Baltic Fleet on a journey halfway around the world to relieve Port Arthur. But instead of improving, the news from the battlefield went from bad to worse. In December 1904, while the naval relief force was sailing off the coast of Africa, Port Arthur surrendered. The Japanese took 25,000 prisoners and captured what was left of Russia's Pacific Fleet.

Up to this point, the Russian masses had taken no part in the political turmoil. The pressures on the government for constitutional change emanated almost exclusively from university students, professional revolutionaries, and zemstvo gentry. This situation changed drastically on January 9, 1905, following events that came to be known as "Bloody Sunday." If the November 1904 Zemstvo Congress was Russia's Estates-General, then Bloody Sunday was her Bastille Day.

The most outstanding participant in the police-sponsored trade unions was a priest, Father George Gapon. A charismatic personality, Gapon established in St. Petersburg several flourishing unions, through which he sought to inculcate in workers Christian principles. Although for radicals, annoyed by his popularity, he was nothing but a police agent, Gapon increasingly identified with his followers and their grievances. In late 1904 it was impossible to tell whether the police were using Gapon or he the police, for by that time he had become the most prominent labor leader in Russia.

Impressed by the Zemstvo Congress and the banquet campaign, Gapon approached the St. Petersburg branch of the Union of Liberation. At its urging, he adopted political objectives for his unions, which until then had been committed exclusively to cultural and spiritual activities. According to his memoirs, he feared that unless the liberal intellectuals received help from workers, they would fail.

In late December 1904, after several workers in Gapon's organizations had been dismissed from the largest industrial plant in St. Petersburg, thousands of workers struck in protest. On January 7, industrial action involved 120,000 workers. Gapon, maintaining close contact with the Union of Liberation, decided to emulate the liberal banquet campaign by staging a procession to present the Tsar with a petition of grievances. Drafted with the help of liberal intellectuals, the petition urged the Tsar to convene a Constituent Assembly and accede to the Union of Liberation's other demands.

The bewildered city administrators authorized the procession on condition that it not come near the Winter Palace (which the Tsar had left the previous day for his country residence). On Sunday morning, January 9, workers assembled in various parts of the city carrying icons, and moved without police interference toward the center. The crowd was calm and resembled a religious procession. Soon, however, the demonstrators ran into armed troops barring the way to the Palace. Pressed from the rear, they failed to disperse when ordered, whereupon the troops fired, killing 200 and wounding 800.

The massacre of a peaceful demonstration sent a wave of revulsion across the country. Organizations of nearly every political hue condemned the government. Several hundred thousand workers went on strike. Both the army and the police savagely repressed the riots that followed, killing numerous protesters.

Nicholas, never a decisive man, wavered. Impressed by the arguments of his more liberal counselors, he agreed after some hesitation to convene an advisory body of the "worthiest men" chosen by the nation. He further consented to invite his subjects to submit "suggestions" on how to improve their lot. A year earlier, these measures might have calmed the situation. Now they no longer sufficed. The liberals, encouraged by the massive support their program had gained, formed a Union of Unions, which combined various professional associations (lawyers, physicians, teachers, engineers, and the like) to demand the abandonment of autocracy in favor of a constitutional regime. Its chairman, the historian Paul Miliukov, would later play a leading role in the liberal party.

The final blow to the monarchy's hopes of saving its autocratic prerogatives was the debacle of the navy. The combined Baltic and Black Sea fleets were ordered to proceed to the Far East even after Port Arthur had fallen. The Japanese navy waited for them in the Strait of Tsushima between Korea and Southern Japan. Benefiting from superior intelligence data and swifter ships, in May 1905 the Japanese dispatched the Russian Fleet to the bottom of the sea. Thus ended any hopes of salvaging something from the disastrous war. Taking advantage of President Theodore Roosevelt's offer to act as intermediary, Russia sent Sergei Witte to Portsmouth, New Hampshire, to negotiate a peace treaty. Thanks to U.S. support and Witte's diplomatic talents, the Russians came out of the negotiations reasonably well.

By the time Witte returned home, a nationwide strike was in the making. After the Tsushima disaster, the Union of Unions decided on a general political strike that would bring the country to a standstill and leave the monarchy no alternative but to surrender to its demands. Its task was facilitated by a surprising decision of the authorities, announced at the end of August 1905, to relax the administration of the universities. Apparently taken in the hope of calming the students in the approaching academic year, this decision restored to the faculties the right to elect rectors and allowed students to hold assemblies, neither of which had been possible under the stringent University Statute of 1884. Even more unexpectedly, to avoid confrontations with the students, the new rules forbade the police to enter university grounds.

Radicals, who until now had been overshadowed by the liberals, at once exploited these concessions. They formulated a strategy for the new academic year which called for transforming the universities into centers of revolutionary activity by holding political rallies with the participation of workers from nearby factories. Mistrusting the young intellectuals, the workers at first viewed these affairs with suspicion, but finding themselves treated with unaccustomed respect, they came and soon gained courage to participate in the rallies. Academic work came to a standstill as universities turned into arenas of political agitation; professors and students who wished to carry on normal academic work were harassed and intimidated. The hope that less stringent regulations would placate the students proved to be a mirage: all they accomplished in fact was to provide the most radical elements with a legal sanctuary.

At the end of September, fresh strikes broke out in central Russia. They began with a work stoppage of Moscow printers, which the printers in St. Petersburg joined. Next came the turn of railroad personnel. At issue were wages and pensions, that is, economic complaints, but the Union of Unions made certain that the workers' organizations affiliated with it did not lose sight of political aims. The work stoppages, aiming at a general strike, were coordinated at the universities, the only place where it was possible to hold political meetings without police interference. The lecture halls, increasingly used for rallies, were attended by thousands of students and nonstudents alike. On October 8, the Union of Unions voted to set up strike committees throughout the country preliminary to a general strike.

On October 9, Witte met with the Tsar. He told him, with unusual candor, that he had two alternatives: appoint a military dictator or make political concessions. Witte realized full well that with the army thousands of miles away, a military dictatorship was out of the question, but he presented it as an option because he knew it was what the Tsar preferred.

6. Sergei Witte at Portsmouth, N.H., summer 1905.

The case for concessions Witte offered in a memorandum. Its contents indicate that Witte accepted both the premises and the program of the Union of Liberation. Repeating almost verbatim the words of Struve on the pages of *Liberation*, he asserted: "The slogan of 'freedom' must become the slogan of government activity. There is no other way of saving the state." The situation was critical. Russia had become dangerously radicalized, and the very foundations of her statehood were in danger.

The advance of human progress is unstoppable. The idea of human freedom will triumph, if not by way of reform, then by way of revolution. But in the latter event it will come to life on the ashes of a thousand years of destroyed history. The Russian *bunt* [rebellion], mindless and pitiless, will sweep away everything, turn everything to dust. What kind of Russia will emerge from this unexampled trial transcends human imagination: the horrors of the Russian *bunt* may surpass everything known to history. It is possible that foreign intervention will tear the country apart. Attempts to put into practice the ideals of theoretical socialism—they will fail but they will be made, no doubt about it—will destroy the family, the expressions of religious faith, property, all the foundations of law.

To avert such a catastrophe, Witte proposed to meet the demands of the liberals and in this manner separate them from the radicals. Take charge of the Liberation Movement, he urged Nicholas. Grant a constitution and a legislative parliament, elected on a democratic franchise with the authority to appoint ministers. He further proposed to improve the lot of workers and ethnic minorities, as well as to grant the country full freedom of speech, press, and assembly.

Nicholas took these revolutionary proposals under advisement, but he hesitated to act on them, partly from a conviction that they meant breaking his coronation pledge to maintain autocracy and partly from fear that they would cause still greater turmoil.

But events were coming to a head, and he soon had no choice in the matter. In the second week of October, Russia was grinding to a halt as employees in indispensable services went on strike. On October 13, a Strike Committee convened at the St. Petersburg Technological Institute; four days later it adopted the name Soviet of Workers' Deputies. Representatives of workers were in attendance, but the leadership of the new institution, destined to have an important future, was firmly in the hands of the radical intelligentsia: the Soviet's Executive Committee consisted of intellectuals designated by the socialist parties. This procedure set a precedent that would be followed by the Petrograd Soviet of 1917.

Nicholas continued to agonize. He asked the Governor-General of St. Petersburg whether order could be restored by force without inflicting many casualties. The Governor-General replied in the negative. Nicholas held repeated consultations with Witte as well as other advisers, one of them his cousin, Grand Duke Nikolai Nikolaevich. In response to the Tsar's offer that he, the Grand Duke, assume dictatorial powers, his cousin said that there simply were no forces available for a military dictatorship; he also threatened to shoot himself if the Tsar did not grant the country political liberties.

On October 17, Witte presented the Tsar with the draft of a Manifesto. It rephrased the resolutions of a Zemstvo Congress held in Moscow a month earlier, which had called for guarantees of civil rights and a legislative parliament (Duma) elected on the basis of universal franchise. That evening Nicholas affixed his signature to a document that came to be known as the October Manifesto. In it he pledged:

(1) To grant the population inviolate foundations of civil liberty [based] on the principles of genuine inviolability of person, the freedom of conscience, speech, assembly, and association;

(2) . . . to extend, in the future, through the new legislature, the principle of universal franchise; and,

(3) To establish as inviolate the rule that no law shall acquire force without the approval of the State Duma and that representatives of the people shall have an effective opportunity to participate in supervising the legality of the actions of the authorities whom we have appointed.

It was the end of autocracy in Russia. Before retiring for the night, Nicholas wrote in his diary: "After such a day, the head is grown heavy and thoughts are confused. May the Lord help us save and pacify Russia."

Two aspects of the October Manifesto call for comment, for otherwise a great deal of the history of the ten-year-long constitutional experiment will be incomprehensible.

First, the October Manifesto was extracted from Nicholas under duress, and for this reason he did not feel morally bound to observe it. Second, the document did not refer to a "constitution." This was no oversight. Nicholas avoided the detested word in order to maintain the illusion that he remained an autocrat even after creating a representative body with legislative powers. He had been assured by his liberal advisers, Witte among them, that he could always revoke what he had conceded. This self-deception—the absurd notion of a limited autocrat—would cause no end of trouble in the years ahead.

The proclamation of the Manifesto, which was read in the churches, led in the cities to tumultuous demonstrations of jubilant crowds. But it also produced bloody pogroms against Jews and intellectuals, who were blamed for forcing the Tsar to give up his autocratic prerogatives. The pogroms, which the authorities did not instigate but also did nothing to prevent, had the unexpected result of encouraging peasants to seize private properties. For, following their own logic, the peasants concluded that the failure of the police to defend Jews from violence and looting gave them license to carry out pogroms against landlord estates. Their purpose was to "smoke out" private owners from the countryside and force them to dispose of their properties at bargain prices. Nicholas was appalled by the continuing unrest and felt deceived by advisers who had assured him that granting a constitution would pacify the country.

The final act of the 1905 Revolution was played out in Moscow. On December 6, the Moscow Soviet, dominated by the Bolsheviks, called for an armed uprising to overthrow the tsarist government, convene a Constituent Assembly, and proclaim a democratic republic. The strategy behind this action, which came to be known as one of "permanent revolution," was formulated by Alexander Helphand (better known by the pseudonym Parvus), who would play an important role in the triumph of Bolshevism in 1917. Parvus argued that socialists should not allow the first stage of the Revolution to solidify "bourgeois" rule but proceed at once to the next, socialist phase. Witte ruthlessly crushed the Moscow uprising, after which Parvus emigrated to Germany.

Appointed Chairman of the Council of Ministers—a post equivalent to Prime Minister though not so designated—Witte made several attempts to bring representatives of moderate public opinion into the cabinet. He failed. Liberals and liberal-conservatives posed impossible conditions for joining the government; Witte thought that their reluctance was due to a fear of assassination. In the end, the new cabinet was staffed exclusively with *chin*-bearing officials. Witte resigned his post in April 1906, feeling that he had lost the Tsar's confidence.

The year 1905 marked the apogee of Russian liberalism—the triumph of its program, its strategy, its tactics. The socialists played in these events an auxiliary role. The liberals' triumph, however, was tenuous. As events were to show, they constituted a minority of the intelligentsia and soon found themselves caught in the deadly cross fire of conservative and radical extremism.

The 1905 Revolution substantially altered Russia's political institutions, but it left political attitudes untouched. The monarchy continued to ignore the implications of the October Manifesto, pretending that nothing had really changed. Although he had granted the new Parliament the power to veto legislation, Nicholas believed it to be nothing more than an advisory body. He received support from street mobs, in which workers participated, eager to punish those who had humiliated him. The socialist intelligentsia, for its part, was more determined than ever to exploit the government's concessions to press on with the next, socialist phase of the Revolution. The experience of 1905 left it more, not less, radical. The terrible weakness of the bonds holding together the mighty Russian Empire became apparent to all. But to the government it spelled the need for firmer authority, whereas to the radicals, and even many liberals, it signaled an opportunity to deliver the existing system its coup de grâce. Not surprisingly, the government and the opposition alike viewed the new parliament not as a vehicle for reaching compromises but as an arena of combat. Sensible voices pleading for cooperation found themselves vilified by both parties.

In the end, Russia had gained nothing more than a breathing spell.

Stolypin

The attitudes with which the monarchy and the opposition emerged from the trials of 1905 did not bode well for the new constitutional order. Both sides lacked the goodwill that is essential for the success of any contractual arrangement, constitution included.

The Crown, according to a contemporary wit, was prepared to live with a constitution provided autocracy remained intact. It regarded the Duma as a factor that complicated the bureaucracy's administrative responsibilities rather than as a partner. Liberal and radical parties, for their part, treated the entire constitutional arrangement as merely an episode in Russia's unstoppable advance toward full-scale democracy.

During the half year that followed the proclamation of the October Manifesto, government experts worked on legislation that would institutionalize its promises. In November 1905, censorship was abolished and Russians received for the first time the right to publish freely. Laws announced in March 1906 guaranteed the freedoms of assembly and association. They made it possible, for the first time in the country's history, to organize political parties and trade unions. However, the practice of imposing martial law on turbulent provinces remained in place, permitting the bureaucracy to violate these freedoms whenever it felt that state security was being endangered.

In April 1906, the authorities made public the text of the constitution, called Fundamental Laws. It was a conservative document that still referred to the Tsar as "autocrat." Russia received a two-chamber parliament. The upper house, the State Council, consisted of a mixture of appointees and representatives of public bodies, such as the Church and Assemblies of the Nobility. The lower house, the State Duma, was made up entirely of elected representatives, chosen on a complicated franchise designed to ensure the preponderance of more conservative elements. All bills, in addition to requiring the signature of the monarch, had to have the consent of both chambers. Both chambers also passed on the annual budget. The October Manifesto's pledge to enable the legislature to supervise the legality of actions of government officials was fulfilled in a limited way by empowering the Duma to subject ministers to public questioning. Otherwise the bureaucracy remained outside parliamentary control.

To the great disappointment of the liberals, the Crown retained the power of appointing ministers: this issue, more than any other, would cause friction between parliament and the monarchy. The Crown also reserved for itself the right to declare war and make peace.

Two other provisions of the 1906 Fundamental Laws call for comment. As in Britain, parliament had a normal term of five years, but the Crown could dissolve it at any time. In modern Britain, as in other constitutional monarchies, the Crown would not dream of resorting to this prerogative unless the government lost a vote of confidence. In Russia, as will be seen, the power of dissolution was used to punish truculent parliaments. Similarly abused was Article 87 of the Fundamental Laws, which empowered the Crown, in emergencies, when parliament was not in session, to rule by decree. The monarchy would use this clause to circumvent the Duma when it had reason to believe it would defy the Crown's wishes.

In some respects, perhaps the single most important prerogative of the Duma was the parliamentary immunity granted its members. Liberal and radical deputies took advantage of this right to engage in intemperate and often inflammatory criticism of the regime. Such criticism lowered still further the prestige of the Crown, stripping it of the aura of omniscience and omnipotence that it had so assiduously cultivated and that the population at large regarded as the hallmark of good government.

Whether one sees the Fundamental Laws of 1906 as a significant advance or as a deceptive half-measure depends on one's criteria. By the standards of the advanced industrial democracies, Russia's constitution certainly left much to be desired. But in terms of her own traditions, it marked a giant step toward democracy. For the first time ever, the Crown allowed representatives elected by its subjects to initiate and veto legislative bills, scrutinize the budget, criticize its policies, and interrogate its ministers. If the constitutional experiment failed to stabilize the country, the fault lay not so much with the constitution as with the unwillingness of the Crown and parliament alike to respect its spirit and its provisions.

Conflicts arose from the day the Duma opened its doors. Because the Socialists-Revolutionaries and the Social-Democrats boycotted the elections, the liberal Constitutional-Democrats, or Kadets, issued from the Union of Liberation and formally organized in October 1905, were the most radical party represented. In the hope of securing a permanent hold on the worker and peasant constituencies, the Kadets adopted a confrontational strategy. Having won the largest number of seats (179 out of 478), including all the seats in St. Petersburg and Moscow, they immediately went on the offensive. They treated the Fundamental Laws as merely a preliminary draft of the country's true constitution, which was one of parliamentary democracy rather than constitutional monarchy: emulating the French Estates-General of 1789, they sought to force the monarchy to its knees. In heated sessions, they called for the abolition of the upper chamber, the right to appoint ministers, the expropriation of large landed estates, and blanket amnesty for political prisoners, including those sentenced for terrorist crimes.

Dismayed by such uncompromising behavior, the Court decided on dissolution. On July 8, 1906, barely three months after it had met, it dissolved the Duma and ordered fresh elections. The Kadet deputies responded to this action, which perhaps violated the spirit of the constitution but certainly not its letter, by withdrawing to the Finnish city of Vyborg, beyond the reach of the Russian police. From there they appealed to the population to refuse to pay taxes and to disregard draft notices. The so-called Vyborg Manifesto was both unconstitutional and futile. The population ignored it, and its only effect was to disenfranchise its signatories, among whom were many of Russia's best-known liberal politicians.

While the country was voting for the Second Duma, St. Petersburg cast about for a strong man capable of taming the rebellious politicians. Its choice fell on Peter Stolypin, the governor of Saratov province, who had attracted attention by his effective handling of peasant disturbances in 1905–6. It was a singularly happy choice, and Stolypin proved to be the outstanding statesman of late Imperial Russia.

Descended from an old servitor family, Stolypin felt total devotion to the monarchy. At the same time, he concluded that Russia could no longer be governed in the old patrimonial manner, as if it were a royal estate. To survive, the Crown had to seek a solid base of social support and lead the country by consent rather than command. He resembled Bismarck in the sense that, while a staunch conservative, he realized that the monarchy had to adapt itself to the dissolution of the traditional estate system and the emergence of the modern nation.

Stolypin wanted to cooperate with the Duma by forming a bloc of loyal supporters and thus isolating the left. But beyond parliamentary maneuvering, he also envisaged bringing into existence a conservative, landowning yeomanry to perform the same stabilizing function it performed in France and some other Continental countries. To this end, he

7. P. A. Stolypin, 1909.

wished to weaken and ultimately abolish the commune in order to transform communal allotments into the private property of the farmers. He
also entertained ambitious plans of modernizing Russia's social services
and ridding the country of the remaining vestiges of the bureaucratic-
police regime.

As long as the monarchy felt threatened by social turmoil and a rebellious parliament, Stolypin enjoyed its unstinting support. But to the
extent that he succeeded in pacifying the country, he ran into hostility
that in the end destroyed him politically. The bureaucracy did not consider him one of its own because he had not reached the top of the ministerial career ladder by ascending step by step, but had leaped directly
from the post of Governor to that of Prime Minister. The Court looked
with misgivings on his parliamentary maneuvers, suspecting self-serving
motives. And the radical left despised him for the ruthlessness with
which he had crushed the revolutionary movement.

The first task Stolypin set for himself after being appointed Minister of the Interior (April 1906) and then Chairman of the Council of Ministers (July 1906) was to quell the agrarian disturbances and the SR terror. The terror continued unabated. It has been estimated that in the course of 1906 and 1907, terrorists killed or maimed 4,500 officials. If private persons are included, the total number of victims of left-wing terrorism rises to 9,000. Stolypin suppressed both political terrorism and rural violence by setting up field courts-martial for civilians to dispense summary justice that often ended in death sentences. These procedures outraged public opinion, but they succeeded in restoring order.

Unlike his predecessors, Stolypin was not content merely to suppress violence, for he regarded it as symptomatic of a deeper malaise. He wanted to strike at its roots. Without waiting for the convocation of the Second Duma, he proceeded, with resort to Article 87, to enact a series of legislative acts bearing on the peasantry. To begin with, he lifted the remaining legal restrictions on the peasants, granting them full freedom of movement and abolishing other relics of serfdom. Next, he persuaded Nicholas to transfer to the Peasant Land Bank quantities of Crown and state land for sale, on easy terms, to the peasants. This was followed by his single most important law, issued in November 1906, which enabled the peasants to withdraw from the commune and set up private farms.

By then, conservative circles had become disenchanted with the commune, which fifty years earlier they had viewed as a bulwark of rural stability. The commune kept on the land marginal elements—families too small or inefficient to succeed—and at the same time hindered large, industrious families from expanding their holdings. The periodic turnover of allotments gave the peasant no stake in his land and encouraged him to exhaust it before he surrendered it in the next repartition. Stolypin had figures to prove that the agrarian problem could not be solved by expropriating private estates, as advocated by liberals and radicals: there simply was not enough land in private possession to meet the needs of the peasants, who were multiplying at a rate that exceeded anything known in Europe. The solution lay rather in more intensive cultivation, which would yield larger harvests. The best means to this end was privatization of peasant landholdings.

The November 1906 law, which is indissolubly associated with Stolypin's name, provided easy procedures for a communal household to declare its desire to withdraw from the commune and claim ownership title to its allotment. This done, it could either sell its land or set up an independent farmstead.

How successful were Stolypin's agrarian reforms? On balance, not very. The peasantry liked the security of the commune and resented Stolypin's law, which threatened the majority that chose to remain in it. Although the law provided that peasants leaving the commune could consolidate their allotments, in many villages they had to take them in scattered strips, which meant that one of the banes of Russian agriculture, strip-farming, continued as before. Between 1906 and 1916, 2.5 million, or 22 percent, of the communal households, holding 14.5 percent of the communal acreage, filed petitions to take title to their allotments. As these figures indicate, those who availed themselves of the new legislation were the poorer peasants; most of them did so in order to sell their allotments. This defeated the purpose of Stolypin's reform, which aimed at creating a strong, self-sufficient class of farmers. On the eve of the 1917 Revolution, only 10 percent of Russian households operated as independent farmsteads. And the latter would vanish in 1917–18, when communal peasants seized privately held land, including that belonging to fellow peasants, and distributed it among themselves. Thus the expected agrarian revolution never occurred.

Stolypin revived Witte's attempts to bring into the cabinet public representatives, including Kadets, but he had no more success. He asked the Kadets to condemn terrorism, but they refused to do so and thereby disqualified themselves from receiving legal status as a political party.

To the Crown's dismay, the Second Duma, which opened in February 1907, turned out to be even more radical than its predecessor. Both the SDs and the SRs made up their minds to participate in the elections with the intention of using parliamentary privileges and immunity to undermine Parliament and radicalize the masses. In April 1907, the Social-Democrats resolved to enter the Duma in order "systematically [to exploit] all conflicts between the government and the Duma as well as within the Duma for the purpose of broadening and deepening the revolutionary movement." The SRs voted to participate in the elections to "utilize the State Duma for organizing and revolutionizing the masses." The Kadets, chastised by their experience the previous year, adopted a more constructive strategy, but they were outflanked on the left by the radical parties, which controlled 222 seats.

Nicholas and his advisers by now had their fill of the Duma and considered abolishing it. They might have gone through with this plan were it not for the fear that foreign financial markets would react negatively and devalue the price of Russian obligations. Enlightened bureaucrats added their weight to these arguments. In the end it was decided to retain the Duma but to revise the electoral law so that the conservative representation would be enhanced and the radical and liberal one correspondingly reduced.

The government dissolved the Second Duma on June 2, 1907, and the next day made public, with reference to Article 87, a new electoral law. It raised the representation of the propertied classes at the expense of peasants, workers, and ethnic minorities. The result was a more conservative and ethnically homogeneous Great Russian legislature. The move was indisputably unconstitutional inasmuch as the Fundamental Laws explicitly forbade the use of Article 87 to alter the franchise. The opposition therefore referred to the electoral law of June 3 as a "coup d'état," but the term seems inappropriate, given that it did not affect the fundamental rights of parliament.

The Third Duma, convened in November 1907, was the only one to serve out its full five-year term. Of the 422 deputies, 154 belonged to the Union of 17th October, whose members, popularly known as Octobrists, espoused a liberal-conservative ideology and were prepared to cooperate with the Crown. One hundred forty-seven deputies belonged to various right-wing and nationalistic groupings. The Kadets were reduced to fifty-four seats, while the socialists ended up with thirty-two. Although the new Duma was far more to the Crown's liking, it was by no means a mere rubber stamp. Stolypin had to engage in a great deal of parliamentary maneuvering to secure passage of some government bills.

The Octobrists, who dominated the Third Duma as the liberals had dominated the First and the socialists the Second, accepted the constitutional arrangement of 1906. If for the liberals the highest good was liberty and for the socialists, equality, for the Octobrists it was legality; in this respect, they were at one with the liberal bureaucracy, which Stolypin represented. Their leader, Alexander Guchkov, combined patriotism with a belief in firm authority and a respect for the law. Cooperation between Stolypin and Guchkov provided the balance that enabled the Third Duma to engage in a great deal of constructive work. It voted on 2,571 bills introduced by the government, initiated 205 bills of its own, and questioned ministers on 157 occasions. Its commissions dealt with agrarian issues, social legislation, and similar subjects. The year 1908 and, even more so, 1909 yielded bountiful harvests that calmed the countryside. With declining violence and renewed industrial development, Russia seemed on the way to full recovery from the ravages of the Revolution. Stolypin stood at the pinnacle of his career.

Yet at this very time the first dark clouds appeared on the horizon. The Court disliked Stolypin's parliamentary maneuvering, suspecting that rather than serving the interests of the Crown, as he claimed, he was building his own power base. After his death, the Tsarina would caution his successor, in a clear reference to Stolypin, "not to seek support in political parties." The more successful Stolypin was, the less were his services required and the more intense grew the Crown's antagonism to him.

Stolypin's actual and projected reforms alienated powerful interests. His agrarian policies annoyed the conservative landed gentry, which did not like the prospect of an independent yeomanry taking its place as the dominant element in the countryside. The bureaucracy objected to his proposals to decentralize the administration and curb the powers of the police. His efforts, though unsuccessful, to grant Jews full civil rights infuriated the extreme right, which had persuaded itself that Jews were the cause of all of Russia's troubles. The liberals and socialists hated him for bolstering the monarchy and repressing terrorism. Assailed from all sides, isolated and increasingly discouraged, Stolypin began to falter and commit political blunders.

His first conflict with the Duma occurred in 1908–9, when the legislature refused the government money to build an expanded navy to replace the one lost in the war with Japan. But the major and ultimately ruinous clash occurred in March 1911 over the issue of extending zemstva to the western provinces of the Empire. On their introduction in 1864, zemstva were not extended to the Empire's western provinces, taken from Poland in the partitions of the eighteenth century. Elections to zemstvo boards were heavily skewed in favor of the landowning class, and in these regions a high proportion of the landed gentry consisted of Poles and other Catholics who were considered hostile. Stolypin concluded that the time had come to repair this omission. He introduced a bill calling for elections to the proposed western zemstva by means of complicated procedures that required Russians and Poles to vote in separate chambers. Jews were to be altogether disenfranchised. It was a minor measure that would have produced hardly a ripple if the reactionaries, hostile to Stolypin and sensing that his standing at Court had weakened, had not chosen it as a pretext to bring him down. The Western Zemstvo bill passed the Duma in May 1910 on a close vote and was sent to the upper chamber, where its passage was virtually a foregone conclusion. But unknown to Stolypin, two Council members obtained from the Tsar permission to have deputies vote on this measure not as directed by the Court but as they themselves preferred. To Stolypin's astonishment and outrage, the Council defeated the bill.

Stolypin tendered his resignation but allowed himself to be dissuaded by the Tsar, who apparently had no inkling of the extent to which he had humiliated his minister. On his suggestion, Nicholas prorogued both chambers for three days, during which the Western Zemstvo bill was promulgated under Article 87. It was a fatal move, one that alienated Stolypin from the Octobrists and did not win him friends at the Court: Nicholas never forgave him for this embarrassment. Stolypin knew that he was politically finished, and so did everyone else.

At the beginning of September 1911, Stolypin followed the Imperial family to Kiev to attend celebrations connected with the unveiling of a monument to Alexander II. The police had received warnings of possible terrorist attacks, and the security precautions were very tight. Stolypin ignored the danger, refusing to wear a bulletproof vest and leaving his bodyguards behind. During the performance in the Kiev opera a terrorist approached and fired point-blank two bullets, one of which lodged in Stolypin's liver. Investigations revealed that the assassin was a double agent, a young man from a well-to-do family who served the police while involved in terrorist circles. He had concocted a story of an alleged attempt that would be made on the life of the Tsar during the opera performance and gained access to the theater in order to identify the would-be terrorist. Neither Nicholas nor his wife appeared despondent over the death of the minister, whom they viewed as expendable now that the regime was again firmly in the saddle.

Stolypin stood head and shoulders above his immediate predecessors and successors in that he combined a vision of the desirable with a sense of the possible; he was a rare blend of statesman and politician. Witte, his closest competitor, was a brilliant and realistic politician, but a follower rather than a leader and something of an opportunist. Stolypin was virtually the only prime minister of the constitutional decade to address the Duma as a partner in the joint endeavor to build a vigorous and great Russia rather than as a royal steward. A monarchist, he viewed himself also as a servant of the nation.

This said, it cannot be realistically claimed, as is done by some Russian conservatives, that had he survived there would have been no revolution. His reforms either failed or were not enacted. His political career was finished before he was struck down by the assassin's bullets, and he would almost certainly have been dismissed before long. Although he lost his life to a revolutionary, Stolypin was politically destroyed by the very people whom he had served and tried to save.

The three years that separated the death of Stolypin from the outbreak of World War I were filled with contradictory trends, some of which pointed to stabilization while others foreshadowed a breakdown.

On the surface, Russia's situation looked promising. Stolypin's repressions and the economic prosperity that happened to accompany them had restored order. Conservatives and radicals agreed, with different emotions, that the monarchy had weathered the Revolution of 1905. The economy was booming. In 1913 iron production, compared with 1900, grew by more than 50 percent, while coal production more than doubled; the nation's exports and imports doubled as well. A French economist forecast in 1912 that if Russia maintained until the middle of the twentieth century the pace of economic growth she had shown since 1900, she would come to dominate Europe politically, economically, and financially. The village was calm. And although there was an increase in industrial strikes, this did not necessarily presage revolution, since similar increases occurred in Great Britain and the United States on the eve of World War I. In Russia, they were an expression of the growing strength of trade unions, which the 1905–6 legislation had made possible. Public opinion began to veer toward the right. Socialism lost its attraction, yielding to patriotism and aesthetics.

And yet, notwithstanding such positive trends, Russia was a troubled and anxious country. Neither the violence of 1905 nor the reforms of Stolypin had solved anything. There was a widespread feeling that the events of 1905 were only a prelude to another round of violence.

To the historian, the most striking—and most ominous—aspect of this period was the prevalence and intensity of hatred: ideological, ethnic, and social. The radicals hated the establishment. The peasants loathed those of their neighbors who had withdrawn from the commune. Ukrainians hated Jews, Muslims hated Armenians, the Kazakh nomads hated and wanted to expel the Russians who had settled in their midst under Stolypin. All these passions were held in check only by the forces of order—the army, the gendarmerie, the police—who themselves were under assault from the left. Since political institutions and processes capable of peacefully resolving these conflicts had failed to emerge, the chances were that sooner or later there would again be recourse to violence, and to the physical extermination of those who happened to stand in the way of one or another of the contending groups.

It was common in those days to speak of Russia living on a "volcano." In 1908 the poet Alexander Blok used another metaphor when he referred to a "bomb" ticking in the heart of Russia. Some tried to ignore it, some to run away from it, others yet to disarm it. To no avail:

> . . . whether we remember or forget, in all of us sit sensations of malaise, fear, catastrophe, explosion . . . We do not know yet precisely what events await us, *but in our hearts the needle of the seismograph has already stirred.*

RUSSIA AT WAR

Her Prospects

J udging by the outcome of the war with Japan, which was defeat followed by revolution, the rulers of Russia would have been wise to stay out of World War I: for the immediate cause of the Revolution of 1917 would be the collapse of Russia's fragile political structure under the strains of a war of attrition. It can be argued, of course, that the deteriorating ability of tsarism to govern and the presence of a militant intelligentsia made revolution inevitable, war or no war. But even if this point is conceded, a revolution under peacetime conditions, with the army on hand to quell disorders, would have been less violent, offering moderate elements a better chance to pick up the reins of power.

Neutrality, however, was not an available option, given the ambitious designs of Wilhelmine Germany on Europe, Russia included. Following the defeat of France in 1870–71, the Germans expected the French sooner or later to seek revenge. Accordingly, they prepared themselves for the contingency of another war, which, they hoped, would establish their unchallenged hegemony on the Continent. Some influential German publicists envisioned reducing Russia to the status of an economic colony that would furnish Germany with cheap labor and raw materials. It was clear to Russia's rulers that if Germany succeeded in crushing France for the second time, it would be their turn next. Tsar Alexander III noted in

1892 that it was imperative for Russia to come to terms with France "and, in the event of a war between France and Germany, at once attack the Germans so as not to give them the time first to beat France and then to turn against us." The French, for their part, realized that they could not defeat Germany single-handedly, and required an ally. The two countries edged toward an alliance in the 1880s; it was formalized in 1894 in a mutual defense treaty committing them to come to each other's aid if attacked by Germany or one of her allies.

Faced with the prospect of a two-front war, the German General Staff worked out an elaborate strategy known as the Schlieffen Plan. As ultimately formulated, it called for Germany to deploy nine-tenths of her forces on the French front, entrusting to the Austro-Hungarian army, stiffened with some German divisions, the task of keeping the Russians at bay while a decision was reached in the west. The German army was to crush the French in forty days—before the Russians had time to mobilize fully—and then quickly shift the bulk of its forces to the east. The precondition of success of the Schlieffen Plan was speed, especially speed of mobilization. It postulated that the Russians would require 105 days to bring their army to full strength, by which time their French allies would be out of the picture.

The French and Russian General Staffs, aware in broad terms of what the Germans intended, worked out a counterstrategy. The Russians promised on the fifteenth day of mobilization, with only one-third of their forces under arms, to strike either at the German troops in East Prussia or at those guarding the approaches to Berlin. The hope was that faced with such an offensive, which endangered their capital city, the Germans would withdraw troops from the west at a critical stage of their operation, with the result that the entire Schlieffen strategy would collapse. The Russians were not entirely happy with the French proposals, for they believed that while the Germans were occupied in the west they could be more useful disposing of the weaker Austro-Hungarian army. Ultimately, a compromise was reached whereby they would simultaneously attack the Germans and the Austrians. It was a bad decision, for Russia did not have adequate forces to fight on two fronts.

In 1912 the Germans were alarmed by the announcement in St. Petersburg of a military modernization plan, to be carried out with the financial assistance of France, whose objective was to reduce Russian mobilization to eighteen days. Once completed, it would have aborted the entire Schlieffen Plan. The prospect caused some Germans to contemplate a preventive war and helps to explain the heedless speed with which they acted in the summer of 1914.

Europe was thus quite poised for war when a tragic but relatively minor incident—the assassination of the successor to the throne of Austria by a Serbian terrorist—provoked hostilities between Austria and Serbia. Although the Serbians were prepared to meet the terms of the Austrian ultimatum, Vienna, encouraged by Berlin, rejected compromise and declared war (July 15/28). The Russians, self-designated protectors of Orthodox Christians, fearful that unless they came to the Serbs' assistance their prestige in the Balkans would suffer irreparable damage, responded by ordering first a partial and then a general mobilization (July 15–17/ 28–30). On July 30, the Germans presented the Russians with an ultimatum demanding that they stop massing troops along their common frontier. They received no answer. That day France and Germany began to mobilize, and on July 19/August 1, Germany declared war on Russia. The following night, without a formal declaration of war against France, German troops crossed into Belgium and Luxembourg, heading for Paris.

How well prepared was Russia for war? The answer depends on the kind of war one has in mind: a short one, measured in months, or a long one, lasting years.

The Russian General Staff was not alone in expecting the next war to be brief. The belief was based both on the experience of Continental wars of the preceding century, in which decisions were usually reached quickly, in a single decisive engagement, and on the conviction that the interdependence of the world's economies precluded a conflict of long duration. For such a quick war Russia was well prepared, given her large standing army.

Matters looked different when Russia's military potential was assessed in terms of hostilities lasting years, such as the American Civil War. Her manpower, deemed inexhaustible, was in fact quite limited, because Russia's unusually high birth rate made for a young population; at the turn of the century, nearly half of it was below draft age. The reserve system, as previously noted, was poorly developed and after the initial mobilization, Russia found herself short of trained cadres. Russian troops were courageous under fire and showed little fear of death, but they had no idea why they were fighting and obeyed only from habit: as soon as authority weakened, they would disobey orders and desert. They had little of the patriotism that enabled Western European troops to stand fast in a four-year carnage. No other army in World War I surrendered to the enemy in such numbers. Russian officers looked down on modern mechanical warfare, believing that it sapped morale: their favorite tactic was storming enemy positions with bayonets and hand grenades. Many of the top commanders were political appointees, chosen for their political reliability and short on combat experience.

Russia's capacity for waging a protracted war looked no better from the economic point of view. Food was plentiful during the war, but transport was not up to the task of carrying it in sufficient quantities from the producing areas in the south and southeast to the grain-consuming cities in the north. Despite its impressive growth during the preceding quarter of a century, Russia's industrial plant simply could not bear comparison with that of the advanced countries of the West. The bulk of her weapons and ammunition was produced in state-controlled manufactures that lacked the capacity to meet the demands of a modern war. At the end of 1914, with mobilization completed, Russia had 6.5 million soldiers under arms but only 4.6 million rifles. Russian industry could at best supply only 27,000 rifles a month. In the first phase of the war, therefore, some Russian soldiers had to wait for their comrades to fall in order to procure weapons. The situation with artillery shells was no better. Russia had allotted 1,000 shells per field gun, but actual consumption greatly exceeded that quantity, with the result that after four months of combat the ordnance depots stood empty. The most that existing manufactures could supply in 1914 was 9,000 shells a month. As a result, within months, many Russian artillery guns stood silent, unable to answer enemy fire.

Transport, too, was cause for concern. In relation to her territory, Russia fell far behind the other major belligerents: she had a mere 1.1 kilometers of railway track for each 100 square kilometers, compared with Germany's 10.6, France's 8.8, and Austria-Hungary's 6.4. Three-quarters of Russia's railways, including the Trans-Siberian, had only a single track. Improvidently, St. Petersburg did not consider the likelihood that in the event of war her major ports would be rendered useless by enemy action—German in the Baltic, and Turkish in the Black Sea—leaving her effectively blockaded. Wartime Russia has been compared to a house to which entry could be gained only by way of the chimney. But even the chimneys were clogged. Aside from Vladivostok, thousands of miles away, Russia was left with only two seaports to the outside world. One, Archangel, was frozen for six months of the year. The other, Murmansk, was ice-free but in 1914 had no railroad: a line connecting it with

Petrograd was begun only in 1915 and completed in January 1917, on the very eve of the Revolution. Consequently, much of the war matériel sent to Russia by the Allies in 1915–17 ended up stockpiled in warehouses at Archangel, Murmansk, and Vladivostok.*

And last but not least, there were the strained relations between government and society that, except for a brief period of patriotic frenzy at the outbreak of the war, hampered the mobilization of the home front. The government was determined not to allow representatives of society to take advantage of the war to encroach on its authority. At times the Russian government found itself waging war on two fronts: a military one against the Germans and Austrians and a political one against domestic opposition. And improbable as it may sound, some monarchists regarded the internal enemy as the more dangerous of the two. Unfortunately for Russia, the attitude of society, as articulated in the Duma, was even more hostile and uncompromising. The liberal and socialist deputies desired military victory, but they were not averse to exploiting the war to weaken the government. In 1915 and 1916, the opposition would refuse to meet the Crown halfway, aware that its difficulties offered parliament unique opportunities to strengthen itself at the monarchy's expense. In a sense, therefore, the liberals and socialists entered into a silent partnership with the Germans, exploiting German victories over the Russians to gain political advantages. In some respects, tsarism's unresolved political crisis lay at the bottom of its military defeats and ultimate collapse.

Wiser heads realized the risks war entailed for the country's domestic stability. Both Witte and Stolypin pleaded for neutrality in a future European conflict. The onetime Minister of the Interior and director of the Police Department, Peter Durnovo, regarded by the intelligentsia as the personification of bureaucratic obtuseness, foresaw with prophetic insight what would happen in the event of war. In a memorandum submitted to the Tsar in February 1914, he predicted that in case of military reverses "a social revolution in its most extreme form will be unavoidable in Russia." It would begin, he said, with all strata of society blaming the government for failures on the battlefield. Duma politicians would capitalize on the government's predicament to incite the masses. The army

---

* It was to overcome this handicap and open access to Russia that on Churchill's initiative in early 1915 the British and Australians landed troops at Gallipoli, at the entrance to the Straits. The expedition, assigned inadequate forces, failed. Had it succeeded, the course of Russian history might have been very different.

8. Nicholas II at army headquarters, September 1914.

would become less dependable after losing in combat its professional cadres. Their replacements, freshly commissioned civilians, would possess neither the authority nor the will to restrain the peasants from rushing home to share in the land seizures. In the ensuing turmoil, the opposition parties, which, in Durnovo's judgment, had no popular support, would fail to assert authority, and Russia "will be thrown into total anarchy, the consequences of which cannot be even foreseen."

The First Year

From the opening day of hostilities, the French bombarded the Russians with appeals to move against the Germans. The German assault on Belgium turned out to be conducted on a broader front and with larger forces than anticipated. French counterattacks against the German center proved unavailing.

Nicholas wanted to assume personal command of the army in the field, but he was dissuaded (for now) by ministers worried by the adverse effect that setbacks at the front would have on his domestic prestige. The command went to Grand Duke Nikolai Nikolaevich.

Responding to French appeals, the Russians sent two armies into East Prussia. It was intended that after destroying the German troops there, they would join forces and advance on Berlin. Although the terrain, full of lakes and forests, favored the defenders, the Russians initially made good progress. But the greater their success, the more careless they grew, communicating in the clear and rushing headlong forward, each commander eager to claim the laurels of victory. The Germans, under Paul von Hindenburg and his Chief of Staff, Erich Ludendorff, bided their time. When they judged it right, they sprang a trap, separating the two Russian armies from each other. To begin with, they annihilated the Second Russian Army, then they mauled the First, forcing it to retreat into Poland. It was a catastrophic defeat, but the Russian command, never particularly concerned about casualties, took it in stride. When the French military attaché expressed sympathy over Russian losses, which amounted to almost a quarter of a million men, Nikolai Nikolaevich responded nonchalantly: "We are happy to make such sacrifices for our allies." But the British attaché, who recounts this incident, thought the Russians had acted less out of concern for the Allies than from plain irresponsibility: They were "just great big-hearted children who had thought out nothing and had stumbled half-asleep into a wasp's nest."

The East Prussian debacle was overshadowed by Russian successes against the Austrians. In an impressive operation, they captured most of Galicia, putting out of commission one-third of the Austro-Hungarian army and placing themselves in a position to advance south into Hungary and east into Silesia.

The next half year on the Eastern front saw intense but inconclusive fighting. It was then, in the winter of 1914–15, that the Russian army first began to experience shortages of military matériel; half of the reinforcements sent to the front had no rifles.

After three months of war, the German High Command faced a bleak prospect. The Schlieffen Plan had failed, largely because it had not made allowances for soldier fatigue and the difficulties of providing the rapidly advancing troops with logistical support. The right wing of the invading army, instead of sweeping south of Paris and trapping the French army as planned, had to shorten its lines by swinging to the north of the French capital. Following the French counteroffensive at the Marne, the German campaign ground to a halt. By the end of 1914, the western front had stabilized as the troops took shelter in trenches. Germany now confronted what she had dreaded most: a prolonged two-front war that she could not win, given the enemy's superiority (now that Britain had joined in) in manpower and resources.

The only remaining hope lay in knocking the Russians out of the war. In late 1914, the German High Command resolved to adopt a defensive stance in the west and to launch, with the onset of spring, a decisive campaign against Russia with the view of forcing her to sue for peace. Acting in the greatest secrecy, the Germans transferred troops to the eastern front. By April 1915, with the buildup completed, the Central Powers enjoyed a considerable advantage over the Russians in manpower and a forty-to-one superiority in artillery. Their strategic plan called for a giant pincer movement, with one German army, assisted by the Austrians, advancing into Poland from the southwest and another striking from the northwest. The objective was to capture the four Russian armies deployed in central Poland.

The German offensive opened in complete surprise on April 15/28 with a sustained artillery barrage that blasted the Russians out of their shallow dugouts. The Russians had to retreat. When he was informed on June 30/July 12 that the German army in the northwest was also beginning to advance, Nikolai Nikolaevich faced a painful decision: whether to stand his ground and risk being trapped or retreat and abandon Poland to the enemy, with all the disastrous political consequences that were certain to follow. He wisely chose the second course. The Russians withdrew, abandoning Poland and surrendering to the enemy 13 percent of the Empire's population. Their army suffered heavy casualties in killed, wounded, and captured. Russia's elite professional officer corps was virtually destroyed. Its replacements, made up mostly of young high-school graduates and university students commissioned on the battlefield, lacked, as Durnovo had foreseen, the respect of the troops. Russian soldiers came to dread the Germans: convinced that the Germans "could do anything," they were prone to take to their heels at the very sight of the enemy.

And yet it can be said that the Germans' impressive victories on the eastern front lost them the war. Their 1915 offensive in Poland achieved neither of its aims, which were to annihilate the Russian army and force Russia to sue for peace. The Russian armies, though severely mauled, eluded capture, and St. Petersburg ignored German peace overtures. The campaigns in the east gave the western front a year of relative stability, which Britain used to build up a citizen army and convert her vast industrial plant to war production. When, in 1916, the Germans resumed offensive operations in the west, they found the enemy well prepared. The disaster of 1915 may well have been Russia's greatest, if unintended, contribution to Allied victory.

But these facts were not apparent to Russian politicians or the public at large; all they saw was that their armies had suffered a humiliating debacle. They clamored for scapegoats. The first to be sacrificed was the Minister of War, General Vladimir Sukhomlinov, who was dismissed for the alleged failure to prepare Russia for the war; later on, he was imprisoned on charges of treason and embezzlement. His replacement, General Aleksei Polivanov, was far better qualified for the post because he understood the nature of modern warfare and, unlike Sukhomlinov, entered into close relations with both politicians and industrialists. But this did not suit the Empress, who complained to her husband that she preferred his predecessor because, although not as smart as Polivanov, he was more "devoted." Other unpopular ministers, too, were let go and replaced with officials of a more liberal cast. Still, some Russian politicians concluded that the problem lay not so much with personalities as with the entire system of war management. This system had to be thoroughly restructured if Russia was to emerge from the war intact. The disasters of 1915 spelled to them the opportunity to complete the 1905 Revolution.

When the Polish campaign began, the Duma was in recess. It had been promised, however, that it would be reconvened if the military situation warranted it. Such a situation now arose. The Empress pleaded with her husband in her quaint English not to summon Parliament:

> . . . oh please dont, its not their business, they want to discuss things not concerning them & bring more discontent—they must be kept away—I assure you only harm will arise—they speak too much. Russia, thank God is not a constitutional country [!], tho' those creatures try to play a part & meddle in affairs they dare not. Do not allow them to press upon you—its fright if one gives in & their heads will go up.

Nicholas, however, ignored his wife's advice and ordered the legislature reassembled for a six-week session on July 19, 1915—the first anniversary, according to the Russian calendar, of the outbreak of the war.

The Duma deputies took advantage of the month and a half that lay ahead to caucus. The small Progressive Party persuaded the Kadets and the moderate conservatives that in her tragic hour Russia required effective authority that only the Duma could provide. Russia's very survival required a confrontation with the monarchy over the distribution of power, especially in the matter of ministerial appointments that the Fundamental Laws of 1906 had reserved for the Crown.

The Duma opened its session as Russian troops were abandoning Warsaw to the Germans. In an atmosphere charged with emotion, deputies attacked the government for incompetence. One of the most aggressive speakers was a thirty-four-year-old radical lawyer, Alexander Kerensky, who, as became known after the Revolution, utilized his parliamentary immunity to organize forces for the overthrow of tsarism. The political crisis came to a head at the end of August, when 300 of the Duma's 420 deputies formed the "Progressive Bloc." The Bloc announced a nine-point program which demanded, in effect, that the Duma be granted the right to veto ministerial appointments. Other clauses called for the release of political and religious prisoners and the abolition of the disabilities imposed on religious minorities, Jews included. Surprisingly, the majority of the ministers expressed a willingness to step down in favor of a cabinet approved by the Duma.

Thus, in August 1915, an extraordinary situation emerged: liberal and conservative legislators, representing nearly three-quarters of a body elected on a very restricted franchise, made common cause with the highest officials appointed by the Tsar to call for something closely resembling parliamentary government—and this in the midst of a war and, it was claimed, for the sake of victory.

Nicholas responded by proroguing the Duma and departing for the front. On this occasion he rejected the advice of his ministers and assumed personal command of Russia's armed forces. He did so from a sense of patriotism and the desire to share the army's hardships in its difficult hour. In late September he dismissed the ministers who had been most vocal in opposing his decision to assume military command. Some contemporaries believed that his actions in August–September 1915, by precluding a peaceful transfer of power from the Crown to the nation's representatives, made a revolution virtually inevitable.

For the time being, however, Nicholas was saved by Germany's decision in September to halt the advance of her armies. Fears that they would march on and occupy Moscow and St. Petersburg did not materialize. This turn of events calmed public opinion for the time being.

Even though he refused to yield more power to society and its representatives, Nicholas agreed to concede a greater role in mobilizing the home front to Duma deputies and members of the business community. He and his monarchist supporters hoped these measures would invigorate the war effort and, at the same time, placate the opposition. In the summer of 1915, several special councils came into being to help organize the production of weapons and resolve difficulties in transport and the supply of food and fuel. Such boards, routine in Western countries, were in Russia a striking innovation; for alongside officials, who traditionally enjoyed a monopoly on government posts, sat deputies of the Duma and State Council as well as representatives of zemstva and Municipal Councils and private businessmen. The most important of the special councils, the Defense Council, had authority to intervene in nongovernmental plants working for defense. It established a Central Military-Industrial Committee which involved in defense production 1,300 small and medium-size industrial establishments previously excluded from it. It also took the unprecedented step of inviting representatives of workers employed by the war industries to help maintain labor discipline, prevent strikes, and resolve worker grievances. This it did with the help of a Central Workers' Group organized on the initiative of the Mensheviks: in early 1917, the Workers' Group would form the nucleus of the Petrograd Soviet. The participation of workers in industrial management and, indirectly, in the management of the war economy was another indicator of the social and political changes that the war had forced on the monarchy.

The Defense Council and the Military-Industrial Committee contributed significantly to improvements in war production, as was demonstrated by the production of artillery shells. Whereas in 1914, Russian defense industries, then fully under state control, could supply at most 108,000 shells a year, in 1915, with the private sector engaged, they turned out 950,000 shells, and in 1916, 1,850,000. On the eve of the February Revolution, shell shortages were a thing of the past.

The third institution created to help the government in the war effort was the All-Russian Union of Zemstvo and Municipal Councils, popularly known as Zemgor. Zemgor helped the civilian population cope with the hardships of war, proving especially effective in dealing with the hundreds of thousands of refugees from the front.

In addition to these quasi-public bodies, volunteer organizations of all kinds sprang up in Russia, including producer and consumer cooperatives.

Thus, in the midst of the war, a new Russia was quietly taking shape: the bureaucracy was losing its monopoly on administration. The development resembled the vigorous growth of saplings in the shade of an old and decaying forest. The participation of citizens without official rank alongside rank holders in government institutions and the introduction of worker representatives into industrial management signified a silent revolution. Conservative bureaucrats were dismayed by the emergence of this "shadow" government. For the same reason, the opposition brimmed with confidence. Kadet leaders boasted that the civic organizations created during the war would demonstrate so convincingly their superiority over the bureaucracy that once peace returned, nothing could stop them from taking charge of the country.

Catastrophe Looms

During the second y
ing weapons shor
an economic nature whic
educated and affluent, to

One of these new p
preceding the outbreak
the world, had been r
government suspende
the ruble into gold and gave the
in quantities needed to cover war costs, wi
reserve. This measure had inflationary implications. The
deficit was aggravated by the government's decision, at the outbreak of
the war, to forbid the sale of alcoholic beverages. The population got
around this prohibition by resorting to moonshine, but the Treasury lost
one-quarter of the revenue it normally collected from taxes on alcohol.
Some of the deficit was made good with loans, mainly from Britain; the
rest was covered with emissions of paper money. In the course of the war,
the quantity of ruble banknotes in circulation increased between four
and six times. The flood of paper money did not immediately affect consumer prices because the suspension of exports initially glutted the market with foodstuffs and other goods. But by the middle of 1915, prices
had begun to move upward, and the following year they rose steeply.

Inflation did not hurt the rural population. On the contrary, as the war
progressed, agricultural produce fetched higher prices and government
allowances to families of soldiers brought the peasants additional
income. Mobilization had syphoned off most of the excess rural inhabitants, enhancing wages for farm labor. By Russian standards, the peasant
was swimming in money. He began to restrict his sown acreage and even
to withhold deliveries of foodstuffs in the hope that they would fetch still
higher prices in the future.

Inflation and food shortages afflicted exclusively the urban population, which had expanded considerably from the influx of war refugees
and workers hired by the defense industries. It is estimated that during
the war, the cities attracted 6 million newcomers. City inhabitants found
it difficult to locate staples, and when they did find them, could not
afford to pay the prices demanded. The Police Department estimated in

e preceding two years wages had doubled,
s had risen by 300 percent.

as the inability of rail transport, burdened to
y demands, to supply the cities with the required

tion of the urban population was, for the time being, of
ature. But in late 1916, the Police Department warned that
e little provocation for economic grievances to assume politi-

Allies, who after the Polish debacle had more or less written off the
ssian army, were agreeably surprised by the vigor of its offensive
against the Austrians in June 1916. The operation soon ran out of steam,
but not before it had severely mauled the enemy. Austria-Hungary stood
on the verge of a collapse from which she was saved, once again, by the
Germans, who dispatched fifteen divisions to the eastern front.

Nicholas paid a heavy price for his ill-advised decision to assume personal command of the armed forces because by departing to headquarters
at Mogilev he lost contact with the political situation at home. Leadership
passed to his wife, who was glad to have him out of the way, since she considered herself better qualified to deal with opposition politicians. In her
letters to him she offered constant reassurance: "Do not fear for what
remains behind. . . . Lovy, I am here, dont laugh at silly old wify, but she has
'trousers' on unseen. . . ." In the final year and a half of the war, Alexandra
exerted great influence on personnel appointments in both the central and
the provincial branches of the administration. She judged candidates for
high office exclusively by the criterion of loyalty to the throne. Ministers
who failed to meet this test were dismissed at a pace that gave rise to the
expression "ministerial leapfrog." Nor was the disorganization of the
administrative apparatus confined to central institutions. Governors, too,
came and went at an alarming speed. In the first nine months of 1916 alone,
forty-three new gubernatorial appointments were made, which meant that
over the course of less than a year most provinces received a new head.

Alexandra did not act on her own but sought the advice of her confi-
dant, Rasputin. Often referred to as a "mad monk," Rasputin was neither
mad nor a monk. He was a peasant healer from Siberia, possibly an
adherent of the Khlysty sect, whose members believed that by sinning
one reduced the quantity of sin abroad in the world. He gained his position at Court because he proved able—by what means is not known—to

9. Rasputin with children in his Siberian village.

stop the bleeding and suffering of the heir to the throne, Alexis, a victim of hemophilia. This disease, transmitted by the mother, was the consuming tragedy of the Imperial family, reinforcing the Tsar's fatalism and his wife's superstition. Rasputin used his influence with the Empress to pocket bribes and to wallow in drunken orgies, but the stories of his sexual prowess are sheer fantasy: a physician who once examined him expressed doubts that he was even capable of the sexual act.

Rasputin acquired political influence only after Nicholas's departure for the front. From August 1915 on, it was impossible either to stay in office or to obtain office without his consent. Nicholas, who did not especially care for Rasputin, tolerated him for the sake of his wife and son and angrily dismissed any suggestion that he be gotten rid of on the grounds that his presence at Court was a "family matter." The Imperial couple also persuaded themselves that Rasputin, who insisted that ordinary Russians loved them, was an authentic voice of the people. He was largely responsible for the growing estrangement from the Court of the conservative monarchists, who felt that he had brought dishonor to the Crown.

One of the victims of Alexandra's and Rasputin's intrigues was Polivanov, the Minister of War, who had pulled the Russian army back from the brink of collapse. He was dismissed because he maintained close relations with both politicians and industrialists. His replacement was an incompetent general with expertise in army footwear. When the public began to complain of treason in high places, he is said to have exclaimed indignantly: "I may be a fool, but I am no traitor!"—a saying that would provide the rhetorical flourish for Miliukov's sensational Duma address of November 1, 1916.

A survey undertaken by the Police Department in October 1916 of the mood in the country painted a gloomy picture. The population's discontent over shortages of basic necessities could easily explode into open rebellion. Especially worrisome was the fact that for the first time in the experience of the security police the anger of the populace was directed not only against the ministers but against the Imperial couple. The Empress was especially disliked and, because of her German origin, widely suspected of betraying Russian military secrets to the enemy.

By the end of 1916, the most conservative elements had grown so disgusted with the doings at Court that they talked of taking steps to "save the monarchy from the monarch." For the first time ever, right-wing elements made overtures to the liberals, hoping through their joint efforts to keep Russia in the war and to forestall social upheavals.

To placate the opposition, Nicholas made what on the face of it seemed a major concession: He named as Minister of the Interior Alexander Protopopov, a businessman and a member of the Progressive Bloc holding no official rank. This appointment, which appeared to be a significant step toward accommodation with the Duma, aroused wild hopes that the monarchy was about to give up its power of selecting ministers. But the move soon revealed itself as a political maneuver. The Court knew Protopopov to be a vain and unprincipled careerist who would do its bidding. The appointment had been made at the recommendation of Alexandra (behind whom stood Rasputin). "Please, take Protopopov as Minister of the Interior," she had urged her husband, "as he is one of the Duma it will make a great effect amongst them & shut their mouths." The effect was short-lived, however: as soon as the Duma realized that Protopopov was little more than a royal steward, it turned against the Crown with heightened fury.

10. Alexander Protopopov.

This became evident when the Duma reconvened in November 1916 to vote on the budget. In September and October, the principal opposition parties, meeting first separately and then jointly, as the Progressive Bloc, worked out a strategy. The deputies felt a sense of great urgency: something had to be done, and done quickly, before the country exploded. The Kadets adopted a very radical platform that called for their spokesman in the Duma, Miliukov, to charge the Prime Minister, Boris Stürmer, with high treason. Stürmer, a dyed-in-the-wool monarchist bureaucrat, was indeed hardly qualified to direct Russia's government at a time of crisis. But there was no evidence, and none has come to light since, that he ever committed any acts remotely resembling treason. He was chosen as a target because of his German name, which aroused suspicions about his loyalty among ignorant chauvinists. Under pressure from the more conservative members of the Progressive Bloc, Miliukov agreed to moderate somewhat his accusations while still leaving no doubt as to their portent.

Stürmer, who had gotten wind of these plans, asked Nicholas for permission, if the situation required it, to dissolve the Duma: unfounded charges of governmental treason in a country at war were in themselves treasonous. But Nicholas, thoroughly discouraged by now, was unable to act decisively. He had difficulty sleeping and felt such revulsion at what he regarded as the unpatriotic behavior of the politicians that he refused to read the press.

The Duma opened on November 1, 1916, in an atmosphere charged with high tension. After opening addresses, Kerensky took the floor to deliver a scurrilous attack on the government, in which he charged that Russia's true enemy was not at the front but at home. He called for the government's overthrow on the grounds that it was betraying the country's interests.

Kerensky's speech did not make much of an impression because he had a reputation for hysteria. Matters stood differently with Miliukov, a self-possessed scholar with a national reputation as leader of the Kadets and editor of the party's newspaper. Miliukov's speech was a skillful blend of innuendo and fact, the purpose of which was to imply without explicitly asserting that Stürmer had committed high treason. To make his point, Miliukov quoted from German and French papers, and hinted that he had at his disposal even more damning evidence which he did not feel at liberty to divulge. He listed in turn one mistake after another that the government had committed, and followed up each time with the rhetorical question, "Is it stupidity or is it treason?" to which each time the chamber lustily responded, "Stupidity!" "Treason!" "Both!"

Miliukov's accusations had no basis: in fact, they were a tissue of lies. Later, in emigration, he admitted as much. His justification for spreading such slander was the need for extreme measures to enable the Progressive Bloc to take charge of the country before it fell apart. In reality, his speech contributed as much as anything the government did or failed to do to inflaming revolutionary passions. Although military censorship forbade the press to cite or even report on it, the speech, reproduced in hundreds of thousands of copies, flooded the country and the front. It persuaded civilians and soldiers alike that "Duma deputy Miliukov had proven that the Empress and Stürmer were selling out Russia to Kaiser Wilhelm." The passions unleashed by Miliukov played a major role in instigating the February Revolution, in which anger over alleged government treason was, at first, a dominant motive.

The Duma sessions that followed brought the authorities little comfort, as speaker after speaker, including monarchists, joined in the attack.

The November sessions of the Duma marked the onset of a revolutionary psychosis—an irrational but intensely felt feeling that "things could not go on like this any longer," that the entire edifice of monarchic Russia had to be pulled down. The psychosis, long prevalent among the radical intelligentsia, now seized the liberal center and even spilled into conservative ranks. An aide of the Tsar speaks in his memoirs of a "widespread conviction that something had to be broken and annihilated—a conviction that tormented people and gave them no peace." Another contemporary wrote in December 1916 of a "siege of authority that has turned into sport."

On November 8, 1916, Nicholas, in a vain effort to appease the Duma, dismissed Stürmer. In his place he appointed a liberal, A. F. Trepov. Trepov attempted to emulate Stolypin and bring the Duma into partnership. He promised to meet many of its demands. But when he appeared in the Duma on November 19 to deliver a programmatic speech, the left greeted him with abusive screams that lasted for forty minutes during which he could not utter a word. When order was finally restored, he delivered a conciliatory address. He asked for help:

> Let us forget our quarrels, let us postpone our feuds. . . . In the name of the government, I declare directly and openly that it wishes to devote its energies to constructive, pragmatic work in cooperation with the legislature.

To no avail. In late December 1916, the Tsar dismissed Trepov, whom the Empress in a private communication called a liar who deserved to be hanged.

While the liberals and radicals wanted a complete constitutional change, the monarchists believed that it would suffice to be rid of the Empress. And to be rid of the Empress, some of them concluded, it was only necessary to remove Rasputin, whom she allegedly needed to preserve her emotional equilibrium. Trepov had tried to bribe Rasputin to leave Petrograd, but the crafty favorite informed Alexandra of this, with the result that his standing at Court rose to unprecedented heights. There was no alternative, therefore, but to assassinate him. The Oxford-educated Prince Felix Iusupov, son of the wealthiest woman in Russia, who was herself a sworn enemy of the Empress, organized the plot, in which he implicated Grand Duke Dmitrii, the Tsar's nephew, and Vladimir Purishkevich, one of the most reactionary deputies in the Duma. Iusupov acted on the premise that

> [the Empress's] spiritual balance depends entirely on Rasputin: the instant he is gone, it will disintegrate. And once the Emperor has been freed of his wife's and Rasputin's influence, everything will change: he will turn into a good constitutional monarch.

On the night of December 16–17, Iusupov lured Rasputin to his luxurious palace and there, together with Purishkevich, shot him. The body was weighed down with chains and thrown into a canal, where it was discovered a few days later.

The murder had on the Imperial couple the opposite effect of the one intended: instead of separating Nicholas and Alexandra, it drove them still closer together. They felt isolated and surrounded by traitors. Nicholas felt revulsion at the thought that a nephew of his should have been implicated in the crime: "I am ashamed before Russia," he wrote, "that the hands of my relatives should be smeared with the blood of this peasant." And when a group of grand dukes and duchesses pleaded with him not to punish Dmitrii, he replied, "No one has the right to engage in murder."

Nicholas returned from the front and spent the next two months with his wife and children leading a quiet life at Tsarskoe Selo, cut off from virtually all social contacts. A frequent visitor to the royal residence said that it resembled a house in mourning. Protopopov delivered reassuring reports that the country was calm and that he had more than adequate forces at his disposal to cope with any disturbances. When occasional visitors warned him of impending disaster, Nicholas listened politely but inattentively, studying his nails or fingering a cigarette. "The Empress and I know that all is in God's hands," he said. "His will be done." Rasputin had predicted more than once that should any harm befall him, the country would be drowned in blood and choked in smoke.

Nicholas's equanimity abandoned him only once. On January 7, 1917, he received a visit from Mikhail Rodzianko, the Chairman of the Duma. He listened impassively to the familiar warnings, but when Rodzianko urged him not to put the people in a position of having "to choose between you and the good of the country," Nicholas "pressed his head between his hands" and said, "Is it possible that for twenty-two years I tried to work for the best, and that for twenty-two years it was all a mistake?"

Having failed to alter the political situation by disposing of Rasputin, the conservatives made up their minds that to save the monarchy they would have to remove the monarch. Several plots were set in motion to abduct Nicholas and force him to abdicate in favor of his twelve-year-old son under a regency of Grand Duke Nikolai Nikolaevich. One of these involved General Mikhail Alekseev, the de facto Commander in Chief of Russia's armed forces. The conspiracies never progressed beyond the talking stage.

Protopopov, however, exuded supreme confidence—a fact that caused some contemporaries to question his sanity. In his spare moments, he liked to communicate with the spirit of Rasputin.

THE FEBRUARY REVOLUTION

After two mild winters, the winter of 1916–17 proved unusually cold; temperatures fell so low that peasant women refused to cart food to the towns. Blizzards disabled locomotives and piled mountains of snow on the railway tracks. The weather had a devastating effect on deliveries to the northern cities, notably distant Petrograd.* Bakeries had to shut their doors for lack of either flour or fuel. Fuel shortages also forced some factories to close and lay off tens of thousands of workers.

The Tsar, reassured by Protopopov that he had the situation in hand, left for the front on February 22: he would return two weeks later as Nicholas Romanov, a private citizen.

Suddenly the weather took a turn for the better, the temperature rising from an average of –14.5° Centigrade (6° F.) to +8 (46° F.), where it would remain until the end of the month. People whom freezing weather had kept confined for weeks to poorly heated rooms, now streamed outdoors to enjoy the sun. Documentary films of the February Revolution show gay crowds under brilliant skies.

The day after Nicholas's departure, disorders broke out in Petrograd. They began with a demonstration on International Woman's Day

---

* Because "St. Petersburg" sounded Germanic to Russian ears, at the outbreak of the war with Germany the city was renamed Petrograd.

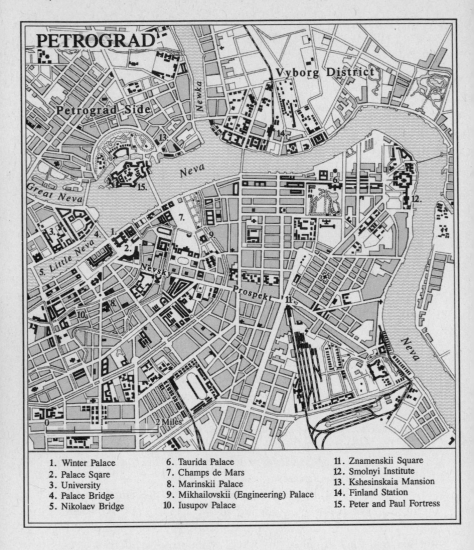

1. Winter Palace
2. Palace Sqare
3. University
4. Palace Bridge
5. Nikolaev Bridge

6. Taurida Palace
7. Champs de Mars
8. Marinskii Palace
9. Mikhailovskii (Engineering) Palace
10. Iusupov Palace

11. Znamenskii Square
12. Smolnyi Institute
13. Kshesinskaia Mansion
14. Finland Station
15. Peter and Paul Fortress

(February 23). The event proceeded peacefully, but even so the authorities had reason to worry because the Cossacks responsible for order seemed to sympathize with the women clamoring for bread. The atmosphere was exacerbated by attacks on the government in the Duma, which had reconvened on February 14. Kerensky and other opposition figures again used inflammatory language to incite the public.

On February 24, the situation in the capital deteriorated when up to 200,000 idle workers, either on strike or locked out, filled the streets. On the city's main thoroughfare, Nevsky Prospekt, crowds shouted "Down with the autocracy!" and "Down with the war!" Here and there, mobs sacked food stores.

The following day the crowds, emboldened by the lack of a vigorous response, grew still more aggressive. Apparently under the influence of radical intellectuals, the demonstrations now assumed a distinctly political character, with red banners making their appearance bearing revolutionary slogans, some of which read "Down with the German Woman!" In several city quarters, gendarmes came under attack.

Alexandra reported to her husband on the day's events as follows:

> This is a *hooligan* movement, young people run & shout that there is no bread, simply to create excitement, along with the workers who prevent others from working. If the weather were very cold they would probably all stay home. But all this will pass and turn calm if only the Duma will behave itself.

The socialists scented revolution in the air. On February 25, the Menshevik Duma deputies discussed forming a "workers' soviet." Up to this point, however, the turmoil had mainly economic causes. The leading Bolshevik in Petrograd, and later the first Soviet Commissar of Labor, Alexander Shliapnikov, dismissed talk of a revolution: "What revolution? Give the workers a pound of bread and the movement will fizzle."

Whatever chance there was of containing the incipient rebellion was destroyed with the arrival in the evening of February 25 of a telegram from Nicholas to the city's military commander demanding that he restore order by force. Nicholas, who continued to receive soothing reports from Protopopov, had no idea how charged the situation in the capital had become. It seemed intolerable to him that while the troops at the front braved hardships and faced the prospect of death, civilians in the rear should be rioting. His order succeeded temporarily in calming the city. On Sunday morning, February 26, troops in combat gear occupied Petrograd and all seemed back to normal.

But it only seemed so. For on that day an incident occurred that completely transformed the situation. In Znamenskii Square, a popular gathering place for political rallies, troops of the Pavlovskii Guard Regiment fired on a crowd that failed to disperse. There were forty civilian casualties. The massacre sparked a mutiny of the Petrograd garrison that

Дни революціи. Знаменская пл. 1917 г.

11. Crowds in Znamenskii Square, Petrograd,
scene of the first violence of the February Revolution.

quickly communicated itself to the workers, producing an explosion that to this day astonishes with its suddenness and scope.

To make these events comprehensible, something needs to be said of the personnel of the Petrograd military garrison and its living conditions. By the summer of 1916, the Russian army, having run out of younger recruits, began to induct men in their thirties and early forties, who believed themselves exempt from the draft. Their resentment was aggravated by the fact that they were billeted in overcrowded urban barracks: in Petrograd, 160,000 men were packed into quarters that in peacetime housed 20,000. After a few weeks' training, supervised by officers recalled from combat, they were dispatched to the front. Sullen and full of grudges, they differed from frontline troops, who, according to foreign eyewitnesses, preserved good morale and discipline. It required little for their disaffection to erupt into violence.

The spark that caused such an eruption was the Znamenskii Square massacre. Immediately after the event, a group of angry workers who had witnessed it made their way to the barracks of the Pavlovskii Guard Regiment. They told the soldiers what their comrades had done. Enraged, some soldiers grabbed guns and proceeded to Znamenskii Square, but on their way there they ran into a detachment of mounted police. Fire was exchanged in which their leader, a young officer, was wounded. Disheartened, the soldiers returned to their barracks. The following night, however, troops of the Pavlovskii Regiment held rallies at which they voted to disobey further orders to fire at civilians. Messen-

gers were sent to other units to gain their support. On the morning of
February 27, three of the city's regiments were in mutiny. In some units,
officers were assaulted and killed. The rebellious soldiers comman-
deered armored cars and cruised the snow-covered streets, waving their
weapons and shouting. Some uniformed policemen were lynched. A
mob sacked the Ministry of the Interior. The red flag went up over the
Winter Palace. In the late afternoon, crowds stormed the headquarters
of the Okhrana, scattering and burning files—suspected police informers were seen to display notable zeal in this work. Arsenals were broken
into and thousands of rifles stolen. There was widespread looting of
shops, restaurants, and private residences. By nighttime, Petrograd was
in the hands of peasants in uniform. Of the 160,000-man garrison, half
were in full mutiny, with the remainder adopting a "neutral" stance. The
military command was powerless to restore order, since it had at its disposal no more than 2,000 loyal troops, 3,500 policemen, and some
mounted Cossacks.

Nicholas still had no idea of the gravity of the situation. He ignored
alarming telegrams from the politicians, believing they were exaggerating
the extent of the mutiny in order to wrest greater power for the Duma.
But his annoyance gave way to anxiety as military commanders in charge
of the capital confirmed that the situation was indeed out of control.

His first impulse was to restore order by force. He instructed an elite
battalion of decorated veterans, stationed at headquarters under General
N. I. Ivanov, to proceed to Petrograd. At the same time, he ordered front
commanders to dispatch eight regiments augmented with machine-gun

12. Petrograd crowds burning emblems of the Imperial regime,
February 1917.

detachments. The size of this force indicates that he had in mind a major operation. Ivanov was to take command of the Petrograd Military District.

It will never be known whether, had Nicholas acted decisively in the days that followed, Ivanov would have succeeded in his mission, because it was aborted. It does not, however, seem to have been as hopeless an undertaking as the politicians and generals, under the politicians' influence, believed. The mutineers were leaderless rabble. When threatened, they instantly panicked and ran for cover. But the Duma leaders convinced first themselves and then the generals that they alone could restore order. In reality, it was their pressure on Nicholas to abdicate that transformed a local mutiny into a nationwide revolution.

Nicholas, anxious to rejoin his family, left Mogilev for Tsarskoe Selo at 5 a.m. on February 28. To avoid interfering with Ivanov's mission, the Imperial train did not proceed directly north but used a circuitous route, heading first east, toward Moscow, and then northwest. Some 170 kilometers from the capital, the train carrying the Tsar and his suite was stopped by an officer who reported that the tracks ahead were in the hands of hostile troops. After a short consultation, it was decided to turn back and head for Pskov, headquarters of the northern front, from which it was possible to communicate with Petrograd (but not Tsarskoe Selo) by teleprinter. The commander of the northern front, General N. V. Ruzskii, was known for his antiroyalist views, a fact that was not without bearing on the course of events during the next, critical twenty-four hours.

After the rioters had done their work, the center of attention shifted to Taurida Palace, the seat of the Duma. The Duma learned that the Tsar had ordered it dissolved. It did not obey this order, but it lacked the courage to flout it openly. It chose, therefore, a cautious middle course by convening, on the morning of February 28, a private meeting of the Progressive Bloc and the Council of Elders. The Duma leaders who had for so long clamored for power lost nerve now that power was within their grasp. They feared inflaming the crowds that filled the vast space in front of Taurida, yet they could not sit on their hands, for the crowds demanded action. After lengthy deliberations they resolved to form an executive bureau of twelve Duma members, still of a private nature, to be known as "The Provisional Committee of Duma Members for the Restoration of Order in the Capital and the Establishment of Relations with Individuals and Institutions." Headed by Rodzianko, the Duma chairman, the Committee initially consisted of ten members of the Progressive Bloc and two socialists, one of them Kerensky. Its ludicrously cumbersome name reflected the timidity of its founders. And, indeed, an

Вред. Испол. Комитеть Государственной Думы

13. The Provisional Committee of the Duma. Sitting on
extreme left, V. N. Lvov, and on extreme right, M. Rodzianko.
Standing second from right, A. F. Kerensky.

eyewitness says that the Provisional Committee—now the de facto government of Russia—was established in a manner that resembled the appointment in normal times of a Fisheries Committee.

Matters stood very differently at the rival center of authority, the Petrograd Soviet, formed on the same day (February 28). It was convened on the initiative of the Mensheviks with the assistance of the Central Workers' Group (see above, p. 66), whose members Protopopov had imprisoned and the mutinous crowd had set free. The Soviet consisted of haphazardly chosen representatives of factories and military units. Electoral procedures followed the traditional practices of Russian popular assemblies, which strove to achieve a community consensus rather than a mathematically accurate reflection of individual opinions. Small shops sent as many representatives as did huge factories. Garrison units followed a similar procedure, with the result that of the Soviet's 3,000 deputies in the second week of its existence, more than 2,000 were soldiers—this in a city that had two or three times as many industrial workers as servicemen. These figures illustrate the extent to which the February Revolution in its initial phase was a soldier mutiny.

The plenary sessions of the Soviet resembled a giant village assembly. There were no agendas or voting procedures. The system adopted was to

14. The Executive Committee (Ispolkom) of the Petrograd Soviet.

allow everyone who demanded to be heard to have his say and then arrive at a decision by acclamation. Because such a body could serve no other purpose than to provide a forum for interminable speeches, and because the intellectuals consciously or unconsciously believed they knew best what was good for the "masses," the decision-making authority of the Soviet soon shifted to its Executive Committee (Ispolkom). This organization was not chosen by the Soviet but, as had been the case in 1905, was made up of nominees of the socialist parties, each of which was allotted three seats. Instead of serving as a true executive organ of the Soviet, therefore, the Ispolkom became a coordinating body of the socialist parties, superimposed on the Soviet and acting in its name.

This fact, little noticed at the time, had three grave consequences. It expanded artificially the representation of the Bolshevik Party, which had a small following among the workers and virtually none among the soldiers. It also strengthened the moderate socialists, who, though popular at the time, would soon lose favor with the population. And, most important, it bureaucratized the Ispolkom, making it a self-appointed executive body that acted independently of the Soviet plenum, whose decisions were predetermined by caucuses of socialist intellectuals.

The Soviet, initially dominated by Mensheviks, adopted the Menshevik doctrine that Russia had to undergo a full-scale "bourgeois" revolution during which the socialists would organize the masses in preparation for the next, socialist phase but stay out of government. On these grounds it refused to send representatives to the Duma Committee. The leaders of the Soviet saw their political mission as confined to ensuring that the "bourgeoisie" did not betray the revolution. In consequence, there arose in Russia a peculiar system of government called *dvoevlastie*, or "dual power," that lasted until October. In theory, the Provisional Committee of the Duma—soon renamed Provisional Government—assumed full governmental responsibility, while the Ispolkom acted as a kind of supreme court of the revolutionary conscience. In reality, the Ispolkom from the outset performed both legislative and executive functions. The arrangement was utterly unrealistic, not only because it vested responsibility in one institution and power in another but also because the parties involved had different objectives. The Duma wanted to contain the Revolution; the Soviet leaders wanted to deepen it. The former would have been happy to arrest the flow of events at the point reached by nightfall of February 27. For the latter, February 27 was a mere prelude to the "true"—that is, socialist—revolution.

Events drove the reluctant Duma leaders to the inexorable conclusion that they had to form a government, even in defiance of the Tsar, for there was no public authority left. This settled, they had to decide how to legitimize its rule. Some advised contacting the Tsar and requesting his consent to form a cabinet. But the majority preferred to turn to the Soviet—that is, the Ispolkom. Understandable as this step was from a practical point of view, given the Soviet's influence over soldiers and workers, from the point of view of legitimacy it had little meaning, since the Ispolkom was a private body made up of nominees of socialist parties, whereas the Duma had been elected.

The socialists on the Ispolkom had no intention of giving the new government carte blanche. During the night of March 1–2, they met with representatives of the Duma, headed by Miliukov, to hammer out a set of policy guidelines that would secure for the new government the Soviet's support. The outcome was an eight-point platform to serve as the basis of the government's activity until the convocation of the Constituent Assembly. Its principal clauses called for amnesty for all political prisoners, terrorists included; immediate preparations for a Constituent Assembly elected on a universal ballot; the dissolution of all police organs; new elections to organs of self-government; military units that had participated in the Revolution to retain their weapons and to receive assurances that they would not be sent to the front.

The document, drawn up by exhausted politicians after all-night discussions, was seriously flawed. The most pernicious were the articles calling for the immediate dissolution of the police and new elections for self-government, which was interpreted to mean the dissolution of the provincial bureaucracy. They abolished in one fell swoop the entire administrative and security structure that had kept the Russian state intact for a century or more. They ensured administrative anarchy. Only slightly less harmful were the clauses concerning the Petrograd garrison, which deprived the government of effective authority over 160,000 disgruntled and armed peasants whom its enemies could turn against it.

Following this accord, the Provisional Committee of the Duma renamed itself the Provisional Government. The cabinet was chaired by Prince G. E. Lvov, an innocuous and indolent civic activist chosen because, as head of the Union of Zemstva and City Councils (Zemgor), he could be said to represent society at large. Lvov understood democracy to mean that all policy decisions were made by the citizens directly affected by them and that government served essentially as a registry office. Convinced of the infinite wisdom of the Russian people, he refused to give any guidance to provincial delegations that came to Petrograd in quest of instructions. The cabinet secretary, Vladimir Nabokov (the father of the novelist), wrote: "I do not recall a single occasion when [Lvov] used a tone of authority or spoke out decisively . . . he was the very embodiment of passivity."

15. Paul Miliukov, leader of the
Constitutional-Democratic Party.

16. Alexander Kerensky.

The two outstanding members of the new government, as well as bitter rivals, were Miliukov, the Minister of Foreign Affairs, and Kerensky, the Minister of Justice.

Miliukov, fifty-eight years old, was a man of unbounded energy. A professional historian, he managed to combine scholarly work with leadership of the Constitutional-Democratic Party as well as editorship of the party's daily paper. His main shortcoming was a lack of political intuition: he would reach, by a purely logical deduction, a certain position and cling to it even after it had become evident to everyone else that it would not work. But as the country's best-known political figure, he had reason to see himself as premier of democratic Russia.

Kerensky was Miliukov's opposite. Only thirty-six years old, he had acquired fame as the leading radical orator in the Duma and as a defense attorney in political trials. A brilliant speaker with no apparent political philosophy, he burned with political ambition. Aware of a physical resemblance to the French emperor, he liked to strike Napoleonic poses. Vain and impulsive where Miliukov was cold and calculating, he rose meteorically and just as meteorically burned out.

As deputy chairman of the Soviet and a member of its Ispolkom, Kerensky was honor-bound to refuse the post of Minister of Justice in the "bourgeois" cabinet. But he found the offer irresistible, and when the Ispolkom denied him permission to accept it, he took his case directly to the crowd. In an impassioned speech to the Soviet, he pledged as Minister never to betray democratic ideals. "I cannot live without the people," he shouted, "and the moment you come to doubt me, kill me!" Having uttered these words, he made ready to faint. The workers and soldiers gave him a rousing ovation. The Ispolkom, compelled to yield, never forgave him the blackmail. Kerensky kept his seat on the Ispolkom and thus became the only person to hold membership in both the Soviet and the Provisional Government.

The February Revolution was, as such things go, a relatively bloodless affair. The total number of casualties has been estimated at between 1,300 and 1,450, of whom 169 were fatalities. More lives would have been lost had not Kerensky, at considerable personal risk, protected tsarist officials from being lynched by crowds inflamed by his own Duma rhetoric. Some 4,000 tsarist officials either turned themselves in or were taken into protective custody. The most important of them were transferred to the Peter and Paul Fortress. The diminutive Protopopov seemed shrunken still smaller from fear as he was driven to the fortress with the guard's gun pressed to his head. Along with many others, he would perish in the Bolshevik "Red Terror."

Ostensibly the organ of "democratic control" of a "bourgeois" government, the Ispolkom at once arrogated to itself legislative functions. It first defied the government with the notorious Order No. 1, which it released on March 1, without so much as consulting it. The document was drawn up by a group of socialist officers and civilians. Ostensibly taken on the initiative of soldiers to rectify their grievances, its real purpose was to emasculate the officer corps, which socialist intellectuals, well versed in revolutionary history, saw as the main breeding ground of counterrevolution. Addressed to the garrison of Petrograd, Order No. 1 was immediately interpreted as applicable to all troops, at the front as well as in the rear. It called for the election in military units of "committees" modeled on the soviets, which were to send representatives to the Petrograd Soviet. Article 3 stipulated that in respect to all political actions, the armed services were subordinated to the Soviet. Article 4 claimed for the Soviet the right to countermand orders of the Provisional Government bearing on military matters. Article 5 provided that company and battalion committees take charge of all military equipment, access to which was to be denied to officers. Only the concluding two articles dealt with the soldiers' rights.

17. N. D. Sokolov drafting Order No. 1, March 1, 1917.

18. A sailor removing an officer's epaulettes.

This extraordinary document, passed in time of war, which the socialists supported, had the effect of politicizing the military and, at the same time, disarming the officers and depriving them of authority over the troops. It thoroughly disorganized the armed forces. The soldier committees, especially those at higher levels, fell into the hands of junior officers, many of them Menshevik, Bolshevik, and Socialist-Revolutionary intellectuals. The government, in effect, lost control of its armed forces and the Soviet became the true master of the country. On March 9, hardly more than a week after the new government had come into being, Guchkov, the Minister of War, cabled General Alekseev to Mogilev:

> The Provisional Government has no real power of any kind and its orders are carried out only to the extent permitted by the Soviet of Workers' and Soldiers' Deputies, which controls the most essential strands of actual power, inasmuch as the troops, railroads, [and] postal services are in its hands. One can state bluntly that the Provisional Government exists only at the sufferance of the Soviet of Workers' and Soldiers' Deputies.

. . .

Nicholas took no part in these events. His last order of any consequence was that of February 25 demanding the suppression of street disorders. Once the command proved unenforceable, the monarchy retreated into the background and power shifted to the Duma and the Soviet. But with the formation of the Provisional Government, the future of the monarchy acquired great urgency. Some ministers—led by Miliukov and Guchkov—wanted to retain the monarchy, if only in a ceremonial capacity, on the grounds that the population identified the state with the person of the monarch and without him would succumb to anarchy. Others felt that given the popular mood, such a course was unrealistic. One of the major factors mitigating against the retention of the monarchy was the fear of Petrograd troops that they would be treated as mutineers and punished. On these grounds, the garrison resolutely opposed the Crown. As for the rest of the country and the frontline troops, no reliable information exists to judge their attitude on this matter.

On his arrival in Pskov on March 1, Nicholas had no thought of abdicating. He began to change his mind under the influence of arguments pressed on him by the generals, who, in turn, responded to the concerns of the politicians that if he wished Russia to stay in the war to the victorious end, he had to step down. General Alekseev, who during the Tsar's absence from Mogilev had assumed the duties of Commander in Chief, feared that the continuation of strikes and mutinies in the capital city would disrupt railway transport and cut off the flow of supplies to the front. There was the further danger that the turmoil would spread to the combat troops deployed only a few hundred kilometers from Petrograd. Having learned of disorders in Moscow, Alekseev wired the Tsar on March 1:

> A revolution in Russia—and it is inevitable once disorders occur in the rear—will mean a disgraceful termination of the war, with all its inevitable consequences, so dire for her. The army is most intimately connected with the life of the rear. It may be confidently stated that disorders in the rear will produce the same effect among the armed forces. It is impossible to ask the army calmly to wage war while a revolution is in progress in the rear. The youthful makeup of the present army and its officer staff, among whom a very high percentage consists of reservists and university students, gives no grounds for presuming that the army will not react to events occurring in Russia.

Alekseev recommended that the Tsar grant the Duma's request to form a cabinet.

Alekseev's telegram, which reached Nicholas shortly before midnight, made on him a deep impression. Under its influence he took two decisions: Rodzianko was to be told that the Duma could proceed with the formation of a cabinet; and General Ivanov was to halt his advance on Petrograd. Having given these instructions, Nicholas retired to the bedroom car to spend a sleepless night.

While the Tsar tossed in bed, worried about his family and wondering whether his concessions would work, General Ruzskii contacted Rodzianko. Their conversation, carried out by means of a teleprinter, lasted four hours. Apprised of the Tsar's instructions, Rodzianko responded that the Tsar seemed to be unaware how far the situation had deteriorated: the garrison was completely out of control, with soldiers firing at one another. Nicholas's concession had become irrelevant; nothing short of his abdication would pacify the rebellious troops. As Ruzskii conversed with the Duma chairman, the tapes of their exchange were forwarded to Alekseev in Mogilev. Stunned by what he read, Alekseev passed them on to the commanders of the fronts and fleets, requesting their opinion of Rodzianko's recommendation. Personally, he advised them, he favored Nicholas's abdication in favor of his minor son, with the Tsar's brother, Grand Duke Michael, assuming the regency.

At 10:45 a.m. on March 2, Ruzskii showed Nicholas the tapes of his conversation with Rodzianko. The Tsar studied them in silence. He said that he would consider abdicating but doubted that the people would understand such a move. He affirmed

> his strong conviction that he had been born for misfortune, that he brought Russia great misfortune. He said that he had realized clearly the previous night that no manifesto [about the Duma ministry] would be of help . . . "If it is necessary, for Russia's good, that I step aside, I am prepared to do so."

Around 2 p.m. Pskov was in receipt of the army and navy commanders' responses to Alekseev's request. All, including Grand Duke Nikolai Nikolaevich, the commander of the Caucasus front, agreed that Nicholas had to give up the Crown. Ruzskii, accompanied by two generals, immediately brought these tapes to the Tsar. Having read them and heard their personal opinions—they concurred with the other commanders—he retired. An hour later he reappeared with the text of an abdication manifesto written by hand on telegraphic blanks, one addressed to Rodzianko, the other to Alekseev. It passed the Crown to Alexis, with the proviso that until he attained maturity, Michael would serve as Regent.

All evidence indicates that Nicholas abdicated from patriotic motives, persuaded by the generals that he had to do so in order to keep Russia in the war and earn her the rewards of victory. Had his foremost concern been staying in power, he would have quickly made peace with Germany—as Lenin would do a year later—and unleashed the frontline troops against the mutineers in Petrograd and Moscow.

Before the abdication document was made public, Ruzskii learned that two Duma deputies, one of them Guchkov, were on their way to Pskov. On being so advised, Nicholas requested that the documents be returned to him: he apparently believed that the two deputies, both well-known monarchists, might bear news that would keep him on the throne. While awaiting their arrival, Nicholas consulted the court physician about his son's illness. Rasputin, he said, had assured him that on reaching thirteen—that is, in the current year, 1917—Alexis would be fully cured of hemophilia. Was that correct? The physician responded that, unfortunately, medicine knew no such miracles. On hearing this, Nicholas changed his mind. Unwilling to part from the ailing boy, he resolved on the spot to pass the Crown to Michael. This impulsive action was the last gasp of the old patrimonial spirit which treated the Crown as the monarch's property. It was both illegal and unrealistic.

The two Duma deputies arrived at 9:45 p.m. and were immediately led to the Tsar's train. They brought no good news: the Duma leadership felt that the Tsar had to abdicate in favor of the tsarevich. Nicholas responded that he had already resolved to do so, but in view of the prospect that his son would never be cured, he would abdicate also in Alexis's name and pass the Crown to Michael. The deputies were stunned by the move, but Nicholas would not budge. He revised his original manifesto to name Michael his successor. The document stressed that he was making the sacrifice to bring Russia victory in the "hard-fought war" over an enemy bent on enslaving Russia.* While the manifesto was being copied, Nicholas acceded to the deputies' request that Lvov assume the post of Chairman of the Council of Ministers, and Grand Duke Nikolai Nikolaevich that of Commander in Chief. Then he departed for Mogilev to take leave of the army. In his diary that night, he wrote: "Left Pskov at 1 a.m. with oppressive feelings about events. All around treason and cowardice and deception."

In the context of the time, Nicholas's abdication was something of an anticlimax, since he had been effectively deposed four days earlier by the Duma and the Petrograd Soviet. But in a broader context, it was an event of the greatest significance. The Tsar was the linchpin of the country's political structure. All the strands of authority converged in his person, and all bureaucratic and military personnel owed allegiance to him. The population saw him as the personification of statehood. His removal left a vacuum: the state vanished.

When Guchkov and his companion reached Petrograd early in the morning of March 3 bearing the Tsar's abdication manifesto, the cabinet was conferring with Michael. The Grand Duke was surprised and annoyed that his brother, without consultation, had appointed him successor to the throne. An emotional scene ensued, with Miliukov pleading that he accept the Crown and Kerensky imploring him to refuse it. The majority of the cabinet supported Kerensky. The decisive factor seems to have been Rodzianko's inability to guarantee Michael's personal safety. In the late afternoon, Michael signed a Manifesto declining the Crown until and unless the Constituent Assembly saw fit to confer it on him.

---

* In Communist histories and those written by Western scholars identified with the "revisionist" school, the roles of the mutinous troops and of concern with the war are minimized if not altogether ignored in order to depict the February Revolution as a social upheaval led by industrial workers and directed against the continuation of the war. Contemporary sources offer no warrant for such an interpretation; they hardly mention workers. They further indicate that the supreme consideration leading to the climactic event, the abdication of Nicholas II, was the desire to pursue the war more effectively.

19. Grand Duke Michael.

The following day, March 4, the two manifestoes were made public. According to eyewitnesses, the population joyfully welcomed their appearance.

Nicholas eventually made his way to Tsarskoe Selo, where he and his family were placed under house arrest. For the next five months he led a quiet life, shoveling snow, reading to his family, and taking brisk walks. The government, wanting him out of the way, negotiated with Britain for asylum. The British at first agreed, but then withdrew the invitation from fear of the Labour Party's objections. The news of yet another act of disloyalty is said to have deeply depressed the ex-Tsar.

The intellectuals who formed Russia's new government had been preparing themselves for the task for many years. But none of them had any administrative experience, and they rejected opportunities to acquire it during and after the 1905 Revolution. They thought of politics as legislating rather than administering. The Provisional Government issued countless laws intended to rectify the abuses of the old regime, but it never created a set of new institutions to replace those it had destroyed. In a country that throughout its history had been accustomed to a centralized government and orders from above, the Provisional Government adopted an extreme form of political laissez-faire—and this in the midst of an unprecedented war, inflation, and agrarian stirrings.

20. Ex-Tsar Nicholas under house arrest
at Tsarskoe Selo, March 1917.

On March 4, in accord with the eight-point program agreed upon with the Ispolkom, the government dissolved the Department of Police, the Okhrana, and the Corps of Gendarmes. It transferred police functions to citizens' militias commanded by elected officers and accountable to zemstva and municipal councils. The following day it dismissed all governors and deputy governors, consigning their responsibilities to chairmen of the provincial zemstvo boards who had never exercised administrative functions. These measures had the effect of destroying the country's entire administrative apparatus. Russia in the spring of 1917 may well represent a unique instance of a government born of revolution dismantling the machinery of administration before it had the chance to replace it with one of its own making.

Initially, this administrative vacuum was not apparent. The entire citizenry, including the most reactionary elements, swore allegiance to the Provisional Government, and it functioned for a while impelled by the sheer momentum of popular enthusiasm. Allied powers, beginning with the United States (March 9), pleased by its pro-war stance, promptly accorded the new government diplomatic recognition. But the display of support from the population and foreign powers was deceptive, encouraging it in the belief that it was firmly in control, whereas it was floating on air. Nabokov, in his recollections of the Provisional Government, wrote: "I primarily remember an atmosphere in which everything experienced seemed unreal."

One aspect of unreality lay in the dual nature of the government. The Ispolkom made it clear at every opportunity that the government existed only on its sufferance and that while the ministers could, in a strictly circumscribed way, engage in "high politics," the Soviet was in charge of day-to-day events. The Ispolkom legislated in every sphere of activity. Yielding to worker pressure, it instituted an eight-hour working day in all enterprises, including those working for defense. On March 3, it ordered the arrest of members of the Imperial family, including Grand Duke Nikolai Nikolaevich. On March 5, it closed "reactionary" newspapers. Two days later, it forbade editors of newspapers and periodicals to publish without express permission of the Soviet—that is, itself. These attempts to restore pre-1905 censorship provoked such an outcry that they had to be rescinded, but it was indicative of the readiness of the socialist intelligentsia, while professing the loftiest democratic ideals, to violate a cardinal principle of democracy: freedom of opinion.

The Ispolkom insisted that the government do nothing of any importance without its approval. It set up a "Contact Commission" of five socialist intellectuals to ensure compliance with this directive. According to Miliukov, the government satisfied all of the Commission's demands.

For reasons stated, the Ispolkom paid particular attention to the armed forces. To "facilitate contact," on March 19 it appointed commissars to the Ministry of War, the army headquarters, and the headquarters of the fronts and fleets. In the frontline zone, orders by the military commanders did not go into effect without prior approval of the Ispolkom and its commissars.

During the first month of its existence, the Petrograd Soviet served only the capital city, but before the end of the month it had expanded its authority to the entire country. After admitting representatives of provincial city soviets and frontline units, it turned into the All-Russian Soviet of Workers' and Soldiers' Deputies, and its Ispolkom renamed itself the All-Russian Central Executive Committee (CEC). The membership of the Ispolkom increased to seventy-two; of this number, twenty-three were Mensheviks, twenty-two SRs, and twelve Bolsheviks. The CEC had in effect supplanted the Soviet. In the first four days of its existence (February 28–March 3), the Soviet plenum met daily. During the remainder of March, it met four times, and in April six. No one paid attention to its raucous proceedings, and its main function was reduced to ratifying, by acclamation, resolutions submitted by the CEC.

Although the Ispolkom and its successor, the CEC, posed as authentic spokesmen of the masses, they had among their members no representatives from peasant organizations. The latter, 80 percent of the population, had their own Peasant Union, which kept aloof from the Soviet. The All-Russian Soviet thus spoke for only a fraction of the country's inhabitants, 10 to 15 percent at best if allowance is made for the peasantry and the "bourgeoisie," neither of which was represented.

The Provisional Government legislated profusely: the legislative industry was the most productive sector of the Russian economy. Unfortunately for it, while laws granting new freedoms were promptly acted on, no one paid attention to laws that imposed new obligations.

On the three most urgent issues confronting it—land reform, the Constituent Assembly, and peace—the government acted in a most dilatory fashion.

Except for areas adjoining the big cities, the news of the Tsar's abdication traveled slowly to the rural districts, held as they were in the grip of winter. Most villages first learned of the Revolution after a delay of four to six weeks—that is, in the first half of April, when the thaw had set in. Their initial reaction was to pounce on the households that had withdrawn from the commune under the Stolypin legislation and bring them back into the fold. The peasants also raided landed estates, cutting down trees and stealing seed grain. There was little personal violence, however. The SRs organized their peasant followers and pleaded with them to exercise patience and await a general decree on land reform. The decree never came.

The government also postponed from month to month the convocation of the Constituent Assembly, in violation of its accord with the Ispolkom and contrary to its own best interests. Only such a body would have been able to give the post-tsarist government uncontestable legitimacy and thus help to protect it from assaults of the extreme right and extreme left. Admittedly, the complexities of devising an equitable electoral procedure under conditions of war and revolution were formidable. Nevertheless, when the July monarchy had collapsed in France in 1848, a Constituent Assembly met in two months. In Germany in late 1918, after the defeat in war and in the midst of social upheavals, the politicians who succeeded the Kaiser would manage to convene a National Assembly in four months. The Russian Provisional Government failed to do so in the eight months it held office. Somehow there were always more urgent matters to attend to. Its delay contributed heavily to the government's overthrow, for it allowed the Bolsheviks to claim that only a Soviet government would guarantee the convocation of the Assembly.

And finally there was the issue of the war. Here the fault lay with the Soviet. In theory, all the parties, the Bolsheviks excepted, favored war to victory. Contrary to widespread misconception, the population in February 1917, and until the onset of the summer, did not oppose the war. During the first weeks of the February Revolution, writes Nicholas Sukhanov, the author of the best eyewitness account of 1917, "the soldier mass in Petrograd not only would not listen to talk of peace, but would not allow it to be uttered, ready to bayonet any incautious 'traitor' and anyone who 'opened the front to the enemy.' " The Bolsheviks, who treated an end to hostilities as a prelude to civil war and the key to power seizure, exercised great caution in their antiwar propaganda. Even so, their unpopularity with the troops is evidenced by the fact that in the elections to the CEC in the Soldiers' Section of the Soviet, held on April 8, not a single Bolshevik won a seat.

In its public pronouncements, the Soviet pursued a highly contradictory policy. It wanted the war to continue even though it considered it "imperialistic." In an "Appeal to the Peoples of the World" on March 15, the Ispolkom called on people everywhere—"bled white and ruined by the monstrous war"—to rise in revolution, pledging that it would "resist with all means the rapacious policy of its [own] ruling class." This left the man on the street thoroughly bewildered. If Russia's "ruling classes" pursued a "rapacious policy," why keep them in power and why allow oneself to be "bled white" in their "monstrous war"? The Provisional Government ignored these pronouncements, pledging to the Allies that Russia would wage war with all her might and declaring its intention to acquire, after victory, Constantinople and the Straits, as the Allies had promised her in 1915. But when pressed by the Soviet, the government retreated, denying that it wanted any foreign conquests.

The February Revolution spread peacefully to the provinces. In most localities, tsarist officials resigned and authority passed either to zemstvos and city councils or to local soviets.

The most striking aspect of the February Revolution was the extraordinary rapidity with which the Russian state fell apart. It was as if the greatest empire in the world had been an artificial construction, without organic unity. The instant the monarch withdrew, the entire structure collapsed in a heap. Kerensky says that there were moments when it seemed to him that

> the word "revolution" [was] quite inapplicable to what happened in Russia . . . A whole world of national and political relationships sank to the bottom, and all at once all existing political and tactical programs, however bold and well conceived, appeared hanging aimlessly and uselessly in space.

And in the words of V. Rozanov:

> Russia wilted in two days. At the very most, three. Even [the newspaper] *The New Times* could not have been shut down as quickly as Russia shut down. It is amazing how she suddenly fell apart, all of her, down to particles, to pieces. Indeed, such an upheaval had never occurred before, not excluding the "Great Migrations of Peoples." . . . There was no Empire, no Church, no army, no working class. And what remained? Strange to say, literally nothing. The base masses remained.

By late April, eight weeks after the Revolution had broken out, Russia was foundering. On April 26, the Provisional Government issued a pathetic appeal in which it conceded that it could no longer run the country.

Russians, having got rid of tsarism, on which they were accustomed to blame all their ills, stood stunned in the midst of their newly gained freedom. They resembled the lady in the Balzac story who had been sick for so long that when finally cured, she believed herself afflicted by a new disease.

PART TWO

The Bolsheviks Conquer Russia

LENIN AND THE ORIGINS OF BOLSHEVISM

O ne need not believe that history is made by "great men" to appreciate the immense importance of Lenin for the Russian Revolution and the regime that emerged from it. It is not only that the power which he accumulated allowed Lenin to exert a decisive influence on events but also that the regime that he established in October 1917 institutionalized, as it were, his personality. The Bolshevik Party was Lenin's creation: as its founder, he conceived it in his own image and, overcoming all opposition from within and without, kept it on the course he had charted. The same party, on seizing power in October 1917, promptly eliminated all rival parties to become Russia's exclusive source of political authority. Communist Russia, therefore, was throughout its seventy-four years to an unusual extent the embodiment of the mind and psyche of one man: his biography and its history are uniquely fused.

Although few historical figures have been so much written about, personal information on Lenin is sparse. Lenin was so unwilling to distinguish himself from his cause or even to allow that he had an existence apart from it (or it from him) that he left virtually no autobiographical data. Almost nothing is known of his early years. The entire body of writings for the first twenty-three years of his life consists of twenty items, nearly all of them petitions, certificates, and other official documents. Nor did he have friends who remembered him as he was in his youth.

Lenin was born Vladimir Ilich Ulianov in April 1870 in the Volga city of Simbirsk, into a conventional, comfortably well-off bureaucratic family. His father, a school inspector, had at the time of his death in 1886 attained the rank of state councillor, which gave him status equal to that of a general and made him a hereditary noble. He was a man of liberal-conservative views and an admirer of Alexander II's reforms. A year after his death, tragedy struck the family for the second time when the eldest son, Alexander, was arrested and executed for plotting to assassinate the Tsar. The Ulianovs suffered ostracism at the hands of local society. Although Communist hagiography depicts the seventeen-year-old Lenin as having turned into a revolutionary because of his brother's execution, the available evidence gives no warrant to this thesis. Lenin was throughout his school years an exemplary student, earning year after year gold medals for his studies as well as behavior. He showed no interest in politics.

It is thanks to this model record that he gained admission to the University of Kazan, from which his family background would otherwise have barred him. The father of Alexander Kerensky, who by a remarkable coincidence served as principal of Lenin's school in Simbirsk, recommended him to the university as a "reticent" and "unsociable" youth but one who "neither in school nor out of it gave his superiors or teachers by a single word or deed any cause to form of him an unfavorable opinion." Had it not been for the foolish persistence of the tsarist regime in treating every act of insubordination as a political crime, Lenin might well have made a career as a prominent bureaucrat.

On entering the university, Lenin was recognized by fellow students as the brother of Alexander, executed earlier that year, and they pulled him into a clandestine political organization. His membership in it came to light when he took part in a rather harmless student rally to protest some university regulations, as a result of which he was expelled. Such savage punishments kept the revolutionary movement supplied with ever-fresh recruits.

Barred from enrolling at any other university, understandably embittered, Lenin spent the next four years in enforced idleness. His mood was so desperate that his mother, who pleaded in vain with the authorities to reinstate him, feared he might commit suicide. It was during this period that he familiarized himself with radical literature and turned into a fanatical revolutionary determined to destroy the state and society that had treated him so shabbily. His radicalism, then and afterward, was rooted not in idealism but in personal resentment. Struve, who had frequent dealings with Lenin during the 1890s, recalled that his

> principal *Einstellung* [disposition] . . . was *hatred*. Lenin took to Marx's doctrine primarily because it found response in that principal *Einstellung* of his mind. The doctrine of class war, relentless and thoroughgoing, aiming at the final destruction and extermination of the enemy, proved congenial to Lenin's emotional attitude to surrounding reality. He hated not only the existing autocracy (the Tsar) and the bureaucracy, not only lawlessness and arbitrary rule of the police, but also their antipodes—the "liberals" and the "bourgeoisie." That hatred had something repulsive and terrible in it; for being rooted in the concrete, I should say even animal, emotions and repulsions, it was at the same time abstract and cold like Lenin's whole being.

In his entire psychological makeup, Lenin differed fundamentally from the typical Russian *intelligent*, who—to employ categories devised by the novelist Ivan Turgenev—qualified as either a Hamlet or a Don Quixote: an ineffectual dreamer or a foolhardy hero. Lenin's personality alienated most people from him. But it also won him the devoted following of a minority.

Initially, like his elder brother, he sympathized with the People's Will. Conversations with veterans of this terrorist organization, exiled to the Volga region where he grew up, taught him how to organize a tightly disciplined, clandestine revolutionary organization and inculcated in him the belief in the necessity of a head-on assault on the tsarist regime—a belief that he retained even after converting to Social-Democracy.

This he did in the early 1890s, under the influence of the great electoral triumphs of the German Social-Democratic Party, and of contacts with the small band of Russian Social-Democratic émigrés in Switzerland. He sought to graft Marxism onto the anarchist People's Will by accepting the Marxist notion that a country could not become socialist until it had gone through a capitalist phase and then declaring that Russia already was in the midst of capitalist development. When, in 1891, the authorities finally relented and allowed him to take the university examination for a law degree in St. Petersburg, Lenin embodied a not untypical (for the time) blend of anarchist-terrorist and Social-Democrat.

By then, the twenty-two-year-old Lenin was a fully formed personality. His short, stocky figure, his premature baldness, his slanted eyes and

high cheekbones, his brusque manner of speaking, often accompanied by
a sarcastic snicker, made a poor impression. His acquaintances then and
later often resorted to the adjective "provincial" to describe him: some
he reminded of a provincial tradesman, others of a provincial grocer or
schoolteacher. But this unattractive individual glowed with an inner fire
that made people quickly forget their first impressions. He knew only
two categories of men: friend and enemy—those who followed him, and
all the rest. Early on, in 1904, long before he joined him, Trotsky compared Lenin to Robespierre in that he recognized but "two parties—that
of good citizens and that of bad citizens." The normal "I/we—you/they"
contrast, translated into an uncompromising dualism, "friend-foe," had
two important historical consequences.

First, it led Lenin to treat all politics as warfare. When, in a rare
moment of candor, he defined peace as "a breathing spell for war," he
inadvertently allowed an insight into the innermost recesses of his mind.
Such a manner of thinking made him constitutionally incapable of compromise, except for tactical purposes. Once Lenin and his followers came
to power, this attitude automatically permeated their regime. The second consequence was an inability to tolerate dissent. Given that he
viewed any group or individual who was not a member of his party as
ipso facto an enemy, and hence a threat, it followed that such a person
had to be silenced and suppressed. Lenin was quite incapable of tolerating criticism; he simply did not hear it. He belonged to that category of
men of whom a French writer a century earlier had said that they know
everything except what one tells them. One either agreed with him or
fought him. Here lay the seeds of the whole totalitarian mentality.

Lenin's absolute conviction of being in the right and his absence of
moral qualms attracted to the Bolshevik Party pseudo-intellectuals who
yearned for certainty in an uncertain world. It especially appealed to the
young, semiliterate peasants who flocked to the city in search of work
and found themselves adrift in a strange, cold world, devoid of the kind
of personal relations they had known in the village. Lenin's party gave
them a sense of belonging; they liked its cohesion and simple slogans.

Lenin's total commitment to revolution had also its attractive side. It
made him rather tolerant of his own followers even when they disagreed
with him on particular issues. It also made for a peculiar kind of modesty:
being fully submerged in his cause, his ego had no need for the kind of
personal adulation commonly associated with dictators. It sufficed for
his cause to triumph.

Lenin had a strong streak of cruelty. He condemned people to death by the thousands without remorse, though also without pleasure. The writer Maxim Gorky, who knew him well, said that for Lenin human beings held "almost no interest . . . he thought only of parties, masses, states. . . ." When, after 1917, Gorky would plead with him to spare the life of this or that condemned person, Lenin seemed genuinely puzzled that his friend should bother him with such trivia. As is usually the case (this held true of Robespierre as well), the obverse of Lenin's cruelty was cowardice. Whenever there was any physical risk he made himself scarce, even if it meant abandoning his troops. And when he finally became head of state, he used his unlimited powers to exorcise his fears by ordering mass executions of real or imagined enemies.

The mature Lenin was of a piece. After he had formulated the theory and practice of Bolshevism, which he did in his early thirties, he surrounded himself with an invisible wall that alien ideas could not penetrate. One either agreed with him or fought him; and disagreement always aroused in Lenin destructive passions. This was his strength as a revolutionary and his weakness as a statesman: formidable in combat, he lacked the human qualities necessary to govern. In the end, this flaw would defeat his efforts to create a new society, for he simply could not comprehend that ordinary people wanted nothing more than to live in peace.

In the fall of 1893, Lenin moved to St. Petersburg, ostensibly to practice law but in reality to earn his spurs as a professional revolutionary. Conversations with Marxists, who at the time were gaining dominance among the youthful intelligentsia, persuaded him to abandon (for the time being) the People's Will ideology and become a full-fledged Social-Democrat. He accepted the notion that revolution would come only as the result of capitalist development and that the immediate task of revolutionaries was to organize workers. Direct contact with workers, however, brought him disappointment, for they turned out to be quite uninterested in politics and unresponsive to revolutionary agitation. Lenin, along with some of his associates, took to distributing leaflets in factories supporting the workers' economic grievances in the hope that this would bring them in conflict with the state authorities and in this manner politicize them. Arrested for this activity, he was sentenced to three years of exile in Siberia, which he spent rather comfortably in a rented cottage with his new bride, Nadezhda Krupskaia, writing, translating, and engaging in vigorous outdoor activity.

The news he received from home, however, brought him no comfort. The Social-Democratic movement was racked by heresies and weakened by splits. He was especially troubled by the emergence of a trend that, acknowledging the apoliticism of the working class as a given, urged socialists to concentrate on trade-union activity. Inasmuch as trade unions accepted the capitalist system, Lenin considered them inherently antirevolutionary. Before his term of exile was up, he formulated a new and highly unorthodox revolutionary theory fully spelled out in *What Is to Be Done?*, a book he published in Germany in 1902.

The basic thesis of Lenin's theory held that the worker, if left to himself, would not make revolution but come to terms with the capitalist. It was the same premise that had inspired Zubatov to found police-sponsored trade unions. "The labor movement, separated from Social-Democracy . . . inevitably turns bourgeois," he wrote. The implication of this startling statement was that unless the workers were led by a socialist party composed of professional revolutionaries, they would betray their class interests (as understood by socialists) and sell out. The proletariat, for its own good, had to be led by a minority of the elect:

> No single class in history has ever attained mastery unless it has produced political leaders . . . capable of organizing the movement and leading it. . . . It is necessary to prepare men who devote to the revolution not only their free evenings, but their entire lives.

Since workers have to earn a living and therefore cannot devote "their entire lives" to the revolutionary movement, it followed from Lenin's premise that the leadership of their cause had to fall on the shoulders of the socialist intelligentsia. This quite un-Marxist inference led to the creation of a party that, both before and after the seizure of power, acted in the name of the workers but without their mandate.

To implement his theory, Lenin reverted to the practices of the People's Will, demanding that the Russian Social-Democratic Party, formally created in 1903, adopt a clandestine and centralized form of organization. All decisions were to be made by the leadership and carried out by its local cells without questioning. When the majority of Social-Democrats rejected this program, Lenin refused to submit and began to build up within the party his own faction that in time would evolve into a separate organization.

Although until 1912 the two factions nominally belonged to the same SD Party, the break between Mensheviks and Bolsheviks occurred as early as 1906–7. The Mensheviks, even as they adhered to the Marxist ideal of a social upheaval, were content, for the time being, to instruct and organize workers. The Bolsheviks prepared cadres for the coming revolution. Neither group had a mass following. At the height of their popularity in 1907, the Bolsheviks had 46,100 members enrolled and the Mensheviks 38,200—this in a country of 150 million inhabitants and some 2 million workers. Soon, however, desertions began and even these modest figures dwindled. In the calmer Stolypin era (1910), by Trotsky's estimate, the two factions had between them 10,000 or fewer adherents. The Bolsheviks had a predominantly Great Russian following, while the Mensheviks attracted more non-Russians, especially Georgians and Jews. At the Fifth Congress of the Party in 1907, 78.3 percent of the Bolsheviks were of Great Russian origin, while their proportion among the Mensheviks was only 34 percent. Intellectuals predominated in both factions. Their directing organs, according to L. Martov, the leader of the Mensheviks, were staffed not by workers, who had no leisure time for such activities, but by intellectuals.

Lenin had differences with the Mensheviks not only over organizational but also over programmatic matters. To make a successful revolution when the time was ripe, in his opinion, one had to rally the largest number of potential opponents of the status quo, including those whose long-term aspirations were inimical to socialism. These were, first and foremost, the peasants and the non-Russian minorities.

Russian Social-Democrats, in common with Western Marxists, treated the peasantry, except for the minority which had no access to land, as a "petty-bourgeois," reactionary class. They opposed the claim of the Russian communes to acquire all privately owned land. Ideally, they wanted the nationalization of the agrarian land with a view toward its ultimate collectivization, under which the peasant would become, like the factory worker, a wage earner working for the state. Lenin shared these views. But thinking as a revolutionary tactician, he felt that the peasants' support was essential and that to gain it there was no harm in granting them, for the time being, their wishes and embracing the Socialist-Revolutionary program that called for the abolition of commerce in land and its transfer to the peasant communes. After power had been won, there would always be time to resolve the land question in a Marxist fashion.

Lenin adopted a similar tactical approach to the national minorities. Like other socialists, he repudiated nationalism and favored assimilation: he rejected any solution, such as federalism or cultural autonomy, that would institutionalize ethnic differences. His program offered the minorities all or nothing: Either assimilate and become Russians or separate and form an independent state. To associates who argued that such a program threatened to Balkanize Russia, Lenin responded with two counterarguments: first, that the economic bonds linking the borderlands with Russia would prevent separation; and, second, that if these proved insufficiently strong to thwart centrifugal impulses, the socialists could always, with appeal to the higher principle of "proletarian self-determination," bring the separated borderlands back into the fold.

Lenin regarded both slogans—land seizure for the peasants, and national self-determination for the minorities—as nothing more than temporary concessions:

> It is the support of an ally against a *given* enemy, and the Social-Democrats provide this support in order to speed the fall of the common enemy, but they expect *nothing for themselves* from these temporary allies and concede them nothing.

The decade that preceded the 1917 Revolution was for the Social-Democrats a period of interminable intrigues and squabbles, many of them involving money.

While the Mensheviks financed their operations with membership dues, Lenin needed much greater sums because he staffed his organizations with full-time revolutionaries. His needs were partly met by contributions from wealthy patrons. At this time, writes Leonid Krasin, Lenin's close associate, "it was regarded as a sign of *bon ton* in more or less radical circles to contribute money to revolutionary parties, and among those who quite regularly paid dues of between 5 and 25 rubles were not only prominent attorneys, engineers and physicians, but also bank directors and government officials." But such contributions from repentant "bourgeois" did not suffice, and the Bolsheviks resorted to bank robberies which they euphemistically called "expropriations." In one notorious burglary carried out in Tiflis in 1907, they stole 250,000 rubles ($125,000). The serial numbers of these banknotes had been registered and attempts to cash them abroad led to the arrest of a number of prominent Bolsheviks, among them Maxim Litvinov, the future Soviet Minister of Foreign Affairs. On one occasion, the Bolsheviks used a combination of blackmail and enticement to appropriate for their treasury the estate of a wealthy Marxist sympathizer, amounting to more than 100,000 rubles, which he had bequeathed to the Social-Democratic Party. According to Martov, the proceeds of such crimes enabled the Bolsheviks to pay their St. Petersburg and Moscow organizations 1,000

21. Lenin, Paris, 1910.

and 5,000 rubles a month, respectively, while the legitimate SD trea-sury's monthly earnings from dues did not exceed 100 rubles. When, in 1910, the Bolsheviks had to turn over their funds to German trustees, their Russian committees vanished into thin air.

Lenin used his moneys to pay salaries, but also to publish Bolshevik papers in Russia. In the sordid contest between the security organs and the revolutionaries, cooperation between the hunters and the hunted was not unknown. So it transpired that in his operations in Russia—some open, others clandestine—Lenin found himself working hand in glove with the police. The Police Department, which by now had infil-trated all the revolutionary parties, was eager to promote friction among and within them. A major responsibility of their secret agents, in addi-tion to reporting on the activities and plans of the revolutionaries, was to exacerbate ideological and personal conflicts in radical circles. The police resolved to exploit Lenin's hostility to the Mensheviks so as to maintain tension between the two factions of the Social-Democratic Party and thus render them less dangerous.

To this end, a police agent by the name of Roman Malinovskii penetrated Bolshevik ranks and became the party's chief spokesman in the Duma. Malinovskii also secured from the police funds to publish Lenin's daily *Pravda*, and appointed a fellow agent as its editor. Lenin's *Pravda* articles were regularly vetted by the police before publication. It is not absolutely clear to this day whether Lenin was ignorant of Malinovskii's police connections or knew of them but thought that he gained more from the relationship than did the authorities. The fact that he angrily rejected information supplied by the Mensheviks and SRs about Malinovskii's background and maintained with him cordial relations even after Malinovskii's police connections had been revealed beyond a shadow of a doubt suggests the latter as the more likely explanation.*

Lenin welcomed the outbreak of World War I because he counted on the masses of workers and peasants to rebel against the carnage and, directed by the socialists, transform the international conflict into a civil war. In January 1913, during one of the recurrent Balkan crises, he wrote to Gorky: "A war between Austria and Russia would be a most useful thing for the revolution (in all of Eastern Europe), but it is not very likely that Franz Joseph and Nicky [Nicholas II] will give us this pleasure [!]." And to his mistress, Inessa Armand, on the outbreak of World War I, he sent a postcard that began: "My dear and dearest friend! Best greetings on the commencement of the revolution in Russia."†

He was living at the time in Cracow, in the Austrian part of Poland, from which he maintained contacts with the Austrian government. In return for financial subsidies, he supported the independence of the Russian Ukraine, which Austria actively promoted as a means of weakening Russia. (Neither then nor later did he urge independence for the Ukrainians of Austria-Hungary.) Interned at the outbreak of hostilities as an enemy alien, he was soon released and escorted to neutral Switzer-

---

* Malinovskii was unmasked in 1914, following which he resigned his seat in the Duma and went abroad. He returned voluntarily to Soviet Russia in November 1918, at the height of the Red Terror, apparently expecting Lenin's support. But Lenin had no further use for him and had him executed.

† The Russian Center for the Preservation and Study of Documents of Modern History (RTsKhIDNI), Moscow, Fond 2, op. 1, delo 3341. Benito Mussolini and other proto-Fascists in Italy entertained identical revolutionary hopes of the Great War. See this author's *Russia under the Bolshevik Regime* (New York, 1994), 250.

land, where he would spend the next two and a half years. After arriving there, he prepared a programmatic statement which advocated the defeat of Russia at the hands of the Germans and Austrians as "the least evil." He was the only prominent European socialist to call for the defeat of his own country.

The support that nearly all European socialist parties gave their national governments at the outbreak of the war unquestionably betrayed their solemn pledges not to help unleash a conflict the main burden of which would fall on the common people. The betrayal provoked a crisis within the international socialist movement, pitting the pro-war majority against a minority with strong Russian representation, which demanded an instant suspension of hostilities. Lenin headed the extreme wing of that minority in that instead of calling for immediate peace, he insisted that the war between nations be transformed into a war between classes.

Lenin's anti-Russian propaganda, his open endorsement of Russia's defeat, attracted the attention of the German government. One of its experts on Russian affairs was Alexander Helphand-Parvus, an expatriate Russian radical who in 1905 had formulated the theory of "permanent revolution" (Chapter II). Disillusioned by the failure of the Revolution of 1905, Parvus concluded that only the German army could rid Russia of tsarism. He emigrated to Germany, where he established contact with the Ministry of Foreign Affairs. After the outbreak of the war, he argued that the interests of Russian revolutionaries and those of the German government coincided insofar as the former could attain their objective—the overthrow of tsarism—only if the German armies crushed the Russians. With official sanction, he contacted Lenin in Zurich in May 1915, but at that point Lenin rejected his advances. He agreed, however, in return for financial help, to supply another German agent, an Estonian nationalist, with reports on internal conditions in Russia sent to him by his followers there. These activities, as well as his relations with the Austrian government, constituted high treason and Lenin maintained about them to the end of his life complete silence. They only came to light after German and Austrian archives were thrown open.

In 1915 and 1916, Lenin participated in two conferences convened in Switzerland by antiwar socialists. In both instances, he and his Bolshevik followers found themselves in a minority in their opposition to appeals for an immediate cease-fire and their insistence that the "imperialist" war be turned into a civil war. The majority held such a slogan to be impractical as well as dangerous: as one delegate pointed out, on their return home the signatories of such a platform would face the death penalty while

Lenin enjoyed the safety of neutral Switzerland. Although defeated, Lenin's motions would provide the programmatic basis of the Third or Communist International, which he would found in Soviet Russia in 1919.

The war years were for Lenin and Krupskaia a time of severe trials, a time of poverty and isolation from Russia. They lived in quarters that bordered on slums, took their meals in the company of prostitutes and criminals, and found themselves abandoned by many past followers who had come to regard Lenin as a dangerous fanatic. The only shaft of light for Lenin during this dark period was his love affair with Inessa Armand, the daughter of two music-hall artists and the wife of a wealthy Russian. She had met Lenin in Paris in 1910 and soon became his mistress under the tolerant eye of Krupskaia. Armand seems to have been the only human being with whom Lenin ever established true intimacy.

For all his talk of civil war, Lenin had little faith in the imminence of revolution. Addressing a gathering of socialist youths in Zurich on January 9/22, 1917, he predicted that while Europe would not escape social upheaval, "we old-timers perhaps shall not live [to see] the decisive battles of the looming revolution." Seven weeks later, tsarism collapsed.

THE OCTOBER COUP

The Bolsheviks' Failed Bids for Power

Although it is customary to speak of two Russian revolutions of 1917—one in February, the other in October—only the first deserves the name. In February 1917, Russia experienced a genuine revolution in that the disorders that brought down the tsarist regime, although neither unprovoked nor unexpected, erupted spontaneously and the Provisional Government that assumed power gained immediate nationwide acceptance. Neither held true of October 1917. The events that led to the overthrow of the Provisional Government were not spontaneous but carefully plotted and staged by a tightly organized conspiracy. It took these conspirators three years of civil war to subdue the majority of the population. October was a classic coup d'état, the capture of governmental authority by a small band, carried out, in deference to the democratic professions of the age, with a show of mass participation, but with hardly any mass involvement.

The Bolshevik coup went through two phases. In the first, during which Lenin assumed direct command, the strategy was to replicate the events of February and bring the government down by street demonstrations. The strategy failed. Trotsky, who took charge in September, while Lenin hid out in Finland, abandoned orchestrated riots. He disguised Bolshevik preparations for the coup behind the facade of an unlawfully convened Second Congress of Soviets and entrusted to special shock troops the task of seizing the nerve centers of the government. In theory, the power seizure was carried out provisionally and on behalf of the soviets, but, in fact, permanently and for the benefit of the Bolshevik Party.

The outbreak of the February Revolution found Lenin in Zurich; he learned of it nearly a week late from a report in a Swiss newspaper. He decided immediately to return to Russia. But how? Given his pronounced pro-German and anti-Russian stand, the Allies would certainly refuse him transit. The other alternative was to travel across Germany to neutral Sweden and from there, by way of Finland, to Petrograd. But this option exposed him to charges of consorting with the enemy at a time when anti-German feeling in Russia ran high.

While raging in Zurich, in the words of Trotsky, like a caged animal, he worried lest his followers in Russia adopt a wrong political course. He feared, with good reason as events were to show, that they would follow the Menshevik line of supporting the Provisional Government instead of working for its immediate overthrow. On March 6/19, he cabled the Petrograd Bolsheviks:

> Our tactics: complete mistrust, no support for the new government. We especially suspect Kerensky. The arming of the proletariat provides the only guarantee. Immediate elections to the Petrograd [Municipal] Duma. No rapprochement with the other parties.

When Lenin sent these instructions to his followers, the Provisional Government had been in office for only one week and had hardly revealed its physiognomy. To the extent that it had, it demonstrated subservience to the socialist Soviet. Lenin's insistence that it be treated with "complete mistrust" and denied support, therefore, had to be due to his disapproval not of what it did but of what it was—a political rival. His order to "arm the proletariat" indicates that he intended to topple it by military insurrection. And the refusal to cooperate with any other party meant that the coup was to be carried out exclusively by the Bolshevik Party.

The party, decimated by the tsarist police, was hardly in a position to realize such an ambitious program. It had nearly no following among the mutinous soldiers, while among the Petrograd workers it had fewer adherents than either the Mensheviks or the SRs. But the Bolsheviks were good at organizing. On March 2, the Petrograd Committee of the party, fresh out of prison, resumed operations and three days later brought out the first issue of *Pravda*, which had been shut down at the outbreak of the war. For their headquarters, the Bolsheviks appropriated the luxurious villa of the ballerina M. F. Kshesinskaia, who in her youth is said to have been the mistress of the tsarevich, the future Nicholas II.

The Petrograd Bolsheviks were inclined to cooperate with the Mensheviks in support of the "bourgeois" Provisional Government but not to join it. This was also the view of leading Bolsheviks, Lev Kamenev and Joseph Stalin, who returned to Petrograd from Siberia under the government's amnesty. The Bolshevik policy, as enunciated by Stalin at the All-Russian Conference of Bolsheviks held in Petrograd between March 28 and April 4, was identical with that of the Mensheviks: control of the Provisional Government and cooperation with other "progressive forces" to thwart the "counterrevolution." The "un-Bolshevik" behavior of the Bolsheviks when on their own and the rapid turnabout after Lenin's arrival demonstrates that the party's conduct was based not on principles that the members could assimilate and apply but on their leader's will. It indicates that the Bolsheviks were bound together not by what they believed but in whom they believed.

The Germans had their own designs on the Russian radicals. In the fall of 1916, Kaiser Wilhelm mused:

> From the strictly military point of view, it is important to detach one or another of the Allied belligerents by means of a separate peace, in order to hurl our full might against the rest. . . . Accordingly, we can organize our war effort only insofar as the internal struggle in Russia exerts influence on the conclusion of peace with us.

This meant exploiting the pro-German, antiwar stand of the radical left, of which Lenin was the undisputed leader.

The principal proponent of the "Lenin card" was Parvus. In 1917 he was living in neutral Denmark, where, as a cover for his intelligence operations, he ran an import company. As his business agent in Stockholm, he employed the Pole Jacob Fürstenberg-Ganetskii, a trusted associate of Lenin's. Intimately familiar with Russian politics—as a political strategist Parvus was Lenin's peer—he assured the German ambassador to Denmark that if let loose, the antiwar left would sow such discord in Russia that in two or three months she would drop out of the war. He singled out for particular attention Lenin, whom he described as "much more raving mad" than Kerensky. With extraordinary foresight, he predicted that once Lenin returned home he would topple the Provisional Government, take charge, and conclude a separate peace. He understood Lenin's lust for power and believed that he would strike a deal to traverse Germany en route to Sweden and Russia. Under Parvus's influence, the German ambassador wired Berlin:

> We must unconditionally seek to create in Russia the greatest possible chaos ... We should do all we can ... to exacerbate the differences between the moderate and extremist parties, because we have the greatest interest in the latter gaining the upper hand, since the Revolution will then become unavoidable and assume forms that must shatter the stability of the Russian state.

Persuaded by these arguments, the German government authorized its embassy in Switzerland to enter into negotiations with the Russian émigrés about transit rights. Lenin, who spoke on the latter's behalf, went to great lengths to ensure that they would not be accused of collaborating with the enemy. The Russians were to be exchanged for German civilian internees in Russia; their train was to enjoy extraterritorial status and exemption from passport controls. Lenin's objectives happened to coincide with those of the Germans and he acted now, as always, on the principle that one struck deals with anyone with whom one shared a passing interest against a common enemy. As for the Germans, what they did in Russia was part of a pattern. In the words of the historian Richard M. Watt:

> For each of their enemies, France, Britain, Italy, and Russia, the Germans had long since worked out a scheme for treason from within. The plans all bore a rough similarity: first, discord by means of the parties of the far left; next, pacifist articles by defeatists either paid or directly inspired by Germany; and, finally, the establishment of an understanding with a prominent political personality who would ultimately take over the weakened enemy government and sue for peace.

For Britain, they employed the Irishman Sir Roger Casement, for France, Joseph Caillaux, and for Russia, Lenin. Casement was hanged, Caillaux ended up in prison, and only Lenin justified the effort.

At 3:20 p.m. on March 27/April 9, thirty-two Russian émigrés left the Zurich railway station for the German frontier. Among the passengers were Lenin, Krupskaia, Grigorii Zinoviev with his wife and child, and Inessa Armand. On its journey across Germany, their train received the highest priority. Contrary to legend it was not sealed, but in conformance with the agreement, no Germans entered the car. On March 30/April 20, the Russians reached the Baltic, where they boarded a steamer bound for Sweden.

In Stockholm, Parvus awaited them. He asked to meet Lenin, but Lenin refused, turning him over to Karl Radek, a close associate, who, being an Austrian citizen, could not be accused of consorting with the enemy. No record exists of Radek's talks with Parvus, but it is virtually certain that the two worked out the terms of German financial support for the Bolsheviks. Following these negotiations, Parvus dashed off to Berlin, where he met with the German State Secretary.

Lenin and his party arrived in Petrograd on April 3 at 11:10 p.m. It happened to be the final day of the All-Russian Bolshevik Conference, and his followers prepared for him a welcome accorded to no other political figure in post-tsarist Russia. As the train pulled into Finland station, a band struck up the "Marseillaise"; outside the terminal stood an armored car illuminated by a projector. Lenin mounted the car to deliver a short message, and then, followed by a crowd, rode to Kshesinskaia's villa. There he delivered a speech whose militancy stupefied everyone present. Its thrust was that the transition from the "bourgeois" phase of the revolution to the socialist one had to be accomplished in a matter of weeks rather than years. Sukhanov, a Menshevik who was in the audience, wrote:

> I cannot forget that speech, like a flash of lightning, which shook and astonished not only me, a heretic accidentally thrown into delirium, but also the true believers. I aver that no one had expected anything like it. It seemed as if all the elemental forces had risen from their lairs and the spirit of universal destruction, which knew no obstacles, no doubts, neither human difficulties nor human calculations, circled in Kshesinskaia's hall above the heads of the enchanted disciples.

Later that day Lenin read to his followers a document which came to be known as "the April Theses." It impressed most members of his audience as written by someone out of touch with reality, if not positively mad. Lenin proposed renunciation of the war; immediate transition to the next phase of the Revolution; denial of any support to the Provisional Government; transfer of all power to the soviets; dissolution of the army in favor of a people's militia; confiscation of landlord property and nationalization of all land; integration of Russia's financial institutions into a single National Bank under soviet supervision; soviet control of production and distribution; and creation of a new International.

The *Pravda* editorial board at first refused to publish Lenin's "Theses." When finally compelled to do so, it accompanied the text with an editorial that disassociated the paper from Lenin's views.

Whatever the Bolsheviks' opinion of their leader's pronouncements, the Germans were delighted. On April 4/17, their agent in Stockholm cabled to Berlin: "Lenin's entry into Russia successful. He is working exactly as we desire."

Lenin was a highly secretive man: treating politics as warfare, he was no more likely to disclose his intentions than a general on the eve of battle. Of his general strategic objective, to be sure, he made no secret; it was his tactics that he kept to himself. And as Benito Mussolini, no mean expert in the art of the coup d'état, confided to a friend: "A State has to be defended not against the program of the revolution but against its tactics."

Like every successful conqueror, Lenin had a keen sense of his enemy's weaknesses. He knew the liberal and socialist intelligentsia for what they were: "vegetarian tigers," to borrow a phrase from Clemenceau, men who for all their revolutionary posturing feared both violence and responsibility. He further realized that the country was seething with resentments and unsatisfied aspirations that, fanned and properly directed, could bring him to power. To achieve this objective, the Bolsheviks had to distance themselves from the government and the other parties in order to appear as the sole alternative to the status quo.

Lenin had studied closely Clausewitz's *On War*, and applied its teachings to politics. As in war, the objective was not merely to defeat the opponent but to destroy him. This meant (1) depriving him of an armed force and (2) dismantling all his institutions. But if he refused to submit, it could also mean his physical annihilation.

The principle guiding Lenin was a dictum that Marx had pronounced rather casually in 1871, following the collapse of the Paris Commune. Analyzing its failure, Marx had concluded that the Communards had committed a fundamental mistake in taking over instead of liquidating the existing political, social, and military structures. Future revolutions would have to proceed differently: "not transfer from one set of hands to another the bureaucratic-military machine, as has been done until now, but *smash* it." These words etched themselves deeply in Lenin's mind because they showed how to avert the counterrevolutionary backlash that had been the undoing of every previous revolution. They explain the destruction he and his successor, Stalin, would visit on their country after gaining power.

The experience of February seems to have persuaded Lenin that the Provisional Government, like tsarism, could be toppled by street action. Unlike then, however, such riots were to be carefully managed by the Bolshevik Party. Lenin adopted for revolutionary ends the military tactic of skirmishing, or *tiraillerie*, devised by Napoleon to ascertain the enemy's weak spots before sending the elite Guard to deliver the decisive blow. In addition to Clausewitz, Lenin studied the work of the French sociologist Gustave Le Bon, *Crowd Psychology*, a pioneering analysis of human behavior in crowds and of the ways to manipulate it. (Le Bon's book provided similar guidance to Mussolini and Hitler.)

In the three months that followed his return to Russia, Lenin acted with reckless impetuosity to bring down the Provisional Government by mobs. He failed, and his last attempt, in July 1917, almost ended in the destruction of the Bolshevik Party. But the skirmishes were not a total loss because they demonstrated the government's indecisiveness, knowledge of which Trotsky would later put to good use. They also served to solidify his movement.*

The first, rather halfhearted, Bolshevik bid for power occurred in April, less than three weeks after Lenin's return. The pretext was a disagreement between the government and the Soviet over war aims. The Soviet wanted to pursue the war till victory, but to conclude it with a peace without "annexations and indemnities." Miliukov, the Foreign Minister, had different ideas, desiring to claim for Russia the Turkish Straits and Constantinople promised her by the Allies in 1915, when they feared that she might drop out of the war. Conflicting signals sent by the government on this matter led to street demonstrations by military units brought out by radical junior officers. The Bolsheviks joined these disturbances under slogans calling for the resignation of the government in favor of the Soviet. General Lavr Kornilov, the Commander of the Petrograd Military District, asked the cabinet for permission to suppress the riot by force, but this was denied, and order was restored by agreement with the Ispolkom. Disgusted with the government's indecisiveness, Kornilov asked to be relieved of his duties and assigned to the front. He would be heard from again.

Evaluating the lessons of April, Lenin concluded that the Bolsheviks had been "insufficiently revolutionary" in their tactics.

The April riots precipitated the first crisis of the new government. In its public appeal at the end of the month (above, p. 97), it conceded that it could no longer administer the country and pleaded with the socialist

---

* According to Eric Hoffer's study of modern dictatorships, "Action is a unifier . . . All mass movements avail themselves of mass action as a means of unification. The conflicts a mass movement seeks and incites serve not only to down its enemies but also to strip its followers of their distinct individuality and render them more soluble in the collective medium." *The True Believer* (New York, 1951), 117, 118–19.

intelligentsia to join the cabinet. The Ispolkom, faithful to the principle of controlling the new authority from the outside, initially rejected the request, but then thought better of it and at the beginning of May reversed itself. After Miliukov and Guchkov had resigned, six socialist representatives of the Soviet accepted ministerial posts in what came to be known as the "Coalition Government." Lvov stayed on as Prime Minister, while Kerensky took over the Ministry of War.

The May accords alleviated the pernicious effects of dual power, but they also created a new problem. By entering the "bourgeois" government, the socialists automatically came to share the blame for everything that went wrong, for they were now part of the establishment. This allowed the Bolsheviks, who refused to join, to pose as the sole alternative to the existing "bourgeois" authority and the true custodians of the Revolution. And since under the hopelessly incompetent administration of liberal and socialist intellectuals events were bound to go from bad to worse, they positioned themselves as the only party able to save Russia.

In May and June 1917, the Bolshevik Party still ran a poor third to the socialist parties: at the First All-Russian Congress of Soviets in early June, it had only 105 seats, compared with 285 for the SRs and 248 for the Mensheviks. At the First Peasant Congress, dominated by the SRs, it had a mere twenty delegates. But the tide was running in its favor.

The Bolsheviks enjoyed several advantages over their rivals. In addition to their unique status as the sole alternative to the status quo and their equally unique paramilitary organization, there are two other assets that deserve emphasis.

Unlike the Mensheviks and the SRs, who mouthed revolutionary slogans but balked when it was time to act on them, the Bolsheviks took their program literally. They were, therefore, able to portray their socialist rivals as hypocrites and pose as the conscience of the Revolution. And, again unlike the socialists, the Bolsheviks thought in global terms and did not much care what happened to Russia, which was for them merely a stepping-stone to a world revolution. They could, therefore, act with complete irresponsibility, promising every group whatever it wanted and encouraging every destructive trend. This neither the SRs nor the Mensheviks, not to speak of the liberals and conservatives, were prepared to do. Later, when in power, the Bolsheviks would promptly renege on all their promises and reconstruct the state in a highly centralized manner. But until then, their unconcern for Russia proved for them an immense, perhaps even decisive, asset.

The rapid disintegration of Russian unity gave the Bolsheviks the opportunity to loosen the Mensheviks' hold on organized labor. As transport and communications disintegrated, and each region, no longer able to rely on the central government, had to take charge of its own affairs, the network of national trade unions weakened. Factory workers now began to shift their loyalties from unions organized horizontally, along professional lines, to those organized vertically, by enterprises. This development promoted syndicalism, a form of anarchism that called for the abolition of the state and for worker control of the national economy. One expression of the trend was the emergence of Factory Committees (Fabzavkomy), which embraced workers of diverse trades working in the same enterprises. The Fabzavkomy initially adopted a moderate stance, helping to improve production, but they soon radicalized, evicting proprietors and their managers and taking charge of factories. Marxists despised syndicalism, since they wanted to vest command of the economy not in workers but in the socialist state. Nevertheless, as was his habit, Lenin now identified himself with syndicalism, joining calls for "worker control" of industry. This gained for his party a strong following among industrial workers: at the First Conference of Petrograd Factory Committees at the end of May, the Bolsheviks controlled at least two-thirds of the delegates.* Later, in 1920, the syndicalist trend within the Communist Party would give Lenin a great deal of trouble and make him resort to purges to rid himself of it. In 1917, however, he wholeheartedly supported the syndicalists.

Since he envisaged the power seizure, in its decisive phase, as a violent act, Lenin organized a private army, called the Red Guard, that he refused to subordinate to the Soviet. He also carried out intense propaganda among the troops, both in city garrisons and at the front, in order to deprive the government of military support during the anticipated coup. The antiwar propaganda was carried out in muted tones, for the troops hated the Germans and Lenin was already under suspicion of being their agent. Bolshevik newspapers distributed in vast quantities to the men in uniform carried a subtle message that was propagandistic rather than agitational in nature: The soldiers were not to lay down their

---

* Even so, few workers joined the Bolshevik Party. On the eve of the Bolshevik coup in the fall of 1917, only 5.3 percent of Russia's industrial workers were members. Z. V. Stepanov, *Rabochie Petrograda v period podgotovki i provedeniia Oktiabr'skogo vooruzhonnogo vosstaniia* (Moscow-Leningrad, 1965), 47–48.

arms, but ponder who wanted war and to what end? (The answer: the "bourgeoisie".)* This was a veiled appeal for civil war. The troops were exhorted under no conditions to let themselves be used against the workers (by which was meant the Bolshevik Party).

Such propaganda, carried by newspapers produced in hundreds of thousands copies, mostly distributed free of charge, required money. This came mainly from Germany, which shared with the Bolsheviks a common interest in taking Russia out of the war. Subversive activities of this nature rarely leave documentary traces. Reliable people in Berlin, using equally reliable intermediaries, delivered cash to Bolshevik agents in neutral Sweden without written requests or receipts passing hands. According to a most authoritative source, the German Minister of Foreign Affairs, Richard von Kühlmann, the architect of Berlin's pro-Bolshevik policy in 1917–1918, the Bolsheviks used German subsidies to pay for party organization and propaganda. On December 3, 1917 (NS), in a confidential internal memorandum, Kühlmann thus summarized his country's contribution to the Bolshevik cause:

> The disruption of the Entente and the subsequent creation of political combinations agreeable to us constitute the most important war aim of our diplomacy. Russia appeared to be the weakest link in the enemy chain. The task therefore was gradually to loosen it, and, when possible, to remove it. This was the purpose of the subversive activity we caused to be carried out in Russia behind the front—in the first place, promotion of separatist tendencies and support of the Bolsheviks. It was not until the Bolsheviks had received from us a steady flow of funds through various channels and under different labels that they were able to build up their main organ, *Pravda*, to conduct energetic propaganda and appreciably to extend the originally narrow basis of their party.

A German socialist with close links to the postwar Weimar government estimated the subsidies to the Bolsheviks to have exceeded 50 million deutsche marks in gold—a sum equivalent to $6–$10 million, which at the time would have purchased nine or more tons of gold. The bulk of the funds seems to have been channeled through a German Embassy official in Stockholm, Kurt Riezler. Riezler paid them to Fürstenberg-Ganetskii, an associate of Lenin's and an employee of Parvus's, who forwarded them to Petrograd to spurious business firms, including a

---

* In the vocabulary of Russian revolutionaries, "agitation" meant an appeal to immediate action, whereas "propaganda" called for planting ideas in subjects' minds which in due course would move them to act on their own.

22. Kerensky visiting the front, summer 1917.

pharmaceutical company run by a member of the Bolshevik Central Committee. The Provisional Government learned of these transactions from French intelligence and kept track of them for possible future use but did not, for the time being, disrupt them.

Although he lacked military experience, Kerensky tackled his duties as Minister of War with admirable vigor. He believed that the survival of democracy in Russia depended on the spirit of the army and that the army's morale would be best raised by a successful offensive. He hoped to duplicate the feat of the French army in 1792, when it stopped and threw back the invading Prussians, rallying the nation behind the revolutionary government. But he also expected that a resounding triumph of Russian arms would enable him to make short shrift of the Bolsheviks, who campaigned relentlessly against his government.

An offensive was scheduled for mid-June. Kerensky's personal contribution to it consisted in rousing the troops with patriotic speeches; these had an enormous immediate effect which evaporated as soon as he departed. The generals, trying to command an increasingly undisciplined army, regarded such rhetoric skeptically, dubbing the Minister "Persuader in Chief." The will to fight was no longer there. According to Kerensky, the Revolution had persuaded the troops that there was no point in fighting. "After three years of bitter suffering," he recalled, "millions of war-weary soldiers were asking themselves: 'Why should I die now when at home a new, freer life is only beginning?'" The malaise was encouraged by the ambivalent attitude of the Soviet, which continued to urge them to fight in the same breath that it condemned the war as "imperialist."

23. Russian soldiers fleeing Germans, July 1917.

The Bolsheviks sought to exploit this war-weariness by staging a second mass demonstration on June 10—this time, with the participants fully armed—in order to embarrass the government and, should the opportunity present itself, overthrow it. The event, which had aroused considerable opposition in the Bolshevik Central Committee as premature, was canceled at the last moment on the insistence of the Soviet. But even as they yielded, the Bolsheviks put the Soviet on notice that in the future they would not be bound by its wishes.

On June 16, the Russian army struck. The brunt of the assault fell on the Southern front, against Lwów and Galicia. But the offensive, in which the Eighth Army under Kornilov distinguished itself, dissipated as soon as the Germans came to the Austrians' aid. At the sight of German uniforms, the Russians fled in panic. The June operation was the dying gasp of the Russian army.

Since the old army engaged in no more significant operations and soon disintegrated, this is an appropriate place to summarize Russian casualties in World War I. These are often greatly exaggerated, as it is sometimes said that they exceeded those of any other belligerent power. The most reliable estimates speak of 1.3 million fatalities, which is equal to the fatalities suffered by the French and Austrians but is one-third fewer than those of the Germans. The Russians, however, lost to the enemy far and away the largest number of prisoners of war—3.9 million—a figure that indicates (when compared with their battlefield casualties) that they surrendered at a rate twelve to fifteen times that of Western soldiers.

The failure of the June offensive affected calamitously the reputation of Kerensky and the Provisional Government, improving correspondingly the fortunes of the antiwar Bolsheviks, who in the prevailing atmosphere of gloom ventured on yet another putsch.

The story of the July events has long been confused, largely because the Communists went to great trouble to conceal their involvement in what turned out to be an unmitigated disaster.

The July riots were triggered by the government's decision to dispatch some units of the Petrograd garrison to the front. The order, which violated the agreement reached four months earlier with the Soviet, angered the troops. The Bolsheviks unleashed a furious propaganda campaign, inciting the garrison to mutiny. They made certain, however, that any riots that broke out would not be spontaneous and unmanaged, as had been the case the previous February, but directed by their own Military Organization, a clandestine command center formed to carry out the coup d'état.

On June 29, as tension rose, Lenin suddenly vanished from Petrograd. He resurfaced in Finland. The ostensible reason for his departure was exhaustion and need of rest. The more likely reason was intelligence furnished by the Bolsheviks' sympathizers in the government that the authorities had sufficient evidence of their dealings with the enemy to bring the party's leaders to trial. Indeed, on July 1 orders went out for the arrest of twenty-eight prominent Bolsheviks, Lenin included.

In Lenin's absence, the Petrograd Bolsheviks concentrated on the Machine Gun Regiment, the largest military unit in the city and the one that gave the authorities the most trouble. On June 30, the regiment learned that it would be disbanded and its soldiers sent to the front. Protest meetings followed at which Bolshevik and anarchist agitators incited the soldiers against the authorities. Similar meetings took place at the nearby naval base of Kronshtadt, an anarchist stronghold. The Bolsheviks vacillated between fomenting a mutiny and restraining the troops, for as much as they wanted a large-scale riot, they also feared that a premature and undirected uprising could give the government the pretext to crush them.

On July 3, the Machine Gun Regiment, having voted to take to the streets, sent emissaries to the other garrison units to request their help. Most refused. Later that day the leading Bolsheviks in Petrograd—Kamenev, Trotsky, and Zinoviev—decided to side with the mutineers. Their plan was to take control of the Workers' Section of the Soviet and proclaim the passage of power to the Soviet, and then—but only then—

notify the Ispolkom of the decision. In line with this plan, they convened an extraordinary session of the Workers' Section. When Zinoviev declared that the Soviet was about to take power, the Mensheviks and SRs walked out, leaving the Bolsheviks in full control. On their motion, the rump body passed a resolution calling for the passage of all power to the Soviet. The Bolshevik Central Committee, meeting late at night, ordered its Military Organization to bring out the mutinous soldiers and sailors in the morning, fully armed, for a demonstration.

The Bolsheviks drew up flexible plans, their actions to be determined by the progress of the mutiny. Mikhail Kalinin, a participant in these events (and many years later President of the Soviet Union), described the Bolshevik attitude as follows:

> Responsible party workers faced a delicate question: "What is this—a demonstration or something more? Perhaps the beginning of the proletarian revolution, the beginning of a power seizure?" . . . [Lenin] would answer: "We will see what happens, now one can't tell anything! . . . This was, indeed, a review of the revolutionary forces, their numbers, their quality, and activism . . . The review could turn into a decisive encounter: everything depended on the correlation of forces and on any number of chance occurrences. In any event, as if for purposes of insurance against unpleasant surprises, the commander's order was: "We shall see." This in no way precluded the possibility of throwing the regiments into battle if the correlation of forces proved favorable, or, on the other hand, of retiring with the least possible losses, which is what actually happened on July 4.*

The armed demonstration began, as planned, with a review of the troops by the Bolsheviks at Kshesinskaia's villa. Lenin, who had come back earlier that morning, addressed them in a short and rather noncommittal speech. The demonstrators then marched through the city center to Taurida Palace, once the seat of the Duma and now of the Soviet. They were directed by the Bolshevik Military Organization, whose units occupied strategic points throughout the capital. The intent was to compel the Soviet to take power: once this was done, the Bolsheviks had no doubt that they would shunt the SRs and Mensheviks aside and take charge.

In the afternoon, a huge crowd assembled in the front of Taurida Palace. Bolshevik speakers, dispersed in its midst, fired provocative questions at the Soviet's socialists as they appeared before them. The stage

---

* Since Lenin was not present in Petrograd on July 3, when the decision to proceed with the putsch was made, Kalinin presumably refers to his responses the following day, when he returned.

24. The events of July 1917.

was set for the final push, but it did not occur because at the crucial moment Lenin lost his nerve. While Bolshevik troops, awaiting his order, stood poised to take over the Taurida and announce the power seizure, he equivocated and thus lost the battle.

The government, under siege and virtually without armed defenders, sat as if paralyzed. It was its good fortune that the Minister of Justice took matters into his own hands and released to the press a small part of the evidence in his possession on Bolshevik dealings with the Germans. The information, which quickly reached the garrison troops, produced on them an electrifying effect. In the late afternoon, army units reached Taurida Palace ready to make short shrift of the Bolsheviks and their followers. The mutineers, along with sympathetic workers, ran for cover. By nightfall, the putsch was over.

For the next several days, during which the city was occupied by frontline troops loyal to the government, the police hunted and arrested Bolsheviks. Lenin and his closest associates were ordered held on charges of "high treason and organizing an armed uprising." Lenin went into hiding in Petrograd, hotly denying from his hideaway having had any intention of launching a coup; a few days later, accompanied by Zinoviev, he fled in disguise first to a rural region near Petrograd and later to Finland. Most of his colleagues were arrested, but the government did not initiate legal proceedings against them because of Soviet objections: the Soviet feared that any action against the Bolsheviks would serve as a pretext to liquidate the socialist parties. Even though the abortive coup had been directed as much against the Soviet as against the Provisional Government, the Soviet felt that its fate was tied to that of the Bolsheviks.

In the aftermath of the July events, Lvov resigned and Kerensky took over the prime ministership, with wide-ranging powers. He offered Kornilov command of the armed forces. He also ordered that units that had participated in the mutiny be disarmed and the garrison reduced. *Pravda* and other Bolshevik publications were barred from the front. Yet despite these energetic steps, Kerensky feared a right-wing, monarchist coup more than a repetition of a Bolshevik putsch. Appeasing the Soviet, he failed to deal the Bolsheviks the coup de grâce they expected. This saved them: later on Trotsky would write that "fortunately our enemies had neither sufficient logical consistency nor determination."

The Coup

I n September 1917, with Lenin in hiding, the command of the Bolshevik forces passed to his associates. Trotsky was the most visible Bolshevik, largely owing to his outstanding rhetorical gifts. The operational direction of the coup was entrusted to the Bolshevik Military Organization headed by N. I. Podvoiskii. Viacheslav Molotov, a Bolshevik insider, recalled many years later that Trotsky had played a "major role" in October but "only as agitator"—he was not invited to participate in organizational matters.* Defying Lenin's pressures for immediate action, his associates adopted a more circumspect strategy, avoiding street riots and disguising the coup as the assumption of power by the Soviet.

Trotsky ideally complemented Lenin. Better read and more flamboyant, a superior speaker and writer, he could galvanize crowds, whereas Lenin's charisma was limited to his followers. But Trotsky was unpopular with the Bolshevik cadres, in part because he had joined the party late and in part because of his insufferable arrogance. During the Revolution and

---

* *Sto sorok besed s Molotovym (Iz dnevnika F. Chueva)* (Moscow, 1991), 162.

25. Leon Trotsky.

the Civil War, he was Lenin's alter ego, an indispensable companion-in-arms. Once victory had been won, he became an embarrassment.

The event that enabled the Bolsheviks to recover from their July debacle was one of the more bizarre episodes of the Russian Revolution. Known to historians as the Kornilov affair, it resulted from a struggle in Kerensky's mind between his sense that as the head of state in a situation of near-anarchy and a looming German offensive he needed the army's support, and his fear as a socialist intellectual that the army was likely to breed a counterrevolutionary Napoleon.*

Kornilov, the son of a Siberian Cossack, had made a rapid career in the army owing to personal courage and his ability to inspire troops. He knew little and cared less about politics; such opinions as he had on the subject were neither conservative nor monarchist but rather "progressive." He was an ardent patriot. He always displayed a tendency to insubordination.

---

* In private conversation with the author, Kerensky conceded that his actions at the time had been strongly influenced by the experience of the French Revolution.

26. General Lavr Kornilov.

Kerensky turned to Kornilov after the July putsch, appointing him Commander in Chief in the hope that he would restore discipline in the armed forces and arrest the German counteroffensive. Kornilov accepted the post but on certain conditions. To restore the army's fighting capacity, he demanded elimination of the most harmful provisions of Order No. 1: the disbanding or at least reduction in power of the army committees the Order had sanctioned and the restoration of disciplinary authority to the officers. He further wanted the reintroduction of the death penalty for desertion or mutiny at the front as well as in the rear. Russian defense industries were to be mobilized more effectively for the war effort.

These conditions incensed Kerensky and nearly caused him to withdraw Kornilov's nomination. Associates dissuaded him, but the seeds of conflict had been sown: in the words of Boris Savinkov, Kerensky's deputy, who knew both men well, Kornilov "loves freedom . . . but Russia comes for him first, and freedom second, while for Kerensky . . . freedom and revolution come first, and Russia second." These differing priorities could not be reconciled.

Negotiations between the two men dragged on for two weeks. Kornilov assumed his new duties only on July 24 after receiving assurances that most of his demands would be met. In fact, however, Kerensky neither could nor would keep his promises to Kornilov. He could not because he was dependent on the Soviet, which viewed Kornilov as an incipient military dictator; and he would not because he soon came to perceive Kornilov as a dangerous rival.

Kerensky procrastinated in implementing the military reforms that Kornilov had made a condition of assuming command. Aware that the Germans were about to resume operations in the Baltic provinces, Kornilov requested permission to meet with the cabinet. The meeting took place on August 3. While he was giving an overview of the situation at the front, Kerensky leaned over and asked him in a whisper to exercise caution; Savinkov made a similar request. This incident shattered Kornilov's faith in the Provisional Government, for it convinced him that there were ministers in the cabinet capable of betraying military secrets to the enemy.

A few days later, Kornilov ordered the Third Cavalry Corps, made up of two Cossack divisions and one division of Caucasian natives, to deploy in a locality roughly equidistant from Petrograd and Moscow. This he did in order to have troops ready to suppress another Bolshevik putsch, and, if it occurred, to disperse the Soviet.

Liberal and conservative politicians began to look up to Kornilov as the country's savior. When he arrived in Moscow on August 14, over Kerensky's objections, to attend a State Conference, he was wildly cheered. For Kerensky, who regarded Kornilov's reception as a personal affront, this incident marked a watershed. According to his subsequent testimony, "after the Moscow conference, it was clear to me that the next attempt at a blow would come from the right and not from the left." His belief received reinforcement from an unrelenting barrage of criticism of his administration in the nonsocialist press. He expected a Bonapartist putsch to come any day, and dismissed the Bolshevik threat as a phantom.

Thus the plot was written; it only remained to find the protagonist.

In the middle of August, Savinkov received from French intelligence information that the Bolsheviks were planning to stage another putsch at the beginning of September in support of a German advance on Petrograd. The information proved to be incorrect, but Kerensky used it to ruin Kornilov. He sent Savinkov to Kornilov's headquarters with a request that he dispatch the Third Cavalry Corps to Petrograd for the purpose of imposing martial law in Petrograd and defending the Provisional Government from any and all assaults, and, in particular, from an assault of the Bolsheviks . . . who, according to information of foreign intelligence, are once again preparing to rise in connection with German landings and an uprising in Finland.

Since Kerensky had stated emphatically more than once both before and after October 1917 that he no longer feared a Bolshevik putsch, this request has to be interpreted as a devious provocation to discredit Kornilov—a popular general who appeared to Kerensky's fevered imagination as the leader of a military cabal.

At this point there occurred one of those incidents that, though trivial in themselves, have weighty historical consequences. Its central figure, Vladimir Lvov, was a man who had failed in everything he had tried but owing to family connections had managed to gain a seat in the last two Dumas, and then to have himself appointed the head of church administration (Procurator of the Holy Synod) in the First Provisional Government. Kerensky dismissed him in July, following which he joined one of the many conservative groups that sprang up at the time to help save the country from catastrophe.

On the morning of August 22, Lvov paid a visit to Kerensky. He implied in veiled terms that he represented an influential party which believed the government should be strengthened with the addition of public figures close to the military. Kerensky subsequently claimed that the instant the interview was over, he dismissed it from his mind.

Lvov, however, proceeded to Mogilev to sound out Kornilov. There he identified himself as an emissary of the Prime Minister sent to request the General's opinion on how to strengthen the government. With a reckless lack of caution, Kornilov neither asked Lvov for his credentials nor contacted Petrograd to confirm his authority to speak on the Prime Minister's behalf. Lvov requested Kornilov's reaction to three alternatives: (1) Kerensky assumes dictatorial powers; (2) a Directory is formed with Kornilov as a member; and (3) Kornilov becomes dictator. Interpreting Lvov's words to mean that Kerensky was offering him dictatorial authority, Kornilov responded that he preferred the third option. He did not crave power, he said, and would work for any legitimate government, but he would not refuse supreme authority if offered it. He went on to say that in view of the danger of an imminent Bolshevik coup in Petrograd, it would be prudent for Kerensky and Savinkov to seek safety in Mogilev.

Lvov rushed back to Petrograd, and the following day (August 26) at 6 p.m. saw Kerensky. Just as in the interview with Kornilov he had posed as a representative of the Prime Minister, so now he pretended to be an agent of the Commander in Chief. Without telling Kerensky what options he had offered Kornilov, he declared that the General demanded dictatorial powers. Kerensky, who had long suspected Kornilov of harboring such ambitions, asked Lvov to put the General's demands in writing. Lvov wrote: "General Kornilov proposes:

1. That martial law be proclaimed in Petrograd.
2. That all military and civil authority be placed in the hands of the Commander in Chief.
3. That all ministers, not excluding the Prime Minister, resign and that provisional executive authority be transferred to deputy ministers until the formation of a cabinet by the Commander in Chief.

The ultimatum was in fact drafted by Lvov and his friends, who believed that a military dictatorship alone could save Russia and attempted to force the issue in this clumsy way.

Kerensky now grew seriously alarmed. Later that evening he contacted Kornilov by teleprinter. The conversation, tapes of which have been preserved, leaves no doubt that the two men were talking at crosspurposes. Kerensky, referring to Kornilov's ultimatum (without spelling it out) and impersonating Lvov, requested that Kornilov confirm it. Kornilov, thinking that the message referred to his request that Kerensky and Savinkov come to Mogilev, did so. Kerensky interpreted Kornilov's confirmation to mean that he demanded dictatorial powers. The most favorable interpretation of the Prime Minister's behavior is that he was exhausted and unable to think straight. But the suspicion lurks that he heard exactly what he wanted to hear.

On the basis of such flimsy evidence, Kerensky made up his mind to finish off Kornilov. Ignoring Savinkov's pleas that he communicate once more with headquarters to clear up what seemed a tragic misunderstanding, Kerensky convened the cabinet and requested dictatorial powers to crush a counterrevolutionary military coup. In the early hours of the morning, Kerensky informed Kornilov that he had been dismissed as Commander in Chief and was to report to Petrograd.

While these events were taking place, Kornilov, ignorant of Kerensky's interpretation of their exchange, proceeded with deployments to help the government suppress the anticipated Bolshevik rising. At 2:40 a.m. he cabled Savinkov: "The [Cavalry] corps is assembling in the environs of Petrograd toward evening of August 28. Request that Petrograd be placed under martial law." If any more proof is needed that Kornilov did not intend a putsch, this cable should furnish it: for surely if he had sent the Cavalry Corps to unseat the government he would hardly have forewarned it of his intention by telegraph. Nor would he have remained behind in Mogilev, entrusting the operation to subordinates.

The receipt, at 7 a.m. on August 27 at headquarters, of Kerensky's telegram dismissing Kornilov threw the generals into confusion. At first they treated the cable as a forgery, not only because it contradicted what Kornilov thought was his understanding with the Prime Minister but also because it was improperly formatted. Subsequently, the generals concluded that perhaps it was genuine but that the Prime Minister had fallen into Bolshevik hands and was acting under duress. On these grounds, Kornilov refused to carry out Kerensky's orders until he had the chance to clarify the situation.

Later that day, Savinkov contacted Kornilov and learned for the first time of Lvov's involvement. But Kerensky would not rescind his orders: he was determined on a break and issued a statement to the press charging Kornilov with treason. Kerensky's accusation threw Kornilov into an uncontrollable rage because it touched his most sensitive nerve, his patriotism. Having read it, he no longer thought of Kerensky as a putative Bolshevik prisoner but as a despicable schemer, the author of a provocation designed to discredit him and the army. He sent the armed forces a message in which he called Kerensky's charges "an out-and-out lie," and recounted the circumstances that had impelled him to act as he did. He called on the people of Russia to rally behind him to save their country, pledging to throw back the Germans and convene a Constituent Assembly. This, at last, was mutiny: Kornilov did rebel, but only after having been wrongly charged with rebellion.

As the Cavalry Corps approached Petrograd, Kerensky issued another statement in which he told the population that Kornilov, acting "treacherously," had stripped the front of troops and sent them against the capital. But to General Alexander Krymov, their commander, he wired that the city was calm and there was no danger of an uprising, for which reason he should immediately halt his advance. He invited Krymov to visit him under guarantees of personal safety. When Krymov showed up, he ordered him to report to the Military-Naval Court. Krymov instead went to a friend's apartment and put a bullet through his heart.

Was there a "Kornilov plot"? Almost certainly not. The available evidence indicates that there was a "Kerensky plot" to discredit the commanding general as the ringleader of an imaginary but widely anticipated counterrevolution, the suppression of which would elevate the Prime

Minister to a position of unrivaled popularity. It cannot be a coincidence that none of the elements present in a genuine coup d'état ever came to light: lists of conspirators, organizational charts, code signals, programs. Neither Kerensky nor the Bolsheviks have ever been able to identify a single person who would admit, or of whom it could be demonstrated, that he was in collusion with Kornilov: and a conspiracy of one is an obvious absurdity. A government commission appointed in October 1917 completed in June 1918 (that is, already under Bolshevik rule) an investigation into the Kornilov Affair. It concluded that the charges of treason and mutiny leveled against the Commander in Chief had no foundation and accused Kerensky of lacking the courage to admit that he had committed a grave mistake.

If it is correct that Kerensky provoked the break with Kornilov to enhance his authority, he not only failed in his purpose but achieved the very opposite. The clash estranged him from both liberal and conservative circles without solidifying his position in the socialist camp. The main beneficiaries of the affair were the Bolsheviks, who had warned all along of the looming counterrevolution. In August, the government, responding to pressures of the Ispolkom, began to release the Bolsheviks who had been held in prison for the July putsch. In municipal elections held the following month, the Bolsheviks showed a dramatic spurt: in Moscow they gained 49.5 percent of the seats, while the Mensheviks and SRs, who between them had held 71.1 percent of the seats since June, now declined to 18.9 percent. Nor was this all. To stop the imaginary invasion of Kornilov, Kerensky appealed to the Bolsheviks for assistance. Of the 40,000 guns distributed to the workers at the time, a good part ended up in the hands of the Bolshevik Red Guard.

A no less important consequence of the Kornilov Affair was a break between Kerensky and the military. For although the officer corps, loyal as always to the government and confused by Kerensky's appeals, would not rally behind Kornilov, it despised the Prime Minister for his treatment of their popular commander, the arrest of many prominent generals accused of conspiring with him, and his pandering to the left. When, in late October, he would appeal to the military to help save his government from the Bolsheviks, he would meet with no response.

It was only a question of time before Kerensky would be overthrown by someone able to provide the country with firm leadership. Such a leader had to come from the left. For whatever the differences dividing them, the parties of the left closed ranks when confronted with the specter of the "counterrevolution," a term that in their definition covered every initiative to restore to Russia an effective government and a credible military force. But since the country had to have both, the initiative to restore order had to emerge from its own ranks: the "counter-revolution" would come disguised as the "true" revolution.

In the meantime, Lenin, in his rural hideaway, busied himself redesigning the world.

From the recollections of Zinoviev, we learn that the two men lived in a field hut, disguised as farm laborers, but maintained communications with Petrograd by means of couriers. Lenin at first thought that he and his party were finished but that even so, his failed efforts could serve as a lesson for future revolutionaries. With this in mind, he resumed work on a book, which he had started in Switzerland and which would come out the following year under the title *State and Revolution*. The thrust of this work, based on a dictum of Marx (see above, p. 118), was that a successful revolution had to "smash" the existing bureaucratic and military machine of the old regime. This was the task of a transitional "proletarian dictatorship." Once it had accomplished its mission, government would wither away: "Under socialism, *all* will govern in turn and quickly become accustomed to no one governing." In dealing with the future economy, Lenin was much more conservative: rather than destroy capitalism, he wanted it harnessed in the service of the socialist state. In this instance, he acted under the influence of German socialists, who argued that advanced, or "finance," capitalism had attained a level of ownership concentration that made it easy to introduce socialism by the simple device of nationalizing banks and syndicates.

The Kornilov Affair gave Lenin fresh hope. He realized how fatal was Kerensky's break with the army, and observed with delight and surprise the Prime Minister rehabilitating and even arming his followers. Nor was it lost on him that the workers and soldiers were drifting away from the soviets—the main base of support of the Mensheviks and Socialists-Revolutionaries—leaving them open to manipulation by a determined minority.

In mid-September, the Bolsheviks gained majorities in the Workers' Sections of both the Moscow and Petrograd soviets. Trotsky, who had been released from prison on bail, took over as chairman of the Petrograd Soviet and immediately proceeded to fashion it into an instrument with which to seize control of the nation's soviets. Ignoring the Ispolkom, he created a parallel pseudonational soviet organization that represented those soviets in which the Bolsheviks had pluralities.

27. Grigorii Zinoviev.

In the more favorable political environment created by the Kornilov Affair and their successes in the soviets, the Bolsheviks renewed discussions of another coup d'état. The July fiasco still fresh in their minds, Kamenev and Zinoviev firmly opposed another "adventure." The Bolsheviks were gaining strength, they conceded, but they remained a minority: even if they managed to seize power, they would soon lose it to the combined forces of the "bourgeois" and the peasant "counterrevolution." They preferred to await the convocation of a Second Congress of Soviets, which would assume power by legitimate means.

Lenin regarded such a course as nothing short of insane. On September 12 and 14, he addressed from Finland two letters to the Central Committee, one called "The Bolsheviks Must Take Power," the other, "Marxism and Insurrection." Having gained majorities in the Petrograd and Moscow soviets, he insisted, "the Bolsheviks can and *must* seize power." Contrary to Kamenev and Zinoviev, they not only could seize it but keep it, too: by offering an immediate peace and encouraging the peasants to appropriate private land, Lenin assured the skeptics, "the Bolsheviks can set up a government that *no one* will overthrow." It was imperative, however, to act swiftly, because the Provisional Government could turn Petrograd over to the Germans or else the war could end. The

28. L. B. Kamenev.

"order of the day" was "*armed insurrection* in Petrograd and Moscow (plus their regions), the conquest of power, the overthrow of the government. We must consider *how* to agitate for this, without so expressing ourselves in print." Once power had been taken in Petrograd and Moscow, the issue would be settled. As for Kamenev's and Zinoviev's suggestion that the party await a popular mandate from the Second Congress of Soviets, he dismissed it as "naive": "no revolution waits for *that*."

The Central Committee was far from convinced: according to Trotsky, none of its members favored an immediate insurrection. On Stalin's motion, Lenin's letters were sent to the party's major regional organizations for their reaction.

Such passivity infuriated Lenin, for he feared that the favorable moment for the insurrection would pass, never to return. On September 29, he sent the Central Committee a third letter, "The Crisis Had Ripened." He was appalled that the Committee chose to await the convocation of the Second Congress of Soviets. "To pass up such a moment and 'await' the Congress of Soviets is *complete idiocy* or *complete treason*." It was necessary to act swiftly and decisively, striking simultaneously in Petrograd, Moscow, and the Baltic Fleet; an unexpected move in Moscow could well "paralyze" the government. "The chances are that we will win with fewer losses than we suffered on July 3–5, because the *troops will not move* against a government of peace."

Lenin's sense of urgency was in good measure inspired by his fear of being preempted by the Constituent Assembly. After interminable delays, on August 9 the government finally scheduled the elections for November 12 and the inaugural session for November 28. An Assembly elected on a democratic franchise was bound to be in large measure a peasant body, which is the same as saying that it would be dominated by the Socialists-Revolutionaries. The only hope the Bolsheviks had of winning any semblance of a popular mandate was provided by the urban soviets, in many of which they had majorities. After the country had pronounced its will through democratic elections, they could no longer pretend to act in the name of the "people." Once they were in power, on the other hand, they would control the situation: as one Bolshevik publication indiscreetly put it, the composition of the Assembly "will strongly depend on who convenes it." Hence the haste. The coup had to be carried out before November 12 or the Bolsheviks would appear to be striking not against a "bourgeois" government but against a government of Socialists-Revolutionaries chosen by the nation.

Although Lenin wanted immediate action, he had to yield to the majority of his associates, who preferred that the coup be carried out in the name of the soviets. Since a genuinely elected national congress of soviets was almost certain to yield a Bolshevik minority, Trotsky and his lieutenants proceeded to convene a congress composed mostly of those soviets in which they had assured majorities. Ignoring the protests of the Ispolkom that it alone had the right to convene congresses of soviets, they created a spurious "Northern Regional Committee" composed of eleven Bolsheviks and six Left SRs (a splinter from the SR Party, temporarily affiliated with them). This committee, arrogating itself the authority of the Ispolkom, invited soviets and military committees to send delegates to the forthcoming Congress. The soviets and army units in which the Bolsheviks had clear majorities received double and triple representation. One provincial soviet was allotted five delegates, which was more than allocated to the city of Kiev, where the Bolsheviks happened to be weak. This was a veritable coup against the legitimate Soviet organization, and the Ispolkom condemned it in the severest terms:

> No other committee has the authority or the right to take upon itself the initiative in convening this congress. The less does this right belong to the

Northern Regional Congress, brought together in violation of all the rules
established for the regional soviets and representing soviets chosen arbi-
trarily and at random.

But much as they objected to Bolshevik procedures, in the end the
socialists of the Ispolkom yielded to them. On September 26, the
Ispolkom agreed to the convocation on October 20 of the Second
Congress chosen on a Bolshevik franchise, on condition that its agenda
be limited to the discussion of the internal situation in the country,
preparations for the Constituent Assembly, and the election of a new
Ispolkom. Later the Ispolkom postponed the date of the Congress to
October 25, to give provincial delegates time to reach the capital. It was
an astonishing and, as it turned out, fatal capitulation. Although aware of
what the Bolsheviks had in mind, the Ispolkom gave them what they
wanted: a handpicked body, packed with their adherents and allies, to
legitimize a coup d'état.

The gathering of pro-Bolshevik soviets, disguised as the Second
Congress of Soviets, was to sanction the Bolshevik coup, which, on
Lenin's insistence, was to be carried out by shock troops of his Military
Organization *before* the Congress met. Their task was to seize strategic
points in the capital and declare the government overthrown. The instru-
ment the Bolsheviks intended to use for this purpose was the Military-
Revolutionary Committee (Milrevkom) created by the Petrograd Soviet
in a moment of panic in early October to defend the city from an expected
German assault.

The precipitating event was a German naval operation in the Gulf of
Riga. When completed in early October with the occupation of three
strategic islands, it created a direct threat to Petrograd. Fearing German
capture, the Russian General Staff proposed to evacuate the government
from Petrograd to Moscow. The Ispolkom condemned this plan, interpreting it as motivated by political considerations, namely the desire of
the Provisional Government to surrender the "capital of the Revolution."
On October 9, a Menshevik deputy moved that the Soviet form a "Committee of Revolutionary Defense" to work out measures for protecting
the city. The Bolsheviks initially voted against this resolution on the
grounds that it would strengthen the Provisional Government. But they
promptly reversed themselves, because they realized that such a committee would have no choice but to rely on their Military Organization, the
only armed force that remained outside government control. This would
enable them to carry out the projected coup in the name of the Soviet and

under its umbrella. Later that day (October 9) the Bolsheviks moved and the Soviet Plenum approved—over Menshevik objections—a motion to form a Revolutionary Committee of Defense to assume charge of the city's security not only against the Germans but also against domestic "counterrevolutionaries." Renamed Military-Revolutionary Committee, the organization was a front of the Bolshevik Military Organization.

There can be no certainty, but it is highly probable that this vote of the Soviet, seemingly so innocuous, prompted the hesitant Bolsheviks to make their move. The decision fell at a clandestine meeting of the Central Committee held during the night of October 10–11. Present were twelve members, including Lenin, who emerged from his place of hiding despite the dangers because he did not trust his lieutenants to act decisively. Three points of view were expressed. Lenin, a faction of one, wanted an immediate seizure of power, independently of the Congress of Soviets. Zinoviev and Kamenev, supported by three others, preferred to postpone the coup to a later, more propitious time. The remaining five members agreed with Trotsky that the time was ripe for a coup but that it should be carried out in conjunction with the Congress of Soviets and in its name. A compromise was struck: The coup would be carried out on the eve of the convocation of the Second Congress on October 25, and the Congress would be asked, after the fact, to ratify it.

Kamenev found this decision unacceptable. He resigned from the Central Committee and the following week, in an interview with a Menshevik newspaper, stated that he and Zinoviev had "firmly argued against the party assuming the initiative in any armed uprisings in the near future." When Lenin read this interview, he demanded the immediate expulsion of the two "strikebreakers": "We cannot tell the capitalists the truth, namely that we have *decided* [to go] on strike [read: stage a coup] and to *conceal* from them the *choice of timing*." The Central Committee failed to act on his demand, but Lenin never quite forgave Kamenev and Zinoviev for their timidity during these critical days.

The Central Committee's tactics called for provoking the government into retaliatory measures that would enable it to launch the coup in the guise of the defense of the Revolution. Trotsky and Stalin later confirmed that this had indeed been the plan. In Trotsky's words:

> In essence, our strategy was offensive. We prepared to assault the government, but our agitation rested on the claim that the enemy was getting ready to disperse the Congress of Soviets and it was necessary mercilessly to repulse him.

And according to Stalin:

> The Revolution [read: the Bolshevik Party] disguised its offensive actions behind a smoke screen of defenses in order to make it easier to attract into its orbit uncertain, hesitant elements.

Mesmerized by Bolshevik audacity, the Mensheviks and SRs resigned themselves to another Bolshevik "adventure," but they were not overly concerned, certain that it would fail like their July putsch. Trotsky, who during these critical days was everywhere at once, waged a war of nerves, one day admitting, the next denying, that an insurrection was under way. He held audiences spellbound with speeches that alternately promised and threatened, extolled and ridiculed.

A survey of the correlation of forces in Petrograd on the eve of the coup indicates that in one sense the pessimists in the Bolshevik camp were right. The critical factor now, as in July, was the attitude of the garrison. As best as can be determined, out of a total force of 240,000 soldiers in the capital and its environs, no more than 10,000 actively supported the Bolsheviks. The rest declared "neutrality" in the looming conflict. But Lenin was fundamentally correct in his assessment, for if he could count on only 4 percent of the garrison, the government had behind it even fewer troops.

The first step of the Milrevkom was to claim control of the garrison on behalf of the Soviet. This it accomplished on October 21–22: it was the first and most decisive move in the coup that fairly settled its outcome. The Milrevkom dispatched some 200 "commissars" to the military units, most of them junior officers who had participated in the July putsch and had recently been released from prison on parole. Next, it convened a meeting of regimental committees. In his address to the group, Trotsky spoke of the threat of a counterrevolution and urged the garrison to support the Soviet and its organ, the Milrevkom. At his request, the meeting passed a harmless-sounding resolution that called for closer relations between the front and the rear.

Armed with this noncommittal statement, a deputation from the Milrevkom went to the headquarters of the Military Staff. Its spokesman, a Bolshevik lieutenant, advised the Commander of the Petrograd Military District that by decision of the garrison, the Staff's orders would henceforth acquire force only if countersigned by the Milrevkom. The troops, of course, had made no such decision, and the deputation was acting on the orders of the Bolshevik Military Organization. After the commander had threatened to have them arrested, the delegates returned to Smolnyi, the new headquarters of the Bolshevik insurrection. A hastily convened assembly—no one knows who attended—approved a Bolshevik resolution that by rejecting the garrison meeting's decision, the Military Staff had turned itself into a weapon of the counterrevolution. The garrison was not to obey its commands unless confirmed by the Milrevkom. This was the deception referred to by Trotsky and Stalin: the Milrevkom concealed its offensive behind the smoke screen of the Revolution's defense. According to Podvoiskii, the Commander of the Bolshevik Military Organization, these steps marked the onset of the armed insurrection.

And still the government temporized. It shut down some Bolshevik papers but did not arrest the Milrevkom, as Kerensky wanted, because the ministers preferred to resolve the new crisis through negotiations. There are doubts about Kerensky's determination, in any event. Some contemporaries claim that the Prime Minister actually hoped that the Bolsheviks would rise in order to give him the opportunity to crush them once and for all. Nor was he too eager to involve the army, for fear of unleashing a right-wing counterrevolution; its zeal in suppressing the Bolsheviks in July is said to have frightened him. Thus, no effective steps were taken to mobilize loyal forces, including some 15,000 officers then living in the capital in idleness. Security precautions were so lax that no one guarded the headquarters of the Military Staff: anyone could enter this nerve center of the government without being asked for identification.

The final phase of the Bolshevik takeover got under way on the morning of October 24, when the Military Staff implemented some half-hearted preventive measures ordered by the government.

In the early hours of October 24, military cadets known as *iunkers* took over guard duty at key points. Two or three detachments went to the Winter Palace, the residence of Kerensky and the meeting place of the cabinet; they were joined by the so-called Woman's Death Battalion of 140 volunteers, some Cossacks, a bicycle unit, and forty war invalids commanded by an officer with artificial legs. Bridges over the Neva were raised to prevent pro-Bolshevik soldiers and workers from penetrating the center of the city. Orders went out to arrest the Bolshevik commissars.

These measures produced an atmosphere of crisis. The streets emptied at around 2:30 p.m. as offices closed and people rushed home.

Lenin, who was hiding out in Petrograd, out of touch with hourly developments, burned with anxiety and impatience. On the evening of October 24, when the uprising was already well under way, he addressed

29. Cadets (*iunkers*) defending the Winter Palace, October 1917.

yet another letter to the Central Committee, saying, "[to] delay the uprising is death . . . everything hangs on a hair."

> It would be perdition or a formality to await the uncertain voting [of the Soviet Congress] of October 25. The people have the right and duty to solve such questions not by voting but by force . . .

Nothing in Lenin's behavior or statements during these critical days indicates that he placed his trust in the masses to carry out the "proletarian revolution." He trusted only in physical force.

Later that evening he made his way to Smolnyi, with his beard shaved off and his face bandaged to look as if he were going to a dentist. He barely escaped arrest by a government patrol by pretending to be drunk. At Smolnyi he hid in one of the back rooms, taking naps on the floor.

That night (October 24–25), Bolshevik units methodically took control of the key points in the city by the simple procedure of posting pickets. *Iunker* guards, told to retire, either withdrew voluntarily or were disarmed. Thus, under cover of darkness, the Milrevkom occupied, one by one, railroad stations, postal, telephone and telegraph offices, banks, and bridges. No resistance was encountered, no shots exchanged. The Bolsheviks seized the Military Staff headquarters in the most casual manner imaginable: according to one participant, "they entered and sat down while those who had been sitting there got up and left; thus the Staff was taken."

Kerensky, isolated with his ministers at the Winter Palace, tried by telephone to secure military help, but none was forthcoming. At 9 a.m., disguised as a Serbian officer, he slipped out and in a car borrowed from a U.S. Embassy official left for the front.

By then the Winter Palace was the only structure that remained in government hands. Lenin insisted that it be captured before the Second Congress of Soviets opened. But the Bolshevik forces, after months of preparation, proved unequal to the task. They had no men willing to brave fire: their 45,000 Red Guards and tens of thousands of alleged supporters in the garrison were nowhere to be seen. At dawn a halfhearted attack was launched, but at the first sound of shots the attackers retreated.

Between 8 and 9 a.m., Lenin made his way to the Bolshevik operations room in Smolnyi, where he drafted, in the name of the Milrevkom, the following declaration:

> TO THE CITIZENS OF RUSSIA!
>
> The Provisional Government has been deposed. Government authority has passed into the hands of an organ of the Petrograd Soviet of Workers' and Soldiers' Deputies, the Military Revolutionary Committee, which stands at the head of the Petrograd proletariat and garrison.
>
> The task for which the people have been struggling—the immediate offer of a democratic peace, the abolition of landlord property in land, worker control over production, the creation of a Soviet Government—this task is assured.
>
> Long Live the Revolution of Workers, Soldiers, and Peasants!

This document, which enjoys pride of place in the corpus of Bolshevik decrees, declared sovereign power over Russia to have been assumed by a body that no one except the Bolshevik Central Committee had authorized to do so. The Petrograd Soviet had formed the Milrevkom to help defend the city from the Germans, not to depose the Provisional Government. The Second Congress of Soviets, unrepresentative as it was, had not even opened when the Bolsheviks began to act in its name. Because the coup was unsanctioned and carried out virtually without violence, the population of Petrograd had no reason to take it to heart. On October 25, life in Petrograd returned to normal as offices and shops reopened, factory workers returned to work, and places of entertainment filled with crowds. No one except a handful of principals knew what had happened—that Petrograd was in the iron grip of armed Bolsheviks and nothing would ever be the same.

The rest of the day was material for comedy. At the front, Kerensky managed to persuade the Third Cavalry Corps—the same that two months earlier he had accused of trying to remove him from office at Kornilov's behest—to advance on Petrograd, but the troops dismounted before reaching the capital and refused to proceed farther. A few days later they fought a desultory battle with Kronshtadt sailors, who forced them to withdraw. The cabinet that Lenin had declared deposed sat in the Malachite Room of the Winter Palace awaiting help. Five thousand Kronshtadt sailors brought in by the Bolsheviks to seize the government's last stronghold had no heart for battle. Lenin did not want to open the Congress of Soviets until the ministers were under arrest, so the delegates milled around. At 6:30 p.m. the Milrevkom gave the cabinet an ultimatum to surrender or face artillery fire from naval and shore batteries. The ministers, awaiting Kerensky's arrival at the head of relief troops, ignored it; they chatted listlessly, talked to friends on the phone, and took naps, dressed in overcoats. At 9 p.m. the cruiser *Aurora* opened fire. Because it had no live ammunition aboard, it shot a single blank salvo and fell silent—just enough to secure a prominent place in the mythology of October. Two hours later the Peter and Paul Fortress opened fire with live shells, but its aim was so inaccurate that of the thirty to thirty-five rounds only two struck the palace, inflicting minor damage.

The defenders of the Winter Palace, discouraged by the failure of relief forces to arrive, began to disperse. When the pro-Bolshevik forces no longer encountered resistance, they penetrated the building through the open windows on the Hermitage side and the unlocked gates facing the Neva. They then overran the vast structure, looting and vandalizing. The *iunkers*, who stayed to the last, were willing to fight, but the ministers wanted no bloodshed and ordered them to surrender. At 2:10 a.m. the cabinet, minus Kerensky, was arrested and escorted under guard to the Peter and Paul Fortress.

Some time before, the Bolsheviks, unable to hold out any longer, had opened the Congress of Soviets in the Assembly Hall of Smolnyi. Present were some 650 delegates, among them 338 Bolsheviks and 98 Left SRs. The two allied parties thus controlled two-thirds of the seats—a representation twice that to which they were entitled, judging by the elections to the Constituent Assembly held three weeks later. The initial hours were spent on raucous debates. Awaiting word that the Winter Palace had fallen, the Bolsheviks gave their socialist opponents the floor. Amid hooting and heckling, the Mensheviks and Socialists-Revolutionaries denounced the Bolshevik coup and demanded immediate negotiations with the Provisional Government. Trotsky dismissed these opponents as "bankrupts," fit for the "garbage heap of history."

This happened around 1 a.m. on October 26. At 3:10 a.m., Kamenev, appointed Chairman of the Presidium, announced that the government had been arrested. At 6 a.m. he adjourned the Congress until the evening.

Lenin now repaired to a friend's apartment to draft key decrees for the Congress's ratification.

The Congress resumed at 10:40 p.m. Lenin, greeted with tumultuous applause, presented the decrees on peace and on land with which he expected to win the support of both soldiers and peasants.

The Decree on Peace was not a legislative act but an appeal to the belligerent powers promptly to open negotiations for a peace without annexations and indemnities, guaranteeing every people the right to "self-determination." The Land Decree was lifted bodily from the program of the Socialist-Revolutionary Party. Instead of calling for the nationalization of all land, as demanded by the Bolsheviks' own program, it directed that it be "socialized"—that is, withdrawn from commerce and transferred to peasant communes. All landed properties, except those owned by peasant-cultivators, were expropriated without compensation.

After these measures had been passed on a voice vote, the organizers presented a slate of officials of the new Provisional Government, designated Council of People's Commissars (Sovnarkom). It was to be a caretaker government to serve only until the Constituent Assembly met. Lenin initially did not want a cabinet post, preferring to act behind the scenes as de facto chairman of the Communist Party's Central Committee, but his colleagues would have none of it and compelled him to assume responsibility for a coup that was in large measure carried out at his insistence. All the commissars belonged to the Bolshevik Party and were subject to its discipline. Lenin became Chairman. A. I. Rykov took over the portfolio of Internal Affairs, and Trotsky that of Foreign Affairs. Stalin received the minor, newly created post of Chairman of Nationality Affairs. The old Ispolkom was dissolved and replaced with one that had 101 members, of whom 62 were Bolsheviks and 29 Left SRs. Kamenev assumed its chairmanship. The decree setting up the Sovnarkom made it accountable to the Ispolkom.

Lenin assured the Congress that all its decisions would be subject to ratification, rejection, or modification by the Constituent Assembly,

30. One of the early meetings of the Council of People's Commissars.
Lenin at center; behind him, with hand to mouth, Stalin.

elections to which were to be held, as ordered by the previous government, on November 12. Its work done, the Congress adjourned.

In Moscow, the takeover proved much more difficult. The pro-
government forces, composed mainly of military cadets and students,
captured the Kremlin. Instead of pressing their advantage, however, the
Committee of Public Safety, chaired by Moscow's mayor, entered into
negotiations with the Bolsheviks, saving them from almost certain
defeat. During the three-day armistice, the Milrevkom assembled reinforcements and attacked at midnight of October 30. In the morning of
November 2, the government ordered its troops to lay down arms.

In the other cities of Russia, the situation followed a bewildering variety of scenarios, the course and outcome of the conflict in each city
depending on the strength and determination of the contending parties.
(In the countryside, at this point, the October coup had no impact except
to intensify land seizures; there it did not make itself felt until the following summer.) In some localities, the Bolsheviks joined hands with the
SRs and Mensheviks to proclaim "soviet" rule; in others, they ejected
their socialist rivals and took power for themselves. By early November,
the new government controlled the heartland of the defunct empire,

Great Russia or, at any rate, the cities of that region. For the present the borderlands as well as the villages remained outside its reach.

The stratagem of carrying out the coup in the name and on behalf of the Soviet concealed from nearly everyone its true significance. The illusion prevailed that the Soviet, the stronger partner in the dual power arrangement that had existed since February, had formally assumed full responsibility, and hence that nothing much had really changed. The illusion gained strength from the fact that the new authority called itself also a Provisional Government. In the original draft of the October 25 announcement declaring the deposition of Kerensky's cabinet, Lenin wrote "Long Live Socialism!" but he had second thoughts and crossed out the phrase, apparently to emphasize (for now) the image of continuity. The earliest official use of the word *socialism* occurred in a document that Lenin drafted on November 2. In the aftermath of the coup, the ruble lost one-half of its exchange value in terms of the U.S. dollar, but shares on the Petrograd Stock Exchange held steady. There was no panic even among the affluent.

The fall of the old Provisional Government caused few regrets: eyewitnesses report that the population reacted to it with complete unconcern. The man on the street seemed to feel that it made no difference who was in charge, since things were so bad they could not possibly get any worse.

BUILDING THE
ONE-PARTY STATE

The regime that Lenin established after coming to power resembled none that had ever existed. The world has known a great variety of governmental systems ranging from communal self-rule to autocracy, but the government of Russia after 1917 fit no previous model. It was a dual authority: an extreme dictatorship exercised by a private body—the "party"—behind the facade of popular self-rule represented by the soviets. The system lent itself equally well to adaptation by radical left and radical right causes. Because it had no precedent, the world required many years to realize its true nature. It was only after the Fascists and the Nazis borrowed Communist political methods for their own purposes that the concept of totalitarianism came into use to define the regime that had first sprung up on Russian soil.

Marx and his followers had given little thought to the state they would set up after coming to power, in good measure because they did not know how to resolve such thorny problems as the relationship between the "dictatorship of the proletariat" and proletarian democracy or how a socialist economy would function without money. They preferred to leave the resolution of these problems to the future. The Bolsheviks similarly ignored such issues because they took it for granted that their revolution would instantly ignite the entire world and free them from the burden of setting up a national government. Lenin's one attempt to project the Communist future in *State and Revolution* was so confused that it has puzzled commentators ever since.

Hence, Russia's new rulers improvised their political system as they went along. Essentially, they imposed on the entire population the rules and procedures they had adopted for their Bolshevik organization when it had been a private and voluntary body, making the private public and the voluntary coercive. Although they never succeeded in providing it with a theoretical foundation, the one-party state proved to be the most enduring and influential of their accomplishments.

While Lenin took it for granted that he and his associates would exercise unlimited power—for he saw the party as the agent chosen by history to lead humanity into the socialist era—he had to make allowance for the fact that he had taken power in the name of "Soviet democracy." The Bolsheviks, it will be recalled, had carried out the October coup not on their own behalf—the party's name did not appear on any proclamation of the Military-Revolutionary Committee—but on behalf of the soviets. This pretense had to be maintained because the country would not have tolerated a one-party dictatorship. Even the delegates to the Second Congress of Soviets, which the Bolsheviks had packed with followers and sympathizers, had no intention of investing them with dictatorial powers. In a poll conducted at the Congress, none of these delegates expressed a preference for one-party rule. This even held true of some of Lenin's closest associates, who envisaged the new government as a coalition of all the socialist parties. Although Lenin initially did not reject such ideas outright, in fact he had no intention of entering into a league with the Mensheviks and SRs, since he considered them compromisers who would slow down and emasculate his revolutionary agenda. His solution was to create a formal edifice of democratic institutions to satisfy the clamor for a popular government but to control it with an iron hand through the Bolshevik Party. Individual Mensheviks and SRs could participate in the new government but only if they broke with their own parties and submitted to Bolshevik discipline.

The introduction of a one-party state required a variety of measures of a destructive as well as constructive nature. First and foremost, the Bolsheviks had to uproot all that remained of the old regime, tsarist as well as "bourgeois" (democratic): the organs of self-government, the political parties and their press, the armed forces, the judiciary system, and the entire economic edifice built on the principle of private property. This purely destructive phase of the Revolution, carried out in fulfillment of Marx's injunction not merely to take over but "smash" the old order, found expression in decrees, but it was accomplished mainly by the spontaneous anarchism of the population, which the Bolsheviks did their utmost to encourage.

Construction of the new order proved a much more difficult task. First, it required curbing anarchic passions. Then it called for the structuring of a new authority designed to resemble folkish, "soviet" democracy but in reality akin to Muscovite patrimonial absolutism. The new government had to free itself from accountability to the soviets, its nominal sovereign, and convert them into supine tools of the Party. It also somehow had to be rid of the Constituent Assembly, to the convocation of which it was solemnly committed but which was certain to remove it from power. All these objectives the Bolsheviks attained within six months of the October putsch.

That the Bolshevik Party was the engine driving the Soviet government no Bolshevik ever questioned. Lenin merely stated a truism when he said in 1921, "Our party is the governmental party and the resolutions which the Party Congress adopts [are] binding on the entire republic." And yet for all its public authority, the Bolshevik Party remained after 1917 what it had been before—namely, a private body. Neither the constitution of 1918 nor that of 1924 made reference to it. Until 1936, when it was first mentioned in the so-called "Stalin constitution," the party liked to depict itself as a spiritual force that led the country not by compulsion but by example.

As a private organization, the party was not subject to external supervision. While it controlled everything, it was itself free of any controls: it remained, until its demise in August 1991, a self-contained and self-perpetuating body, accountable only to itself.

The rolls of the party—renamed "Communist Party" in March 1918—grew exponentially: in February 1917, it had 23,600 members; in 1919, 250,000; in March 1921, 730,000 (including candidate members). Most of the new adherents, to be sure, were careerists who joined in order to benefit from the privileges traditionally associated in Russia with government service. Lenin realized this, but he had no choice in the matter because he desperately needed personnel to manage all the spheres of life over which his party had assumed control. At the same time, he made certain that key posts in the party and government went to the "Old Guard," Bolsheviks who had joined before 1917.

Until mid-1919, the party retained the casual structure of its underground years, but as its ranks expanded it received a more formal organization. In March 1919, the Central Committee, the party's highest organ, created two new offices alongside the Secretariat: the Politburo, to reach rapid decisions on urgent policy matters, and the Orgburo, to deal with the party's personnel. Lenin was the undisputed head of the party, although it had no formal chairman. In the first year, he often had to fight his associates to have his way, sometimes with resort to threats of resignation. But by late 1918, he no longer faced opposition. As Kamenev told the Menshevik Nicholas Sukhanov:

> I become ever more convinced that Lenin never makes a mistake. In the end, he is always right. How many times it seemed that he had blundered, in his prognosis or political line—and always, in the end, his prognosis and his line turned out to have been correct.

Lenin and his lieutenants served in a double capacity: they ran the party, the country's true legislature, and also the Sovnarkom, the country's supreme executive. As a rule, important decisions were first made in the Central Committee or the Politburo, then submitted for discussion to the Sovnarkom, often with the participation of non-Bolshevik experts. Such discussions always confined themselves to the best means of implementing party decisions, taking the decisions themselves for granted. This duplication of offices became a characteristic feature of the totalitarian regime.

The destructive phase of the Bolshevik Revolution is best defined by the term *duvan*, a Turkish word adopted by the Cossacks to mean "division of spoils," such as the Cossacks used to carry out after raids on Turkish and Persian settlements. In the fall and winter of 1917–18, all Russia became the object of duvan. The main commodity divided was agrarian land. Similar pilferage also took place in industry, where workers took over factories. Frontline soldiers, who after October deserted in droves, before heading for home broke into arsenals and storehouses and took whatever they could carry. Thus preoccupied, the peasants, workers, and soldiers lost the little interest they had in politics.

The duvan was not limited to material goods; it also applied to political power. The population of what had been the Russian Empire tore apart the state, the product of 600 years of historical development. By the spring of 1918, the largest state in the world had disintegrated into many overlapping entities, large and small, each claiming sovereignty over its territory. As in the Middle Ages, Russia turned into a realm of self-governing principalities.

The first to detach themselves were the borderland areas inhabited by non-Russians. Beginning with Finland, which declared its independence in December 1917, one ethnic group after another went its separate way, sometimes justifying its action with the right of "national self-determination" proclaimed by the new government.* But the centrifugal forces also affected Russia proper, as provinces, regions, and even cities asserted independence from central authority. The Bolshevik acceptance of the anarchist principle of soviet rule encouraged this process. According to one contemporary source, in June 1918 there existed on the territory of what had been the Russian Empire at least thirty-three sovereign "governments."

The Bolsheviks, whose long-range objective called for a highly centralized state, for the time being did not interfere with these centrifugal trends because they promoted the disintegration of the old political and economic systems. In March 1918, the government approved a new constitution of the Russian Soviet Federated Socialist Republic (RSFSR) which, drafted with the help of the Left SRs, had a strong anarchist flavor. That it was not meant to be taken seriously is evident from the fact that while vesting (nominally) all power in the soviets, it did not define the distribution of power among the village soviets, district soviets, and provincial soviets, nor between the soviets and the central government. The Bolshevik Party, the true source of all authority, went unmentioned.

To gain full freedom of action, Lenin and Trotsky had to rid themselves as quickly as possible of accountability to the Central Executive Committee (CEC).† It was on Lenin's own initiative that the Second Congress of Soviets, which had created the Council of People's Commissars (Sovnarkom), gave the Central Executive Committee control over its actions and composition. But Lenin's real intention was to have the Sovnarkom, of which he was chairman, bear exclusive responsibility to the Central Committee of the party, of which he was undisputed leader. The contradiction between declaratory and intended practice led to the first and only constitutional clash in the history of Soviet Russia.

The socialists on the CEC appointed by the Bolsheviks in late October thought of it as a kind of socialist Duma empowered to monitor the activities of the new Provisional Government, nominate its members, and legislate. Lenin, who treated such "formalism" with contempt, ignored the CEC from his first day in office. The potential conflict between him and

---

* This subject will be treated at greater length in Chapter XII.

† The Central Executive Committee (CEC, previously known as Ispolkom) was the highest organ of the nation's soviets—that is, the *state*. The Central Committee directed the *party*.

the CEC broke into the open with the release of two controversial decrees, neither of which had been submitted to the CEC for approval. One, made public on October 27, dealt with the press. Although signed by Lenin, it was actually drafted by Anatolii Lunacharskii, the Commissar of Enlightenment. It called for the shutting down of the "counterrevolutionary" press, by which were meant all newspapers that refused to acknowledge the legitimacy of the October coup—in effect, the entire press except for the organs of the Bolsheviks and Left SRs.

Anticipating that this decree and others that they had in mind would provoke strong opposition in the CEC, the Bolsheviks issued another law regulating their relations with the Sovnarkom. Called "Concerning the Procedure for the Ratification and Promulgation of Laws," it authorized the Sovnarkom to legislate by decree. The CEC could ratify or abrogate these decrees, but only retroactively. This measure, modeled on Article 87 of the tsarist Fundamental Laws, was drafted by Lenin's principal economic adviser, Iurii Larin.

The socialists in the CEC reacted to these developments with alarm, since they violated the provisions under which the Sovnarkom had been created and reduced its own role to that of a rubber stamp. The issue came to a head at a meeting of the CEC on November 4, when—again for the first and last time—Lenin and Trotsky, like pre-revolutionary ministers, appeared before the CEC to defend the legality of their actions. The Left SRs on the CEC demanded that the government immediately cease ruling by decree. Lenin dismissed this argument as an expression of "bourgeois formalism." Trotsky echoed him, asserting that since Soviet Russia no longer had antagonistic classes she had no need of a "conventional parliamentary machinery." The government and the "masses," he went on, were linked not by formal institutions and procedures but by a "vital and direct bond." This reasoning failed to persuade the non-Bolshevik minority on the CEC; even some of its Bolshevik members felt uneasy. A Left SR introduced a motion which stated that the CEC found the explanations of the Chairman of the Sovnarkom unsatisfactory. A Bolshevik countermotion stated that the

> Soviet Parliament cannot refuse the Council of People's Commissars the right to issue, without prior discussion in the Central Executive Committee, urgent decrees within the framework of the general program of the All-Russian Congress of Soviets.

The Left SR motion was defeated 25–20; the low vote resulted from the defection of nine Bolsheviks, four of them Commissars, who announced that they were resigning their posts to protest Lenin's refusal to form a coalition government. (All returned to the fold shortly afterward.)

But a negative victory did not satisfy Lenin; he wanted it affirmed explicitly that his government had the right to rule by decree, as stated in the Bolshevik motion. A preliminary head count indicated that a vote on the motion would produce a tie (23–23). To break it, Lenin and Trotsky announced that they would take part in the voting—an action equivalent to serving as their own judges. If Russia's "parliamentarians" had had more experience, they would have refused to participate in such a travesty and walked out. But they stayed and voted. The Bolshevik motion carried 25–23, the decisive two votes being cast by Lenin and Trotsky. By this simple procedure, the two Bolshevik leaders arrogated to themselves full legislative authority and transformed the CEC and the Congress of Soviets, which it represented, from legislative into consultative bodies. It was a watershed in the history of the Soviet constitution.

Later that day the Sovnarkom announced that its decrees acquired the force of law as soon as they were published in the official *Gazette of the Provisional Workers' and Peasants' Government*. The CEC was allowed for a while longer to debate government policies but without having the power to alter them. By the summer of 1918, when the non-Bolsheviks were ejected from it (below, p. 165), the CEC turned into an echo chamber in which Bolshevik deputies routinely "ratified" the decisions of the Sovnarkom, which, in turn, executed the wishes of the Bolshevik Central Committee. It met less and less frequently; in all of 1921, it would convene only three times.

Henceforth, Russia was ruled by decree, as she had been before 1905 by Imperial *ukazy*. As in pre-revolutionary days, laws went into effect when the head of state—then the Tsar, now Lenin—affixed to them his signature. Such practices would have been entirely understandable to a Nicholas I or an Alexander III. The system of legislation the Bolsheviks set in place within two weeks of the October coup, for all its revolutionary rhetoric, marked a reversion to the autocratic practices of tsarist Russia before the Manifesto of October 17, 1905. They simply wiped out the eleven intervening years of constitutionalism.

One of the problems the new regime had in securing legitimacy—at any rate, in its own eyes—derived from the fact that although it claimed to be the government not only of workers but also of peasants, peasant organizations had boycotted the Second Congress of Soviets. The Congress of Peasants' Deputies, dominated by the Socialists-Revolutionaries, refused to recognize the October coup. To break this resistance the Bolsheviks entered into an alliance with the Left Socialists-Revolutionaries, a splinter group of the main party, headed by an ex-terrorist, Maria Spiridonova. The Left SRs supported the Bolsheviks' coup even though they objected to many of their subsequent actions.

The Congress of Peasants' Deputies scheduled to meet in late November: the meeting was virtually certain to condemn the October coup. To forestall this turn of events, the Bolsheviks entered into secret negotiations with the Left SRs, holding out the promise of seats in the Sovnarkom and other concessions in return for the Left SRs' assistance in splitting the Peasant Congress. The Left SRs helped ensure that the Mandate Commission of the forthcoming Congress gave them and the Bolsheviks disproportionately generous representation. Then, after it had opened, they helped disrupt its proceedings. Spiridonova, elected Chairman of the Congress, invalidated a formal resolution adopted by the majority that designated the Constituent Assembly the supreme legislature of the new regime. Then she and her followers joined the Bolsheviks in walking out of the Congress. The Bolsheviks ordered the dissolution of the legitimate Congress and declared the rump representation of Bolsheviks and Left SRs the sole voice of the peasantry, following which they merged the latter with the Soviet of Workers' and Soldiers' Deputies. Thus perished the institution that represented the nation's peasants.

As a reward, the Bolsheviks made several concessions to the Left SRs. They allotted them five minor portfolios in the Sovnarkom as well as some other posts, including the deputy chairmanship of the newly formed security police, the Cheka. More important still, they agreed to the SRs' demand to convene the Constituent Assembly.

The first to resist the October coup was the intelligentsia. This group, which had contributed so heavily to the breakdown of the old order and had hindered with its irresponsible behavior the construction, on its ruins, of an effective democracy, now stood up to the Bolsheviks. Writers, artists, academics, journalists, lawyers, as well as government officials and white-collar employees of private enterprises refused to carry on their responsibilities as long as the Bolsheviks remained in power. A Committee for the Salvation of the Fatherland and the Revolution, which sprang up in Petrograd, organized a general strike of government employees. When the new Commissars appeared in the ministries to assume their duties, they found either idle officials or no one at all except doormen and charwomen. Trotsky had an embarrassing experience when on November 9—two weeks after receiving his appointment—he ventured to visit the Ministry of Foreign Affairs. This is how a contemporary newspaper described the incident:

> Yesterday, the new "minister" Trotsky, came to the Ministry of Foreign Affairs. Having assembled all the officials, he said: "I am Trotsky, the new Minister of Foreign Affairs." He was greeted with ironic laughter. To this he paid no attention and told them to go back to work. They went . . . but to their own homes, with the intention of not returning to the office as long as Trotsky remained head of the ministry.

Postal and telegraph workers walked out vowing not to resume work until the Bolsheviks had yielded power to a coalition government. Other office employees, including those working for private banks, followed suit.

For the Bolsheviks, the most humiliating aspect of this protest was the refusal of the personnel at the State Bank and Treasury to honor their requests for money. After being repeatedly frustrated, they sent an armed guard, which rounded up the officers of the State Bank and forced them to open the vault, from which they removed 5 million rubles. The whole operation resembled a holdup.

In the second half of November, Lenin ordered a counteroffensive against striking government officials. One by one, armed men occupied public institutions in Petrograd and compelled their staffs, under threat of severe punishment, to work for them. Those who refused were dismissed and replaced with junior personnel. But the strike of white-collar employees was effectively broken only in January 1918, following the dispersal of the Constituent Assembly, when it became apparent even to the most sanguine democrats that the Bolsheviks would neither share power nor surrender it.

The meetings of the Sovnarkom in the first months of the Bolshevik dictatorship resembled gatherings of old-time revolutionaries. Simon Liberman, a Menshevik timber expert who participated in them, left the following description:

> A peculiar atmosphere prevailed at the conferences of the highest administrative councils of Soviet Russia, presided over by Lenin. Despite all the efforts of an officious secretary to impart to each session the character of a cabinet meeting, we could not help feeling that here we were, attending another sitting of an underground revolutionary committee! For years we had belonged to various underground organizations. All of this seemed so familiar. Many of the commissars remained seated in their topcoats or greatcoats; most of them wore the forbidding leather jackets. In the wintertime some wore felt boots and thick sweaters. They remained thus clothed throughout the meetings.

One of the commissars, Alexander Tsiurupa, was nearly always ill; he attended these meetings in a semi-reclining position, his feet stretched out on a nearby table. A number of Lenin's aides would not take their seats at the conference table but shoved their chairs helter-skelter all over the room. Lenin alone invariably took his seat at the head of the table as the presiding officer of the occasion. He did so in a neat, almost decorous way. Fotieva, as his personal secretary, sat beside him.

Irritated by the unpunctuality and verbosity of his colleagues, Lenin established a strict regime, setting fines for lateness: five rubles for less than half an hour, ten for more. When others spoke, he would frequently thumb through a book and deliver his judgment after the speaker had stopped.*

To free themselves completely from popular control, the Bolsheviks still had one major hurdle to clear, and that was the Constituent Assembly, which, in the words of one contemporary, "stuck like a bone" in their throat.

By early December 1917, the Bolsheviks had succeeded in (1) shunting aside the legitimate All-Russian Congress of Soviets and unseating its Executive Committee (CEC), (2) depriving the new CEC, which they had formed, of legislative functions and control over ministerial appointments, and (3) splitting the Peasants' Congress and replacing it with a handpicked body of their own adherents and sympathizers. None of these actions, important as they were for the future of Russia, aroused the interests of the population at large because they took place in distant Petrograd and involved complex organizational issues that were beyond most people's comprehension. Matters stood differently with the Constituent Assembly, which was to be elected by all adult citizens. So, at any rate, it seemed in the fall of 1917.

One of the arguments the Bolsheviks used to justify the October coup was that it alone would ensure the convocation of the Constituent Assembly since, as they maintained, the "bourgeois" Provisional Government, frightened of the radicalism of the masses, would never allow it to meet. As late as October 27, the Bolshevik organ, *Pravda*, told its readers that the new government "alone is capable of leading the country to

---

* Jay Lovestone, a founder of the American Communist Party, told the author that on one occasion when meeting with Lenin he referred to three-by-five cards. Lenin wanted to know their purpose. When Lovestone explained that to save Lenin's time, he had written down on them what he meant to say, Lenin said that communism would come to Russia when Russians learned to use three-by-five cards.

a Constituent Assembly." In reality, the new government dreaded the Assembly and desperately sought to find ways either to prevent it from convening or, if that proved politically impossible, to render it harmless.

The Bolsheviks honored their pledge to hold elections for the Assembly; these took place in Petrograd on November 12–14, and in the rest of the country in the second half of the month. Eligible, according to criteria established by the defunct Provisional Government, were all male and female citizens twenty years of age and over; for men in uniform, the voting age was lowered to eighteen. The turnout was impressive: in Petrograd and Moscow some 70 percent of those eligible went to the polls, and in some rural areas the figure reached 100 percent. According to the most reliable estimate, 44.4 million persons cast ballots. On December 1, Lenin declared: "If one views the Constituent Assembly apart from the conditions of the class struggle which verges on civil war, then, as of now, we know of no institution which more perfectly expresses the will of the people."

The results of the voting cannot be precisely determined because of the large number of parties involved and because in many localities they formed electoral blocs; in Petrograd alone, nineteen parties competed. The largest number of votes—17.9 million, or 40.4 percent—went to the Socialists-Revolutionaries. Next came the Bolsheviks—with 10.6 million, or 24.0 percent. The Mensheviks and Left SRs were all but wiped out. The Constitutional-Democrats, as the most important nonsocialist party running, garnered the bulk of the nonsocialist vote (2.1 million, or 4.7 percent). In regions outside Russia proper, the voters favored nationalist parties, many of them affiliated with their Russian counterparts; thus in the Ukraine, the Ukrainian Socialists-Revolutionaries gained 3.4 million votes, and in Georgia, the Georgian Mensheviks came out on top with 662,000 votes.

The Bolsheviks, who had occasionally hoped against hope that they would gain a majority, were not dismayed by the results. They won the bulk of the workers' vote and did well among the troops, groups that would be especially useful to them once the Civil War got under way. They were unhappy, however, with the strong showing of the Kadets: for although nationwide the liberals gained less than one vote in twenty, they won much of the city vote, running a close second to the Bolsheviks and in some cities besting them. To the extent that the political future of Russia was expected to be decided in the cities, the Kadets were much more dangerous to the new rulers than the SRs, with their huge but soft rural constituency.

What to do next? In their inner councils, the Bolsheviks spent a great deal of time debating how to neutralize the Assembly. Some urged that it be canceled; others (Lenin included) suggested that it be allowed to meet but be made subject to the principle of "recall," under which non-Bolshevik deputies would be unseated on the grounds that in the altered historic conditions they no longer represented the voters. While mulling this question over, Lenin ordered the Kadets outlawed and their leaders arrested as "enemies of the people." The liberals were the first political party to be suppressed by the Bolshevik government.

In the end, by virtue of the arrangement made with the Left SRs, it was decided to allow the Assembly to convene but divest it of legislative authority and promptly disband it. Lenin, who on December 1 had pronounced it as "perfectly" expressing the people's will, on December 12 insisted that the slogan "All Power to the Constituent Assembly" had become counterrevolutionary. The Assembly had either to ratify the resolutions of the Second Congress of Soviets as well as the decrees of the Sovnarkom or face "the most energetic, rapid, firm, and decisive measures on the part of Soviet authority." This was a sentence of death on the Assembly. In all the public pronouncements that followed, the Bolshevik spokesmen, who in October had insisted that soviet rule alone would ensure the convocation of the Assembly, now argued that support of the Assembly was tantamount to rejection of the soviets.

The socialists reacted to this argument with a massive counterpropaganda campaign. The Union for the Defense of the Constituent Assembly sent agitators to factories and barracks to obtain the signatures of workers and soldiers, including those who had voted the Bolshevik ticket, on appeals upholding the Assembly. The SRs and Mensheviks, who ran the Union, hoped that evidence of massive support would inhibit the Bolsheviks from using force against the Assembly. A few socialists thought psychological warfare was not enough. They wanted to meet force with force and persuaded some units of the Petrograd garrison to participate on the opening day of the Assembly, set for January 5, in an armed demonstration in its favor. The organizers of this demonstration requested authorization from the Central Committee of the SR Party. They received an unequivocal "no" for an answer; they were told that Bolshevism was a "disease" of the masses that required time to overcome and that an armed demonstration would be a dangerous "adventure." The Central Committee would only countenance a peaceful procession, without weapons. Informed of this decision, the soldiers refused to face the pro-Bolshevik units unarmed and backed out of the demonstration.

On January 4, Lenin appointed Podvoiskii, the ex-chairman of the Bolshevik Military Organization, which had carried out the October coup, head of an Extraordinary Military Staff to deal with the Assembly. Podvoiskii placed Petrograd under martial law and forbade public assemblies. *Pravda* warned that any gatherings in the vicinity of Taurida Palace, where the Assembly was to meet, would be dispersed by force. On January 5 the Bolshevik organ carried a headline: TODAY THE HYE-NAS OF CAPITAL AND THEIR HIRELINGS WANT TO SEIZE POWER FROM SOVIET HANDS.

On Friday, January 5, Petrograd, especially the area adjoining Taurida, resembled a military encampment as troops armed to their teeth deployed around the palace and on the streets leading to it. The principal force consisted of Latvian riflemen, who had adopted a pro-Bolshevik stance and in the next two years would render the new government invaluable services both in the interior of the country and on the front of the Civil War.*

The unarmed demonstration in favor of the Assembly began to advance toward the Taurida at 10 a.m. Before it could reach its destination, it was fired upon by Bolshevik units and broken up.

Lenin arrived at Taurida at 1 p.m. to supervise the dispersal of the Assembly. According to his secretary, he was "excited and pale as a corpse. . . . In this extreme white paleness of his face and neck, his head appeared even larger, his eyes were distended and aflame, burning with a steady fire." It was, indeed, a decisive moment, when the fate of the young Bolshevik dictatorship hung in the balance.

Lenin, who sat on the side and took no part in the proceedings, postponed the opening of the session from noon to 4 p.m. to make certain that the pro-Assembly crowds had been scattered. The Bolshevik tactic relied on disruption. From the opening bell, Bolshevik deputies and armed guards booed and jeered opposition speakers; some pointed guns at them. Many of the sailors and soldiers were drunk on vodka dispensed by the Palace buffet. When their motion, asking the Assembly to renounce the right to legislate and to confine itself to ratifying Bolshevik decrees, went down in defeat, the Bolsheviks declared the Assembly "counterrevolutionary" and left.

---

* Latvia had a strong Social-Democratic movement, anti-German in its orientation. On a per capita basis, Latvians were more strongly represented in the Bolshevik Party than any other nationality. Because of their loyalty, the Bolsheviks allowed them—and them alone of the old army—to serve in separate military formations.

On Lenin's instructions, the Assembly was allowed to carry on for a while longer. Shortly after 4 a.m. an anarchist sailor, acting on orders of Lenin's deputy in charge of Taurida security, mounted the tribune and demanded of the chairman, the SR Victor Chernov, that the meeting be adjourned on the grounds that the guards were tired. More troops poured into the assembly hall, looking menacing. Chernov kept the proceedings going for another two hours, and then (at 6 a.m. on January 6) adjourned it until 5 that afternoon. But there was to be no second session because the following morning Iakov Sverdlov, Chairman of the CEC and Lenin's right-hand man, officially dissolved the Assembly. That day *Pravda* came out with banner headlines:

THE HIRELINGS OF BANKERS, CAPITALISTS, AND LANDLORDS ... THE SLAVES OF THE AMERICAN DOLLAR, THE BACKSTABBERS — THE RIGHT SR'S — DEMAND IN THE CONSTITUENT ASSEMBLY ALL POWER FOR THEMSELVES AND THEIR MASTERS — ENEMIES OF THE PEOPLE ... BUT THE WORKERS, PEASANTS, AND SOLDIERS WILL NOT FALL FOR THE BAIT OF LIES OF THE MOST EVIL ENEMIES OF SOCIALISM. IN THE NAME OF THE SOCIALIST REVOLUTION AND THE SOCIALIST SOVIET REPUBLIC THEY WILL SWEEP AWAY ITS OPEN AND HIDDEN ASSASSINS.

This was the first time that opposition to Bolshevism was linked to American money.

Two days later (January 8), the Bolsheviks opened their counterassembly, labeled "Third Congress of Soviets." Here no one could defy them because they had reserved for themselves and the Left SRs 94 percent of the seats. This gathering duly ratified all Bolshevik laws and resolutions. The new government now dropped the adjective "Provisional" from its name and established itself as the permanent government of Russia and her possessions.

The dissolution of the Assembly met with surprising indifference: there was none of the popular fury that in France in 1789 had greeted rumors that Louis XVI was about to dissolve the National Assembly, precipitating the assault on the Bastille. After a year of near-anarchy, Russians were exhausted; they yearned for peace and order, no matter how purchased. The Bolsheviks had gambled on that mood and won. After January 5, no one could any longer delude himself that Lenin's men could be talked into abandoning power.

An immediate result of the dissolution was the collapse of the boycott of government and white-collar employees, as the strikers drifted back to work, some driven by personal need, others acting in the belief that they could influence events better from the inside. The psychology of the opposition now suffered a fatal break; it is as if brutality and the blatant disregard of the nation's will legitimized the new autocracy. The Bolshevik claim to power was consummated only now, for the October coup had been carried out under false pretenses. On January 5, the Bolsheviks made it unmistakably clear that they did not have to listen to the voice of the people because they were the "people." In the words of Lenin, "The dispersal of the Constituent Assembly by Soviet authority [was] the complete and candid liquidation of formal democracy in the name of the revolutionary dictatorship." "Formal democracy" in this context meant the will of the nation's majority as expressed in elections.

The response to this historic event on the part of the population at large and the intelligentsia boded ill for the country's future. Russia, events confirmed once again, lacked a sense of national cohesion capable of inspiring the population to give up immediate and personal interests for the sake of the common good. The "masses" demonstrated that they understood only private and local interests, the heady joys of the *duvan*. In accordance with the Russian proverb "He who grabs the stick is corporal," they conceded power to the boldest and most ruthless claimant.

No less troublesome was the reaction of the socialist intelligentsia, who, having gained a solid electoral victory, could have acted confident of the country's backing. But they doomed themselves by their refusal, under any circumstances, to resort to force against the Bolsheviks, whom they denounced as usurpers but treated as comrades. Trotsky later taunted socialist intellectuals, saying that they had come to Taurida Palace equipped with candles in case the Bolsheviks cut off electricity and with sandwiches in case they deprived them of food. But they would neither carry guns nor allow their supporters to do so. When, following the dissolution of the Assembly, a group of soldiers approached the socialist deputies with the offer to restore it by force of arms, the horrified intellectuals implored them to do nothing of the kind: better to let the Constituent Assembly die a quiet death than to provoke a civil war. Such people no one would risk following.

This suicidal behavior was attributed not only to an abhorrence of physical violence and faith in the inevitable advance of democracy, independent of human actions, but to the ever-present dread of counterrevolution. The socialists felt themselves bound to the Bolsheviks by a common commitment to the new order; much as they condemned Bolshevik methods, they shared their objectives. In the nonsocialist enemies of the Bolsheviks they saw also their own enemies. As a Menshevik newspaper put it one day after the Bolshevik coup: "It is essential, above all, to take into account the tragic fact that any violent liquidation of the Bolshevik coup will, at the same time, result inevitably in the liquidation of all the conquests of the Russian Revolution." After the dispersal of the Constituent Assembly, the same paper wrote, justifying inaction: "The fate of our revolution is closely tied to that of the Bolshevik movement." This way of thinking paralyzed the socialist intelligentsia's will to act before the coup, during, and afterward. The notion that the true counterrevolutionaries were the Bolsheviks eluded them to the end, for they judged by slogans rather than deeds.

Unlike their opponents, the Bolsheviks learned a great deal from these events. They learned that in areas under their control they need fear no organized armed resistance: their rivals, though supported by three-fourths of the population, were disunited, leaderless, and, above all, unwilling to stand up and fight. This experience accustomed the Bolsheviks to resort to violence as a matter of course whenever they ran into defiance and to "solve" problems by physically "liquidating" those who caused them. The machine gun became for them the principal instrument of political persuasion. The unrestrained brutality with which they henceforth ruled Russia stemmed in large measure from the knowledge, gained on January 5, 1918, that they could do so with impunity.

And by the spring of 1918, they had to resort to force with ever greater frequency, for they had now lost even the support of these soldiers and workers who had followed them in the autumn. In the elections to the soviets held at that time, they fared poorly; in all the cities for which records exist, they suffered defeat at the hands of Mensheviks and SRs. The regime handled this embarrassment in two ways: it disqualified Mensheviks and SRs from running in soviet elections, and it forced repeated elections until the desired majorities were obtained. The workers, with tepid Menshevik support, attempted to counter these moves by forming their own organization of Worker Plenipotentiaries, independent of the discredited soviets, but this body was soon suppressed and its leaders arrested.

Thus ended the autonomy of the soviets, the right of workers to their own representation, and what remained of the multiparty system. These measures, enacted in June and July 1918, completed the foundations of the one-party dictatorship.

THE REVOLUTION
INTERNATIONALIZED

VIII

> To obtain an armistice now means *to conquer the whole world.*
>
> —LENIN IN SEPTEMBER 1917

Brest-Litovsk

The Bolsheviks' concerns after October were first to solidify their power in Petrograd and then, as rapidly as possible, to expand it nationwide and globally. But to attain these objectives they had to have peace. In Lenin's judgment, unless his government promptly concluded an armistice, it would not survive. Then, as before the October coup, his anxiety centered on the armed forces: if Russia stayed in the war, in his words, "the peasant army, unbearably exhausted by the war . . . will overthrow the socialist workers' government." The Bolsheviks had to have a *peredyshka*, a "breathing spell," to consolidate their authority, to organize an administration, and to build a new, revolutionary army.

Lenin was prepared to make peace with the Central Powers on almost any terms as long as they left him in power. This was by no means the prevalent view in Bolshevik ranks. The resistance that he encountered among his associates grew out of the belief (which he shared) that the Bolshevik regime could survive only if a revolution broke out in Western Europe and the conviction (which he did not fully share) that this was bound to happen momentarily. To Lenin's critics in the party, making peace with "imperialist" Germany meant a betrayal of international socialism and, implicitly, of their own cause. Instead of making peace with Germany, Russia should proceed to revolutionize it. Lenin disagreed:

Our tactics ought to rest . . . [on the principle] how to ensure more reliably and hopefully for the socialist revolution the possibility of consolidating itself or even surviving in one country until such time as other countries joined in.

Trotsky and Nicholas Bukharin, who led the opposition, argued that Lenin was deceiving himself: the Central Powers would not grant the new regime a respite to consolidate; rather, peace would help consolidate the Central Powers. Let the Germans invade Russia, they said. They would merely rouse the people and infect them with revolutionary fervor. With reference to the events of 1792 in France, Lenin's opponents argued that the nation's resistance would "stir the souls of the working classes abroad" and put an end to the "nightmare of imperialism." On this issue the Bolshevik Party split in the winter of 1917–18 right down the middle: most of the time Lenin found himself in a minority, sometimes a minority of one.

The Bolsheviks neither could nor would subscribe to the principles of international law and diplomacy that Western Europe had worked out during the preceding 400 years. In particular, they rejected the notion that states respected one another's sovereignty and dealt with one another only at the governmental level. As revolutionaries, they recognized neither the principle of sovereignty nor the legitimacy of existing governments. But because for the time being—that is, until the outbreak of the global revolution—they had to have dealings with "bourgeois" states, if only to forestall concerted action against themselves, they developed a dual foreign policy. On one level—that of the state—they maintained formally correct foreign relations, observing accepted diplomatic standards. On another level—that of the party—they pursued a highly unorthodox foreign policy, appealing, over the heads of governments, directly to their citizens with inflammatory slogans. When foreign powers protested such behavior, the Commissariat of Foreign Affairs would respond that the Bolshevik Party was a private organization for which the Soviet government bore no responsibility. The subterfuge deceived few, but it provided an excuse for foreign states that for one reason or another found it expedient to have dealings with the Soviet government.

While intervening freely in the internal affairs of other countries, the Bolsheviks indignantly rejected as "imperialism" any such interference on the part of foreign governments in their own country.

As noted (above, p. 147) the Second Congress of Soviets passed Lenin's "Decree on Peace," which proposed an immediate armistice to all belligerent powers. This proposal it coupled with an appeal to the workers of England, France, and Germany to help Soviet Russia "complete . . . the task of liberating the toiling and exploited masses of the population from all slavery and all exploitation." George Kennan has labeled this "decree" an act of "demonstrative diplomacy" intended to "embarrass other governments and stir up opposition among their own people." The Bolsheviks issued other declarations of a similar nature, urging foreign citizens to rise up in rebellion.

The Peace Decree was transmitted on November 9 to the Allies, who rejected it out of hand as a propaganda ploy, whereupon Trotsky notified the Central Powers of Russia's readiness to open negotiations.

The policy of cultivating the Bolsheviks now paid the Germans handsome dividends: some of them believed they were about to witness a repetition of the "miracle" of 1762, when the accession of the pro-Prussian Peter III in St. Petersburg saved Prussia from certain destruction. The prospect of a separate peace revived hopes of victory over France and Britain before the United States could train and deploy significant forces on the Continent. Ludendorff immediately drew up plans for what he expected to be a decisive offensive on the western front, using hundreds of thousands of troops transferred from the east.

On the surface, in its dealings with Soviet Russia, Germany had all the advantages, for she had an efficient government and a formidable army, whereas the Russians had neither. In actuality, the correlation of forces was not quite so one-sided. The Allied blockade had brought the Central Powers to the brink of famine. Austria-Hungary seemed to be breathing her last: the Austrian Foreign Minister told the Germans that his country probably would not hold out until the next harvest. The Germans suffered a further handicap from their ignorance of the Bolsheviks, whom they treated as a band of disheveled and quixotic utopians. The Bolsheviks, however, knew a great deal about the German ruling class, having lived in their country for many years and gained familiarity with their domestic conditions. This knowledge enabled them time and again to outwit the Germans.

Many German politicians and intellectuals hoped to transform defeated Russia into a kind of surrogate Africa, a colonial dependency that would supply them with cheap raw materials and manufacturing facilities. To this end, they desired to break up the Russian Empire along ethnic lines and establish in what remained—the Great Russian provinces—a government that would be too weak to resist their pressures for economic concessions. From the perspective of these ambitions, nothing suited Berlin better than a Bolshevik regime. German internal communications in 1918 are replete with arguments that no matter how odious the Bolsheviks were, they had to be kept in power because their incompetence and unpopularity kept Russia in a state of permanent turmoil. In June 1918, an influential German political writer, Paul Rohrbach, answered those of his compatriots who had developed doubts about the wisdom of continuing to back Lenin:

> The Bolsheviks are ruining Great Russia, the source of any potential future Russian danger, root and branch. They have already lifted most of that anxiety which we might have felt about Great Russia, and we should do all we can to keep them as long as possible doing their work which is so useful to us.

On this basis, a tacit alliance developed between two unlikely partners—radical Russia and monarchist Germany—that would last until Germany's surrender in November 1918 and then reemerge again in the early 1920s. It failed to rescue the Kaiser, but it did save Lenin.

The Germans and Austrians promptly accepted the Russian offer of an armistice with the understanding that it would be followed by peace talks. On November 18/December 1, 1917, a Russian delegation, headed by Adolf Ioffe, an ex-Menshevik and a friend of Trotsky's, departed for Brest-Litovsk, the headquarters of the German High Command on the eastern front. The German delegation was led by von Kühlmann, the foreign minister who had played a key role in arranging for Lenin's transit from Switzerland.

As soon as the armistice had been agreed upon and the fighting stopped, the Russians unleashed a vigorous propaganda campaign aimed at German troops on the eastern front, encouraging them to fraternize with their onetime enemy and inciting them against their government. The Russian tactic at Brest was to procrastinate for as long as possible, using the talks as a forum from which to appeal to the German population with revolutionary slogans. The campaign was not without effect, for in late January 1918 strikes broke out in a number of German cities among workers, who demanded an immediate peace without annexations or reparations.

Once the armistice talks had adjourned (December 15/28, 1917), the Germans began to wonder about the Russians' true intentions: Were they seeking to make peace or to gain time to unleash a worldwide social revolution? The military, which correctly concluded that the Bolsheviks were playing for time, demanded an end to the charade. In a letter to the

31. The signing of the armistice at Brest (November23/
December 6, 1917). Sitting on the right, Kamenev,
and behind him (concealed), Ioffe. On the German side,
sitting fourth from left, General Hoffmann.

32. Russian and German troops fraternizing, winter 1917–18.

Kaiser of January 7 (December 25), General von Hindenburg criticized the "weak" and "conciliatory" tactics of German diplomats in Brest, which created the impression that Germany desperately needed peace. Such an impression, in his view, adversely affected the army's morale. The Kaiser concurred, and when the talks resumed on December 27/January 9, the German attitude had stiffened. Without seeking Russian consent, the Germans unilaterally recognized the sovereignty of the Ukraine, preliminary to signing a separate peace treaty with her. A shocked Trotsky, who had replaced Ioffe as head of the Russian delegation, protested in vain.*

He experienced still greater shock when the Germans unfolded a map showing the revised boundary between the two countries. It called for the separation of Poland, the Ukraine, Lithuania, and Latvia. Trotsky responded that these terms were unacceptable to his government. On January 5/18, which happened to be the very day the Bolsheviks dispersed the Constituent Assembly, he said the Soviet government believed that a people's will was best determined by means of a referendum. Following which he departed for Petrograd.

The German terms threw the Bolshevik high command into disarray. Bukharin, voicing the wishes of the party rank and file, wanted the negotiations broken off in order to ignite a popular uprising against the imperialists. Trotsky, who held a position similar to Bukharin's, came up with the slogan "neither war nor peace," by which he meant breaking off the talks and unilaterally declaring Russia's hostilities with the Central Powers at an end. The Germans would then be free to do what they wanted to do and what no force was capable of preventing them from doing in any event—annex vast territories—but in the process they would reveal to their own people and to the rest of the world the brutality of their imperialism.

Lenin—supported by Kamenev, Zinoviev, and Stalin—declared such a policy utopian. Russia had no army with which to stop the Germans should they decide to occupy Moscow and Petrograd, toppling the Bolshevik government. He pleaded for the acceptance of a humiliating peace as absolutely essential for the survival of the new regime.

---

* Germany and Austria-Hungary signed separate peace treaties with the Ukraine in February and installed there a puppet government that helped them collect foodstuffs for shipment home. Germany compelled Soviet Russia, as part of the peace settlement in March 1918, to recognize Ukrainian independence, but the proposed peace treaty between Moscow and Kiev never materialized.

At the Central Committee meeting that followed Trotsky's return from Brest, Lenin suffered a narrow defeat. Trotsky was instructed to return to Brest and there pursue his tactic of "neither peace nor war," dragging out the talks for as long as possible in the hope that a German revolution would break out any day. But by now the Germans had seen through the Russian stratagem. On February 9–10 (NS), von Kühlmann, acting on the Kaiser's instructions, presented the Russians with an ultimatum: they were to sign the German peace terms without further discussion or delays or the negotiations would be broken off and the German army would march into Russia. Trotsky responded that he would not sign the proffered document but that, peace treaty or no, Russia considered herself to be out of the war and would demobilize her army. Then he reboarded his train and headed for home.

The Russian ploy threw the Germans into utter confusion. They had by now no doubt that the Bolsheviks were using the peace talks as a diversion, but they could not decide what conclusions to draw from this fact. Continue the fruitless talks? Compel the Bolsheviks by military action to accept their ultimatum? Or march on Petrograd and remove them from power?

Von Kühlmann counseled patience; he feared that German workers would respond to a resumption of hostilities on the eastern front with fresh disturbances. He also worried about Austria dropping out of the war. But the generals who had gained the Kaiser's ear, convinced that the Bolsheviks were both weak and undependable partners, demanded resolute action. According to Hindenburg, unless decisive steps were taken in the east, the war in the west could drag on for a long time. He wanted to "smash the Russians [and] topple their government." The Kaiser sided with the generals: the Bolsheviks, whom he now came to view as members of a worldwide "Jewish-Freemasonic conspiracy," had to go. The Russians were accordingly advised that the German army would end the armistice and recommence military operations against them at midday on February 17.

The information about the projected German offensive reached Petrograd on the afternoon of February 17. At a meeting of the Central Committee, Lenin renewed his plea to return to Brest and capitulate, but he was again defeated by a single vote. The majority wanted to wait and see whether the Germans would carry out their threat: if they did and no revolution broke out in Germany and Austria, there would always be time to bow to the inevitable.

The Germans, true to their word, advanced into western Russia, occupying one city after another without firing a shot.

For Lenin, this was the last straw: the failure of the remnant of the Russian army to offer even token resistance meant that he had no bargaining chips left. He was convinced—possibly on the basis of information supplied by German sympathizers—that the enemy intended to occupy the two capital cities and liquidate his regime. At a meeting of the Central Committee on February 18, at which his motion once again lost by a single vote, Trotsky eventually came to his rescue by switching sides. As a consequence, Lenin's proposal carried 7–6. The Germans were advised that the Russian delegation would return to Brest and sign on the dotted line.

Then came another shock. The Germans and the Austrians did not halt their advance into Russia but marched on, occupying still more cities, apparently aiming at Petrograd and Moscow. Panic-stricken, Lenin issued, on February 21–22, a decree that was to have far-reaching consequences. Titled "The Socialist Fatherland in Danger," it declared that the Germans were bent on liquidating the socialist government and restoring the monarchy in Russia. To defend the Revolution, urgent measures had to be taken. One of these called for the formation of forced-labor battalions made up of "all able-bodied members of the bourgeois class" to dig trenches; resisters would be shot. The other clause read: "Enemy agents, speculators, burglars, hooligans, counter-revolutionary agitators, German spies are to be executed on the spot." This provision introduced irrevocable penalties for crimes that were nowhere precisely defined; nothing was said about trials or even hearings for the accused. In effect, the decree gave the new security organ, the Cheka, the license to kill. It marked the onset of the Bolshevik terror.

About the only asset Lenin still had left in the crisis which he had foreseen but could not prevent, were the Allies. The latter had only one interest in Russia: to keep her in the war. Who the Bolsheviks were and what they stood for concerned them little. Nor did they worry about Bolshevik fraternization policies or their subversive appeals to workers, neither of which had found a response in their countries. The Allied attitude was unambiguous: the Bolshevik regime was an enemy if it made peace with the Central Powers but a friend and an ally if it stayed in the fight. In the words of Arthur Balfour, Britain's Foreign Secretary, as long as the Russians fought the Germans, their cause was Britain's cause. The United States adopted a similar stand.

After the Russians had opened peace talks with the Germans, the Allies withdrew their diplomatic missions from Petrograd to the provincial town of Vologda and dealt with Lenin's government through several unofficial intermediaries. The latter accepted Bolshevik assurances that the Bolsheviks would stay in the war if offered Western economic and military assistance. When, on February 21, Trotsky contacted the French to inquire about aid against the Germans, he received a prompt answer from the French ambassador: "In your resistance to Germany you may count on the military and financial cooperation of France." With Lenin's approval, the Sovnarkom formally requested such aid, and negotiations opened to determine the form it would take. Kamenev left for Paris to assume the post of Soviet diplomatic representative (he was turned back).

Whether the Germans had gotten wind of these dealings or by mere coincidence, their long-awaited response arrived on the very morning that the Sovnarkom voted to seek Allied help. As Lenin had warned, they now made even more onerous demands, which included an indemnity and a variety of economic concessions. Their note was phrased as an ultimatum that required an answer within forty-eight hours, following which a maximum of seventy-two hours was allowed for the signing of the treaty.

For the next two days, the Bolshevik leadership sat in almost continual session. All the old arguments were rehearsed. Lenin ultimately prevailed over the majority by threatening to resign all his posts in the party and government unless the German terms were accepted. The Germans were notified that a delegation was en route to Brest.

Because he did not trust the Germans to stop their aggression even after their terms had been unconditionally accepted, Lenin thought it prudent to transfer the capital from Petrograd to Moscow. The relocation of government personnel took place in the first half of March. Lenin himself sneaked out of Petrograd on the night of March 10–11 in a train guarded by Latvians. The journey was organized in deepest secrecy and only his sister greeted him on arrival. He established his residence and office in the medieval Kremlin fortress; several of his commissars did likewise. Security arrangements of the complex were entrusted to the Latvians.

Although it was based on considerations of security, Lenin's decision to move the capital to Moscow and install himself in the Kremlin had a deeper significance: it symbolized, as it were, a rejection of the pro-Western course initiated by Peter the Great in favor of the older, Muscovite tradition. It also reflected the new leaders' morbid fear for their personal security. To appreciate the significance of these actions, one must imagine a British prime minister moving out of Downing Street and transferring his residence and office as well as those of his ministers to the Tower of London to govern from there under the protection of Sikh guards.

The terms of the Brest-Litovsk Treaty, which the Russians signed on March 3, were extremely burdensome. They give an idea of what the Allies would have faced had they lost the war. Russia had to make major territorial concessions which deprived her of the conquests made in the west since the middle of the seventeenth century. She had to give up Poland, Finland, and the Ukraine, as well as Lithuania, Latvia, Estonia, and Transcaucasia. These were some of the most populous and affluent regions of the Russian Empire, containing 26 percent of its population and 28 percent of its industrial plant, as well as three-quarters of its coal and iron deposits. Here grew 37 percent of the country's grain harvest. In addition, Russia had to make major economic concessions which, in effect, exempted citizens of the Central Powers in the country from Communist nationalization decrees. She had to demobilize her armed forces.

No Russian government had ever surrendered so much land or granted a foreign power such privileges. The population overwhelmingly rejected the treaty and, in one historian's judgment, Lenin became the most vilified man in Europe. One of the consequences of the Brest-Litovsk Treaty was that the Left SRs, who had strenuously opposed it, withdrew from the Sovnarkom. For all practical purposes, in theory as well as practice, the government of Russia henceforth became the exclusive preserve of Communists. In addition, by taking his country out of the war at a critical stage, Lenin earned the enmity of the Allies, who felt betrayed and now faced the prospect of defeat.

Lenin has been widely credited with prophetic vision in accepting a humiliating treaty which gave him the time he needed to organize his government, and which collapsed of its own weight once Germany surrendered to the Allies on November 11, 1918. When the Bolsheviks renounced the Brest-Litovsk Treaty two days later, Lenin's stock in Bolshevik ranks rose to unprecedented heights. Nothing he had done contributed more to his reputation for infallibility; he never again had to threaten resignation to have his way.

And yet there is nothing to indicate that in pressuring his colleagues to accept the German ultimatum Lenin had foreseen Germany's defeat. Quite the contrary. In the spring and summer of 1918, he seems to have shared the optimism of the German High Command that they were about to deal the Allies a crushing defeat. Bolshevik faith in Germany's victory is evidenced by the elaborate economic and military accords that Moscow concluded with Berlin in August 1918, accords viewed by both countries as preliminary to a formal alliance (below, p. 188). On September 30, when Imperial Germany was on the verge of collapse, Lenin authorized the transfer to Berlin of assets valued at 312.5 million marks, as stipulated by the August agreement. The inescapable conclusion from this evidence is that Lenin bowed to the German *Diktat* not because he believed that Germany would not long benefit from it but because he expected Germany to win the war and wanted to be on the winning side.

The circumstances surrounding the Brest-Litovsk Treaty furnish the classic model of what was to become Soviet foreign policy for the next seventy years. Its principles may be summarized as follows:

1. The highest priority at all times is to be assigned to the retention of political power—that is, sovereign authority and control of the state apparatus over some part—no matter how small—of one's national territory. This is the irreducible minimum. No price is too high to secure it; for its sake anything and everything can be sacrificed: human lives, land and resources, national honor. The premise behind this principle is that time works for communism, for which reason whatever is given up today will be regained tomorrow.

2. Ever since Russia underwent the October Revolution, which turned her into the focal point of world socialism, her security and interests have taken precedence over the security and interests of any other country, cause, or party, including those of the "international proletariat."

3. To purchase temporary advantages, it is permissible to make peace with "imperialist" countries, but such peace must be treated as an armed truce, to be broken when the situation changes in one's favor. History teaches, Lenin said in arguing for the ratification of the Brest-Litovsk Treaty, that peace is nothing but "a breathing spell for war." As long as capitalism exists, he declared in May 1918, international agreements are but "scraps of paper." Even in periods of nominal peace, hostilities should be pursued by covert means to undermine governments with which one has signed peace agreements.

4. Politics being warfare, foreign policy must always be conducted unemotionally, with the closest attention being paid to the correlation of forces. In Lenin's words:

> We have great revolutionary experience, and from that experience we have learned that it is necessary to follow the tactics of relentless advance whenever objective conditions allow it . . . But we have to adopt the tactic of

procrastination, the slow gathering of forces when the objective conditions do not offer the possibility of making an appeal to the general relentless advance.

Yet another fundamental principle of Bolshevik foreign policy was to be revealed after the signing of the Brest-Litovsk Treaty: the principle that Bolshevik interests abroad (as at home) had to be promoted by the application of the "divide and rule" principle:

> the most circumspect, careful, cautious, skillful exploitation of every, even the smallest "crack" among one's enemies, of every conflict of interest among the bourgeoisie of the various countries, among the various group-ings or species of the bourgeoisie within individual countries . . .

Foreign Involvement

Although in time the Russian Revolution would exert an even greater influence on world history than the French, initially it attracted much less attention. This was due to the fact that unlike France, which in its day had been the leading power on the Continent—politically, militarily, as well as culturally—Russia lay on Europe's periphery. An agrarian country, half in Asia, it was treated by Europe as largely irrelevant to its own concerns: Russia's turmoil of 1917 appeared to it as marking her belated entry into the modern age rather than a serious threat to the estab-lished world order. Second, the Russian Revolution occurred in the midst of the greatest, most destructive war in history, which totally absorbed the attention of contemporaries. Today it is easy to forget to what extent that war overshadowed everything else—a war that claimed the lives of mil-lions of young men and dissipated assets accumulated over generations. The post-October events in Russia attracted attention exclusively for their potential effect on the outcome of the global conflict: for the Germans, they carried a message of hope; for the Allies, a portent of disaster.

None of the great powers had an interest in overthrowing the Bolshe-vik regime. For reasons that have been adduced, the Germans supported it in every possible way and on several occasions pulled it back from the brink of disaster. The Allies at first courted it and, when the courtship failed, tried to reactivate the eastern front with such forces as they could muster, both Russian and foreign.

Lenin was convinced that immediately after the hostilities had ceased the great powers would bury their differences and launch a concerted drive against his regime. His fears proved groundless. Only the British intervened actively on the side of the anti-Bolshevik forces, and they did so in a halfhearted manner, largely on the initiative of one man, Winston Churchill. The effort was never seriously pursued, because the forces of accommodation in a West exhausted by the World War were far stronger than those calling for intervention, and by the early 1920s the European powers would make their peace with Communist Russia.

But even if the West was not much interested in Bolshevism, the Bolsheviks had a vital interest in the West. The Bolsheviks had good reasons to believe that their Revolution would fail if it remained confined to their country. From the instant they took power they appealed to the workers of the world to rise up against their governments, backing these appeals with lavish appropriations of funds for propaganda and agitation. They involved the Germans in their domestic affairs, using them against the Allies when convenient and the Allies against the Germans whenever the situation changed. The principle, enunciated by Lenin, of exploiting all "cracks" in the "bourgeois" camp entailed constant intrusion abroad. The widespread notion of a calculated and methodical Allied "intervention" in Soviet Russia is one of the many myths that needs dispelling: there was not one foreign intervention in the Russian Revolution but many reciprocal interventions, and no one intervened abroad more zealously than the Communists themselves.

On March 23, 1918, the Germans launched their long-awaited offensive in the West. Since the armistice with Russia, Ludendorff had transferred a half-million men from the Eastern front; he was prepared to sacrifice twice that many German lives to capture Paris.

The Bolsheviks utilized the post-armistice lull to build their own army. They needed a military force to defend themselves from the anticipated capitalist crusade, but also to carry the Revolution abroad. According to Lenin, the country required an effective army because it faced a succession of wars:

> The existence of the Soviet Republic alongside the imperialist states over the long run is unthinkable. In the end, either the one or the other will triumph. And until that end will have arrived, a series of the most terrible conflicts between the Soviet Republic and the bourgeois governments is unavoidable. This means that the ruling class, the proletariat, if it only wishes to rule and is to rule, must demonstrate this [intent] also with its military organization.

But the formation of a new, Soviet army had to overcome several obstacles. The demobilized soldiers had no desire to return to the ranks. Resort to conscription would in any event produce an army manned overwhelmingly by peasants, a class the Bolsheviks viewed as hostile to their cause. The officers of the old army were considered counterrevolutionary. The preferred solution was a worker militia, but given that Russia in 1918 had only between 1 and 2 million workers, such a force could not possibly fulfill the defensive and offensive missions envisioned for it. So the Bolsheviks procrastinated. The old General Staff, raised in the spirit of unquestioning obedience to authority, went over to them almost bodily; it formed the command nucleus of the future Red Army. Moscow also pursued for a while longer negotiations with the Allies for military assistance. But none of these efforts yielded significant results, and until the autumn of 1918 the only effective force on the Bolshevik side was 35,000 Latvian riflemen who were shunted from one endangered spot to another.

In the meantime, the Allies, having given up hope of Soviet collaboration against the Germans, landed token forces on Russian territory. The first landings took place at Murmansk in March 1918 at the request of the local soviet and with Moscow's sanction. Additional forces disembarked later in Murmansk and Archangel. Their immediate mission was to defend these ports from the Germans and Finns, and to protect the stores of war material accumulated there since 1916. Their long-term, strategic assignment was to serve as the advance guard of a reconstituted Eastern Army. In April, the Japanese sent a contingent of troops to Vladivostok, ostensibly to join this inter-Allied force but in reality to establish a Japanese presence in the Russian Far East with a view toward annexation.

Moscow viewed these Allied moves, especially the Japanese initiatives, with considerable anxiety. Impressed by the successes of their spring offensive in France, it drew closer to the Germans.

Toward the end of April, Russia and Germany exchanged ambassadors. The German mission to Moscow was headed by Count Wilhelm von Mirbach, a career diplomat with previous service in St. Petersburg. His right hand, Kurt Riezler, was a young philosopher who in 1917 had been posted in Stockholm to serve as the conduit for German subsidies to the Bolsheviks. The two diplomats found the situation in Soviet Russia depressing: they cautioned Berlin not to rely exclusively on the Communists, who seemed on the verge of collapse, a situation that threatened to leave Germany without any base of support in that country. On June 3, Mirbach advised Berlin that to keep the Communists in power he needed 3 million marks a month. The Foreign Ministry acquiesced to his request, allocating his embassy 40 million marks for "Russian work." Of the 9 million the embassy actually spent, approximately one-half went to the Soviet government, which received tranches in June, July, and August; the remainder was disbursed among other groups, including the liberal government of Siberia. Riezler also established contact with the clandestine anti-Bolshevik "Right Center," made up of conservative politicians and generals who had concluded that Bolshevism presented a greater threat to Russia than did Germany. A stumbling block to closer relations with such conservative elements, however, was the Brest-Litovsk Treaty, which all the anti-Bolshevik groups wanted revised as a precondition of collaboration with the Germans.

Ioffe in Berlin took over the old Imperial Embassy, which the Germans had maintained in perfect shape since its closure on the outbreak of the war. The Soviet diplomatic representation was no ordinary embassy but rather a revolutionary outpost deep in enemy territory. It had three principal missions, all of which it successfully carried out. One was to neutralize the German generals who wanted the Bolshevik government liquidated. This Ioffe accomplished by holding out before the German business community dazzling prospects of profits in Soviet Russia. His second task was to encourage and assist revolutionary forces in Germany and neighboring countries. The third was to gather political and economic intelligence.

Ioffe was able to pursue these objectives with remarkable brazenness because he enjoyed the protection of the German Foreign Ministry, which thought it worth almost any price to keep the Bolsheviks afloat.

In his dealings with big business, Ioffe, assisted by Leonid Krasin, who had excellent German connections, urged the Germans to ignore the "maximalist" slogans emanating from Moscow: this, he assured them, was mere rhetoric. The Bolsheviks were realists who desired nothing better than good relations with Germany. To complaints that the Russians engaged in subversive propaganda, Ioffe responded that it was "the action of the Russian Communist Party and not the government." Hard-headed businessmen fell for this ploy in part because they wanted to believe it and in part because they could not conceive that anyone in his right mind could take Bolshevik slogans seriously. The Krupps, the Thyssens and the Stinneses, all future supporters of Hitler, pressured their government to maintain good relations with the new rulers of Russia in order to secure German hegemony over that country. The coalition of diplomats, industrialists, and bankers managed to neutralize the military.

At the same time, Ioffe established close links with the most extreme radical elements in Germany, exploiting his mission's diplomatic immunity to spread revolutionary propaganda and eventually supply such elements with money and even weapons. In 1919 he thus described his activities in Berlin:

> The [Embassy] directed and subsidized more than ten left-socialist parties . . . All of Germany was covered with a network of illegal revolutionary organizations: hundreds of thousands of revolutionary pamphlets and proclamations were printed and distributed every week in the rear and at the front.

According to Ioffe, some of this material was brought by couriers from Russia, but the bulk was printed in Germany, with his embassy's help.

While pursuing these subversive activities abroad, the Bolsheviks themselves faced the threat of internal subversion.

During World War I, the Russian army had captured some 50,000 to 60,000 Czech and Slovak prisoners serving in the Austrian army. For the most part, they were anti-German and anti-Hungarian in sentiment and socialist in ideology. The Provisional Government formed from them national units that fought in the June 1917 campaign. The others were kept in prisoner-of-war camps in the Ukraine. After the signing of the Brest-Litvosk Treaty, the Czechs and Slovaks wanted to leave Russia as quickly as possible from fear of being captured by the Germans or Austrians and punished as deserters. Moscow agreed, and in March 1918 contingents of prisoners, formed into a Czechoslovak Legion, began to ship eastward, toward Vladivostok, where they were to board ships bound for France. Thomas Masaryk, the head of the Czechoslovak National Council in Paris, arranged with the Bolsheviks that his troops would travel armed to defend themselves from bandits. He gave them strict orders not to meddle in internal Russian affairs.

At first the evacuation proceeded smoothly. The Czechs and Slovaks traveled in good order in well-equipped and fully armed trains. On May 14, however, in the city of Cheliabinsk, east of the Urals, an altercation occurred at a railway station between Czech and Hungarian POWs in which a Hungarian was killed. When the Cheliabinsk soviet arrested some Czechs, their comrades seized the local arsenal and demanded their release. The Cheliabinsk soviet complied.

Up to this point the Czechs and Slovaks were quite sympathetic to Russian revolutionaries, the Bolsheviks included. It was largely Trotsky's tactless behavior that changed their attitude. As soon as he learned what had happened at Cheliabinsk, Trotsky, recently appointed Commissar of War and eager to demonstrate his authority, ordered the Legion to surrender its weapons and discontinue the evacuation; its men were to join either the Red Army or "labor battalions." Resisters faced confinement in concentration camps.* A gathering of the Czech Revolutionary Army in Cheliabinsk rejected Trotsky's ultimatum. Convinced that the Bolsheviks were acting under Berlin's pressure and intended to turn them over to the Germans, they seized control of the Trans-Siberian to ensure unimpeded access to Vladivostok and evacuation to France. At the end of May and the beginning of June, the Legion captured a number of important cities along the railroad. Trotsky's inept directive, which he had no means of enforcing, turned the armed Czechs and Slovaks from tacit friends into open enemies and presented Moscow with a serious military challenge.

This challenge had also a political dimension. The area occupied by the Czechs, notably the provinces along the mid-Volga, were a stronghold of the Socialists-Revolutionaries. As soon as the Czechs had expelled the Bolsheviks, the SRs emerged into the open and formed in Samara a Committee of the Constituent Assembly, popularly known as Komuch, made up of SR deputies to the dissolved Assembly. Declaring themselves the sole legitimate government of Russia, they claimed authority over all the territories liberated by the Czechoslovak Legion. They restored civil liberties but kept in force the Bolshevik Land Decree which Lenin had copied from their own program. In areas east of the Urals, there arose another independent government that claimed authority over Siberia.

To meet these challenges, the Bolsheviks now tackled in earnest the task of forming a regular army. Ex-tsarist generals in their employ as well as French advisers had been urging them for some time to give up the idea of a volunteer worker militia and go over to general conscription. On May 29, 1918—one week after the Czechoslovak Legion had defied its orders and rebelled—Moscow announced a general mobilization of workers and miners. Two months later, all male citizens between the ages of eighteen and forty were declared liable for military service, and all officers of the old army aged twenty-six to thirty-one were ordered to register.

Such was the origin of the Red Army. Organized with the assistance of professional officers and soon commanded almost exclusively by them, in its structure and discipline it eventually modeled itself on the Imperial army. Its main innovation was the institution of political "commissars,"

---

* This seems to be the earliest mention of concentration camps in an official Soviet document.

staffed by reliable Bolsheviks, who were to ensure the officers' loyalty. On July 29, with the bluster that made him so unpopular, Trotsky assured those worried about the dependability of former tsarist officers, now relabeled "military specialists," that any officer who contemplated betraying Soviet Russia would be shot out of hand. "Next to every specialist," he said, "there should stand a commissar, one on the right and another to the left, revolver in hand." On another occasion he warned that if any officer behaved disloyally, all that would remain of him would be a "wet spot."

The Red Army quickly became the pampered child of the new regime, receiving higher pay and bread rations than did workers.

But the Red Army was only an embryo and the fate of Soviet Russia lay largely in foreign hands, especially those of Imperial Germany. The moneys which Berlin paid to Moscow helped it survive financially at a time when it had little other income, since the tax system had collapsed. The knowledge that Germany supported the Bolsheviks inhibited internal opposition. Few doubted that if Germany so chose, she could remove the Bolsheviks from power; Trotsky himself conceded that much. In the summer of 1918, the survival of the Bolshevik regime depended on Germany, or, to be more precise, on Wilhelm II.

The Kaiser received contradictory advice. The Moscow embassy joined the generals in their anti-Bolshevik stand. After the Czechoslovak rising, Mirbach and Riezler lost all faith in Lenin's government and urged Berlin to seek in Russia an alternate source of support. Things had deteriorated to the point where Riezler had to bribe the Latvians to remain in Bolshevik service, for they considered defecting. The Foreign Office disassociated itself from the views of its Moscow mission and insisted that the Bolsheviks were Germany's most dependable client because they and they alone accepted the terms of the Brest-Litovsk Treaty and because they kept Russia in permanent turmoil. A German Foreign Office memorandum thus summarized the pro-Bolshevik case:

> In regard to Great Russia, we have only one overriding interest: to promote the forces of decomposition and to keep the country weak for a long time to come . . . It is in our interest soon genuinely to normalize relations with Russia in order to seize the country's economy. The more we mix into this country's internal affairs, the wider will grow the chasm that already separates us from Russia. . . . It must not be overlooked that the Brest-Litovsk Treaty was ratified only by the Bolsheviks and not even by all of them. . . . It is, therefore, in our interest to have the Bolsheviks remain at the helm for the time being. In order to stay in power, they will, for now,

do all they can to maintain toward us the appearance of loyalty and to respect the peace. On the other hand, their leaders, being Jewish businessmen, will before long give up their theories in favor of profitable commercial and transportation deals. Here we must proceed slowly but purposefully. Russia's transport, industry, and entire national economy must fall into our hands.

Von Kühlmann, who vigorously supported this viewpoint, urged that Berlin assure the Russians it had no designs on Petrograd so as to enable them to shift the Latvian troops guarding that city to the east, to fight the Czechs.

The two opposing viewpoints were laid out before Wilhelm on June 28 by an official of the Foreign Office. The impulsive Kaiser settled on the first option presented to him, which was that of the Foreign Office. He instructed that the Russians be told they could safely withdraw troops from Petrograd to fight the Czechs and that, "without foreclosing future opportunities," support be extended to the Soviet government as the only party that accepted the Brest-Litovsk Treaty.

The immediate effect of this decision was to enable the Red command to transfer three Latvian regiments to the Eastern front, where they helped stem the Czechoslovak advance. In early September, the Latvians would recapture from the Czechs Kazan and Simbirsk: these victories, the first of their kind, would do much to boost sagging morale in the Kremlin. On Kühlmann's instructions, Riezler broke off negotiations with the Right Center and concentrated on bolstering Lenin's regime. The Kaiser's decision thus enabled the Bolsheviks to weather the most critical period in their early history. It would have cost the Germans little effort to seize Petrograd and Moscow and install a puppet Russian government, as they had done in the Ukraine. Wilhelm's ruling at the end of June ended that possibility once and for all: six weeks later, when their offensive in the west had ground to a halt, the Germans no longer had the ability to intervene in Russian affairs.

The Kaiser's action was good news for Moscow. The bad news was that the Left SRs, the Bolsheviks' only allies, were growing restless. Romantic revolutionaries, they craved excitement—the euphoria of October and the ecstasy of February 1918, when they had helped rouse the masses against the invading Germans. They treated the post-October Bolsheviks as contemptible compromisers who by signing the Brest-Litovsk Treaty had betrayed the Revolution. Their leader, Maria Spiridonova, wrote: "It is painful now . . . to realize that the Bolsheviks, with whom until now I have worked side by side, alongside whom I have

33. Maria Spiridonova, second from left.

fought on the same barricades... have adopted the policies of the Kerensky government." The Left SRs resolved to provoke a war between Soviet Russia and Germany in order to end the policy of compromises and revive the country's revolutionary ardor.

To this end they began openly to build up a military force of their own. The Cheka, busy chasing peasant "bagmen" engaged in the illicit grain trade and harassing demobilized officers, knew nothing of these preparations. Its ignorance can partly be explained by the fact that a Left SR served as deputy to Felix Dzerzhinskii, the head of the Cheka. Much of the Left SR plot was hatched in the headquarters of the security police in the Lubianka.

The Left SRs naïvely believed that if they assassinated her Ambassador, Germany would declare war on Soviet Russia and force the Bolsheviks, whom they intended to leave in power, to return to the revolutionary path. With the help of Cheka accomplices, on July 6 two Left SRs, pretending to come on government business, penetrated the German Embassy. They murdered Mirbach and fled, leaving behind the forged Cheka papers with which they had gained admission. This was a signal for a general uprising of the pro-Left SR forces in the capital. The latter seized a number of strategic points in the city but made no attempt to displace the Bolsheviks. To Dzerzhinskii, the head of the Cheka, whom they had taken prisoner, one Left SR said:

> You stand before a fait accompli. The Brest Treaty is annulled; war with Germany is unavoidable. We do not want power.... We will go underground. You can keep power, but you must stop being lackeys of Mirbach. Let Germany occupy Russia up to the Volga.

Lenin, who had every reason to believe that he had been betrayed by his security organ, ordered the Cheka dissolved. (The order was later rescinded.) As the military units stationed in Moscow showed no inclination to come to the government's aid, Lenin had to turn to the Latvians. Under the command of I. I. Vatsetis, they suppressed the rebellion the next day. Hundreds of Left SRs were arrested in Moscow and other cities. To placate the Germans, the government announced that 200 of them had been shot, among them Spiridonova. In reality, the Left SRs were treated with singular indulgence, largely from fear that if punished they would respond with a wave of terrorism against the Bolshevik leaders. Spiridonova was jailed and then freed; she spent the rest of her life in and out of prison, until her execution in 1941 in an Orel prison as the Germans were about to capture the city.

Contrary to Left SR expectations, Berlin reconciled itself to the murder of its ambassador and sent a replacement. The new envoy, Karl Helfferich, so feared for his life that he left the embassy only once during his two-week tenure.

By a remarkable coincidence, another anti-Bolshevik rebellion broke out on the very same day, July 6, in the northeastern city of Iaroslavl and two smaller towns nearby. It was the work of Boris Savinkov, the most efficient and courageous of the anti-Bolshevik conspirators. In his youth a fanatical revolutionary-terrorist, Savinkov turned patriotic with the outbreak of World War I. In 1917 he served as Kerensky's deputy and played a major role in the Kornilov Affair. Subsequently, he joined General Alekseev, the founder of the White Volunteer Army, who sent him to Soviet Russia to recruit officers and obtain financial and political assistance.*

Savinkov, an experienced conspirator, organized a secret skeletal force of 5,000 officers whose mission it was to emerge from the underground and spring into action on the approach of the Volunteer Army. He was desperately short of money and in constant dread of betrayal: in May 1918, the jilted mistress of one of his officers revealed the organization to the Cheka, with the result that more than one hundred members were arrested and later executed. Short of funds and afraid of losing his officers, Savinkov decided to strike. He initially chose Moscow as his objective but shifted to Iaroslavl out of fear of German intervention. In view

---

* The White armies, which began to take shape in the winter of 1917–18, are described in Chapter XI.

of persistent rumors that the Allies were planning additional landings in the north of Russia, he selected the middle Volga as the locale of his insurrection because from there he could establish contact with the Czechoslovak Legion as well as Allied troops. He subsequently claimed that Allied representatives had promised him that if he held out for four days a force from Archangel would relieve him, following which the combined Anglo-French-Russian army would advance on Moscow. This statement cannot be confirmed from any archival source and is rather suspect. More likely, Savinkov counted on his success inspiring an anti-Communist rebellion throughout Russia.

At 2 a.m. on July 6, Savinkov's deputy raised the banner of rebellion in Iaroslavl; two other nearby cities rose shortly afterward. The latter uprisings were quickly suppressed, but Iaroslavl held out for sixteen days. On its recapture, the Communists executed 350 participants, most of them officers. Savinkov managed to escape. For a while he served in Kolchak's White Army, and after its fall, made his way to the West. There he organized various anti-Communist plots, none of which succeeded. After Lenin's death, he was lured back to Russia by a spurious anti-Communist organization created by the successor to the Cheka, the GPU. He was promptly arrested and tried. Because of his cooperation with the authorities, his death sentence was commuted to ten years' imprisonment. He died the following year under suspicious circumstances, allegedly by his own hand, but probably at the hands of the GPU.

For Kurt Riezler, who took charge of the German Embassy before the arrival of Mirbach's replacement, these rebellions spelled the demise of the Bolshevik regime. On July 19, he wired Berlin: "The Bolsheviks are dead. The corpse lives [!] because the grave diggers cannot agree who is to bury it." He initiated talks with the commander of the Latvian riflemen, Vatsetis, who gave him to understand that, if promised amnesty, his men were ready to abandon the Bolsheviks and return home, to German-occupied Latvia. He also resumed negotiations with the Right Center. But Berlin vetoed these plans and kept faith with Lenin.

The mood in the Kremlin was gloomy enough when it learned, on August 1, that a British naval force had appeared off Archangel and landed 8,500 men. More than half of this force consisted of Americans whom President Wilson had sent reluctantly, bowing to British pressure, to help evacuate the Czechoslovak Legion by the shorter, northern route. British General F. C. Poole, who commanded the force, had orders to resist German "influence and penetration," to help Russians willing to fight alongside the Allies, and to link up with the Czechoslovak Legion. Fifteen thousand additional troops disembarked at Murmansk. American troops also landed in Vladivostok. None of these forces were to interfere in internal Russian matters, let alone seek to overthrow the existing regime. Their mission was to reactivate the eastern front, for which purpose Allied military experts calculated, 30,000 men would suffice.

But this was not known in Moscow. Interpreting the landings as the vanguard of a massive Allied intervention, the Kremlin lost its head and threw itself into German arms. On August 1, the first day of Allied operations off Archangel, George Chicherin, the Commissar of Foreign Affairs, paid a visit to Helfferich, the new German Ambassador. He told him that he had come directly from a cabinet meeting to request, on its behalf, German military intervention in Russia. This was to take two forms: (1) German military units were to protect Petrograd from possible Allied assault and from there advance on Murmansk and Archangel to expel the Allied expeditionary forces; and (2) German units in the Ukraine were to launch an offensive against the Whites' Volunteer Army.

Berlin accepted these proposals. On August 27, the two countries signed a Supplemental Treaty that spelled out in detail the economic provisions of the Brest-Litovsk Treaty. Soviet Russia undertook to pay Germany large reparations to compensate her for losses suffered as a result of measures taken against her nationals by both the tsarist and Soviet governments, as well as for the costs of the upkeep of Russian prisoners of war. The various privileges of German citizens and corporations in Russia were confirmed.

But the Supplemental Treaty also contained three secret clauses that were made public only years later. Germany met the Russian request of active military intervention against the Allies in Murmansk and against the Volunteer Army. In addition, she also committed herself to expelling from the oil center of Baku in Azerbaijan a British force that had occupied it in early August. None of these operations materialized because Germany collapsed before they could get underway.

At the beginning of October 1918, when Berlin requested that President Wilson use his good offices to arrange an armistice, the international situation changed radically. Moscow's friends in Berlin lost their positions because the new government desired to distance itself from the Bolsheviks. By this time, Ioffe and his staff were openly working for a German revolution. As he later boasted, his embassy's work increasingly assumed the character of decisive revolutionary preparations for an armed uprising. Apart from conspiratorial groups of Spartacists, in Germany, and specifically in Berlin, there existed since the January [1918] strike—of course, illegally—soviets of workers' deputies . . . With these soviets the embassy maintained constant communication . . . the striving of the German proletariat to arm itself was entirely legitimate and sensible and the embassy assisted it in every way.

By now even the German Foreign Office had had its fill of Soviet interference and in early November ordered the Soviet Embassy closed. Before his departure, Ioffe left a member of the Independent Social-Democratic Party and a virtual resident of the Soviet mission 500,000 marks and 150,000 rubles to supplement the 10 million rubles previously allocated "for the needs of the German revolution."

On November 13, two days after the armistice on the western front went into effect, Moscow unilaterally abrogated both the Brest-Litovsk Treaty and the Supplemental Treaty. As part of the Versailles settlement, the Allies also compelled Germany to renounce the Brest-Litovsk Treaty.

The Russian Revolution was never a local event confined to its country of origin: from the moment the February Revolution erupted, it became internationalized, and, this for two reasons.

Russia had been a major theater of war. Its unilateral withdrawal from the war affected the most vital interests of both belligerent blocs. As long as the hostilities continued, therefore, neither side could be indifferent to what happened to Russia. The Bolsheviks contributed to their country's involvement in the conflict by playing the belligerent camps against each other. In the spring of 1918, they discussed with the Allies the formation on their territory of an anti-German multinational army; they agreed to the occupation of Murmansk; and they invited help in building an army of their own. In the fall, they requested German military intervention to recapture the northern ports and crush the Volunteer Army. Time and again, Germany had to intervene, with political support and money, to prevent the Bolshevik regime from collapsing. According to Riezler, who stood at the center of these events, his country intervened on three separate occasions to save Lenin's government. Helfferich, referring to the Soviet regime's crisis in the summer of 1918, conceded in his memoirs that "the strongest supporter of the Bolshevik regime during this critical time, if unconsciously and unintentionally, was the German Government." In view of these facts, it cannot be seriously maintained that foreign powers "intervened" in Russia in 1917–18 for the purpose of toppling the Bolsheviks from power. They intervened, first and foremost, in order to tip the balance of power on the western front in their favor, either by renewing the fighting in Russia, in the case of the Allies or by keeping it quiescent, in the case of the Central Powers. The Bolsheviks actively participated in this foreign involvement and invited help now from this party, now from that, depending on their transient interests. German "intervention," which they welcomed and solicited, more than likely saved them from suffering the fate of the Provisional Government.*

Second, the Bolsheviks from the outset declared national borders in the era of social revolution and global class war to be irrelevant. They appealed to foreign nationals to rise and overthrow their governments; they allocated state funds for this purpose; and where they were in a position to do so, which for the time being was mainly Germany, actively promoted revolution. By challenging the legitimacy of all foreign governments, they invited all foreign governments to challenge the legitimacy of their own. If in fact no power chose to avail itself of that right in 1917–18, it was because none of them had an interest in so doing. The Germans found that the Bolsheviks served their purposes and propped them up whenever they ran into trouble; the Allies were busy fighting for their lives. The question posed by the historian Richard K. Debo—"How . . . did the Soviet government, bereft of significant military force in the midst of what was until then mankind's most destructive war, succeed in surviving the first year of revolution?"—answers itself: this most destructive war completely overshadowed Russian events and robbed its participants of any interest in diverting forces to topple the Soviet government.

One further thing needs to be said about foreign involvement on Russian soil in 1917–18. In all the talk of what the Allies did *in* Russia, which really was not much, it is usually forgotten what they did *for* Russia, which was a great deal. After Russia had reneged on her commitments and left them to fight the Central Powers on their own, the Allies suffered immense human and material losses. Once Russia dropped out, the Germans withdrew from the inactive eastern front enough divisions to augment their effectives in the west by nearly one-fourth. These reinforcements enabled them to mount a ferocious offensive. In the great battles on the western front in the spring and summer of 1918—St.

---

* Allied intervention in 1919, after the armistice, had, of course, different motives. This subject will be discussed in Chapter XI.

Quentin, the Lys, the Aisne, the Marne, Château-Thierry—the British, French, and Americans lost hundreds of thousands of men. This sacrifice finally brought Germany to her knees. And the defeat of Germany, to which they contributed nothing, not only enabled the Soviet government to annul the Brest-Litovsk Treaty and to recover most of the lands it had been forced to surrender under its terms but also saved Russia from being converted into a colony, a kind of Eurasian Africa, the fate Imperial Germany had intended for her.

WAR COMMUNISM

IX

The Creation of a Command Economy

Shortly after Lenin's death in 1924, Trotsky recalled that on taking power Lenin wrote:

> "The triumph of socialism in Russia [required] a certain interval of time, *no less than a few months*." At present [Trotsky continued] such words seem completely incomprehensible: was this not a slip of the pen, did he not mean to speak of a few years or decades? But no: this was not a slip of the pen . . . I recall very distinctly that in the first period, at Smolnyi, at meetings of the Council of People's Commissars, Lenin invariably repeated that we shall have socialism in half a year and become the mightiest state.

This utopian notion of Lenin's was grounded in the belief, shared by all socialists, that the capitalist system, driven as it is by private profit, is not only unjust but irrational and hence inherently unproductive. Socialism, by allocating human and material resources in a rational manner, with regard to their maximal utility, should be able to attain unprecedented levels of efficiency.

This was the reasoning that lay behind the economic policies of the Bolsheviks between 1918 and 1921 known as "War Communism." Later, after they had caused a catastrophic decline in Russia's economy, these policies would be rationalized as emergency measures necessitated by the Civil War: the expression "War Communism" was coined for this purpose in 1921. But earlier statements of Bolshevik leaders leave no doubt that the needs of the Civil War were at best a secondary consideration: indeed, some of the measures introduced under War Communism impeded the war effort. We have it on the authority of Trotsky that the objective of War Communism was "realizing genuine communism." And in October 1921, when the attempt failed and had to be abandoned, Lenin frankly admitted:

> We counted—or, perhaps it will be more correct to say, we assumed without adequate calculation—on the [ability] of the proletarian state to organize by direct command the state production and distribution of goods in a Communist manner in a country of small peasants. Life has demonstrated our mistake.

War Communism, which reached its apogee in the winter of 1920–21, when the Civil War was over, involved a number of sweeping measures designed to place the entire economy of Russia—her labor force as well as her productive capacity and distribution network—under the exclusive management of the state, or, more precisely, the Communist Party. The process of expropriation began with real estate. The Land Decree of October 26, 1917, deprived non-peasants of their landed properties. A decree nationalizing urban real estate followed. In January 1918, the Communist government repudiated all state debts, domestic as well as foreign. A decree of May 1918 abolished inheritance, and another, issued the following month, nationalized industry. These measures did away with the private ownership of capital and other productive assets; they implemented the dictum of Marx and Engels that the quintessence of communism was the abolition of private property.

The specific provisions of War Communism fall under five headings:

1. The nationalization of the means of production and transport;
2. The liquidation of private commerce through the nationalization of retail and wholesale trade, and its replacement by a government-controlled distribution system;
3. The abolition of money as a unit of exchange and accounting in favor of state-regulated barter;
4. The imposition on the entire economy of a single plan;
5. The introduction of compulsory labor for all able-bodied male adults, and, on occasion, also women and children.

War Communism had several sources of inspiration. There was the example of Germany's War Socialism, an innovative regulation of the nation's economy that enabled her to withstand a tight blockade and hold out for four years against overwhelming odds. There were the theories of certain socialist authorities who thought the high level of ownership concentrated in the hands of banks made it possible, by the simple device of bank nationalization, to lay the foundations of a socialist economy. And there was the model of the medieval Russian patrimonial state, that, though long gone, left a compelling cultural legacy: to the mass of Russians, state ownership of the economy seemed more natural than abstract property rights and the whole complex of phenomena labeled "capitalism."

Lenin originally thought he could attain his economic objectives with the cooperation of big business. His early plans called for "State Capitalism," modeled on the example of wartime Germany. Under this system the capitalist sector in industry would be left intact but forced to work for the state, which would thus reap the benefits of advanced methods of capitalist organization and technology. But this proposal ran into the opposition of Left Communists, influential party members who denounced it as opportunistic. Lenin might have overcome their opposition were it not for the highly unpopular Brest-Litovsk Treaty, which for the Left Communists represented a betrayal of the Revolution. To appease them, Lenin abandoned State Capitalism in favor of War Communism, but he did so with considerable misgivings.

The theorists and architects of War Communism had only a nodding acquaintance with the discipline of economics and none whatever with business management. Their knowledge of the subject derived exclusively from the reading of socialist literature. Not one of them had run an enterprise or earned a ruble from manufacture or trade. This inexperience gave their imagination unlimited scope. What Sukhanov said of Iurii Larin, the most influential of Lenin's early economic advisers, applied to all of them: "a poor cavalryman who knew no obstacles to the leaps of his fantasy, a cruel experimenter, a specialist in all branches of state administration, a dilettante in all his specialties." That such rank amateurs would undertake to turn upside down the economy of tens of millions, subjecting it to innovations never attempted anywhere even on a small scale, says something of the judgment of the people who in October 1917 seized power in Russia.

Their irresponsibility was nowhere more evident than in their obstinate attempts to introduce a moneyless economy.

Marx wrote a great deal of sophisticated nonsense about the nature and function of money, defining it variously as "the alienated ability of mankind," "crystallized labor," and a "monster" that disengages itself from man, its creator, and comes to dominate him. These ideas had a natural appeal to radical intellectuals who neither had money nor knew how to earn it but craved the power and pleasures it affords. In their zeal to liquidate everything associated with capitalism, they overlooked the fact that some unit of measurement, whether or not it is called "money," has to exist in every society which practices the division of labor and the exchange of goods and services.

Under the spell of these ideas, the Bolsheviks both overrated and underrated the role of money. They overrated it in respect to "capitalist" economies, which they viewed as totally dominated by financial institutions. They underrated it in respect to "socialist" economies, which they believed could dispense with it. In the words of two authoritative Bolshevik writers, Nicholas Bukharin and Evgenii Preobrazhenskii, "Communist society will know nothing of money." The Soviet Commissar of Finance on one occasion declared his job redundant: "Finance should not exist in a socialist community and I must, therefore, apologize for speaking on the subject."

The Bolsheviks tried, in the first instance, to abolish money by deliberately fostering an inflation that would render it worthless. This they did by issuing banknotes as fast as the printing presses could turn them out. They used what came to be known as "colored paper" to extract grain from the peasants and to pay the salaries of the expanding ranks of government employees. But they considered banknotes a temporary expedient that would be abandoned once agriculture had been collectivized and the nation's labor force received pay entirely in goods and services.

At the time of the Bolshevik coup, paper money circulating in Russia amounted to 19.6 billion rubles. The bulk of it consisted of Imperial rubles, popularly known as *Nikolaevki*. There were also notes issued by the Provisional Government called *Kerenki*—simple talons, printed on one side, without serial number, signature, or name of issuer, displaying only the ruble value and a warning of punishment for counterfeiting. After taking over the State Bank and Treasury, the Bolsheviks continued to print Kerenkis without altering their appearance. Until February 1919, they produced no currency of their own, presumably because they believed that the population, especially the peasants, would refuse to accept it. Since the tax system had broken down completely, the Bolsheviks printed banknotes in ever larger quantities. By January 1919, Soviet

Russia had in circulation 61.3 billion rubles, two-thirds of them newly issued Kerenkis. The following month, the government produced the first Soviet money, called "accounting tokens." This new currency circulated alongside Nikolaevkis and Kerenkis, but at a deep discount to them. In early 1919, inflation, though increasingly severe, still fell quite short of the grotesque dimensions that lay ahead. Compared with 1917, prices had gone up fifteen times.

Then the dam burst. In May 1919, the State Bank was authorized to print as much money as in its judgment the national economy required. Henceforth, the manufacture of "colored paper" became Soviet Russia's largest and perhaps only growth industry. In the course of 1919, the quantity of money in circulation nearly quadrupled (to 225 billion). In 1920 it nearly quintupled (to 1.2 trillion), and in the following year it increased more than thirteen times (to 16 trillion). The nadir came in 1922, when banknotes in circulation attained nearly 2 quadrillion.

Paper money became virtually worthless except for the Imperial rubles, which were hoarded. But since people could not carry on without some unit to determine value, they resorted to money substitutes, most commonly bread and salt. If the price of goods, in ruble terms, in 1913 is taken as 1.0, the corresponding figure for the end of 1922 was 100 million.

The Left Communists exulted. At the Tenth Party Congress, held in March 1921, before inflation had reached its apogee, Preobrazhenskii boasted that whereas the paper "assignats" issued by the French revolutionaries had depreciated 500 times, the Soviet ruble had already fallen to 1/20,000th of its value: "This means," he said, "that we have beaten the French Revolution 40 to 1."

Students of economic history had more than once demonstrated that money was an indispensable adjunct of all economic activity, capitalist as well as socialist. The Bolsheviks eventually discovered the truth of this observation. Their gravest problem with a moneyless economy was settling accounts among the nationalized enterprises. They took various measures to cope with this difficulty, but none worked. In the end, in 1921–22, with the return to more conventional economic practices under the New Economic Policy, they would introduce a conventional currency based on gold; The vision of a moneyless economy would be abandoned forever.

The new regime had no more success with economic planning. In March 1918, Lenin spoke of the need to transform "the whole of the state economic mechanism into a single huge machine, into an economic organism that will work in such a way as to enable hundreds of millions of people to be guided by a single plan." According to Trotsky:

> The socialist organization of the economy begins with the liquidation of the market, and that means the liquidation of its regulator—the "free" play of the laws of supply and demand. The inevitable result—namely the subordination of production to the needs of society—must be achieved by the *unity of the economic plan*, which, in principle, covers all the branches of production.

To formulate and implement an economic plan, the Party created in December 1917, a Supreme Council of the National Economy. Subordinated to the Sovnarkom, it was to enjoy the same monopoly in regard to the country's economy that the Communist Party enjoyed in the realm of politics. The intention was to make it a kind of universal cartel to oversee human as well as material resources and employ them in the most efficient manner. Its authority, however, turned out to be largely fictitious. For one thing, agriculture, the country's principal source of productive wealth, although nominally nationalized, was managed not by the state but by the peasant-cultivators. Second, Soviet Russia had always had a black market caused by shortages of consumer goods and unrealistic pricing policies. The influence of the Supreme Economic Council was confined to industry, nearly all of which had been nationalized under War Communism. The process, initially random, was systematized with a decree of June 28, 1918, which ordered the nationalization, without recompense, of industrial enterprises and railroad companies with capital of 1 million rubles or more. The managerial staffs of these industries were ordered to remain in their posts under the threat of severe penalties. Gradually smaller businesses were subjected to the same treatment, and by the fall of 1920, the Council nominally oversaw 37,000 enterprises with a work force of 2 million; 13.9 percent of these enterprises had a single employee and nearly half lacked mechanical equipment. The Supreme Economic Council—the "trust of trusts"—generated an immense bureaucracy. It was subdivided into agencies organized vertically (functionally) and horizontally (territorially). The vertical organizations, trusts called *glavki* or *tsentry*, modeled on similar German wartime organizations, assumed charge of specific branches of industry. They bore melodious acronyms, such as Glavlak, Glavsol, and Glavbum, for the paint, salt and paper industries, respectively. In addition, the Council had a network of provincial branches. The organizational chart of the Council resembled a celestial map on which the Presidium represented the sun and the *glavki* with their regional agencies the planets and their moons. The huge staff, much of it non-Bolshevik, attracted intellectuals whom it offered jobs that demanded no political commitment and made them feel they were serving not the regime but the people. One example of bureaucratic featherbedding was the Benzene Trust (Glavanil), which had on its payroll 50 officials to supervise a single plant employing 150 workers. Of necessity, the regime had to engage in these positions administrators and technical specialists who before the Revolution had worked in the same industries as owners or managers. In the fall of 1919, one observer noted that at the head of many Moscow *glavki* and *tsentry*

> sit former employees and responsible officials and managers of business, and the unprepared visitor . . . who is personally acquainted with the former commercial and industrial world would be surprised to see previous owners of big leather factories sitting in Glavkhozh [the leather trust], big manufacturers in the central textile organization, and so on.

Abroad, this gigantic enterprise of "socialist construction" made a great impression. Soviet propaganda in the West spoke glowingly of the "rationalization" of Russian industry, but it stressed intent rather than performance. Inside Russia, it was frankly admitted that the entire undertaking had accomplished next to nothing. In 1921, Trotsky estimated that "at best" 5–10 percent of industry had been successfully centralized. And in *Pravda*'s blunt words of late 1920, "there is no economic plan." The situation described by a Soviet economist in November 1918 held equally true two years later:

> Not a single *glavk* or *tsentr* disposes of adequate and exhaustive data which would enable it to proceed with the genuine regulation of the country's industry and production. Dozens of organizations carry out parallel and identical work of collecting similar information, with the result that they gather totally dissimilar data . . . The accounting is conducted inaccurately, and sometimes up to 80 and 90 percent of the inventoried items escape the control of the relevant organization. The items which are unaccounted for become the object of wild and unrestrained speculation, passing from hand to hand dozens of times until they finally reach the consumer.

The Bolsheviks had more success in overcoming the managerial anarchy resulting from the introduction during 1917–18, with their blessing, of "workers' control." The collegiate manner of administering industrial enterprises under which inexperienced workers and trade-union officials enjoyed a decisive voice bore a great deal of responsibility for the drastic decline of industrial productivity under War Communism. As early as the spring of 1918, Lenin and Trotsky spoke of the need to entrust executive authority to individual managers. The workers, however, resisted such a change, for they came to regard "workers' control" as one the great achievements of the Revolution. With the end of the Civil War, the government could disregard their protests and by late 1921, nine out of ten Soviet factories had chief executive officers, many of them holdovers from the old regime.

Still, no administrative measures could slow the relentless decline of industrial productivity caused by party meddling, economic hardship confronting the workforce, and lack of incentives. There are various indexes of this decline. Overall large-scale industrial production, compared with that of 1913, fell by 82 percent. Taking 1913 production as 100, the output of coal had declined by 1920 to 27.0, that of iron to 2.4, cotton yarn to 5.1, and petroleum to 42.7. The productivity of the Russian worker (measured in constant rubles) had dropped to 26. The number of employed industrial workers, with 1918 taken as 100, was down in 1921 to 49. In sum, under War Communism, the Russian "proletariat" declined by one-half, industrial output by three-quarters, and industrial productivity by 70 percent. Surveying the wreckage, Lenin in 1921 raged: "What is the proletariat? It is the class engaged in large-scale industry. And where is large-scale industry? What kind of a proletariat is this? Where is your [!] industry? Why is it idle?" The answer to these rhetorical questions was that the utopian programs which Lenin had approved had all but destroyed Russian industry and reduced by one half Russia's industrial labor force. But during this time of rapid deindustrialization, the expenses of maintaining the bureaucracy in charge of industry grew by leaps and bonds: the personnel of the Supreme Economic Council expanded 100-fold—from 318 employees in March 1918 to 30,000 in 1921.

A central plank of War Communism was the liquidation of the market—the institution that, according to one Communist theorist, constituted "the nidus of infection from which constantly ooze the germs of capitalism." To Marxists, the market is the heart of the capitalist economy, as money is its lifeblood. The choking off of the free exchange of products and services, therefore, constituted a central plank of Bolshevik economic policy which they doggedly pursued in disregard of its obvious drawbacks. The elimination of the free market and the centralization, under state auspices, of distribution were not, as is often erroneously asserted, responses to shortages caused by the Revolution and the Civil

War but initiatives directed against the capitalist system; it is they that caused the shortages.

According to Communist intentions the distribution of commodities was to be concentrated in the hands of the Commissariat of Supply, or Komprod. Komprod collected and distributed such foodstuffs as the government managed to extract from the peasantry. It was also supposed to receive for purposes of distribution and barter other consumer goods. For distribution, Komprod relied partly on its own outlets but mainly on the network of pre-revolutionary cooperatives, which the Bolsheviks retained with some reluctance after nationalizing them and removing from their directing staffs SRs and Mensheviks. All inhabitants of a given area were required to join "consumer communes," which upon the presentation of ration cards would provide them with food and other necessities. These cards came in several categories, the most generous of which were issued to workers in heavy industry; members of the "bourgeoisie" received at best one-quarter of a worker's ration and often nothing.* The system lent itself to no end of abuses: in Petrograd in 1918, for example, one-third more ration cards were issued than there were inhabitants, and in 1920, the Commissariat of Supply distributed ration cards to 21.9 million urban residents, whereas they actually numbered only 12.3 million.

In the words of Milton Friedman, the more significant an economic theory, "the more unrealistic the assumption." The Soviet attempts to monopolize trade amply corroborated this aphorism. Instead of eliminating the market, War Communism split it in two: a state sector, which sold at nominal prices or distributed—free of charge—consumer goods by ration cards, and, alongside it, an illicit private sector, which followed the laws of supply and demand. To the astonishment of Bolshevik theoreticians, the more the nationalized sector expanded, the larger loomed what one of them called its "irremovable shadow," the free sector. Indeed, the free sector battened on the state sector, because a large part of the consumer goods the workers purchased at token prices or received gratis found its way to the black market.

The government inaugurated free public services in October 1920, with a decree exempting Soviet institutions from paying for the use of telegraph, telephone, and mail; the following year, these services were made available free of charge to all citizens. Beginning in January 1921, residents

---

* Possession of a card entitling the holder to the lowest ration served the Cheka as a means of identifying members of the "bourgeoisie." They were the natural objects of terror and extortion.

of nationalized apartments no longer had to pay rent. In the winter of 1920–21, Komprod was estimated to have assumed responsibility for supplying, free or at nominal cost, the basic needs of 38 million people.

Obviously such generosity was possible only as long as the new regime had at its disposal assets inherited from tsarism. It could dispense with rents because it neither repaired existing residences nor built new ones. At the height of War Communism, the government repaired and constructed a mere 2,601 buildings out of a half million. It could distribute food for next to nothing because it appropriated supplies from its producers for next to nothing. Clearly, such a situation could not continue forever, as buildings crumbled and peasants refused to grow surplus food.

In the meantime, the private sector burgeoned. The bulk of the food consumed by the urban population under War Communism came from the illegal free market, supplied by peasant "bagmen" who braved the Cheka to sell their produce directly to the consumer. It has been ascertained that of the foodstuffs consumed in Russian cities in the winter of 1919–20, as measured by their caloric value, the free market furnished between 66 and 80 percent. The government thus found itself in the absurd situation in which strict enforcement of its rules against private trade would have caused the urban population to starve to death. It had no choice, therefore, but to tolerate the numerous black markets that sprouted in all the cities, where goods were sold at negotiated prices, making a mockery of its resolution to abolish, once and for all, the laws of supply and demand.

In October 1917, the Bolsheviks had seized power in Petrograd in the name of the "proletariat." This being the case, one might have expected them to immediately set about improving if not the economic condition of workers, then at least their social and legal status. In actuality, they deprived Russian workers of all the rights they had gained under tsarism, including the rights to elect their union officials and to strike.

Obviously a regimented economy with central planning of production and state monopoly of commerce could not coexist with a free market in labor. Labor, too, had to be regimented. Trotsky, who often spelled out what Lenin thought, put the matter as follows: "One may say that man is rather a lazy creature. As a general rule, he strives to avoid work. . . . The only way to attract the labor force required for economic tasks is to introduce *compulsory labor service*."

Before the Revolution, the Bolsheviks, in common with other socialists, idealized the industrial worker as a creature endowed with unique moral qualities. Political responsibility quickly dispelled these illusions: the worker turned out to be neither better nor worse than anyone else, and just as concerned with his personal well-being. At the Eleventh Party Congress (March 1922), Lenin went so far as to deny that Russia even had a "proletariat" in the true sense of the word, insinuating that most of the employees of Russian factories took jobs to avoid military service. In response to which Alexander Shliapnikov, the most prominent Bolshevik of worker origin, congratulated Lenin on "being the vanguard of a nonexistent class."

The regime introduced compulsory labor for the entire population. For the bourgeoisie, this spelled servitude in work battalions formed to carry out disagreeable or dangerous tasks with execution hanging over its head as punishment for shirking. For workers and others with technical skills, it meant mobilization for state service. Drafted workers were sent, like soldiers, wherever they were needed without regard for their personal preferences. The Commissariat of Labor stated in 1922 that it "supplied labor according to plan and, consequently, without taking into account the individual peculiarities or wishes of the worker. . . ."

In a regime based on compulsory labor, free trade unions were, of course, an anomaly. Their abolition was justified on the grounds that since Soviet Russia was a "worker's state," the worker could have no interests distinct from those of the state; in obeying the state, he obeyed, in effect, himself, even if he happened to think otherwise. From this premise it followed that the function of unions was to serve the state. This is how Trotsky defined their proper role:

> In the socialist state under construction, trade unions are needed not to struggle for better working conditions—this is the task of the social and political organization as a whole—but to organize the working class for the purpose of production: to educate, discipline, allocate, collect, attach individual categories [of workers] and individual workers to their jobs for a set period: in a word, hand in hand with the government, in an authoritative manner, to bring workers into the framework of a single economic plan.

The Factory Committees, once a basis of Communist strength, gradually faded from the picture as professional specialists assumed managerial responsibility. Trade unions, in which the Bolsheviks had to compete with the Mensheviks, survived but they no longer represented their members. Treated as organs of the state, they lost the right to elect officials: as in all other branches of the administration, these were appointed by the Party. They also lost the right to strike, which was declared redundant on the grounds that it made no sense for workers to strike against themselves.

The Left Communists could not fail to realize that their ambitious economic plans had failed: instead of raising productivity to unprecedented heights, War Communism had reduced it to levels that threatened Russia's very survival. They were not disheartened, however. Bukharin, a leading Left Communist, boasted that War Communism performed a positive role in that it thoroughly demolished the legacy of capitalism, clearing the way for communism. Others argued that its failures were due to the maintenance of a dual economy under which agriculture remained in private hands and the management of the economy was entrusted to "bourgeois specialists." The remedy was to collectivize agriculture and train cadres of proletarian specialists who would make it possible to proceed in earnest with the construction of socialism.

But whatever the explanation or excuse, two facts were indisputable. Soviet Russia had lived during her first three years largely on inherited capital, capital that had been dissipated by the end of 1920. And her economy had suffered, in the words of L. Kritsman, one of the architects of War Communism and its first historian, a calamity "unparalleled in the history of mankind."

The War Against the Village

Perhaps the greatest paradox of the October coup d'état was that it sought to introduce a "dictatorship of the proletariat" in a country in which industrial workers (including self-employed artisans) constituted at most 2 percent of those gainfully employed, while 75 to 80 percent of the population consisted of peasants. And, as we have noted, peasants, in the judgment of Marxists, were a "petty bourgeois" class, inimical to the "proletariat." This fact and this perception ensured that the Communists would have to govern not by consent but by coercion.

Although for tactical reasons, before and during 1917, Lenin had encouraged peasant land seizures, once in power he was quite determined to prevent the Russian peasantry from turning into what it had been in Europe—namely, a conservative force and a bulwark of the "counterrevolution." Over the long run, the only way to achieve this objective was by means of collectivization, which would abolish both private and communal landholding and transform peasants into state employees. *Pravda* in November 1918 predicted that the so-called "middle peasantry," that is, that vast majority of peasants who neither availed themselves of the labor of others nor sold their own labor—would be dragged into collective farms "kicking and screaming" as soon as the new regime was in a position to do so.

Until then, in Lenin's view, it was necessary to (1) assert state control over the food supply by means of forced exactions of produce and a strictly implemented monopoly on the grain trade; and (2) insert Communist power bases into the countryside. These objectives entailed nothing less than a declaration of war on the village. Such a war the Bolsheviks launched in the summer of 1918. The campaign against the peasantry, virtually ignored in both Communist and Western historiography, constituted a critical phase in the Bolshevik conquest of Russia. Lenin himself attached to it the greatest importance: he felt that it ensured that his Revolution, unlike all the previous ones, would not stop halfway and then slide back into "reaction."

By the spring of 1918, the peasants had distributed among themselves virtually all the private, noncommunal land—not only that belonging to landlords, private investors, the church and the monasteries, but also that acquired by fellow peasants who had taken advantage of the Stolypin legislation to set up private farms. As a rule, the communes would not share their loot with peasants from other districts, preferring, if they had an excess, to leave it in the possession of owners for future expropriation.

Their acquisitions, although not negligible, fell far short of expectations. Before the Revolution, peasants had envisioned obtaining from a nationwide repartition anywhere from 5 to 15 hectares. As best as can be determined, they actually obtained, on the average, 0.4 hectares, or one acre of arable per communal adult. These acquisitions were very unequally distributed, since private landholding was more prevalent in some parts of the country—essentially, the borderlands—than in others. 53 percent of the communes gained nothing. Of the remainder, some received large increments, others minuscule ones. The peasants, skeptical that the land they had appropriated was really theirs, since it did not come from the Tsar, its rightful owner, kept it apart from their traditional allotments or turned it over to landless peasants if forced by the authorities to share the loot with them.

The Soviet regime would later boast that it had distributed to the peasants, free of charge, 23 million hectares of arable land. In reality, the handout was neither so large nor free. Before the Revolution the peasants had accumulated sizable savings, some of which they deposited in government banks and some of which they kept at home. By contemporary estimates, this money amounted to 12–13 billion rubles. Although deposits in state savings banks were exempt from the government's nationalization decrees, they were wiped out, along with the hoards kept at home, by inflationary policies, which reduced them to virtually nothing. If these losses are taken into account, the peasantry paid 600 pre–1918 rubles for the average allotment of one acre. Before the Revolution, a parcel of this size would have cost 64.4 rubles.

Some peasants also paid for the new allotments in another way—namely, in the loss of private holdings. Approximately one-third of the land held in private possession before the Revolution belonged to peasants and Cossacks. Most of it was appropriated by the communes. In 1927, on the eve of collectivization, 95.3 percent of the country's land was held communally; only 3.4 percent remained in private ownership. (The remaining 1.3 percent belonged to state-run collectives.)

In view of these facts, it is misleading to claim that the Russian peasantry gained from the Revolution, free of charge, large quantities of agricultural land. Its gains were neither free nor generous. The rural population must not be treated as a homogeneous entity: the term "Russian peasantry" is an abstraction that covers millions of individuals, some of whom had succeeded, by dint of industry, thrift, or business sense, in amassing capital which they held in cash or invested in land. All this cash and nearly all this land they now lost. Once these factors are taken into account, it becomes clear that the peasant greatly overpaid for the land that he had seized under the Communists.

The rise in prices on agricultural produce, which began during World War I and continued at an accelerated pace after the February Revolution, encouraged peasants to withhold much of their surplus from the market, for they expected to obtain still higher returns later. The Provisional Government tried to ensure the supply of food to the cities by passing a law that required the peasant to turn all surplus grain at fixed prices over to the state. The law remained a dead letter until the Bolsheviks came to power; it was one of the very few pieces of pre-October legislation which they kept in force. The prices they paid for the surplus grain, however, became increasingly irrelevant due to shortages and inflation: thus in August 1918, the official tariff allowed approximately one ruble per kilogram of grain, whereas on the free market it fetched eighteen rubles in Moscow and twenty-six in Petrograd. A similar disparity between fixed and free-market prices affected other staples, such as meat and potatoes, which became controlled commodities in January 1919. The peasant responded to this policy both by hoarding his produce and curtailing his acreage.

In the course of 1918, Moscow introduced forced exactions of grain. In practice, this meant that bands of armed men invaded the countryside to scour for food: they confiscated everything that they chose to declare as "surplus"—that is, in theory, whatever the peasant had left after feeding his family and cattle and providing for seed. The norms were entirely arbitrary. The "food detachments," acting on the assumption that the peasant concealed his surplus, took whatever they could lay their hands on: some of it they carted to government collection points; the rest they divided among themselves.

This policy acquired a systematic character in May, when the Kremlin made up its mind that the time had come to conquer the Great Russian village. For all practical purposes, the countryside had remained outside the reach of the Communist Party, which had no cells there to convey its orders and no rural soviets to implement them. A survey conducted in 1919 indicated that there were only 1,585 Communists in the rural districts of central Russia. Behind the campaign against the village lay a complex set of motives—political, social, and economic—although to gain the support of the urban population, stress was placed almost exclusively on the economic aspect—namely, the need to force the kulaks, or rich peasants, to disgorge their hoards of food.

Food shortages in the cities had, indeed, assumed alarming dimensions. The holders of the highest ration coupons received daily allowances of a few ounces of bread; the others got next to nothing. In May, as the campaign against the village got under way, Zinoviev announced in regard to the "bourgeoisie":

> We shall give them 1/16th of a pound a day so they won't forget the smell of bread. But if we must go over to milled straw, then we shall put the bourgeoisie on it first of all.

The government, however, had political considerations uppermost on its mind. In announcing the drive to insiders on the Central Executive Committee in May 1918, Iakor Sverdlov, its chairman, spoke not of food but of power:

If we can say that revolutionary Soviet authority is sufficiently strong in the cities . . . the same cannot be said in regard to the village . . . For that reason we must most seriously confront the question of differentiation of the village, the question of creating in the village two contrasting and hostile forces . . . Only if we succeed in splitting the village into two irreconcilably hostile camps, if we are able to inflame there the same civil war that had taken place not so long ago in the cities . . . only then will we be in a position to say that we will do that to the village that we are able to do for the city.

This extraordinary pronouncement meant that the Bolsheviks had made up their minds to gain control of the countryside by inciting one part of the rural population against the other, unleashing a civil war among citizens living peacefully side by side. The assault troops were to consist of urban workers as well as poor and landless peasants; the "enemy" was the "kulaks," the rural "bourgeoisie."

Lenin hated whomever he perceived as the "bourgeoisie" with a destructive passion that fully equaled Hitler's hatred of the Jews; nothing short of their total annihilation would satisfy him. The trouble was that whereas Hitler was able to produce "racial" criteria to determine who was a Jew, no standards existed by which to define a "kulak." The term *kulak* itself, rarely used by the peasants themselves, had no precise meaning, being loosely applied to enterprising peasants—those who in present-day American slang would be called "go-getters." The difficulty of designating kulaks with any precision became apparent in the summer of 1918, when commissars in charge of inciting the poor peasants against their richer neighbors reported that in the villages under their jurisdiction 40 percent if not a majority of peasants were kulaks.

But Lenin had to have a class enemy in order to divide the village against itself. Hence he produced quite unrealistic figures in order to claim advanced "class differentiation" in the Russian village, according to which there were 15 million (or 75 percent) peasant families who would qualify as "poor," 3 million (15 percent) who belonged to the "middle" category, and 2 million (10 percent) who could be designated "rich." Were this really the case, it would have been a simple matter to set the poor against the rich and overwhelm them. But even by Lenin's own criteria, both the "poor" and the "rich" peasants constituted a far smaller proportion of rural households that these figures indicated. Contemporary statistics show that the "poor" constituted less than 4 percent of the rural population and the rich (kulaks) 2 percent—the remaining 94 percent belonged to the "middle" category of self-employed farmers. The regime chose to overlook these figures and categorized any peasant, no matter what his economic status, who resisted food exactions and otherwise displayed overt hostility toward it as a kulak.

The agrarian decrees which the Bolsheviks issued in May and June 1918 had a threefold purpose: (1) to destroy the politically active peasants, almost to a man followers of the SRs, by designating them as kulaks; (2) to create a network of rural soviets, run by Communists; and (3) to extract the maximum of food for the cities and armed forces. The offensive, which bore all the earmarks of a regular military operation, was envisaged as a two-pronged campaign: from within by means of a fifth column of destitute peasants organized into Committees of the Poor, or *kombedy*; and from without by means of "food detachments" made up of armed civilians, assisted by military units, who were to march on the village and extract from the kulaks their hoard. Lenin instructed the Commissariat of War to transform itself into a "Military-Supply Commissariat" and actively assist in the operation. (At the time, the extent of the Czechoslovak threat was not yet apparent.) Eventually 75,000 soldiers joined 50,000 armed civilians in combating the nation's food producers.

The Russian peasant had never experienced anything like this; even under serfdom what he produced had been his unquestioned property. He resisted the assault as best he could, assisted by demobilized soldiers who had returned to the village. Threatened with machine guns and beaten with whips, he responded to violence with violence.

As the government pressed its campaign, the countryside rose up in a revolt that in extent and numbers involved exceeded anything known in Russian history. The historian Vladimir Brovkin estimates that the "magnitude of the Bolshevik war with the peasants on the internal front eclipsed by far the frontline civil war against the [anti-Bolshevik] Whites." The Cheka reported that in 1918 there occurred 245 rural "uprisings" that claimed the lives of 875 Bolsheviks and 1,821 rebels. In addition, 2,431 rebels were said to have been executed. But these figures represent only a fraction of the casualties suffered on both sides, especially when the nationwide peasant revolt reached its climax in 1920 (see Chapter XV).

Lenin was beside himself with fury at the peasants' defiance and at the meager results of the grain-collecting campaign. In August he ordered peasants caught selling food to be turned over to Revolutionary Tribunals and, if armed, to be shot. In an appeal to industrial workers the same month, he exhorted them to "the last, decisive battle":

> The kulak insanely detests Soviet authority and is prepared to suffocate, to carve up hundreds of thousands of workers ... The kulaks are the most beastly, the coarsest, the most savage exploiters ... These bloodsuckers

have waxed rich during the war . . . These spiders have grown fat at the expense of peasants, impoverished by the war, of hungry workers. These leeches have drunk the blood of toilers, growing the richer the more the worker starved in the cities and factories. These vampires have gathered and continue to gather in their hands the lands of landlords, enslaving, time and again, the poor peasants. Merciless war against these kulaks! Death to them.*

Such outbursts of murderous rage reflected the failure of the campaign. For not only were the quantities of food extracted small (what was left over after the food collectors took their share) but the effort to split the village proved unavailing. Whatever divided the peasants, when confronted with an outside force they closed ranks. Despite generous promises to poor peasants that they would get a share of the loot which they helped to locate, they refused to denounce fellow peasants. Rural "class differentiation" proved a mirage of Marxist intellectuals.

The peasants also resisted the establishment of village soviets, preferring their traditional village councils. When forced to join soviets, they elected to the administrative posts their village headmen, invariably followers of the SRs. Although tens of thousands of rural soviets came into being in 1918–19, most of them led a paper existence. The village stubbornly clung to its own ways.

Forced food exactions prompted the peasant to restrict the sown acreage; he did so on the rational but, as it turned out, not entirely realistic premise that the less surplus he had, the less food would be taken from him. In the grain-growing areas, the acreage under cultivation in 1920, compared with 1913, decreased by 12.5 percent. At the same time, yields per acre fell by 30 percent, largely due to a shortage of draft horses, which had been requisitioned by the armed forces. A 12.5 percent decline in acreage accompanied by a 30 percent decline in yields meant that the grain output equaled only 60 percent of its prewar figure. It required only a spell of bad weather for famine to stalk the country.

True famine, Asiatic famine in which millions would perish, lay in the future. In the meantime, Russia suffered from a condition of permanent undernourishment that drained energy and the very will to live. It also

---

* The English philosopher Bertrand Russell, who met with Lenin in 1920, recorded their conversation as follows: "When I put a question to him about socialism in agriculture, he explained with glee how he had incited the poorer peasants against the richer ones, 'and they soon hanged them from the nearest tree—ha! ha! ha!' His guffaw at the thought of those massacred made my blood run cold."

carried off large numbers of the old and the very young, as well as the ill of all ages. Applying pre-revolutionary criteria, according to which an annual bread consumption below 200 kilograms spelled hunger, in 1919–20 the inhabitant of northern Russia went permanently hungry. If Russian cities at this time did not witness mass starvation, it was owing to the fortuitous coincidence that just as this was about to happen, the Bolsheviks won the Civil War and reconquered Siberia, the North Caucasus, and the Ukraine, which, having escaped Bolshevism, had managed to accumulate rich stores of grain.

Agrarian experts argued already under War Communism that these policies were counterproductive, that there were better means of extracting food from the peasant than through brutal confiscations. These methods would be adopted in March 1921 with the introduction of an agrarian tax in kind. But Lenin resorted to them only when, faced with mass famine and nationwide rebellions, he saw no alternative. His stubborn refusal to accept economic realities had its roots in political considerations: he wanted to subdue the village at all costs and as quickly as possible to prevent it undermining his control of the cities.

Judging by his public pronouncements, he believed he had attained this objective. In December 1918, he boasted that during the preceding year the regime had solved problems that "in previous revolutions had presented the greatest impediment to the work of socialism." The rural "bourgeoisie," with whom the Bolsheviks had allied themselves in the fight for power, now came under the attack of the combined forces of the urban proletariat and the village poor. This meant that the kind of backsliding common to Western revolutions no longer threatened Russia. Hence, he concluded, the campaign against the kulaks, "had incomparably deeper and greater significance" than the October Revolution itself.

Of course, this was wild exaggeration: the Bolshevization of the village of which Lenin spoke would be accomplished only ten years later, by Stalin. But, as in so many other respects, it was Lenin who had charted Stalin's course.

RED TERROR

Violence is the last resort of incompetents.

—AUTHOR UNKNOWN

The Murder of the Imperial Family

The ex-Emperor Nicholas II, along with his wife and children, spent the five months that followed his abdication under house arrest at Tsarskoe Selo, the Imperial residence near Petrograd. At the end of July, anticipating a German assault on Petrograd, Kerensky thought it prudent to send the family away from the capital so they could not be used in monarchist plots. He chose as the place of exile the western Siberian city of Tobolsk. They were installed in the Governor's mansion, where they lived in reasonable comfort, attended by a large body of retainers and servants, and able to communicate with the outside world.

The Bolsheviks on coming to power at first ignored the Romanovs, but they became concerned about them in March 1918 following the conclusion of the Brest-Litovsk Treaty, which brought the regime terrible odium and aroused fears of a monarchist restoration. A few days after the Treaty had been ratified, Lenin ordered Grand Duke Michael exiled from Petrograd to Perm, west of the Urals. Soon all other members of the Imperial family who were not in prison received similar orders.

For a while, Moscow considered holding a public trial of the ex-Emperor, patterned on that which the Convention had given Louis XVI. In April it dispatched a trusted Bolshevik by the name of Vasilii Iakovlev (Miachin) to Tobolsk to escort Nicholas to Moscow. Communists in

34. Ipatev's house—the "House of Special Designation":
The murders occurred in the basement room
with the arched-frame window on the lower left.

western Siberia and the Urals, however, mistrusting Iakovlev and suspecting him of wanting to abduct the Imperial family to Japan, aborted
his mission. After negotiations with Moscow, the details of which remain
unclear to this day, Iakovlev handed the ex-Tsar, his wife, and one of
their daughters over to the Ekaterinburg Soviet, which incarcerated
them under conditions of the tightest security in a requisitioned private
residence.* Their house was surrounded by two high palisades and protected by guards armed with machine guns and revolvers. But although
occasionally humiliated by their guards and isolated from the outside
world, they were not maltreated and bore their misfortune with a resignation rooted in religious faith.

By the advent of summer 1918, the situation of the Bolshevik regime
had deteriorated to the point where a public trial of the ex-Tsar seemed
unrealistic. With the outbreak of the rebellion of the Czechoslovak
Legion, the entire Ural region became endangered. The government, of
course, could have transported the Imperial family to Moscow, but it
apparently feared German interference on behalf of the Empress and her
daughters, whom Berlin regarded as German nationals. Leaving them in

---

* Alexis, who was suffering from a painful bout of hemophilia, was left, for the time being,
in Tobolsk, together with three of his sisters. They rejoined the family in Ekaterinburg at the end
of May.

Ekaterinburg, on the other hand, raised the specter of Nicholas's being liberated and turned into a symbol of anti-Bolshevik resistance at a time when Bolshevik fortunes were at a very low ebb. To prevent this, Lenin decided to have the ex-Tsar executed. The Cheka initially planned to kill the family during a bogus attempt at escape orchestrated by the Cheka. When this plan failed because the prisoners refused to cooperate, an elaborate story was fabricated that placed the onus for the execution on the Ekaterinburg Soviet, allegedly acting to prevent Nicholas from being abducted by the approaching Czechs.

A rehearsal for the murder of the Imperial family took place in nearby Perm, where Grand Duke Michael, the next in line to the throne, resided as a private citizen under police surveillance. During the night of June 12–13, the Cheka staged a spurious monarchist "abduction" of Michael. In fact, he was taken to a forest outside Perm and shot, along with his English secretary. At the very same time, Soviet papers carried false reports that a Red Army soldier, acting on his own, had killed the ex-Tsar. This was a test of foreign reactions. The fact that neither foreign governments nor the foreign press displayed much concern probably sealed the fate of the Romanovs.

In the middle of June, one week after the murder of Michael, the Imperial family received what purported to be a secret communication from royalist officers informing them that steps were being taken to have them abducted. Written in bad French, this was the first of four such messages, produced by the local office of the Cheka with the view of staging an escape during which the Romanovs would be shot. The family, believing the messages to be authentic, prepared to cooperate, but the scheme had to be given up when Nicholas and Alexandra insisted, perhaps fearing a trap, that they would not flee but would only allow themselves to be carried off by their would-be rescuers.

In view of these developments, the Ekaterinburg Cheka decided on a mass execution. Although no document exists to this effect—Lenin was far too experienced a conspirator to commit such orders to paper—we know from the testimony of Trotsky that the decision, indeed, was his. In 1935, while living abroad, Trotsky read in an émigré newspaper an account of the Ekaterinburg events. This prodded his memory, and he wrote in his diary:

> My next visit to Moscow took place after Ekaterinburg had already fallen [i.e., after July 25, 1918]. Speaking with Sverdlov, I asked in passing: "Oh yes, and where is the Tsar?" "Finished," he replied. "He has been shot." "And where is the family?" "The family along with him." "All?" I asked,

apparently with a trace of surprise. "All," Sverdlov responded. "Why?" He awaited my reaction. I made no reply. "And who decided the matter?" I inquired. "We decided it here. Ilich [Lenin] thought that we should not leave the Whites a live banner, especially under the present difficult circumstances . . ." I asked no more questions and considered the matter closed.*

At the beginning of July, the guard of the prisoners was replaced by a Cheka unit staffed by Hungarian Communists.

The Imperial family spent July 16 in their customary manner. Judging by the last entry in Alexandra's diary, written at 11 p.m. as the family retired for the night, they had no premonition of what was about to happen.

They were awakened at 1:30 a.m. and told that in view of the unrest in the city and occasional random shooting, they would be removed to the basement. At 2 a.m. under heavy guard, the seven Romanovs, their physician, lady-in-waiting, and two servants descended to the lower floor. A short time later, the commandant of the house, a Chekist by the name of Iakov Iurovskii, entered the crowded room accompanied by a squad of armed guards. From his recently discovered recollections of the event, this is what ensued:

> When the party entered, [I] told the Romanovs that in view of the fact that their relatives continued their offensive against Soviet Russia, the Executive Committee of the Ural Soviet had decided to shoot them. Nicholas turned his back to the detachment and faced his family. Then, as if collecting himself, he turned around, asking "What? What?" [I] rapidly repeated what I had said and ordered the detachment to get ready. Its members had been previously instructed whom to shoot and to aim directly at the heart to avoid much blood and finish more quickly. Nicholas said nothing more. He turned again toward his family. The others shouted some incoherent exclamations. All this lasted a few seconds. Then commenced the shooting which lasted for two or three minutes. [I] killed Nicholas on the spot.

The young Alexis, who lay on the floor in a pool of blood but still breathing, was dispatched by Iurovskii with two shots in the head. The whole "procedure," as Iurovskii calls it, took twenty minutes.

The bodies were carried to a truck and taken out of town to a place previously chosen for the purpose. There they were stripped. It was dis-

---

* From circumstantial evidence, it appears that Lenin ordered only the ex-Tsar killed. The decision to murder his family and four retainers as well seems to have been taken locally.

35. The murderer of Nicholas II, Iurovskii, with his family.

covered that three of the girls had sewn into their corsets large quantities
of diamonds; Iurovskii had considerable difficulty preventing the executioners from stealing them. The bodies were soaked with sulfuric acid
and kerosene, and then burned. The remains were buried in a shallow
grave that was not discovered until 1989.*

According to eyewitnesses, the population at large reacted to the news
of Nicholas's death with utter indifference. In the words of a German
Embassy attaché: "Even decent and cool-headed circles are too accustomed to horrors, too immersed in their own worries and wants, to feel
something special."

Nicholas was not the first reigning monarch in history to be executed.
Two other European kings had lost their lives in revolutionary upheavals: Charles I in 1649 and Louis XVI in 1793. Yet, as is true of
much else that concerns the Russian Revolution, while the superficial
features of events are familiar, all else is unique. Charles I was tried by
a High Court of Justice and had the opportunity to defend himself. The
trial was open; the execution took place in public view. The same was

---

* To placate the Germans, the Bolsheviks announced only the execution of Nicholas, claiming that the Empress and her children had been evacuated to a safe place. This deception, in
which the regime persisted for the next ten years, gave rise to all sorts of legends, the best known
of which concerns the alleged survival of the youngest daughter, Grand Duchess Anastasia.
There is absolutely no conceivable way Anastasia or any other member of the Imperial family
could have survived the massacre. A message from the Ekaterinburg Soviet to the Kremlin
advised it that the entire family had perished. Trotsky's diary confirms this information.

true of Louis XVI, whose fate was settled by a vote of the convention. Nicholas was neither charged nor tried. The Soviet government, which condemned him to death, never published the relevant documents. In the Russian case, the victims were not only the deposed monarch but also his wife, children, and domestic staff. The deed, perpetrated in the dead of night, resembled more a gangster-type massacre than an execution in the legal sense of the word.

In view of the tens of thousands of lives which the Cheka would claim in the years that followed the Ekaterinburg tragedy, and the millions killed by its successors, the death of eleven prisoners hardly qualifies as an extraordinary event. And yet the massacre had a deep symbolic significance. First, it was unnecessary. If the Bolsheviks had really worried about the ex-Tsar becoming a tool of the counterrevolution, they had ample time to remove him and his family to Moscow, where they would have been out of reach of the Czechs or any other enemy. If this was not done, the reason lies in the political needs of the Bolshevik government. In July 1918 it was a "living corpse," in the words of a German resident in Moscow, under assault from all sides and abandoned by many of its adherents. To keep a hold on its dwindling following, it needed blood. This much was conceded by Trotsky in his recollections of these events. "The decision" to execute the ex-Tsar and his family, he wrote,

> was not only expedient but necessary. The severity of this punishment showed everyone that we would continue to fight mercilessly, stopping at nothing. The execution of the Tsar's family was needed not only to frighten, horrify, and instill a sense of hopelessness in the enemy but also to shake up our own ranks, to demonstrate that there was no retreating, that ahead lay either total victory or total doom.

Like the protagonists in Dostoevsky's *Possessed*, the Bolsheviks had to murder to bind their wavering supporters with the bond of collective guilt. The more innocent victims the Bolshevik government had on its conscience, the more the Bolshevik rank and file had to realize that there was no faltering and no compromising, that they were inextricably chained to their leaders. The Ekaterinburg massacre brought the Soviet regime one step closer to full-scale "Red Terror," formally inaugurated six weeks later, many of whose victims would consist of hostages executed not because they had committed crimes but because, in Trotsky's words, their death "was needed."

When a government arrogates to itself the power to kill its citizens not for what they have done but because their death is "needed," it enters an entirely new ethical realm, crossing the threshold of genocide. The same reasoning that had led the Bolsheviks to condemn to death the Romanovs would later be applied in Russia and elsewhere to millions of nameless beings who happened to stand in the way of one or another design for a new "world order."

Mass Terror

A political party that in free elections received less than a quarter of the vote, that treated as foe any individual or group that refused to acknowledge its right to rule and carry out the most extraordinary social and economic experiments, that regarded a priori nine-tenths of the population—peasants and "bourgeoisie"—as class enemies, such a party could not rule by consent but had to make permanent use of terror. In this matter it had no choice if it wished to stay in power. Terror was built into the very procedures and objectives of the Bolshevik regime, and for this reason—unlike its Jacobin prototype, which lasted only a year—it extended throughout its existence. And terror meant not only summary executions but a pervasive atmosphere of lawlessness in which the ruling minority had all the rights and the ruled majority none, which impressed on ordinary citizens a sense of utter powerlessness. In the words of Isaac Steinberg, a Left SR who served for a while as Lenin's Commissar of Justice, it was a "heavy, suffocating cloak thrown from above over the country's entire population, a cloak woven of mistrust, lurking vigilance, and lust for revenge." It affected and deformed everybody's life, day in and day out.

Followers and apologists for Lenin liked to justify his reliance on terror as a regrettable necessity. Thus Angelica Balabanoff, the first Secretary of the Communist International but by no means an uncritical follower, wrote:

> Unfortunate though it might be, the terror and repression which had been inaugurated by the Bolsheviks had been forced upon them by foreign intervention and by Russian reactionaries determined to defend their privileges and reestablish the old order.

Such an apology raises more questions than it answers. The Bolsheviks founded the Cheka, the main agency of terror, in December 1917, before there was either any foreign intervention or organized domestic

36. Isaac Steinberg.

opposition. A handwritten note by Lenin found in the Central Party Archive, undated but, judging by its contents, written shortly before the Cheka came into being, probably in November 1917, makes this amply clear. Addressed to N. N. Krestinskii, the Secretary of the Bolshevik Party, it reads:

> I suggest that we constitute immediately (initially, it can be done in secret) a commission to formulate exceptional measures (in the spirit of Larin: Larin is right). Let us say you + Larin + Vladimirskii (or Dzerzhinskii) + Rykov? or Miliutin? To prepare in secret the terror: essential and *urgent*. And on Tuesday we shall decide: to formalize it through the Sovnarkom or in some other way.[6]

Although Lenin preferred to direct the terror from behind the scenes and had subordinates sign the relevant decrees, it was he personally who made all the major decisions. Indeed, he had repeatedly to goad his reluctant associates and subordinates to overcome their scruples and act with "merciless" brutality. His writings, those published as well as those still reposing in archives, are replete with exhortations to hang and shoot not only as punishment but as a prophylactic.

An example of his predilection for terror comes from the recollections of Isaac Steinberg. Along with the other Left SRs, Steinberg criticized in the Sovnarkom Lenin's decree "The Socialist Fatherland in Danger," which ordered summary executions for several categories of undefined crimes, including "counterrevolutionary agitation" (above, p. 173). "I objected, he writes:

> that this cruel threat killed the whole pathos of the manifesto. Lenin replied with derision, "On the contrary, herein lies true revolutionary pathos. Do you really believe that we can be victorious without the most cruel revolutionary terror?"
>
> It was difficult to argue with Lenin on this score, and we soon reached an impasse. We were discussing a harsh police measure with far-reaching terroristic potentialities. Lenin resented my opposition in the name of revolutionary justice. So I called out in exasperation, "Then why do we bother with a Commissariat of Justice? Let's call it frankly the *Commissariat for Social Extermination* and be done with it!" Lenin's face suddenly brightened and he replied, "Well put . . . that's exactly what it should be . . . but we can't say that."

The first step in the introduction of mass terror was the abolition of law and its replacement by something called "revolutionary conscience." Nothing like it had ever existed: Soviet Russia was the first state in history to outlaw law. This measure permitted the authorities to dispose of any individual who stood in their way. It implemented Lenin's definition of the "dictatorship of the proletariat" as "rule unrestricted by law."

A decree issued on November 22, 1917, dissolved nearly all courts and abolished the professions associated with the judiciary system, including the legal profession. It did not explicitly invalidate the laws on the statute books—this was to come one year later. But it produced the same effect by instructing judges of the local courts, which were retained, to be "guided in making decisions and passing sentences by the laws of the overthrown government only to the extent that they have not been annulled by the Revolution and do not contradict the revolutionary conscience and the revolutionary sense of legality."

In March 1918, the regime replaced local tribunals with People's Courts to deal with all kinds of crimes except those of a political nature. A ruling of November 1918 forbade judges of People's Courts to refer to laws enacted before October 1917 and absolved them from having to observe formal procedures. Their sole criterion was to be the "socialist sense of justice."

Political crimes were handled by Revolutionary Tribunals introduced in November 1917 on the model of identically named institutions of the French Revolution. The category of "political crimes" embraced a wide variety of economic activities considered harmful to the interests of the state. Judges, who had the power to mete out capital punishment, required no formal education, merely the ability to read and write.

The millions living under the Bolshevik rule found themselves from the first days of the new regime in a situation without historic precedent, since even the most primitive societies acknowledge and respect customs that, if not called law, by informing their members of what they can and cannot do, perform the same function. Soviet Russia from 1917 to 1922 had separate courts for ordinary crimes and for crimes against the state, but no laws to guide either of them; citizens were tried by judges lacking in professional qualifications for crimes that were nowhere defined. The principles *nullum crimen sine lege* and *nulla poena sine lege*—"no crime without a law" and "no punishment without a law"—which had traditionally guided Western jurisprudence (and Russia's since 1864) went overboard. The judiciary changed from an institution that dispensed justice to an agency of terror. This was exactly Lenin's intention: in 1922, when he finally gave Soviet Russia a Criminal Code, he would instruct the Commissariat of Justice that the task of the Communist judiciary was to provide a *"justification* of terror . . . The court is not to eliminate terror . . . but to substantiate it and legitimize it. . . ."

But free as they were to mete out punishment at their whim, even these pseudocourts were too slow and cumbersome for Lenin, who noted with disgust that their judges, inspired by a Russian aversion to capital punishment, hesitated to pass death sentences. Hence he came to rely increasingly on the secret police, staffed with social outcasts who had no such qualms.

The Cheka came into being in virtual secrecy on December 7, 1917. It was created for the express purpose of implementing the policy of terror mandated by Lenin's directive (cited above, p. 218). The name was an acronym for "Extraordinary Commission to Fight the Counterrevolution and Sabotage." Its existence and functions were not recorded in the Collection of Laws and Ordinances for 1917–18. For a long time it was a crime to publish any information about this organization without its consent. In its structure and methods the Cheka modeled itself on the tsarist Department of the Police, not a few of whose employees it hired, except that it enjoyed incomparably broader powers.

The Cheka had on its payroll many non-Russians because Lenin regarded his own people as ill-suited for such work. *"Soft, too soft is the Russian,"* he was heard to complain. "He is incapable of applying the harsh measures of revolutionary terror." Hence he chose as the Cheka's head a

37. Feliks Dzerzhinskii.

Pole, Felix Dzerzhinskii, a professional revolutionary raised in the spirit of Polish nationalism, who in his youth had passionately hated the Russians for what they had done to his people. Having spent many years languishing in tsarist prisons and performing hard labor, he was filled with resentment against those responsible for his misfortunes. Lean and ascetic, he carried out Lenin's instructions with a religious dedication, sending people before firing squads with the same joyless compulsion with which, centuries earlier, inquisitors had ordered heretics burned at the stake. Among his associates were many Latvians, Jews, and Armenians.

The Cheka's powers grew incrementally in the course of 1918, in proportion to the regime's growing sense of insecurity. After the Left SRs had quit the government, and especially after their July putsch, the Cheka cast off its remaining constraints and resorted increasingly to summary executions. Its arbitrary powers, however, became truly unlimited only in September 1918, after a nearly successful attempt on Lenin's life that inaugurated the Red Terror in the full sense of that term.

No tsar, even at the height of radical terrorism, was as fearful of his life and as well protected as Lenin. He almost never traveled outside Moscow except to go to his requisitioned country estate nearby. He revisited Petrograd, the scene of his triumph, only once and always surrounded himself with Latvian guards. Before September 1918, no serious attempts on his life were made because the Socialist-Revolutionary

38. Fannie Kaplan.

Central Committee, the terrorist organization par excellence, rejected terrorism against the Bolsheviks, partly from confidence that they would mend their ways and partly from fear of reprisals.

Not all SRs, however, shared this inhibition, and in the summer of 1918 a plot to assassinate Lenin and Trotsky took shape in Moscow under the very nose of the Cheka.

It was the custom of Bolshevik leaders on Friday afternoons and evenings to address workers and Party members on topics of current concern. For security reasons, Lenin's appearances were usually not announced beforehand. On Friday, August 30, Lenin spoke to the workers of the Mikhelson Factory in Moscow. After delivering a customary diatribe against Western "imperialists," he made his way through a dense crowd to the car parked in the courtyard. There he was buttonholed by a woman who complained about Soviet food policy. As he was speaking with her, one foot on the running board, three shots rang out. They were fired by another woman who stood, unnoticed, nearby. She turned and ran, but then stopped and allowed herself to be apprehended.

Lenin was driven at top speed to the Kremlin. A physical examination revealed two wounds: one, relatively harmless, lodged in the arm, the other, potentially fatal, at the juncture of the jaw and neck. He was bleeding profusely and seemed to be breathing his last.

In the next several hours, the female terrorist underwent examination by Cheka personnel. She gave her name as Fannie Kaplan. For terrorist activities in her youth she had been exiled to Siberia, where she met Spiridonova and other SRs. She said she had made up her mind to assassinate Lenin to punish him for dispersing the Constituent Assembly and signing the Brest-Litovsk Treaty.

While Fannie Kaplan was being interrogated at the Lubianka, a team of physicians attended to Lenin, who, even as he hovered between life and death, had enough presence of mind to make certain his doctors were Bolsheviks.

Questioning revealed that Kaplan had acted on her own (which did not prevent the authorities from immediately implicating the leadership of the SR Party). Unable to discover a plot, the authorities ordered her executed. She was shot in the back in the Kremlin courtyard by the commandant of the guards and her remains destroyed.

Lenin recovered rather quickly and in October returned to his desk. But he overworked himself and had to take prolonged rests in his country dacha. In early 1919, he resumed full-time work.

Because the attempt on Lenin's life coincided with the assassination the same day in Petrograd of the head of the local Cheka, M. S. Uritskii, the Bolsheviks concluded that they were confronting an organized wave of terrorism. To thwart it, they launched a campaign of "Red Terror." Two decrees were issued, one on September 4, the other on September 5. Although signed, respectively, by the Commissars of the Interior and of Justice, it is virtually certain they were initiated and authorized by Lenin, who is known on these two days, despite his wounds, to have signed other state papers. The decree of September 4 ordered an immediate stop to the policy of "slackness and mollycoddling" of the regime's enemies:

> All Right SRs known to local soviets must be immediately arrested. It is necessary to take from among the bourgeoisie and officers numerous hostages. In the event of the least attempts at resistance or the least stir in White Guard circles, resort must be had at once to mass executions. . . . Not the slightest hesitation, not the slightest indecisiveness, in the application of mass terror.

The decree of September 5 ordered "class enemies" to be committed to concentration camps and all persons linked to "White Guard organizations, conspiracies, and seditious actions" to be summarily executed.

The Cheka and its provincial branches immediately proceeded to take and shoot hostages. In Petrograd, Zinoviev ordered the mass execution of 512 hostages, mostly individuals associated with the tsarist regime who had spent months in jail and therefore could have had no connection with the terrorist attack on Lenin. In Moscow, Dzerzhinskii executed several tsarist ministers, including Protopopov. Curiously, no SRs were executed, even though they had been charged with masterminding Kaplan's assassination attempt: fear of SR counterreprisals was very real.

A kind of murderous psychosis seized the Bolsheviks. The Red Army newspaper incited the population to pogroms in these words:

> Without mercy, without sparing, we will kill our enemies by the scores of hundreds, let them be thousands, let them drown in their own blood. For the blood of Lenin and Uritskii . . . let there be floods of blood of the bourgeoisie—more blood, as much as possible.

And Zinoviev, addressing a gathering of Communists in mid-September, said:

> We must carry with us 90 million out of the 100 million of Soviet Russia's inhabitants. As for the rest, we have nothing to say to them. They must be annihilated.

These words, by one of the highest officials of the regime, spelled a death sentence for 10 million human beings.

The Red Terror acquired a momentum of its own, as frightened Communists killed blindly to defend themselves from real and imaginary enemies. Guilt ceased to matter. N. V. Krylenko, then an official of the Commissariat of Justice and later, in 1936, its head, put the matter bluntly: "We must execute not only the guilty. Execution of the innocent will impress the masses even more." An idea of what such a philosophy meant in practice can be gleaned from the recollections of a member of the Kiev Cheka:

> If a prisoner kept in the Lukianov jail was suddenly summoned to the "Cheka," then there could be no doubt as to the reason for the haste. Officially, the inmate learned of his fate only when—usually at 1 a.m., the time of executions—the cell resounded with a shouted roster of those wanted "for questioning." He was taken to the prison department, the chancery, where he signed in the appropriate place a registration card, usually without reading what was on it. Usually, after the doomed person had signed, it was added: so-and-so has been informed of his sentence. In fact, this was something of a lie because after the prisoners had left their cells they were not treated "tenderly" and told with relish what fate awaited them. Here the inmate was ordered to undress and then was led out for the sentence to be executed. . . . For executions there was set up a special garden by the house at 40 Institute Street . . . where the Provincial Cheka had moved. . . .

[T]he executioner—the commandant, or his deputy, sometimes one of his assistants, and occasionally a Cheka "amateur"—led the naked victim into this garden and ordered him to lie flat on the ground. Then with a shot in the nape of the neck he dispatched him. The executions were carried out with revolvers, usually Colts. Because the shot was fired at such close range, the skull of the victim usually burst into pieces. The next victim was brought in a like manner, laid by the side of the previous one, who was usually in a state of agony. When the number of victims became too large for the garden to hold, fresh victims were placed on top of the previous ones or else shot at the garden's entrance . . . The victims usually went to execution without resisting. What they went through cannot be imagined even approximately . . . Most of the victims usually requested a chance to say goodbye; and because there was no one else, they embraced and kissed their executioners.

After a few months of such indiscriminate bloodletting, even stalwart Communists began to feel qualms. They were motivated not so much by humanitarian impulses as by fear—justified, as time was to show—that the terror could eventually turn against them. What else were they to make of the boasts of Chekists that they owed loyalty to no one but their own organization and that "if they felt like it" they could arrest anyone, Lenin included? In response to their criticism, Lenin, while lavishing praise on the Cheka for its services to the Revolution, curbed somewhat its powers. In early 1919, the indiscriminate terror was suspended but the practice of taking hostages continued, as did summary executions of confirmed or suspected opponents of the regime.

Fannie Kaplan's shots had another consequence as well: they inspired a policy of deifying Lenin that, after his death, would turn into a veritable state-sponsored Oriental cult.

Lenin was modest in his wants and took no pleasure in the glorification of his person. But his followers needed to place him on a pedestal, partly because to their subjects the state had meaning only if embodied in the person of a ruler and partly because Lenin was the engine that propelled the regime. Raised to the status of a demigod, he and he alone could bestow legitimacy on a political organization whose only operative principle was to follow his orders.

And so it happened that after August 30, 1918, Russians, who until then had known very little of their dictator, found themselves subjected to a veritable flood of Leniniana that extolled him as the "leader by the Grace of God" (Zinoviev) and, indeed, the new Christ. Lenin's recovery was depicted as a miracle and explained by history's determination, through the agency of Lenin, to bring mankind freedom and equality. When, after his death in 1924, his successors had him mummified and displayed to the public in a mausoleum, they merely institutionalized a process of deification that had been well under way while he was still alive.

By 1920 Soviet Russia had become a true police state in the sense that the security police, virtually a state within the state, spread its tentacles everywhere, including the mammoth apparatus created to manage the nationalized economy. The Cheka gradually took over the supervision of a broad variety of activities not customarily associated with state security. To enforce ordinances against "speculation"—in other words, private commerce—it took charge of railroads and other forms of transport. In April 1921, Dzerzhinskii, who in 1919 had been appointed Commissar of the Interior, was named Commissar of Communications. To thwart possible "sabotage" by the many "bourgeois specialists" working in the bureaucracy and economic enterprises, the Cheka placed its agents in every branch of the administration. It steadily enlarged its military force, separate from the Red Army, until in mid-1920 it numbered nearly a quarter of a million men.

Among the Cheka's most important responsibilities was organizing and administering "concentration camps," an institution which the Bolsheviks did not quite invent but which they gave a novel and uniquely sinister meaning. In its fully developed form, the concentration camp, along with the one-party state and the omnipotent political police, was Bolshevism's principal contribution to the political practices of the twentieth century.

Concentration camps first came into existence during colonial wars waged at the turn of the century: by the Spaniards in Cuba, the Americans in the Philippines, and the British in South Africa. In all three cases, the camps served to isolate the native population from the guerrillas. Brutal as they were, these prototypes had been envisaged as emergency measures and, indeed, closed down upon the conclusion of military operations. Soviet concentration camps—as well as their clones in subsequent totalitarian regimes—although identically named, had a fundamentally different character and purpose. First, they were directed against not foreign enemies but domestic opponents. Second, they were permanent. Third, they performed important economic functions, supplying the regime with slave labor.

Trotsky first mentioned concentration camps in mid-1918, in connection with the Czechoslovak rebellion and the induction of ex-Imperial officers (above, pp. 181–82). In August 1918, he and Lenin ordered the construction of permanent concentration camps. The decree on Red Terror of September 5, 1918, explicitly provided for "safeguarding of the Soviet Republic from class enemies by isolating them in concentration camps."

In the spring of the following year, elaborate rules were laid down to regulate concentration camps. Every provincial city was ordered to construct a facility capable of housing 300 or more inmates. The prisoners were to perform physical labor which was to cover the costs of operating the camp: "Responsibility for deficits will be borne by the administration and the inmates. . . ." Attempts to escape were severely punished: to discourage them, the camp authorities were empowered to institute "collective responsibility," which made the prisoners accountable with their lives for each other.

At the end of 1920, Soviet Russia had 84 concentration camps that held approximately 50,000 prisoners; three years later, that number had increased to 315 camps with 70,000 prisoners.

Thus came into existence a central institution of the totalitarian regime. According to Andrzej Kaminski:

> Trotsky and Lenin were the inventors and the creators of the new form of the concentration camp. [This means not only] that they created establishments called "concentration camps." . . . The leaders of Soviet communism also created a specific method of legal reasoning, a network of concepts that implicitly incorporated a gigantic system of concentration camps, which Stalin merely organized technically and developed. Compared with the concentration camps of Trotsky and Lenin, the Stalinist ones represented merely a gigantic form of implementation. And, of course, the Nazis found in the former as well as the latter ready-made models, which they had only to develop. The German counterparts promptly seized upon these models. On March 13, 1921, the then little-known Adolf Hitler wrote in the *Völkischer Beobachter*: "One prevents the Jewish corruption of our people, if necessary, by confining its instigators to concentration camps." On December 8 of that year, in a speech to the National Club in Berlin, Hitler expressed his intention of creating concentration camps upon taking power.

The Red Terror had many aspects, but the historian's first and foremost concern must be with its victims. Their number cannot be established even approximately; estimates range from 50,000 to 140,000. All one can say with certainty is that if the victims of the Jacobin terror numbered in

39. Dzerzhinskii and Stalin.

the thousands, Lenin's terror claimed tens of thousands of lives. The casualties of the next wave of terror, launched by Stalin and Hitler, would be counted in the millions.

To what purpose the carnage?

Dzerzhinskii, echoed by Lenin, liked to boast that the terror and its agency, the Cheka, had saved the Revolution. This claim is probably correct, as long as "the Revolution" is identified with the Bolshevik dictatorship. There exists no lack of evidence that by the autumn of 1918, when the Bolsheviks launched a systematic terror campaign, they were rejected by all strata of the population except their own apparatus. Under these circumstances, "merciless terror" was indeed the only way of preserving the regime.

This terror had to be not only "merciless" (can one even conceive of a "merciful" terror?) but indiscriminate. If the opponents of the Bolsheviks had been an identifiable minority, they could have been targeted for surgical removal. But in Soviet Russia it was the regime and its supporters that constituted a minority. To stay in power, they had first to atomize society and then destroy in it the very will to act independently. The Red Terror gave the population to understand that under a regime that felt no compunctions about executing innocents, innocence was no guarantee of survival: the only hope lay in total self-effacement, combined with a fatalistic acceptance of whatever happened. Once society disintegrated into an agglomeration of human atoms, each fearful of attracting attention and concerned exclusively with physical survival, then it ceased to matter what anyone thought, for the government had the entire sphere of public activity to itself. Only under these conditions could a few hundred thousand subjugate 100 or more million.

But such conduct did not come cheaply to its practitioners. To stay in power against the wishes of the overwhelming majority of their subjects, the Bolsheviks had to distort that power beyond all recognition. Terror may have saved Communism, but it totally corroded its soul.

In November 1918, when the Great War came to an end, the Bolsheviks controlled twenty-seven provinces of European Russia, inhabited by some 70 million people, or one-half of the Empire's prewar population. The borderlands—Poland, Finland, the Baltic region, the Ukraine, Transcaucasia, central Asia, and Siberia—had either separated themselves and formed sovereign states or were under the control of anti-Bolshevik Whites. The Communist realm encompassed the defunct Empire's heartland, populated almost exclusively by Great Russians. Ahead lay a civil war in the course of which Moscow would reconquer by force of arms most but not all of its borderland areas and try to spread its regime to Europe, the Middle East, and East Asia. The Revolution would enter another phase, that of expansion.

The first year of Bolshevik rule left Russians not only cowed by the unprecedented application of largely random terror but thoroughly bewildered. Those who had lived through it experienced a complete reevaluation of all values: whatever had been good and rewarded was now evil and punished. The traditional values of faith in God, charity, tolerance, patriotism, and thrift were denounced by the new regime as unacceptable legacies of a doomed civilization. Killing and robbing, slander and lying were good if committed for the sake of the proper cause as defined by the new regime. Nothing made sense. The perplexity of contemporaries is reflected in the ruminations published during the summer of 1918 in one of the few relatively independent dailies still allowed to appear:

> There was a time when a man lived somewhere beyond the Narva Gate, in the morning drank tea from a samovar placed in front of him. For dinner, he emptied half a bottle of vodka and read *The Petrograd Rag*. When once a year someone was murdered, he was indignant for a whole week, at the very least. And now . . .
>
> About murders, dear sir, they have stopped writing: on the contrary, they inform us that the day before only thirty people have been bumped off and another hundred robbed. . . . This means that everything is in order. And whatever happens, it is better not even to look out of the window.

Today they parade with red flags, tomorrow with banners, then again with red flags, and then again with banners. Today Kornilov has been killed, tomorrow he is resurrected. The day after Kornilov is not Kornilov but Dutov, and Dutov is Kornilov, and they are, all of them, neither officers nor Cossacks nor even Russians but Czechs. And where these Czechs came from, no one knows . . . We fight them, they fight us. Nicholas Romanov has been killed, he has not been killed. Who killed whom, who fled where, why the Volga is no longer the Volga and the Ukraine no longer Russia. Why the Germans promise to return to us the Crimea, where did the Hetman come from, what Hetman, why does he have a boil under his nose . . . Why aren't we in an insane asylum?

So unnatural were the new conditions, they so outraged common sense and decency, that the vast majority of the population viewed the regime responsible for them as a terrible and inexplicable cataclysm which could not be resisted but had to be endured until it would vanish as suddenly and inexplicably as it had come. As time would show, however, these expectations were mistaken. Russians and the people under their rule would know no respite: those who experienced and survived the Revolution would never see the return of normalcy. The Revolution was only the beginning of their sorrows.

PART THREE

*Russia under
the Bolshevik Regime*

THE CIVIL WAR

The First Battles: 1918

I n its treatment of the Civil War, much as in the case of War
Communism and the Red Terror, the Soviet government and the
historians in its employ insisted on depicting it as something that
was forced on the new regime by its enemies. But the historical record
indicates the contrary to be true—namely that in this case, too, the Bolsheviks acted rather than reacted; they wanted a Civil War and did everything in their power to promote it. Lenin not only expected civil war to
break out in his own country and around the globe after he had taken
power, but he took power in order to unleash such a war. For him, the
October coup d'état would have been a futile adventure if its only result
were a change of regimes in Russia. Ten years before the Revolution,
analyzing the lessons of the Paris Commune, he had agreed with Marx in
attributing its collapse to the failure of the Communards to initiate just
such a war. From the instant World War I broke out he denounced paci-
fist socialists, who demanded an end to the fighting. True revolutionaries did not want peace: "This is a slogan of philistines and priests. The
proletarian slogan must be: civil war." Trotsky stated this even more
bluntly: "Soviet authority is organized civil war."

In speaking of the Russian Civil War one ordinarily refers to the military conflict between the Red and White armies, and this conflict will
form the subject of the present chapter. But this is only one of its dimen-

sions. The Bolsheviks did not acknowledge national boundaries, and in the usage of the time, "civil war" referred, first and foremost, to the political and social struggle between the Bolshevik regime and its own citizenry. In this broader sense of the term, the imposition of a one-party dictatorship and the incitement to class war in the villages, described in Chapters VII and IX, lay at the very heart of the Russian Civil War. So did the "Red Terror."

The Civil War, in the military sense of the word, was fought on three principal fronts—the southern, eastern, and, northwestern. It went through three phases. The first lasted one year, from the Bolshevik coup until the armistice on the Western front. It was characterized by rapidly shifting front lines and intermittent engagements of small units. During this phase, foreign troops—the Czechoslovaks on the anti-Bolshevik side and the Latvians on the Bolshevik one—dominated the fighting.

The second and decisive stage extended over nine months, from March to November 1919. Initially, the White armies made impressive advances and seemed within reach of victory, but for reasons that will be spelled out, the tide of battle changed dramatically as the Red Army crushed first the Siberian forces of Admiral Kolchak (June–November 1919) and then the Southern Army of General Denikin and the Northwestern Army of General Iudenich (October–November, 1919). The battles fought during this phase involved hundreds of thousands of regular troops.

The concluding phase of the war was the anticlimactic Crimean episode under General Wrangel. The evacuation of the remainder of the Southern Army to Constantinople in November 1920 marked the end of the Russian Civil War in the military sense; in the political and social senses it would go on for years.

The Bolsheviks from the outset labeled their military opponents "Whites" or "White Guards," on the example of the counterrevolutionary armies of the French Revolution (white being the color of the Bourbons). The name stuck. But it must be stressed that none of the so-called White armies in Russia fought for the restoration of the monarchy; all committed themselves to reconvening a Constituent Assembly and all enforced on territories under their control the laws of the Provisional Government. Furthermore, no member of the tsarist dynasty claimed the throne while the war was in progress. At the same time, it must be acknowledged that most White officers harbored strong pro-monarchist sympathies.

The Russian Civil War bore little resemblance to the campaigns of World War I. It had few fixed fronts. Troops were in constant flux, moving mainly along railroad lines and leaving large unoccupied spaces in between. Armies emerged suddenly and just as suddenly crumbled and vanished. Units advancing with seemingly irresistible momentum turned into rabble on meeting determined resistance. The front lines were thinly held; it was not uncommon for divisions of several thousand troops to defend a front of 200 kilometers. Such fluidity makes it next to impossible to depict the progress of the war in graphic terms, the more so that in the rear of the principal combatants operated independent bands of "Greens" (peasant partisans) and "Blacks" (anarchists), who were hostile to both the Reds and Whites. Some maps of the Civil War resemble a Jackson Pollock painting, with white, red, green, and black lines running in all directions and dissecting at random.

Since the Red Army won the Civil War, it is tempting to attribute to it superior leadership and motivation. While subjective factors undeniably contributed to the outcome, scrutiny of the correlation of forces indicates that the decisive factors were of an objective nature. The ability of the Whites to hold their own against overwhelming odds and at one point to seem near victory suggests that, contrary to conventional wisdom, it is they who enjoyed superior generalship and morale. They lost because they were outnumbered and outgunned.

The critical advantage the Reds enjoyed was that they were one and their enemies many. They had a single military command that operated under the direction of a political oligarchy. The Whites had no government; their several armies were widely separated and most of the time out of touch with each other. To make matters worse, each of the major White armies was composed of diverse ethnic groups that fought for their own objectives: the Cossacks, in particular, who made up a significant part of the White forces, followed orders only when it suited them and showed greater concern for their homelands than for Russia.

The Reds also enjoyed an immense advantage in that they controlled the center of what had been the Russian Empire, whereas their opponents operated from the country's periphery. This brought the Red Army several benefits.

To begin with, they had at their disposal far larger human resources than did their opponents because the area they controlled was the country's most densely populated. When the Civil War got under way, the Bolsheviks ruled some 70 million people, whereas Kolchak and Denikin, except for brief periods, governed no more than 8 or 9 million each. In the fall of 1919, when the decisive battles of the Civil War took place, the Red Army had nearly 3 million men under arms; the combined effectives of the White armies never exceeded 250,000. In the critical engage-

ments, the Red Army enjoyed at least a 2–1 superiority in man power
and sometimes double that.

The man power available to the Red Army was not only larger but
ethnically homogeneous. The population of Soviet Russia in 1918 and
1919 was nine-tenths Great Russian. The areas of operation of the
White armies had a high proportion of ethnic minorities, including Cossacks, who, although Orthodox and Slav, considered themselves a people
apart. Russian patriotic slogans did not much appeal to these diverse
minorities.

Another advantage the Red Army enjoyed was immense superiority in
military hardware. First of all, the Bolsheviks inherited the rich stores of
the Imperial army. An inventory taken by the Communists in December
1917 showed that the arsenals of the old army held 2.5 million rifles, 1.2
billion rounds of small ammunition, 12,000 field guns, and 28 million
artillery shells. Nearly all this weaponry went to equip the Red Army.
Second, most war industries were located in Great Russia and worked
for the Red Army. As a result, in the final stages of the Civil War, the Red
Army attained a higher ratio of artillery and machine guns to man power
than had prevailed in the tsarist army. The Whites, who had access neither to tsarist arsenals nor to defense industries, depended almost exclusively on what the Allies, mainly the British, saw fit to send them.

The Red and White forces differed in another respect that also
redounded to the Communists' advantage. The Red Army was the military arm of a civilian government, whereas the White armies were a military force that also had to act as a government. The White generals were
ill prepared to cope with this responsibility, for they had no administrative experience and had been raised in the tradition of an army that disdained politics and thought it below an officer's dignity to become
involved in them. They believed that injecting politics into their movement would cause unnecessary divisions. Told by one of his civilian advisers that he needed a clear political program and laws to implement it,
Kolchak replied: "No, leave this alone, work only for the army. Don't you
understand that no matter what fine laws you write, if we lose, they will
all the same shoot us?" But the Civil War was primarily a political conflict, a struggle for power and not a conventional war. Their exclusive
concentration on military operations, their unwillingness to go beyond
rudimentary administration, made the White commanders appear more
reactionary than they really were and handed their opponents a powerful
propaganda weapon.

40. General Alekseev.

· · ·

The first White force to form was the Volunteer Army founded in the Don Cossack region by General M. V. Alekseev. Alekseev was anything but a reactionary monarchist; he had been implicated in plots to dethrone Nicholas II and had played a decisive role in persuading him to abdicate. He was a Russian patriot who felt that his country had a moral duty to keep faith with the Allies by staying in the war to fight the Germans and their Bolshevik puppets. After the Bolshevik coup he fled to Rostov on the Don, where he recruited volunteers for a regenerated Russian army. He received some financial help from the Allies, but the sums were small because until the ratification of the Brest-Litovsk Treaty, the Allies, hoping to dissuade Soviet Russia from signing a separate peace, courted her new rulers. Soon anti-Bolshevik officers and politicians made their way to Rostov—among them Kornilov, who assumed command of the Volunteer Army.

News of the formation of a hostile army rang alarm bells in Petrograd. A motley force was assembled and sent against the Volunteers, forcing the Whites, numbering 3,000 men, to evacuate Rostov and seek refuge in the Kuban Steppe. During the so-called Ice March, they had to

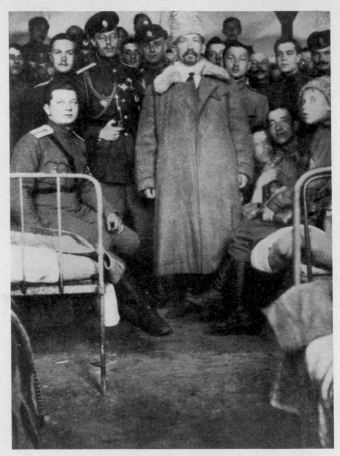

41. Kornilov with young volunteers.

engage in continual fighting against pro-Bolshevik deserters and "out-landers," in the course of which Kornilov, the most popular White com-mander, lost his life.* He was replaced by General Anton Denikin. The Volunteers did manage to recruit numerous Kuban Cossacks, however, and by early spring they were in a far stronger position because after two months of Bolshevik rule the local population became more sympathetic

---

* "Outlanders" (*inogorodnye*) were peasants living in the Cossack regions, not members of Cossack communities. They either had small land allotments or no land at all and eagerly awaited the opportunity to seize Cossack possessions. They formed the core of Bolshevik supporters in this area.

42. General Denikin.

to them. They recaptured Rostov and established there a solid base of operations.

With the approach of spring 1918, Denikin had to decide on his next move. Alekseev wanted the Volunteer Army to join the Don Cossacks in an assault on Tsaritsyn because its capture would make it possible to link up with the Czechs and the Siberian People's Army. Once united, the anti-Bolshevik forces of the east and south could forge a single front from the Black Sea to the Urals. But Denikin had other ideas. He preferred to march his army once again southward, into the Kuban Steppe, in order to liquidate Bolshevik and pro-Bolshevik forces in his rear and recruit more Kuban cavalry. The Don Cossacks attacked Tsaritsyn on their own in November and December 1918, but failed to capture it.*

Denikin's second Kuban campaign attained its objective. In September 1918, when it concluded, the Volunteer Army numbered 35,000–40,000 men (up to 60 percent of them Kuban Cossacks). These successes prompted the Bolsheviks in August to request German military intervention against the Volunteer Army (above, p. 188). With his rear

---

* The battle for Tsaritsyn in 1918 marked the beginning of the feud between Stalin and Trotsky. Stalin, whom Lenin had dispatched to this region to collect food, had himself appointed to the Revolutionary-Military Council of the southern front and interfered with the local commanders' operational decisions. His meddling and the terror against ex-tsarist officers that accompanied it prompted Trotsky to request Stalin's recall. Stalin later claimed credit for the successful defense of Tsaritsyn and had the city renamed Stalingrad.

Main Fronts of the Civil War

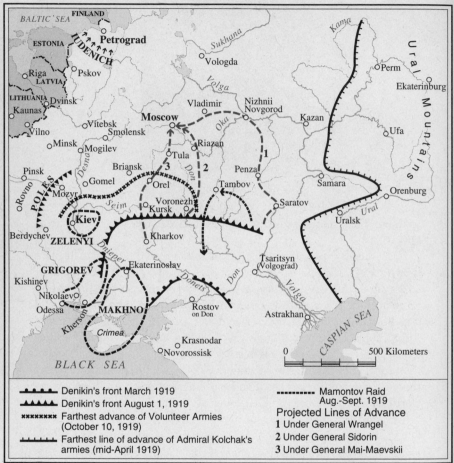

Denikin's front March 1919
Denikin's front August 1, 1919
Farthest advance of Volunteer Armies (October 10, 1919)
Farthest line of advance of Admiral Kolchak's armies (mid-April 1919)
Mamontov Raid Aug.-Sept. 1919
Projected Lines of Advance
1 Under General Wrangel
2 Under General Sidorin
3 Under General Mai-Maevskii

secure, Denikin felt free to plan a major and possibly decisive campaign aimed at Moscow the following spring. It has been argued, however, that by failing to move against Tsaritsyn and join up with the Eastern Army, he missed a unique opportunity to forge a united anti-Bolshevik front.

The Volunteer Army paid minimal attention to administrative responsibilities. The generals had neither the taste for civilian affairs nor qualified personnel. They entrusted administrative authority largely to fellow

43. Stalin in Tsaritsyn, 1918.

officers, who were to be guided by laws issued prior to October 25, 1917. Essentially, the population was left to its own devices, which spelled not so much democracy as anarchy. Shortly before his death in October 1918, Alekseev created an advisory body of civilian politicians and experts, dominated by Kadets. Its resolutions, however, were not binding on the military commanders. Responding to British pressures, Denikin issued a vague liberal program, calling, among other things, for the convocation of a Constituent Assembly, but neither he nor his fellow generals believed that such pronouncements mattered much one way or the other.

More debilitating still was the loose discipline that prevailed in the Southern Army, for which Denikin must bear personal responsibility. When the head of the British military mission complained to him that widespread corruption made it impossible properly to supply frontline troops, Denikin responded: "I can do nothing with my army. I am glad when it carries out my combat orders." Marauding, looting and, later, pogroms were commonplace and went unpunished. This held true not so much of the Volunteers, a disciplined minority, as of the Cossacks and the conscripts drafted in 1919.

While the Volunteer Army formed in the south, another White force took shape in Siberia. It owed its emergence in large measure to the rebellion of the Czechoslovak Legion, which had liberated Siberia and most of the mid-Volga from Bolshevik control. A regional government came into being in Tomsk, which claimed authority over Siberia. In February 1918, it declared independence. The Siberian government, which later moved to Omsk, was a coalition of moderate Socialists-Revolutionaries and Constitutional-Democrats closely affiliated with the powerful Siberian cooperative movement. It annulled Soviet laws and restored appropriated land to its owners. It established one of the few efficient administrations on the territory of what had been the Russian Empire.

In the mid-Volga, in the provinces militarily controlled by the Czechs, political authority was claimed by a Committee of the Constituent Assembly (Komuch), located in Samara and composed almost exclusively of SR deputies in the old Assembly. Komuch pursued a more radical course than did the middle-of-the-road Siberian government, keeping in force much of the Bolshevik social legislation. It regarded itself as the only legitimate authority in Russia and took steps, which never material-ized, to reconvene the Constituent Assembly.

Both the Siberian government and Komuch formed armies of volun-teers, later augmented by conscripts. They relied heavily, however, on the Czechoslovak Legion, which the Allied Supreme Council in the summer of 1918 designated an integral part of the Allied armed forces. It was to serve as the nucleus of the projected multinational army in Russia.

Allied missions did everything in their power to persuade the Siberian government and Komuch to merge into a single authoritative govern-ment. Their pressure resulted in the formation in September 1918 of a five-man Directory, made up of SRs and SR sympathizers. The new body had little influence because the SRs of what had been the Komuch engaged in ceaseless intrigues against the Siberians. The situation grew worse in late September, when the Left SRs, led by Victor Chernov, who had not been invited to join the Directory, declared the agreement between Komuch and the Siberians an act of treason. There was an air of unreality about the Directory, and throughout its two-month exis-tence rumors circulated that it would be overthrown. Its position weak-ened appreciably after October 18, 1918, when the Czechoslovak National Council in Paris proclaimed that nation's independence. As soon as they learned of this declaration, the Czechs and Slovaks in Rus-sia withdrew from the fighting, leaving the defense of the mid-Volga and Siberia to the very inferior Russian People's Army. At French urging, the remnant of the Legion agreed to guard a segment of the Trans-Siberian Railway.

44. Admiral Kolchak.

It was only a matter of time before the Directory fell. The conservative officers of the People's Army viewed with disgust the intrigues of the socialists in the government, which reminded them of the disruptive work of the soviets in 1917. The spark that caused the rebellion was a proclamation of the SR Central Committee in late October calling on democratic forces to arm themselves to prevent an imminent counter-revolution. The officers regarded this act as high treason. They conspired to topple the Directory and replace it with a military dictator. On the night of November 17–18, officers of this group arrested the Directory, following which power passed to the cabinet of ministers. After brief deliberation, the cabinet chose as "Supreme Ruler" the forty-five-year-old Admiral Alexander Kolchak, the Directory's Minister of War.

Kolchak had enjoyed a distinguished career as a naval officer and a Polar explorer. Devoid of political ambitions, he accepted the proffered post with a heavy heart, as a patriotic duty. He was chosen largely because of his good relations with the British, who considered him the most energetic and dedicated of the White leaders. But except for integrity and selfless devotion to the task of liberating Russia from the Bolsheviks, he had no qualifications for the post that was thrust upon him. As a naval officer, he knew next to nothing of land warfare. He disliked politics and politicians. He felt ill at ease in the company of others and suffered from bouts of depression. A tragic quality attended his year-long dictatorship, which he did not seek and which, after fleeting triumphs, would end in death before a Bolshevik firing squad.

The events that transpired in Omsk in November 1918 pushed the socialists into Bolshevik arms. They had pursued since the October coup an unrealistic policy of pretending to be a third force, distinct from the Reds and Whites, expecting the inevitable (in their view) failure of both to drop power in their laps. The Left SRs and the so-called Mensheviks-Internationalists headed by L. Martov supported the Bolsheviks, albeit with qualifications. The mainstream (or Right) SRs played a dominant role in the anti-Bolshevik Komuch and Directory. But the Omsk coup robbed them of the last hope of reaping the fruits of their victory in the elections to the Constituent Assembly a year earlier, and they now defected to Moscow. During the winter of 1918–19, the leaders of the SR Party held talks with Bolshevik representatives that in February 1919 produced an agreement. The SRs renounced all attempts to remove the Communist regime by force. An SR conference held in Moscow in June 1919 instructed the Party's members in areas under White control to go underground and launch a campaign of terror against Denikin and Kolchak. The Mensheviks acted in a less openly hostile manner, but they, too, made their peace with the Soviet regime and offered to help defend it. As a reward for this new policy, both the SRs and the Mensheviks were allowed to rejoin the soviets, from which they had been expelled the previous spring. The partnership would last only until the end of the Civil War, at which time Lenin would once again turn against his erstwhile socialist allies.

The Climax: 1919–1920

The campaigns that would decide the outcome of the Civil War opened in the spring of 1919 and ended eight months later with a decisive defeat of the Whites.

In the fall of 1918, the Soviet government overcame its scruples about forming a professional army and proceeded in earnest to mobilize ex-tsarist officers and peasants.

The decision to entrust commanding positions in the new Red Army to tsarist veterans was not taken lightly and was made only after overcoming fierce resistance from the Bolshevik Old Guard. There seemed to be no choice. On October 1, 1918, Lenin ordered the creation of an army of 3 million "to help the international workers' revolution." A force of this size—double that of the tsarist army in peacetime—could not be commanded by Communist civilians and the small cadre of professional military officers friendly to the new regime. The pool of veteran officers was large (250,000) and socially diversified, since a high proportion consisted of young men commissioned during World War I. The Russian officer corps on the eve of the Revolution was anything but elitist: of the 220,000 lieutenants who had received commissions during the war, 80 percent were of peasant origin and 50 percent had not completed secondary schooling. They were, nevertheless, suspected and persecuted. With their salaries and pensions cut off, they had difficulty making ends meet and many eagerly responded to orders recalling them to active service. The others were inducted under threats of heavy penalties not only

45. Trotsky and Commander in Chief S. S. Kamenev.

for themselves but for their families as well. (In a secret instruction, Trotsky ordered that only those officers be mobilized who had immediate families living on Soviet territory; the latter were to serve as hostages.)

The new Red Army was directed by a Military Revolutionary Council of the Republic (Revvoensovet) operating directly under the Central Committee of the Communist Party. Trotsky, in his capacity as Commissar of War, chaired it. The Revvoensovet was to establish general supervision over the armed forces and remain in constant communication with them, but it was not to interfere with the military decisions of the professional officers. The Council had on its staff the Commander in Chief, a "military specialist" with broad authority in strategic and operational matters. His decisions acquired force, however, only after being countersigned by a civilian member of the Council. Under the Commander served the Field Staff of generals of the old army, which worked out the operational plans.

During the course of the Civil War some 75,000 ex-Imperial officers served in the Red Army, including 775 generals of the Imperial General Staff. Ex-tsarist officers made up 85 percent of the commanders of fronts, 82 percent of the commanders of armies, and 70 percent of the commanders of divisions. The extent to which the tsarist officers corps was integrated into the new, Soviet one, is illustrated by the fact that the two last tsarist Ministers of War and one Minister of War of the Provisional Government donned Red Army uniforms.

Trotsky is depicted by his biographer, Isaac Deutscher, as the man who "had founded a great army and guided it to victory." In fact, his contribution was more modest. The decision to create a peasant army staffed by ex-tsarist officers was made not personally by him but by the Central Committee; and credit for the Red Army's victory belongs to ex-tsarist officers. Trotsky had no military experience, and his strategic sense left a great deal to be desired.* A Soviet officer turned historian, General Dmitrii Volkogonov, who had access to the archival sources on Trotsky's activities during the Civil War, concluded that in military matters he was a "dilettante."

---

* For example, in late 1918, anticipating massive Allied landings in the Ukraine, he wanted to concentrate the armed forces there rather than in the Urals, where Kolchak was making rapid progress. Fortunately for the Communist regime, he was overruled. A year later, he conceived a fantastic plan of forming a cavalry army in the Urals to invade India—this at a time when the Red Army was fighting for its life against Denikin. This proposal was ignored. In October 1919, as the Red Army stood poised to deliver a crushing blow to the Southern White Army, he wrote a lengthy letter to the Central Committee savagely criticizing its deployments and strategy.

Trotsky's contribution lay elsewhere. He provided political linkage and political oversight, the lack of which was a major shortcoming of the White armies. Touring the front in his private train, he could assess the situation on the spot and, cutting through red tape, solve shortages of manpower and matériel. He was also a spellbinding speaker, able to galvanize dispirited troops; in this respect, like Kerensky, he could be called "Persuader in Chief." His directives to the troops had no operational significance, consisting mostly of exhortations topped with exclamation marks: "Southern front, pull yourself together!"; "Round them up!"; "Proletarians, to horse!"; "For shame!"; "Don't waste time!"; "Once more, don't waste time"; and the like. He was responsible for introducing a draconian discipline, spelled out below, which verged on regular terror.

As for Lenin, his military contribution was largely confined to sending alarmist messages to frontline commanders and commissars, demanding that they either hold the line at all costs, "to the last drop of blood," or charge and smash the enemy, otherwise the Revolution was lost. He also never tired of urging his officers to terrorize the civilian population. "Try to punish Latvia and Estonia by military means," he suggested to Trotsky's deputy "(for instance . . . somewhere penetrate the border even for one verst and hang 100 to 1000 of their officials and rich people)". In February 1920, he threatened to "slaughter" the entire population of Maikop and Groznyi if the local oil fields were sabotaged. On August 30, 1918—hours before he himself was shot and nearly killed—Lenin wrote Trotsky in connection with the poor performance of Red forces at Kazan that it might not be a bad idea to execute Vatsetis, the Commander of the eastern front, for "further delay or failure." This was the same Vatsetis who two months earlier had saved him and his government from the Left SR rebellion.

The Red Army suffered serious morale problems. These are clearly reflected in the rate of desertions.* Between October 1918 and April 1919, nearly 1 million men failed to respond to draft orders. The number of desertions between June 1919 and June 1920 is estimated by Communist sources at 2.6 million; in the second half of 1919, each month more soldiers fled the Red Army than the Volunteer Army had in its ranks. The punishments for desertion were very severe, but obviously they could not be rigorously enforced or they would have resulted in the extermination

---

* In the Soviet definition, failure to report for induction as well as temporary absence (absence without leave) qualified as desertion.

of more than half of the Red Army. Most deserters were returned to their units. In the second half of 1919, 612 men in uniform were executed; in 1921, after the Civil War was over and military operations were directed mainly against peasant guerrillas, executions numbered 4,337.

Another indication of the problems of loyalty and morale can be found in the extraordinarily severe disciplinary measures adopted by the Red Army. Trotsky, their author, justified them as follows:

> One cannot build an army without repression. One cannot lead human masses to their death without the commanding officers having at their disposal the death penalty. As long as the evil tailless apes called human beings, proud of their technology, build armies and wage war, so long will commanders present soldiers with [the choice of] possible death in front and certain death in the rear.

The severest measures applied to officers: their families were treated as hostages and they themselves were summarily shot for merely acting in a suspicious manner. In August 1918, Trotsky ordered that in case of "unjustified" retreat, the commissar of the front was to be executed first, followed by its military commander. Draftees were also subject to extreme punitive measures. On entering active service, they had to acknowledge that their comrades not only could but had the duty to shoot them on the spot if they fled from the field of battle, failed to carry out orders, or even complained of food shortages. Implementing his notion of facing the troops with "possible death in front and certain death in the rear," Trotsky created armed "barring detachments" composed of dependable troops with a high proportion of Communists to patrol roads in the rear of the combat zone. Such draconian measures exceeded anything known in the tsarist armies even in the days of serfdom. They had no counterpart in the White armies; Red Army prisoners and deserters are said to have been astonished at the lax discipline on the White side.

The Red Army accompanied such punishments with intensive propaganda. Trains distributing leaflets constantly toured the front. Printing presses turned out posters and newspapers for the troops. The thrust of this effort was to convince the soldiers that a White victory would spell the restoration of the monarchy, the return of landlords, and pogroms of workers.

Although the involvement of the so-called "foreign interventionists" in the Russian Civil War is usually exaggerated out of all proportion, the war's course cannot be understood unless this factor is taken into account.

Unquestionably, were it not for the military assistance provided to the Whites, notably by Britain, the Red Army would have triumphed much earlier. At the same time, two facts must be borne in mind. First, there was never any concerted foreign action on Russian soil; the participants pursued their own, often conflicting, objectives and, furthermore, acted in response to disparate domestic interest groups, some of which favored intervention while others opposed it. Second, except for Great Britain in 1919, the foreign powers did not intend to topple the Communist government. In the first year of the Civil War they intervened exclusively to reactivate the eastern front—with Bolshevik help if possible, without it if necessary. In the second and decisive year of the Civil War, when the guns in the west had fallen silent, intervention lost its clear purpose. Soon afterward, the United States and France disengaged and withdrew. The Japanese stayed on: they did so, however, not to fight the Red Army but to annex Russia's Maritime Provinces. This left England, which lent support to the White armies until the fall of 1919. England acted mainly at the instigation of Winston Churchill, one of the few European statesmen to understand the implications a Communist victory would have for England and world peace. This said, it must be stressed that the Civil War was a fratricidal struggle of Russians; while they lost millions, in military and civilian casualties, the British, who alone engaged in combat, suffered some 400 fatalities.*

The key person involved in the Allied intervention was the British Prime Minister, David Lloyd George, who acted in concert with the American President, Woodrow Wilson. In his memoirs, Lloyd George wrote:

> I would have dealt with the Soviets as the *de facto* Government of Russia. So would President Wilson. But we both agreed that we could not carry our colleagues at the Congress, nor the public opinion of our own countries which was frightened by Bolshevik violence and feared its spread.

True as this statement is, the influences acting on Lloyd George were more diverse and his motives more complicated than it suggests.

At home he had to contend with pressures from opposite sides of the political spectrum. The conservative spokesman in the matter, Churchill, wanted nothing less than an international crusade to dislodge the Bol-

---

* Exclusive of the Czechoslovaks and Latvians, who also "intervened" in a manner of speaking; the latter, fighting for the Bolsheviks, lost many thousands.

sheviks. Since the Liberal Lloyd George headed a coalition government, he could not ignore Churchill. On the other side, he confronted mounting Labour Party and Trade Union Congress antagonism to involvement in Russia, which they saw as directed ultimately against themselves. The Prime Minister therefore compromised: he intervened, but he did so in a halfhearted manner and disengaged as soon as he decently could.

Lloyd George justified his reluctance to give the Whites effective aid and diplomatic recognition with the arguments that the French Revolution had demonstrated the futility of attempts to suppress revolution by military force; that the Bolsheviks were certain to be toppled internally if they failed to gain popular support; and that their ability to hold on to power demonstrated that they did, in fact, enjoy such support. But he also had weightier reasons against intervening in the Whites' behalf, namely a belief that the Bolsheviks represented less of a menace to Britain than would a restored national Russia. Thus in December 1918, he told the War Cabinet that he did not think a Bolshevik Russia "was by any means such a danger as the old Russian Empire, with all its aggressive officials and millions of troops." A year later he would voice a similar opinion in public. This line of argument closely resembled that advanced by the German proponents of a pro-Bolshevik policy in 1918 and later by the head of the Polish republic, Joseph Pilsudski. President Wilson shared these sentiments, which grew out of preconceptions rather than knowledge of the actual situation in Russia.

Initially, Lloyd George and Woodrow Wilson tried to bring the warring sides in the Russian Civil War to the negotiating table. They believed it was essential to restore stability in Russia because otherwise it would be impossible to redraw the borders of Eastern Europe, let alone achieve a durable peace. A secret mission by an American amateur diplomat, William Bullitt, sent to Moscow for this purpose in March 1919, yielded no result. While the Soviet government showed itself eager to negotiate an armistice in order to forestall an anticipated Allied onslaught, the Whites rejected the proposal out of hand. A subsequent attempt to convene a peace conference at Prinkipo, an island off Constantinople, also failed. Lloyd George therefore reluctantly agreed to intervention. The rules he laid down in early 1919 spelled out the terms:

"1. There must be no attempt to conquer Bolshevik Russia by
     force of arms.
 2. Support would only be continued as long as it was clear
     that in the area controlled by Kolchak and Denikin the
     population was anti-Bolshevik in sentiment.

> 3. The anti-Bolshevik armies must not be used to restore the
> old tsarist regime . . . [and] reimpos[e] on the peasants the
> old feudal conditions [!] under which they held their
> land."

British aid consisted primarily of military supplies and instructors, whose principal beneficiary was Admiral Kolchak. On occasion, British combat troops rendered help to the Whites by attacking Red naval targets as well as operating a few combat tanks and reconnaissance planes. In the fall of 1919, British experts estimated the total value of this assistance at £100 million (or $500 million)—a figure Churchill considered to be vastly exaggerated on the grounds that British aid consisted largely of World War I surplus that was of no further use to Britain and had little monetary value.

Churchill was the most ardent advocate of military intervention not only in England but in all Europe. He had concluded that World War I had ushered in a new historical era in which narrowly national interests and conflicts would yield to supranational and ideological interests and conflicts. This conviction enabled him to grasp the implications first of Communism and then of National Socialism sooner and better than any other statesman. He regarded communism as an unadulterated evil, a satanic force. The White cause was to him also Britain's cause. In September 1919, when Britain was about to abandon the Whites, he wrote:

> It is a delusion to suppose that all this year we have been fighting the battles of the anti-Bolshevik Russians. On the contrary, they have been fighting ours, and this truth will become painfully apparent from the moment that they are exterminated and the Bolshevik are supreme over the whole vast territories of the Russian Empire.

Churchill's anxiety about the triumph of communism in Russia was motivated by geopolitical considerations. A disciple of H. J. Mackinder, the founder of geopolitics, he feared that Russian Communists' control of the Eurasian "heartland" could give them world dominance, especially if they joined forces with Germany and Japan:

> If we abandon Russia, Germany and Japan will not. The new states which it is hoped to bring into being in the East of Europe will be crushed between Russian Bolshevism and Germany. Germany will regain by her influence over Russia far more than she has lost in colonies overseas and provinces in the West. Japan will no doubt arrive at a somewhat similar solution at the other end of the Trans-Siberian Railway. In five years, or even less, it will be apparent that the whole fruits of our victories have been lost at the Peace Conference, that the League of Nations is an impotent

mockery, that Germany is stronger than ever, and that British interests in India are perilously affected. After all our victories we shall have quitted the field in humiliation and defeat.

But Churchill had no supporters in the cabinet, and his warnings went largely unheeded. Indeed, well founded as his fears and predictions were, his remedy—massive military intervention, preferably on an international scale—was entirely unrealistic given the exhausted state of Europe after the Great War.

France's position in regard to Russia was uncomplicated. Two objectives dictated it: preventing a Russo-German rapprochement and compensation for the immense losses that France had suffered from Bolshevik defaults and expropriations. France did not believe in a White victory. Marshal Foch, the commander in chief of Allied forces in 1918, explained his country's skepticism when he said that he attached no "great importance to the army of Denikin, because armies do not exist by themselves. . . . They must have behind them a government, legislation, and an organized country. It is better to have a government without an army than an army without a government." Uncompromisingly hostile as France was to the Kremlin, she did next to nothing to help its opponents. A small multinational force which she sent to southern Russia in March 1919 evacuated as soon as it had been trounced by Ukrainian brigands allied with the Red Army. Instead of intervening in Russia, France concentrated on separating Russia from Germany by means of a "barbed wire fence" of friendly states anchored on Poland.

The United States intervened in 1918, most reluctantly and under British pressure, partly to prevent valuable military supplies in Russia's northern ports from falling into German hands, partly to assist in the evacuation of the Czechoslovak Legion, and partly to prevent the Japanese from seizing eastern Siberia. At no time did U.S. troops on Russian soil engage in combat.

The Japanese, who landed troops in Vladivostok on the pretext of protecting their citizens and joining the inter-Allied force on the eastern front, had strictly predatory objectives. They not only did not help Kolchak but made his life difficult because they knew that were he to triumph, they would have to withdraw. They relied on local Cossack warlords, who terrorized the population of the Far East and kept the region out of Kolchak's control.

In the spring of 1919, Kolchak mounted a major offensive in the direction of the Volga River. Its prospects were greatly reduced by poor command and disorganization of the rear. Kolchak proved to be a total disaster as an administrator. A bloated staff of 2,000 officers headquartered in Omsk planned operations for an army of 140,000 troops. Supplies destined for the front were regularly pilfered; some units drew rations for three times the number of men they actually had in their ranks. British uniforms and other marketable goods were rerouted to consumers. Speculators sold weapons and ammunition to the enemy. Omsk wits referred to the head of the British military mission, General Alfred Knox, as the Quartermaster General of the Red Army; he even received a spurious letter from Trotsky, originating in the same circles, expressing gratitude for his help in equipping Red troops. No one paid attention to the civilian population. As late as October 1919, when his army was well on its way to extinction, Kolchak told a civilian associate who pleaded for greater attention to politics:

> You know that I view as useless all your civil laws. . . . I have set myself a
> high goal: to crush the Red Army. I am Commander in Chief and do not
> concern myself with reforms. Write only those laws which are necessary at
> present and leave the rest to the Constituent Assembly.

Kolchak's offensive made excellent progress. The Red Army opposing it had little fighting spirit and suffered from the combined effects of White propaganda and peasant rebellions in its rear. It was also outnumbered, because Moscow, anticipating massive Allied landings in the Black Sea, neglected the eastern front. By the middle of April, the Whites were 100 kilometers or less from the Volga, having occupied in a few weeks 300,000 square kilometers inhabited by more than 5 million people.

The Red command, realizing its mistake, now reversed itself and assigned the highest priority to the eastern front. It shipped sizable reinforcements there, and by June the Red Army in the east enjoyed a numerical preponderance, which grew in the months that followed.

At this point Kolchak thought it important to secure Western recognition as the legitimate bearer of Russian state authority because the Russian population took more seriously a contender backed by the powers that had won the World War. (Similarly, in 1918 the perception that they enjoyed German support had a discouraging effect on the Bolsheviks' opponents.) The Supreme Allied Council posed a variety of conditions for recognition, including acknowledgment of Russia's foreign debts. Kolchak accepted nearly all of them. He also recognized as valid all the "pledges and decrees" of the 1917 Provisional Government. Even so, recognition was delayed, in good measure because President Wilson, who in Russian affairs deferred to the anti-White Alexander Kerensky, mistrusted Kolchak's democratic professions. In mid-June, when the Supreme Allied Council met in Paris to decide what to do about Kolchak, Kolchak's armies were in retreat. They never recovered. And recognition never came.

In the spring of 1919, when Kolchak stood at the peak of his fortunes, the Volunteer Army was mired in the Cossack hinterland. Denikin had drawn up plans for a campaign against Tsaritsyn and Astrakhan to effect a junction with Kolchak. But he abandoned these plans because in March and April the Red Army had mauled the Don Cossacks and threatened to invade the Don region, where the Volunteer Army had its base. On March 12, the southern front of the Red Army received instructions to attack the Donbas to clear out the Whites. But beyond this objective, as has recently become known, the Red Army was also to "liquidate" the Cossacks. A secret directive from Moscow demanded

> the complete, rapid, decisive annihilation of Cossackdom as a separate economic group, the destruction of its economic foundations, the physical extermination of its officials and officers, and altogether the Cossack elite.

Trotsky directed that the "nests of the dishonorable traitors and turncoats be extirpated. . . . The Cains must be exterminated." The use of the verb "exterminate" in regard to a whole socioethnic group anticipated action later designated as genocide. The program was carried out in 1920–21, at the conclusion of the Civil War.

Denikin faced a painful choice: either abandon the Donbas and link up with Kolchak or give up the idea of joining Kolchak to save the Donbas. He chose the second alternative, overruling some of his senior officers, including General Peter Wrangel, the Commander of the Caucasian Army and possibly the ablest White officer. He then divided the army in two; a smaller force under Wrangel was to capture Tsaritsyn, while the bulk of the army moved into the Donbas.

Denikin's decision has been criticized on the grounds that it lost him for the second time the opportunity to join forces with Kolchak. For while Wrangel did capture Tsaritsyn at the end of June following a brilliant campaign, Kolchak's forces were by then in retreat and the linkup could not be effected. The Volunteers, for their part, won spectacular victories in the Donbas, from where they pushed into the Ukraine, capturing in June Kharkov and Ekaterinoslav.

The Red counteroffensive in the east opened at the end of April with a drive against Ufa. Ufa fell on June 9. The Red Army then pressed east-

46. Tukhachevskii.

ward. The tide of battle took a decisive turn in late June, when the Fifth Army crossed the Urals, the only natural barrier in the region. Its commander, the twenty-seven-year-old Michael Tukhachevskii, was an aristocrat whose military record included service with the elite Semenovskii Guards. Once the Red Army spread east of the Urals—it captured Cheliabinsk at the end of July—the outnumbered White forces on the central front could not contain them and had to pull back their right and left flanks. Kolchak's offensive had been repulsed. The news had a shattering effect on his British supporters. When he learned of the fall of Cheliabinsk, Lord Curzon, the British Foreign Secretary, noted: "A lost cause." Indeed, the Siberian army, even while fighting a brave rearguard action, could not arrest the Red offensive and kept falling back toward Omsk. It was unable to replace its casualties, while the Red Army disposed of virtually inexhaustible reserves.

The center of the Civil War now shifted to the south, where Denikin advanced with a seemingly irresistible momentum, mauling the Red Army and conquering most of the Ukraine.

Arriving in Tsaritsyn a few days after its capture, Denikin held a staff meeting to decide on the next campaign. On July 3 he issued Order No. 08878, known as the Moscow Directive. It designated as the army's next and presumably final objective the capture of the capital city. This was to be accomplished by a three-pronged attack. Wrangel was to lead his

Caucasian Army on the right flank and advance on Moscow from the northeast. The Don Cossacks were to man the central front. The main force, composed of the Volunteer Army, other Cossack units, and recruits, was to proceed by the most direct route to Moscow by way of Kursk, Orel, and Tula. Wrangel once again criticized the disposition of forces, arguing that the main thrust should be in his sector. According to Wrangel, having heard him out, Denikin said: "I see! You want to be the first to set foot in Moscow!"

The scheme was an all-or-nothing play. The normally overcautious Denikin had to gamble both because the Red Army was growing by leaps and bounds and British support was likely to cease before the onset of winter. At the time of the Moscow Directive, the Red Army had in the south 180,000 men, while his own force numbered 85,000. During the decisive battles in October and November, the Red Army received 60,000 reinforcements.

The campaigns that followed were distinguished by great brutality. Captured White officers were frequently tortured. In one case, the Commander in Chief of the Red Army, S. S. Kamenev, ordered that "no prisoners be taken." The Whites also executed many captured Red commanders and commissars, but they do not seem to have engaged in torture.

Denikin's armies continued to advance throughout August and September. In the lead were the three Volunteer divisions, which on September 20 captured Kursk. But as it expanded, the White front grew thinner; 1,000 kilometers long, it resembled a wedge, the base of which rested on Kiev in the west and Tsaritsyn in the east, with the tip at Kursk. It was porous; one historian described it as a "series of patrols with occasional columns of slowly advancing troops devoid of reserves." The only compact sector lay in the north, where 10,000 troops manned a front twelve kilometers wide. They were to achieve the decisive breakthrough and capture Moscow.

Much as the White leaders tried to avoid politics and relegate them to the future, after victory had been won, some political issues would not wait. Foremost of these was the status of the non-Russian borderlands, most of which had separated themselves in 1917–18 and proclaimed independence. The White generals favored the restoration of the Empire. Their slogan was "Russia one and indivisible," because, in the words of Denikin, no one would risk his life for a federated Russia. Whenever they were pressed to recognize the independence of regions that had once formed part of the Empire, the White leaders equivocated, claiming they had no authority to deprive the Russian state of territory, and simply left this issue to the Constituent Assembly. This policy cost them dearly.

Politically, the most important of the peoples who had taken advantage of the Russian turmoil to claim sovereignty were the Poles and the Finns.

Of all European statesmen, the Polish leader Pilsudski knew the Russians best, especially the Russian socialists with whom he had worked in his youth: in 1887 he was arrested and exiled to Siberia for participating in the same plot to assassinate Alexander III that had cost Lenin's brother his life. He understood perfectly well that Poland could now assert her independence only because her traditional enemies, Germany and Russia, were crippled—one by defeat in war, the other by revolution. It was also clear to him that sooner or later these two great powers would recover and once again threaten Poland. To ensure his country's future, he wanted to extend Poland's frontiers far to the east and create between her and Russia a protective wall of buffer states. Just as France saw in Poland the linchpin of her security chain east of Germany, so Pilsudski envisaged an independent Ukraine as the bulwark of Poland's security against Russia.

Pilsudski sounded Denikin out on Poland's future. The answers he received did not satisfy him. Personally, the White commander and his political advisers were prepared to acknowledge Polish independence, but only within the borders of the so-called "Congress Poland" created by the Congress of Vienna in 1815, comprising Warsaw and the provinces immediately adjoining it. Even such a truncated Poland would have to await formal recognition from the future Constituent Assembly. Pilsudski concluded that from Poland's point of view, a Bolshevik victory in the Civil War would be a lesser evil than a White one, given that the latter was likely to end in the restoration of a nationalistic and expansionist Russian Empire.

Poland's involvement in the Russian Civil War was a matter of some consequence, since Polish troops, which in 1919 had penetrated several hundred kilometers into Belorussia and the Ukraine, could tip the scales one way or the other. Denikin, fairly confident of victory in the summer of 1919, saw no reason to yield to the Poles on the matter of independence and borders. He assumed that Pilsudski would in any event side with him out of hostility to bolshevism. The Communist government, on the other hand, fighting for its life and unconcerned with borders that, in its view, would become irrelevant in the approaching world revolution, was prepared to make as many concessions in this matter as were required to ensure Poland's neutrality in the Russian Civil War.

Using a Polish Communist as an intermediary, Moscow and Warsaw opened in the middle of July 1919 secret negotiations. Ostensibly, the two countries discussed exchanges of prisoners. In fact, the talks concerned the borders between the two countries and Poland's willingness, in return for a satisfactory border arrangement, to refrain from aiding Denikin. The Communist negotiator assured the Poles that Moscow would concede to them any frontiers they desired. This was all Pilsudski needed to hear. On his instructions, toward the end of October 1919, the Polish representative told his Russian counterpart: "We need you to defeat Denikin. Take your regiments and send them against Denikin and Iudenich. We shall not touch you." True to their word, at this very time, when Red and White forces were locked in combat in the western Ukraine, Polish forces deployed in the rear of the Reds did not stir. Pilsudski's pledge of noninterference rendered an invaluable service to the Red Army, allowing it to withdraw 43,000 troops from the Polish front and send them against Denikin. Pilsudski subsequently boasted that his deliberate inaction may well have decided the outcome of the Russian Civil War. Denikin concurred, and so did Tukhachevskii. At the same time, Pilsudski drew up plans to attack the Bolsheviks the instant they had disposed of Denikin.

The Whites' unwillingness to recognize the independence of Finland had an equally disastrous effect on their operations in the northwest, where a small army under General N. N. Iudenich came very close to capturing Petrograd. Finland had proclaimed her independence on November 4, 1917 (NS). Lenin's government promptly recognized Finland's sovereignty and just as promptly proceeded to stage a coup against her government using the Russian garrison and indigenous Communists. The Finnish leader, General Carl Mannerheim, organized a national resistance force which succeeded in expelling the Communists from northern Finland but lacked the strength to clear them from the south, where the capital, Helsinki, was located. In April 1918, the Germans, ignoring Mannerheim's objections, landed troops in Finland and crushed the Communist rebellion.

Iudenich, who had formed a small White volunteer army in Estonia with British help, asked the Finns in early 1919 to join it or at least allow it to assault Petrograd by the most direct route, across the Karelian Isthmus. Mannerheim hesitated to grant this request, in part because Britain and the other Allies gave him no strong indications that they supported Iudenich but largely because Kolchak, Iudenich's superior, refused to recognize Finland's independence. When Iudenich, on his own authority, agreed to grant such recognition, Kolchak repudiated him. The Finns then refused to allow Iudenich to attack Petrograd from their territory, forcing him to advance from Estonia which greatly complicated his task.

Acknowledging Finnish independence would have been little more than a formality, given that Finland was a fully sovereign state and recognized as such by a number of foreign countries, including France, Germany, and Soviet Russia. This was another example of the political insensitivity of the White generals, whose exclusive concern was with military operations.

The collapse of Kolchak, on whom they had pinned their hopes, was a bitter pill for that small group of British statesmen who favored intervention. Lloyd George, who opposed intervention even as he embraced it, now publicly began to voice skepticism about continued support for the Whites. "If Denikin really had the people behind him," he said, "the Bolsheviks could never overcome him"—as if trial by battle were a form of balloting. In early August 1919, the War Cabinet resolved to offer Denikin a "final packet" of aid, nearly all of it to consist of "nonmarketable" goods; he was to be told that nothing more would be forthcoming. This happened at a time when Denikin was closer than ever to victory. On October 7, as the Volunteer Army approached Orel, 300 kilometers from Moscow, and Iudenich was staging his drive on Petrograd, the British cabinet agreed on a "Final Contribution to General Denikin" totaling £14 million ($70 million), all but £3 million of which was to consist of surplus war matériel.

Thus were sown the seeds of betrayal. After Kolchak's defeat, Britain's heart was no longer in intervention and the government sought ways to extricate itself from Russia. There could be no doubt that as soon as Denikin suffered the first reverses in his advance on Moscow, he would be abandoned.

The Civil War was accompanied by frightful pogroms in the Ukrainian lands west of the Dnieper River. Not since the mid-seventeenth century, when the Ukraine was overrun by Cossacks rebelling against the Poles, had the Jews suffered such persecution. They marked a prelude to the genocide which the Germans would carry out a quarter of a century later.

With the exception of a small minority of Jews who had completed higher education or amassed sizable fortunes, all Jewish inhabitants of the Russian Empire had to reside in the towns of the so-called Pale of Settlement, an area carved out of the provinces of the defunct Polish Commonwealth, which Russia had acquired in the partitions of the eighteenth century. In this regional ghetto they were inscribed on the rolls of the burgher estate and the vast majority had to make a living by trade or artisanship. Because they experienced unusually rapid demographic growth, Russian Jews found themselves in an increasingly desperate economic situation. Many emigrated to Europe and the Americas. For those who stayed, avenues of noncommercial advancement were either completely closed—they could not enroll in either the civil service or the officer corps—or severely restricted (e.g., by means of admission quotas to the universities). As a result of such discrimination, a disproportionate number of Jewish youths joined the revolutionary movement. Some farsighted Russian statesmen, Stolypin among them, favored abolishing the medieval restrictions on the Jews, but such proposals foundered in the face of opposition by anti-Semites at the Court and in the bureaucracy.

The Pale of Settlement died a natural death during World War I when tens of thousands of Jews living near the combat zone were expelled to the interior of Russia on suspicion of harboring pro-German sympathies. The Provisional Government abolished all remaining restrictions on them. In 1917 and the years immediately following, Jews for the first time in Russian history appeared as government functionaries both in and outside the old Pale of Settlement. Thus it happened that following the Revolution, Jews suddenly showed up in parts of the country where they had never been seen before, namely Russia proper, and in capacities they had never before exercised. It was a fatal conjunction that for Russians the appearance of the Jews coincided with the miseries of communism. In the words of a contemporary Jewish intellectual:

Previously, Russians have never seen Jews in positions of authority: neither as governor, nor as policeman, nor even as postal employee. Even then, there had been, of course, better times and worse times, but the Russian people lived, worked, and disposed of the fruits of their labor, the Russian nation grew and enriched itself, the Russian name was great and awe-inspiring. Now the Jew is on every corner and on all rungs of power. . . . The Russian sees him now as judge and executioner. He encounters Jews at every step—not Communists, but people as hapless as he himself, yet giving orders, working for the Soviet regime; and this regime, after all, is everywhere, one cannot escape it. And this regime, had it emerged from the lowest depths of hell, could not be more malevolent or brazen. Is it any wonder that the Russian, comparing the past with the present, concludes that the present regime is Jewish and therefore so diabolical?

The consequence of this identification was the outbreak of a virulent anti-Semitism, first in Russia and then abroad. Just as socialism was the ideology of the intelligentsia and nationalism that of the old civil and military establishment, so Judeophobia became the ideology of the masses. The connection between Jews and communism, made in the aftermath of the Revolution and exported from Russia to Weimar Germany by extreme nationalists and Baltic Germans was instantly assimilated by Hitler and made into a cardinal tenet of Nazism.

The paradox inherent in this situation was that although they were widely perceived as working for the benefit of their own people, Bolsheviks of Jewish origin not only did not think of themselves as Jews but resented any suggestions to this effect. They were renegades who saw in communism an escape from their Jewishness. The historian of Soviet Jewry Nora Levin writes:

> Bolshevism attracted marginal Jews, poised between two worlds—the Jewish and the Gentile—who created a new homeland for themselves, a community of ideologists bent on remaking the world in their own image. These Jews quite deliberately and consciously broke with the restrictive social, religious and cultural life of the Jews of the Pale of Settlement and attacked the secular culture of Jewish socialists and Zionists. Having abandoned their own origins and identity, yet not finding, or sharing, or being fully admitted to Russian life (except in the world of the party) the Jewish Bolsheviks found their ideological home in revolutionary universalism.

Trotsky—the satanic "Bronstein" of Russian anti-Semites—reacted with unrestrained fury whenever anyone presumed to refer to him as a Jew. When a visiting Jewish delegation appealed to him to help fellow Jews, he responded angrily: "I am not a Jew but an internationalist." On another occasion he said that Jews interested him no more than Bulgarians. In the fall of 1919, when Jews in the Ukraine perished by the thousands in pogroms, he seemed not to notice even though he was there. Another Jewish Communist, Karl Radek, went so far as to confide in a German journalist that he would like to "exterminate" all Jews.

The White Army of the south did not display anti-Semitism during the first year of its existence: Jews fought in its ranks and participated in the Ice March. This changed in the winter of 1918–19, partly because Jews were widely blamed for the Red Terror—especially the murder of Nicholas II and his family—and partly because once the Germans had withdrawn, Russian anti-Communists needed another scapegoat for bolshevism, which they would not admit had Russian roots. At the same time, it must be stressed that the Volunteer Army did not engage in pogroms; these were almost exclusively the work of Ukrainian freebooters and Cossacks serving in White ranks who treated the Civil War as an occasion for plunder.

Anti-Jewish excesses began in 1918 during the German occupation of the Ukraine; they intensified after the Germans withdrew. The worst episodes occurred in 1919 during two peak periods, the first in May and the second in August–October. White Cossacks participated only in the last and most savage phase. Until they made their appearance in the central Ukraine in August, the pogroms were perpetrated by the bands of the Ukrainian nationalist Semën Petlura, and other outlaws who terrorized the region.

The pogroms followed a pattern. As a rule, they involved not the local population but outsiders. Their primary objective was plunder; physical violence against Jews served mainly to extort money, although mindless sadism was not unknown. On breaking into a Jewish household, the bandits would demand money and valuables. If these were not forthcoming, they would resort to force. Most killings resulted from the refusal or inability of the victims to pay up. The perpetrators would load the furniture and other household goods on military trains for shipment to the Don, Kuban and, Terek regions; what they could not carry, they smashed or distributed to peasants who stood by with carts and sacks. Nearly everywhere, rape accompanied the pogroms; the victims were often put to death. Sometimes the pogroms had a religious character, resulting in the desecration of Jewish houses of worship, the destruction of Torah scrolls and other religious objects, but on the whole religion played a smaller role than did economic and sexual motives.

A careful reckoning of the pogroms by Jewish organizations indicates that the worst were perpetrated by Ukrainian freebooters. According to these analyses, the Civil War witnessed 1,236 instances of anti-Jewish violence, of which 887 are classified as pogroms and the rest as "excesses"—that is, violence that did not assume mass dimensions. Of this total number, the followers of Petlura committed 493, or 40 percent; independent Ukrainian warlords ("atamans"), 307 (25 percent); Denikin's troops, 213 (17 percent); and the Red Army, 106 (8.5 percent). (On the last, historians have been strikingly silent.)

While it is, therefore, incorrect to lay wholesale blame for the massacres of the Jews on the White Army, it is true that Denikin and his commanders remained passive in the face of the atrocities perpetrated by their Cossack allies. These not only stained the reputation of his army but contributed greatly to its demoralization. Personally, the commander of the Southern Army was not a typical anti-Semite of the time: at any rate, in his five-volume chronicle of the Civil War he does not blame Jews either for communism or his defeat. On the contrary: he expresses remorse at their treatment in his army as well as for the pogroms. He was a weak, politically inexperienced man who had little control over his troops. He yielded to the pressures of his anti-Semitic officers from fear of appearing pro-Jewish and from a sense of the futility of fighting against prevailing passions. In June 1919, he told a Jewish delegation which urged him to issue a declaration condemning the pogroms that "words here were powerless, that any unnecessary clamor in regard to this question will only make the situation of Jews harder, irritating the masses and bringing out the customary accusation of 'selling out to the Yids.' " On a few occasions Denikin and his subordinates tried to punish those who engaged in violence against the Jews, but instructions to this effect could not be enforced in view of the prevailing psychosis. In Kiev, for instance, when a White general ordered courts-martial for officers involved in a pogrom and had three of them sentenced to death, he had to rescind the sentence when other officers threatened to avenge their execution with a pogrom against Kievan Jews in which hundreds would perish.

The anti-Semitism of the White armies has been well documented and publicized. Little attention, however, has been paid to Soviet reactions to anti-Jewish excesses, which were remarkably muted. The Bolsheviks did not tolerate pogroms on their territory because they knew that anti-Semitism often concealed anti-communism. But for the same reason, they did not go out of their way to publicize anti-Semitic violence on the White side so as not to play into the hands of those who accused them of serving "Jewish" interests. They also pretended not to notice pogroms carried out by their own troops. In the secret archive of Lenin, recently opened to scholars, there is a document containing his instruction to local communists following the reoccupation of the Ukraine in late 1919. It contains the following clause:

> Jews (refer to them politely as "Jewish petty bourgeoisie") and city people in the Ukraine are to be managed with an iron rod: transfer them to the front, do not let them into government organs (perhaps only in insignificant percentages in very special circumstances under class control).[7]

The only prominent figure to condemn the pogroms outright and unequivocally was the head of the Orthodox Church, Patriarch Tikhon, who in an epistle dated July 21, 1919, denounced violence against Jews as bringing "dishonor to the perpetrators, dishonor to the Holy Church."

The number of fatalities suffered in the pogroms of 1918–20 cannot be established with any precision, but it was high. Evidence indicates that 31,071 of the victims were given a proper burial. These figures do not include those whose remains were burned or left unburied. Hence it is generally assumed that the number of victims was double or even triple that figure—somewhere between 50,000 and 100,000. In addition, the Jewish population of the Ukraine was left destitute. In every respect except for the absence of a central organization to direct the slaughter and the looting, the pogroms of the Russian Civil War anticipated the Holocaust. They left a legacy that two decades later would lead to the systematic mass murder of Jews at the hands of the Nazis: the deadly identification of communism with Jewry.

This identification gained wide acceptance at the time not only in extreme right-wing circles of Russia and Germany but also among otherwise enlightened Englishmen and Americans, laying the psychological groundwork for Hitler's "Final Solution." The *Protocols of the Elders of Zion,* a forgery purporting to spell out the Jewish strategy for subjugating the gentile world, became at the time an international best-seller because it seemed to explain what otherwise seemed inexplicable—namely, the phenomenon of communism. Fantastic stories spread by Russian extremists to the effect that all the Soviet leaders (except Lenin) were Jews found credence abroad. Suffice it to say that Sir Eyre Crowe, one of the most senior officials in the British Foreign Office, responding to a memorandum from Chaim Weizmann, the future President of Israel, protesting the pogroms, observed "that what may appear to Mr. Weizmann to be outrages against Jews, may in the eyes of the Ukrainians be retaliation against the horrors committed by the Bolsheviks who are all organized and directed by Jews."

What are the facts? Jews undeniably played both in the Bolshevik Party and the Soviet apparatus a role disproportionate to their share of the population. They were also disproportionately represented among Communists in Western Europe and in the Communist International. But then Jews are a very active people, prominent in many fields of endeavor. If they were conspicuous in Communist circles, they were no less so in capitalist ones, not to speak of the performing arts, literature, and science. Although they constitute less than 0.3 percent of the world's population, in the first seventy years of the Nobel Prizes (1901–1970) Jews won one in four awards in physiology and medicine, and one in five in physics. According to Mussolini, four of the seven founders of the Fascist Party were Jews; indeed, initially, Jews constituted a higher percentage of Fascist Party members than did any other Italian group.[8] Hitler said they were among the early financial supporters of the Nazi movement.

Nor must it be deduced from the prominence of Jews in the early Communist government that Russian Jewry was pro-Communist. It must never be overlooked that during the Revolution and the Civil War, the Bolshevik Party was very much a minority party, a self-selected body whose membership did not reflect the opinions of the population: Lenin himself admitted that Communists constituted but a "drop of water" in the nation's "sea." In other words, while not a few Communists were Jews, few Jews were Communists. When in 1917 Russian Jewry had the opportunity to express its political preferences, it voted not for the Bolsheviks but either for the Zionists or for the parties of democratic socialism. The elections to the Constituent Assembly indicate that Bolshevik support came not from the area of Jewish concentration, the old Pale of Settlement, but from the armed forces and the cities of Great Russia. A census of the Communist Party conducted in 1922 showed that only 959 Jewish members had joined it before 1917.

In the course of the Civil War, the Jewish population, caught in the Red-White conflict, gradually came to side with the Communist regime from the instinct of self-preservation. When the Whites first entered the Ukraine Jews welcomed them, for they had suffered grievously under the preceding, Communist regime if not as Jews then as "bourgeois." They quickly became disenchanted with White policies that excluded Jews from the administration and tolerated pogroms. Thereafter, Jews looked to the Red Army, which had both Jewish officers and commissars, for protection. Thus a vicious circle was set in motion: Jews were persecuted for allegedly being pro-Communist, which had the effect of turning them pro-Communist for the sake of survival; this shift of allegiance served to justify further persecution.

For all practical purposes, in November 1919 Admiral Kolchak's army turned into a rabble concerned solely with survival. Thousands of officers, accompanied by their wives and mistresses, as well as hordes of soldiers and civilians, rushed headlong eastward. All streamed toward Omsk in the hope that it would be defended: the influx of refugees swelled the city's population from 120,000 to more than a half million. The wounded and the ill were abandoned to their fate. In the no-man's-land between the advancing Red and the retreating White armies, marauders—mostly Cossacks—robbed, killed, and raped.

> When the main body of [Kolchak's] trooped arrived in Omsk they found unspeakable conditions. Refugees overflowed the streets, the railroad station, the public buildings. The roads were hub-deep in mud. Soldiers and their families begged from house to house for bread. Officers' wives turned

into prostitutes to stave off hunger. Thousands who had money spent it on drunken debauches in the cafés. Mothers and babies froze to death upon the sidewalks. Children were separated from their parents and orphans died by the score in the vain search for food and warmth. Many of the stores were robbed and others closed through fear. Military bands attempted a semblance of gaiety in the public houses but to no avail. Omsk was inundated in a sea of misery . . . The condition of the wounded was beyond description. Suffering men often lay two in a bed and in some hospitals and public buildings they were placed on the floor. Bandages were improvised out of sheeting, tablecloths, and women's underclothing. Antiseptics and opiates were almost nonexistent.

Typhus was rampant; entire trains, filled with the sick, dying, and dead, littered the Trans-Siberian Railway.

Kolchak had intended to defend Omsk, but he was dissuaded and left the city for Irkutsk on November 13, 1919, just ahead of the approaching Red Army. He traveled in six trains, one of which, made up of twenty-nine cars, carried the Russian Treasury's gold and other valuables which the Bolsheviks had evacuated to Kazan and the Czechs had captured. The Czechs and Slovaks, who controlled the railroad, scoured the countryside, looting everything in sight. They shunted Kolchak's convoy to sidings to let their own trains pass. At the end of December, seven weeks after he had left Omsk, Kolchak was stranded 500 kilometers west of Irkutsk, forsaken by virtually everyone and kept incommunicado by his Czech guards.

At this time, a coalition of left-wing groups dominated by Socialists-Revolutionaries staged a coup in Irkutsk. They formed a Political Center, which declared Kolchak deposed and proclaimed itself the government of Siberia. On learning of these events on January 4, 1920, Kolchak announced his resignation, placing himself and his hoard under the protection of the Czechs. The Czechs undertook to escort him to Irkutsk and there turn him over to the Allied missions.

What happened subsequently has never been satisfactorily explained. As best as can be determined, Kolchak was betrayed by the Commander of the Czechoslovak Legion and the head of the French military mission, with the result that instead of receiving Allied protection, he was handed over to the Irkutsk Political Center. The latter organization soon resigned in favor of a Bolshevik Military-Revolutionary Committee. In exchange for Kolchak and his gold, the Czechs were allowed to proceed to Vladivostok and from there to embark for home. Kolchak, his twenty-six-year-old mistress, and his Prime Minister were put in prison.

The Bolsheviks formed a commission to interrogate Kolchak. It sat from January 21 to February 6, 1920. The investigation, a cross between an inquest and a trial, terminated abruptly on February 6, when the Irkutsk Revkom condemned Kolchak to death. The official explanation, issued several weeks later, held that Kolchak was about to be abducted by White troops commanded by General V. O. Kappel. But a coded document, first located in the Trotsky Archive at Harvard, raises serious doubts about this explanation and suggests that the execution was ordered by Lenin. Scribbled on the back of an envelope and addressed to the Chairman of the Siberian Military-Revolutionary Committee, it read:

> Do not release any information about Kolchak; print absolutely nothing but after we have occupied Irkutsk send a strictly official telegram explaining that the local authorities, before our arrival, had acted in such and such a way under the influence of the threat from Kappel and the danger of White Guard plots in Irkutsk.

The whole procedure ordered by Lenin closely resembled that which he had employed to camouflage the murder of the Imperial family—the killing allegedly done on the initiative of local authorities from fear that the prisoner would be abducted, and the Center learning of it only after the fact.

Kolchak and his Prime Minister were removed from their cells in the middle of the night (February 6–7) and shot. Their bodies were pushed under the ice of a nearby river.

In the south and northwest, matters seemed for a while to look up for the Whites, only to end in an identical disaster.

On September 12, 1919, Denikin ordered his armies "from the Volga to the Romanian border" to advance on Moscow. On September 20, the Volunteer Army seized Kursk. According to Viacheslav Molotov, then a secretary of the Central Committee, at this time Lenin told associates that the Soviet government was done for and the Party would go underground.[9] Dzerzhinskii instructed the Cheka to divide its 12,000 hostages into several categories in order to determine whom to execute first to prevent them from falling into White hands.

In their march on the capital, the Whites were aided by intelligence obtained from a clandestine organization called National Center. Directed by a liberal lawyer, N. N. Shchepkin, the Center provided information on the mood of the population and advice on what slogans to use to win it over. Its branch office in Petrograd supplied Iudenich with military intelligence. A series of fortuitous accidents helped the Cheka to uncover the Center. In September 1919 its leaders, Shchepkin included, were executed.

The Southern Army went from victory to victory, piercing the defense perimeter set up by the enemy. On October 13–14, the Volunteer Army captured Orel. It was the high-water mark of the White advance, which brought it within 300 kilometers of Moscow. At this very time, the troops of Iudenich were fighting in Gatchina, within sight of Petrograd. Denikin's next objective was Tula, the last major city on the road to the capital and an important center of arms production. But mass mobilization and troop transfers from the Polish front, secured by arrangement with Pilsudski, gave the Red Army an insuperable numerical advantage in the decisive battles that lay ahead.

On October 11, 1919, while the fighting in the south was reaching a climax. Iudenich launched his second offensive against Petrograd. He made good progress against superior enemy forces. On October 16, his army stood at Tsarskoe Selo, the old Imperial residence, a mere twenty-five kilometers from Petrograd. The Whites, whose ranks included many officers serving as ordinary soldiers, fought brilliantly, using the night as cover to disorient and frighten the enemy and creating the impression that he was greatly outnumbered. The appearance of the few tanks at their disposal threw the Reds into headlong flight. The operation was assisted by the British navy, which provided artillery cover and bombed Kronshtadt, sinking or severely damaging eleven Soviet vessels, including two battleships.

Lenin was prepared to abandon Petrograd and gave secret orders to evacuate the old capital, but Trotsky and Stalin persuaded him to defend it because of the detrimental effect its fall would have on morale. In the only instance during the Civil War in which he personally participated in combat, Trotsky took charge of the city's defenses. He ordered barricades to be built. In rousing speeches to the disheartened troops, he made light of the enemy and his tanks. He decisively turned the situation around. Lenin's advice was useless: on October 22, he urged Trotsky to mobilize "10 thousand or so of the bourgeoisie, post machine guns in their rear, [have] a few hundred shot and assure a real mass assault on Iudenich."

On October 20, Iudenich's troops reached the suburbs of Petrograd. Trotsky, mounted on a horse, rallied the fleeing troops and led them back into battle. A critical factor in Iudenich's defeat was the failure of one of his officers, eager to be the first to enter liberated Petrograd, to obey orders to cut the railroad line to Moscow. This permitted the Red command to dispatch reinforcements.

On October 21, the Seventh Red Army counterattacked. It quickly pierced the White lines, which had no reserves. When the Fifteenth Red Army began to advance from the south, Iudenich's army had no choice

47. Budënnyi and Egorov.

but to retreat to Estonia, where it was disarmed. In the months that followed, Soviet Russia signed peace treaties with the three Baltic republics
as well as Finland.

Toward the end of September 1919, the Red High Command assembled
in great secrecy west of Orel a "Striking Group" of shock troops. Its
nucleus was the Latvian Rifle Division, clad in the familiar leather jackets,
which had been transferred from the western front and was, once again,
to render the Communist regime invaluable services. The commander in
charge of the southern front, A. I. Egorov, a career officer with a Socialist-
Revolutionary background, reinforced the Striking Group with a newly
formed cavalry corps under Semën Budënnyi, an "outlander" from the
Don region who passionately hated the Cossacks. Deployed east of
Voronezh, it was to attack the Volunteer Army from the east.

On October 18–19, as the Volunteer Army pushed toward Tula, the
Second and Third Latvian Brigades of the Striking Group launched a
surprise attack against the left flank of the Volunteer Army. In pitched
battles the Latvians defeated the exhausted Volunteers and on October
20 forced them to abandon Orel. In this engagement, the Latvians lost
in killed and wounded over 50 percent of their officers and up to 40 percent of their soldiers.

The Volunteer Army found itself in a perilous but not hopeless situation when suddenly from the east appeared another threat, Budënnyi's Cavalry Corps reinforced by 12,000–15,000 infantry. On October 19, Budënnyi defeated the Don Cossacks defending Voronezh and occupied the city. On October 29, he crossed the Don and attacked the strategically important railroad junction of Kastornoe. Fierce fighting went on for two weeks. The Red Army captured Kastornoe on November 15, sealing the fate of the White advance on Moscow. The Volunteer Army fell back toward Kursk. Its commander, a capable soldier but given to drink and womanizing, was replaced by Wrangel.

In the midst of these reverses, another heavy blow fell on the Whites. On November 8, Lloyd George declared in a public speech that bolshevism could not be defeated by force of arms and that Britain "cannot . . . afford to continue so costly an intervention in an interminable civil war." On November 17, in an address to the House of Commons, he recalled Disraeli's warning of a "great, gigantic, colossal, growing Russia rolling onwards like a glacier toward Persia and the borders of Afghanistan and India as the greatest menace the British Empire could be confronted with." Kolchak's and Denikin's struggle for "a reunited Russia," he asserted, was not in Britain's best interest.

According to Denikin, these words had a devastating impact on his troops. This assessment is confirmed by a British eyewitness, the journalist C. E. Bechhofer:

> The effect of Mr George's speeches was electrical. Until that moment, the Volunteers and their supporters had comforted themselves with the idea that they were fighting one of the final phases of the Great War, with England still the first of their Allies. Now they suddenly realized with horror that England considered the War as over and the conflict in Russia as merely a civil conflict. In a couple of days the whole atmosphere in South Russia was changed. Whatever firmness of purposes there had previously been, was now so undermined that the worst became possible. Mr George's opinion that the Volunteer cause was doomed helped to make this doom almost certain.

On November 17, the Whites pulled out of Kursk. At this time they learned that three days earlier Kolchak had abandoned Omsk. They kept retreating at an ever faster pace. In mid-December, after Kharkov and Kiev had fallen, their retreat turned into a rout. Events now followed the same pattern they had in Siberia, with mobs of soldiers and civilians fleeing in panic southward, toward the Black Sea. The masses converged on Novorossiisk, the principal Allied port, hoping to evacuate on Allied ships. Here, in the midst of a raging typhus epidemic, with the Bolshevik

Critical Battles

OCTOBER–NOVEMBER 1919

cavalry waiting in the outskirts, dreadful scenes were enacted as people pleaded to be taken on ships that could accommodate only a fraction of them. When the ships set sail and the Red cavalry entered Novorossiisk, hundreds paid immediately with their lives and tens of thousands were shipped to concentration camps. Cossack settlements were devastated and masses of their inhabitants deported. By 1921 in some areas, the Cossack population had declined by half. Ten years later, during collectivization, Cossackdom was abolished.

On arriving in the Crimea on April 2, 1920, White generals compelled Denikin to resign his command. A poll of senior officers unanimously chose Wrangel as his successor. Wrangel, who had retired and was living in Constantinople, immediately boarded an English ship bound for the Crimea. He carried with him a note from the British High Commissioner demanding that the Whites cease forthwith the "unequal struggle." Britain promised to grant asylum to the top White officers and to intercede with Moscow for a general amnesty for those left behind. Should the Whites reject the offer, the note stated, the British government would "cease to furnish [them] . . . with any help or subvention of any kind from that time on."

Wrangel had no illusions about carrying on the struggle against the millions-strong Red Army, but he was unwilling to abandon to its mercy hundreds of thousand of White troops and anti-Communist civilians who had taken refuge in the Crimea. He received a respite from the Polish invasion of the Soviet Ukraine which occurred three weeks after he had assumed command (see below, p. 292). The Red Army, which did not want to fight a two-front war, suspended its operations against the Crimea. Wrangel utilized the time to restore discipline in the army. He also formulated a program of reforms meant to transform the Crimea into a democratic and socially progressive state that would serve Russians as a model once communism collapsed. But when the Poles and Russians suspended hostilities (October 18, 1920), his cause was doomed. Two days later, the Red Army launched offensive operations against the Crimea. On November 14, Wrangel's remnant evacuated on British and French ships to Constantinople. From there, the military and civilian refugees scattered across Europe, joining the 1 million émigrés from Soviet Russia who had preceded them.

It is commonplace among historians to attribute the White defeat to a failure to win mass support and to explain this failure by their unwillingness to adopt liberal social and political platforms. This proposition

48. General Wrangel.

assumes that civil war is a kind of popularity contest in which the preferences of the majority decide the issue. In reality, the Russian Civil War was waged by minuscule minorities with the population at large bearing the brunt but without being politically involved—the attitude of the "masses" was described by contemporaries as "a plague on both your houses." The peasantry, in particular, may have been alienated by the absence of a clear White policy on their land seizures, but it was no less angered by Bolshevik food confiscations. Eyewitnesses report that when living under the Reds, the population longed for the Whites, but after experiencing White rule they wanted the Reds back. In many ways the so-called Green bands, which fought both the Reds and the Whites, best expressed the feelings of the Russians and Ukrainians in the Civil War.*

---

* To understand how little it takes in Russia to sway the country in extreme directions, one need only recall the events of August 1991 and October 1993. In the first instance, a few thousand civilians, aided by small army contingents, thwarted a military coup to restore communism. The result was the collapse of the Soviet Union and the dissolution of the Communist Party. In October 1993, a few thousand soldiers, assembled with great difficulty, enabled President Yeltsin to liquidate the parliamentary opposition. On both occasions, which ended seventy years of Communist rule, the overwhelming majority of the people, the "masses," stood by, withholding support from both parties to the conflict and passively awaiting the outcome.

Thus in the ultimate analysis, the Red triumph has to be accounted for by the "objective" factors mentioned previously—namely, control of the center of Russia with its vastly superior human and military resources, and the unity of command.

The human casualties of the Civil War were staggering, most of them due to epidemics and hunger. Combat fatalities of the Red Army—mainly suffered on the home front fighting peasants—have been estimated at 1 million. White battlefield casualties are even less precise, but one demographer calculates them at 127,000. This figure does not include White prisoners of war who were executed after being captured or died from maltreatment in concentration camps.

To the combat fatalities must be added the civilian victims of epidemics as well those who perished from malnutrition, the cold, and suicide; infectious diseases alone are estimated to have claimed more than 2 million lives.

Finally, to the demographic losses must be added the loss of citizens who fled abroad; they numbered between 1½ and 2 million. While the majority went to France and Germany, each of which took in 400,000 émigrés, Russians found new homes in every country around the world. They constituted a high proportion of the educated elite that had run Russia before the Revolution. Although, expecting to return, they treated their sojourn as no more than a temporary exile, with few exceptions they ended their days abroad. This exodus represented for Russia a loss in talent, knowledge, and experience that defies quantification.

THE NEW EMPIRE

Although one conventionally speaks of the "Russian" Revolution and the "Russian" Civil War, the country in which these events took place was an empire in which Russians proper (Great Russians) constituted a minority. The first nationwide census, conducted in 1897, showed that this empire (exclusive of the Grand Duchy of Finland) had 125 million inhabitants. Of that number, 56 million were Great Russians, 22 million Ukrainians, and 6 million Belorussians. But even this count inflated the size of the dominant nationality, because the census takers tabulated not ethnic affiliation but native language: according to subsequent censuses, a considerable number of non-Russians (in 1926, 8.2 percent) considered Russian their mother tongue and were listed as Russians. In terms of ethnic origin, at the time of the Revolution, Great Russians numbered probably no more than 52 million, or 42 percent of the Empire's population.

The 1897 census recorded 85 distinct linguistic groups, the smallest of which numbered in the hundreds. Interesting as such groups may be to the anthropologist or ethnographer, for the historian they are of marginal importance. From a political point of view, the minorities of the Russian Empire numbered fewer than a dozen.

The largest of them, the Ukrainians, had close affinities to the Great Russians in terms of language and religion, but having lived for nearly five centuries under Catholic Poland, developed differently. The same, if to a smaller extent, held true of the Belorussians. Both nations had much briefer experience with the three institutions that shaped the lives of Great Russians: patrimonial autocracy, serfdom, and communal land-holding. At the turn of the century neither was yet a fully formed nation, and such sense of national identity as they possessed remained confined to a thin layer of the intelligentsia. The Ukrainian nationalist movement, encouraged and financed by the Austrians in the interest of weakening Russia, acquired a broader constituency only during the Revolution and Civil War.

Politically, the most troublesome ethnic group were the 8 million Poles. By 1900, St. Petersburg had deprived them of all rights to self-rule and administered them as if Poland, once a great European power, were but another Russian province. It is difficult to understand how the Russians hoped to keep an ancient people, culturally much superior to the mass of their own population, in permanent subjection. But they acted as if they could because of Poland's geopolitical importance to them as an outpost in Europe.

Next to the Slavs, in terms of numbers, came various Turco-Tatar groups professing Islam—mainly in its Sunni form—who were scattered from the Black Sea to the Pacific. They concentrated in three regions. The largest of these was central Asia (the Steppe and Turkestan), inhab-ited by 7 million Muslims, all of them, except the Shiite Tajiks, Sunnis speaking Turkic dialects. Another Muslim grouping, and the earliest to come under Russian rule, comprised Turks living along the mid-Volga and in the Urals. They were the Tatars, a partly commercial, partly agrar-ian people, and 1.3 million largely nomadic Bashkirs. A third area of Muslim concentration lay in the Caucasus and the Crimean Peninsula. Muslims totaled 14–15 million, or 11 percent of the Empire's population.

Russia acquired Finland in 1809 as a present from her ally, Napoleon. She formed in the Russian Empire an autonomous entity with her own legislature; the Tsar, an autocrat in all his other possessions, ruled the Finns as a constitutional monarch. This arrangement began to fall apart at the turn of the century owing to violations of the Finnish constitution by Russian officials. The inhabitants of Finland enjoyed exemption from Russian laws and from conscription by the Russian army.

In the Baltic areas, then known as Livonia, Courland, and Estonia, Germans constituted the dominant element by virtue of their control of the land and commerce. The Latvians and Estonians formed a lower class of peasants and workers. Lithuanians made up a third ethnic group in the Baltic provinces.

The Georgians (1.4 million in 1897) and Armenians (1.2 million) constituted an Orthodox Christian minority in a predominantly Muslim region. In Georgia, native Mensheviks dominated the political scene; several of them played also prominent roles in the Russian Social-Democratic Party. The leading Armenian political organization, Dashnaktsutiun, had a nationalist orientation and strove to unite with the larger Armenian population living under Ottoman rule across the border.

The 5 million Jews made up a category of their own because of the unique discriminatory laws to which they were subject. Their status was due in part to religious intolerance and in part to the fear of the officials charged with internal security that capitalist entrepreneurship, at which Jews excelled, would upset social stability if given free rein. Nearly all of them lived in the Pale of Settlement, which encompassed Poland, the western Ukraine, Belorussia, and Lithuania.

Apart from the Poles, who would be satisfied with nothing short of sovereignty and, to a lesser extent, the Finns, the ethnic minorities did not give the Imperial authorities much trouble. What came to be known as the "nationalities problem" presented as yet more of a potential than a tangible threat to the Empire's unity.

The 1905 Revolution and the constitutional regime that emerged from it stimulated ethnic awareness. During 1905 and 1906, representatives of the major ethnic groups held congresses to air grievances and formulate demands. In the electoral campaigns to the Duma, many minorities ran their own candidates, usually in affiliation with Russian socialist parties or the liberal Constitutional-Democrats. In their programs, the minority parties (the Poles always excepted) confined themselves to calls for greater territorial or cultural autonomy within the framework of the Russian Empire. Independence did not as yet figure among their demands.

Considering the importance which ethnic issues were to acquire, it is surprising how little attention Russians paid to them: even politically active intellectuals treated nationality and nationalism as marginal matters, essentially responses to discrimination that were bound to disappear with the introduction of political and social democracy. This lack of awareness can be explained by a combination of historical and geographic factors. Unlike the European empires, which came into being only after the formation of national states, the Russian Empire grew concurrently with the Russian state; historically, the two processes—state-building and empire-building—were virtually indistinguishable. Furthermore, since Russia is not a maritime nation, her colonial possessions were territorially contiguous rather than—as in the case of Europe—separated by oceans. This geographic factor further blurred the distinction between metropolis and imperial domain. To the extent that they gave the matter any thought, educated Russians expected the minorities to assimilate, and their country, like the United States, to fuse into a single nation. The analogy had little to recommend it, since unlike the United States, which except for native Indians and imported African slaves, was inhabited by immigrants, the Russian Empire consisted of historic regions conquered by force of arms.

The nationality question arose in an acute from within days of the outbreak of the February Revolution. The collapse of tsarism gave the ethnic groups the opportunity not only to articulate their demands but to insist on their prompt satisfaction. Grievances that in the provinces inhabited by solid Russian majorities assumed economic or social forms of expression, in the predominantly non-Russian regions found outlets in nationalism. Thus, to cite but one example, to the Kazakh-Kirghiz nomads of central Asia, the Russian colonists who had taken over their pastures and turned them into arable land appeared not as a hostile class but as an ethnic enemy.

The first to stir were the Ukrainians, who on March 4, 1917, formed in Kiev a regional soviet called the Rada. Initially moderate in their demands, the Ukrainian nationalist leaders became increasingly radical as central authority in Russia crumbled. On June 10, the Rada declared itself the only body empowered to speak on behalf of the Ukrainian people. Before long, it began to act as if it were a quasi-sovereign authority. In August 1917, the Provisional Government had to acknowledge the Rada's claims.

At this stage, Ukrainian separatism was largely a movement of the intelligentsia, encouraged and financially supported by the Austrians and Germans. But in the course of 1917 it acquired a mass following because the Ukrainian peasantry did not want to share its land—superior in quality—with the landless and land-poor Russians. Responding to this mood, Ukrainian politicians insisted that the distribution of land in their region be decided by the Ukrainians themselves.

The Muslims held in May 1917, in Moscow, an All-Russian Muslim Congress. Inasmuch as the Islamic population lived in scattered settlements rather than in a compact mass, its political representatives were divided in their demands. The Volga Tatars wanted cultural autonomy within a unitary Russian state. Others preferred a federal arrangement. Submitted to a vote, the federal platform won a decisive majority. The Congress set up a National Central Council (Shura) for Russia's Muslims.

However, as a result of the general disintegration of Russian statehood during the course of 1917, Muslim central institutions weakened and the center of political activity shifted to the regions. In the Steppe, a national Kazakh-Kirghiz party called Alash Orda came up with demands of autonomy for its people and the restoration to them of the lands seized by Russian and Ukrainian settlers. In some areas of the Steppe, fighting broke out among native Turks and the Slavic newcomers.

Farther south, in Turkestan, where Muslims outnumbered Russians 17 to 1, a Muslim Central Committee formed in April 1917. As happened in the Steppe, the Slavs buried their differences to form a united front against the natives. The Congress of Soviets, which in early November 1917 carried out the Bolshevik coup in Tashkent, the capital of Turkestan, passed a resolution barring Muslims from the soviets. In 1918–19, central Asia would be the scene of violent clashes in which social conflicts assumed a racial character.

In the Caucasus the political situation, complicated enough by an unusually intricate ethnic structure, was further aggravated by the intervention of the Germans and Turks.

Georgia was a stronghold of Social Democracy, and the Georgian intellectuals linked their national aspirations to Russian democratic movements: the striving for independence emerged here only after the Bolshevik coup in Russia had dashed hopes that the country would institute a democratic government. The majority of Armenians lived in the Ottoman Empire. During World War I, the Ottoman government, charging them with disloyalty, ordered their expulsion. During the mass deportations of Armenians from eastern Anatolia, hundreds of thousands lost their lives. In 1917–18, the Armenians found themselves in an exceedingly precarious situation and they looked for protection to other Christian nations, including the United States. Absent such support, they were not averse to Russian hegemony even if it meant Bolshevization. The Azeri Turks had close affinities to the Azeris living across the border in northern Iran. During the war, they secretly sympathized with the Ottoman Empire. In addition to these three major ethnic groups, there were numerous smaller Muslim communities in the valleys of the Caucasian Mountains.

One week after taking power in Petrograd, the Bolsheviks issued, over the signatures of Lenin and Stalin (the latter in his capacity as Commissar of Nationalities) a "Declaration of Rights of the Peoples of Russia." It granted, without conditions or qualifications, every nation the right to separate itself from Russia and proclaim its independence. This pledge implemented Lenin's nationalities theory. This theory (see Chapter V) assumed that the ethnic minorities were too closely integrated into the Russian economy to take advantage of the right of self-determination: Lenin viewed it mainly as a psychological device that would make them feel that they remained part of Russia of their own free will.

Events disappointed Lenin's expectations and compelled him almost immediately to renege on his pledges. In late 1917 and early 1918, one borderland region after another, anxious to escape Bolshevik rule and the Civil War, declared its independence. The Germans and Austrians encouraged this trend. In February 1918, Germany and Austria recognized the sovereignty of the Ukraine and compelled Moscow to follow suit. Finland, Lithuania, Latvia, and Estonia went their separate ways as well. Transcaucasia declared itself an independent federation in April 1918. Central Asia alone remained under Russian control, owing to the local Slavic population's loyalty to the homeland.

What was he to do? Lenin, who like any able military commander had no difficulty modifying tactics when the situation required it, resolved to abandon—in effect, though not in name—the principle of national self-determination in favor of federalism, which in the past he had always rejected on the grounds that it institutionalized ethnic differences. The federalism he had in mind was to be not genuine federalism, which grants member states equal status and meaningful authority over their territories, but a peculiar brand of pseudo-federalism that provided neither equality nor authority. Under the one-party regime, the exclusive source of legislative, executive, and judiciary authority throughout the Communist domain was the Communist Party. While the state would be divided along ethnic lines to give the non-Russians the feeling that they enjoyed sovereignty, the Communist Party—one, undivided, and centered in Moscow—would exercise effective control over the "federation." It is this model that Lenin adopted and in 1922–24 incorporated into the constitution of the new state, the Union of Soviet Socialist Republics. He assumed that as other countries went Communist, they would join the U.S.S.R. on the same principles in order to constitute in time a single commonwealth spanning the globe.

The situation in the Ukraine in 1919 was so chaotic and volatile as to defy description. As soon as the Germans had evacuated, the puppet government they had installed there collapsed. Two major contenders struggled for control: Ukrainian nationalists under Semën Petlura, based in Kiev, and pro-Russian Communists centered in Kharkov. Neither group, however, controlled much of the country, large areas of which were divided among warlords preoccupied with plunder and pogroms. In the summer of 1919, Denikin's armies seized most of the Ukraine. When the Whites were routed (November–December 1919), the Red Army retook this region and installed a Communist regime. But this regime split immediately into two rival factions, one fully submissive to Moscow, the other of a more independent bent. In 1920, the Cheka carried out massive arrests and executions on Ukrainian territory, liquidating, in the process, the local warlords.

The Bolsheviks had virtually no following among Muslims. They courted them assiduously not only because they wanted to gain influence among the Islamic inhabitants of Russia but also because they considered it essential for their strategy of worldwide revolution to win over and radicalize the Middle East. This objective frequently caused friction between Moscow and the Slavic population of the predominantly Muslim regions. Thus, overcoming the resistance of local Russians, Moscow granted autonomy to the Tatars and Bashkirs. This right turned out to be quite meaningless, and in 1920 the mid-Volga witnessed anti-Bolshevik revolts that required considerable effort to suppress.

Much the same held true of central Asia, where local Slavs, determined to preserve the colonial regime, sabotaged Moscow's initiatives on behalf of the native population. They crushed an attempt by Muslims to establish a national government in Kokand and destroyed the city by fire. To such repressive policies, the Muslims responded with guerrilla warfare. The partisans, known as Basmachis, raided Communist outposts and Russian settlements. This warfare, which reached its apogee in 1920–22, was not fully brought under control until the end of the decade.

The most prominent early Muslim convert to communism was a onetime Tatar schoolteacher, Mirza Sultan-Galiev. A protégé of Stalin's, he made a rapid career in the Party but soon developed doubts about the cause he had joined. Observing the treatment of the Muslims at the hands of the Communists, especially in central Asia, and the willingness of Slavs of diverse classes to bury their differences and join forces against them, he began to question whether communism would liberate the world's colonial peoples. The true division of mankind, it occurred to him, was not between the "bourgeoisie" and the "proletariat," but between the exploiting imperial nations, of which Russia was one, and their colonial subjects. The latter were the true "proletariat" because once in power, the working class of the imperialist nations behaved exactly as did the "bourgeoisie." From this premise he drew the conclusion that the colonial peoples should impose a "dictatorship" on their colonial masters—the Europeans. Such heretical ideas, which anticipated the ideology of Mao Zedong, the leadership of the Russian Communist Party found entirely unacceptable: Sultan-Galiev was expelled, imprisoned, and ultimately executed. He is said to have been the first victim of Stalin's purges.

In 1918, the Caucasus fell under the influence of the Germans and the Turks. The Germans were primarily interested in Georgian manganese deposits and the oil fields of Baku. The Turks had their own designs on the region. The two powers established spheres of influence, with the Germans dominant in Tiflis and the Turks in Baku. At their urging, in late May 1918 the Transcaucasian Federation dissolved as Georgia, Armenia, and Azerbaijan proclaimed separate statehood.

Georgia proved the most successful of these successor states. The Mensheviks, who headed the Georgian government for the next three years, were better educated and had wider international connections than did the leaders of neighboring republics. Implementing a land-reform program, they expropriated and distributed among farmers landed estates in excess of forty acres. They also nationalized large industrial enterprises and transport. Georgia had conflicts with the Abkhazians and Ossetians—Islamic minorities living on territory Georgia claimed—but on balance she coped reasonably well with the responsibilities of independence.

Moscow had never given up its claims to Transcaucasia, an area that before the Revolution had supplied Russia with two-thirds of her petroleum, three-quarters of her manganese, one-fourth of her copper, and a high share of her subtropical produce. It only awaited an opportune moment to reabsorb it. The conquest was carried out in two stages—the first in April 1920, the second in February 1921—by a perfected strategy that combined military aggression from without with internal subversion. The critical factors that enabled Moscow to reassert dominion over Transcaucasia were the hands-off policy adopted by the great powers, notably Britain, and the friendly neutrality of the leader of

Turkey, Kemal Atatürk. Kemal disavowed the Panislamic and Panturkic ambitions of the defunct Ottoman state, and in exchange for Moscow's pledge to refrain from Communist agitation in Turkey and support against the Allies, acquiesced in Russia's reconquest of the Caucasus.

Preparations for the Caucasian campaign got under way in mid-March 1920 when Lenin ordered the seizure of Azerbaijan and Georgia. The following month, the Central Committee of the Russian Communist Party formed a Caucasian Bureau (Kavbiuro), headed by a close friend of Stalin's, the Georgian Sergo Ordzhonikidze, to impose Soviet rule on the Caucasus and from there extend assistance to "anti-imperialist" movements in the Middle East. The Kavbiuro worked closely with the command of the Eleventh Red Army, which was to carry out the operation.

Azerbaijan fell first. At noon on April 27, 1920, representatives of the Azerbaijani Communist Party handed the Baku government an ultimatum to surrender power within twelve hours. Before the time was up, the Eleventh Army crossed the border, and the next day, unopposed, entered Baku. Ordzhonikidze introduced at once a reign of terror arresting and executing a number of Azerbaijani politicians, including the Prime Minister and Chief of Staff of the deposed government.

Without stopping, the Eleventh Army continued to advance on the capitals of Armenia and Georgia. But the invasion of these countries had to be aborted because on April 25 a combined Polish-Ukrainian force invaded the Ukraine (below, p. 292). On May 4, Lenin ordered Ordzhonikidze to pull back the troops that had penetrated Georgia. Three days later, the Soviet government signed a treaty with Georgia in which it recognized her independence and pledged to refrain from interfering in her internal affairs. In a secret clause, Georgia consented to the legalization of the Communist Party. Sergei Kirov, whom Moscow appointed as its envoy to Tiflis, immediately proceeded to lay the groundwork for the future conquest of Georgia. In June, Moscow signed a similar treaty with Armenia. Thanks to the war with Poland, the two republics received a temporary reprieve.

The campaign against the Caucasus resumed in December 1920, following the suspension of hostilities between Russia and Poland.

The Sovietization of Armenia occurred in the midst of Armenia's territorial dispute with Turkey over eastern Anatolia, areas which the Allies in the peace settlement had assigned to the Turks but which the Armenians claimed as their own and continued to occupy. In late September 1920, the Turks counterattacked. The tide of battle turned in Turkey's favor. Moscow lost no time in exploiting Armenia's predicament. On November 27, Lenin and Stalin instructed Ordzhonikidze to move into Armenia to stop the Turkish advance. Two days later, the Soviet diplomatic mission in Erevan presented the Armenian government, dominated by the Dashnaktsutiun Party, with an ultimatum demanding the immediate transfer of authority to a "Revolutionary Committee of the Soviet Socialist Republic of Armenia" located on Azerbaijani territory. The Armenians not only agreed but welcomed the Soviet intrusion, which promised to save them from the Turks. In December 1920, Armenia became a Soviet republic, initially ruled by a coalition of Dashnaks and Communists.

Georgia was surrounded. Under the terms of the May 1920 treaty with Soviet Russia, Tiflis had released from jail nearly 1,000 Georgian Communists who now busied themselves preparing an armed insurrection. In December 1920, Ordzhonikidze, in partnership with Stalin, had everything in readiness for an invasion, but Moscow ordered him to hold back. Lenin had grave doubts about the wisdom of assaulting Georgia. The Commander in Chief of the Red Army, S. S. Kamenev, strongly opposed such an operation on the grounds that the Eleventh Army had been depleted by desertions and could not be reinforced because troops were needed in Russia to fight rebellious peasants. Foreign-policy considerations also mitigated against invasion. In early 1921, the Politburo, faced with the collapse of the national economy and massive rural uprisings, contemplated abandoning War Communism in favor of a more liberal economic policy. The latter required extensive Western credits and investments that could be withheld as punishment for aggression against Georgia.

Georgia might have survived but for the relentless pressure on Lenin by Stalin and Ordzhonikidze, who were eager to conquer their native land. Given to understand that the Allies considered Georgia to lie in the Russian sphere of influence, Lenin yielded to these pressures. On January 26, Ordzhonikidze finally received the green light. This, the last Soviet territorial conquest until 1939, followed what by now had become a classic pattern. First, on February 11–12, 1921, came a "rebellion" of the disaffected masses, staged by the Kavbiuro in a region contested between Georgia and Armenia. Then came friendly help from the Eleventh Army. On February 16, units of this army crossed the Georgian frontier from Azerbaijan and advanced on Tiflis. Budënnyi's Cavalry joined in the operation. The Georgians resisted as best they could, but, overwhelmed, on February 25 surrendered Tiflis. The rest of the country gave up the unequal fight, especially after the Mensheviks, prior to departing for the West, signed an accord with the Bolsheviks to retain for Georgia Batumi, to which the Turks laid claim.

Even after the optimists were proven right, Lenin worried about the Sovietization of Georgia. He knew of the popularity of the Menshevik government and had little confidence in Ordzhonikidze's diplomatic skills. He repeatedly warned his Caucasian viceroy to exercise the utmost tact in dealing with the defeated enemy as well as with local Communists. This advice Ordzhonikidze and his patron, Stalin, chose to ignore, igniting conflicts with the population at large as well as with Georgian Communists that before long would precipitate a major crisis in the ranks of the Russian Communist Party.*

With the conquest of Georgia, Soviet Russia acquired the borders that she would retain until September 1939. Formally composed of six independent republics, the country was a constitutional anomaly, since neither the relations among its constituent republics nor the role of the Russian Communist Party in the new multinational state was even approximately defined. The shape of the new state, from which emerged the Union of Soviet Socialist Republics, was determined only in 1922–24. It became the subject of heated disagreements between the dying Lenin and the ascendant Stalin.

---

* See Chapter XV.

COMMUNISM FOR EXPORT

D uring the five years when Lenin was in charge, the foreign policy of Soviet Russia was an adjunct of the policies of the Russian Communist Party. As such, it was intended to serve, first and foremost, the interests of the global revolution. It cannot be stressed strongly enough or often enough that the Bolsheviks seized power in Russia not to change Russia but to use her as a springboard from which to change the world. "We assert," Lenin said in May 1918, "that the interests of socialism, the interests of world revolution, are superior to national interests, to the interests of the state." The founders of the Communist regime felt that their revolution could not survive for long unless it promptly spread abroad. This belief rested on two premises. One was that the vastly stronger "capitalist" camp would unite to overwhelm the revolutionary outpost by a combination of economic sanctions and military aggression. The other held that even if this did not happen, or if it did happen but Russian Communists succeeded in repulsing the assault, they would still face insuperable difficulties trying to run an isolated Communist state surrounded by enemies and inhabited by a backward and hostile peasantry.

So much for the theory. In practice, since Soviet Russia was the first and for a long time the only Communist country in the world, the Bolsheviks came to regard the interests of Russia as identical with those of world communism. And as their expectations of world revolution receded—this happened by 1921—they had no alternative but to assign the interests of Soviet Russia the highest priority: for after all, communism was a reality in Russia, whereas everywhere else it was but a hope.

As the government of a country that had its own national interests and, at the same time, served as the headquarters of a supranational revolution, a cause that knew no boundaries, the Bolshevik regime developed further its two-tiered foreign policy. The Commissariat of Foreign Affairs, acting in the name of the Soviet state, maintained, as before, formally correct relations with those foreign powers that were prepared to have dealings with it. The task of promoting world revolution devolved on a new body, the Third or Communist International (Comintern), founded in March 1919. Formally, the Comintern was independent of both the Soviet government and the Russian Communist Party; in reality, it was a department of the latter's Central Committee. The separation of the two entities enabled Moscow to conduct a policy of concurrent "peaceful coexistence" and subversion.

The Comintern had two tasks, one offensive, the other defensive: to promote revolution abroad and, at the same time, to neutralize the efforts of "capitalist" countries to launch a crusade against Soviet Russia. It had more success in its defensive than its offensive mission. Appealing with political slogans to socialists and liberals abroad, and with prospects of lucrative business to foreign entrepreneurs, the Comintern's agents managed to thwart anti-Communist initiatives under the slogan "hands off Russia." By the early 1920s, virtually all European countries had established diplomatic and commercial relations with a government they had initially treated as an outlaw. But every revolution which the Comintern tried to stage, whether in Europe, the Middle East, or the Far East, ended in disaster. Lenin's failure to carry the Revolution abroad, especially to the industrialized countries, virtually ensured that Soviet Russia would revert to her native autocratic and bureaucratic traditions. It made all but inevitable the ascendancy of Stalin, who concluded early that the prospects of global revolution were close to nil—at any rate, until the outbreak of another world war—and concentrated on building up his power base at home.

Lenin attempted to export the Revolution to Finland and the Baltic countries while World War I was still in progress, but the effort got under way in earnest only after the November 1918 armistice. The defeated Central Powers, in a state of anarchy and on the verge of famine,

49. Radek on the eve of World War I.

offered an especially inviting target. In January 1919, Lenin dispatched to Germany Karl Radek, who had numerous contacts there and knew intimately her internal situation. Radek took charge of the Spartacus League formed from the radical wing of the radical Independent Social-Democratic Party (USPD), founded by Karl Liebknecht and Rosa Luxemburg. Disregarding the hesitations of the Spartacists, he appealed to German soldiers and workers to boycott the elections to the National Assembly and to overthrow the interim socialist government.

This strategy, based on the experience of October 1917 in Russia, misfired because the German socialists, avoiding the mistakes of Kerensky and the Soviet, moved vigorously to crush the attempt by a minority to defy the nation's will. When, on January 5, 1919, the Spartacists and the USPD staged a revolt in Berlin, the government appealed to veterans to form volunteer detachments. These units liquidated the uprising in ten days. Luxemburg and Liebknecht were arrested and murdered; Radek wound up in prison.

Ignoring this setback, the German Communists attempted to seize power in other cities. The high point of these putsches was the proclamation on April 7, 1919, in Munich of a Bavarian Socialist Republic. Following Lenin's instructions, its program, emulating Russian models, called for arming the workers, expropriating banks, confiscating "kulak" lands, and creating a security police empowered to take hostages. The strategy showed a remarkable ignorance of German workers' inbred respect for the state and private property. These efforts, too, suffered a fiasco.

Only in Hungary did the Communists achieve momentary success, and this for reasons that had more to do with nationalism than socialism.

Hungary, which had fought in the war on the losing side, formed in late 1918 a liberal government. However, when the Allies assigned Transylvania, a region populated by a large Hungarian minority, to Romania, the liberal government turned to the Communists for help. At this time, the leading Communist in Hungary was Béla Kun, who had been sent there by Moscow supposedly to arrange for the repatriation of Russian POWs but in reality to serve as its agent. The liberals approached Kun, who was serving time in jail for Communist agitation, with an offer to form a coalition government. The hope was that such a government could procure the Red Army's help against the Romanians. Béla Kun became the head of a government dominated by Communists which carried out radical social and economic reforms, accompanied by terror. When in April 1919 the Romanians invaded Hungary and Soviet help failed to materialize, Hungarian disenchantment was complete. Kun had to flee, yielding to a successor government headed by Admiral Nicholas Horthy, a conservative and an anti-Communist.

Kun's attempt to stage a revolution in neighboring Austria never got off the ground.

Thus the three efforts to promote revolutionary upheavals in central Europe at a time when conditions for it were uniquely propitious went down in defeat. Although Moscow, hailing each as the beginning of a world conflagration, had stinted on neither money nor personnel, it gained nothing. European workers and peasants turned out to be made of very different stuff from their Russian counterparts. Indeed, such initiatives produced the very opposite result from that intended: they discredited communism and played into the hands of nationalist extremists. "The main results of that mistaken policy," writes Neil McInnes, "were to terrify the Western ruling classes and many of the middle classes with the specter of revolution, and at the same time provide them with a convenient model, in Bolshevism, for a counterrevolutionary force, which was fascism."

In March 1919 responsibility for foreign subversion, until then exercised by the Commissariat of Foreign Affairs, was transferred to the Communist International. This organization came into existence at a hastily convened congress. The representatives of the "international proletariat" who attended were either Russian Communists or foreign-

50. The capitalist pig squirming. The sign reads "Third International."

ers living in Russia: of the thirty-five delegates, only five came from abroad, and only one carried a mandate. The expectations of its founders knew no bounds. Zinoviev, whom Lenin appointed Comintern Chairman, exulted in the summer of 1919:

> The movement advances with such dizzying speed that one can confidently say: in a year we shall already have forgotten that Europe had to fight for Communism, because a year hence all Europe shall be Communist. And the struggle for Communism will shift to America, and perhaps also to Asia and other parts of the world.

In its first year, the Comintern led a paper existence. It became an operational and well-financed organization only after its Second Congress,

51. Lenin and Central Commitee Secretary, E. D. Stasova, at the
Second Congress of the Comintern.

held in the summer of 1920. Foreign Communists and sympathizers
were far better represented this time; attending were 217 delegates from
thirty-six countries. Next to the Russians, who had one-third of the delegates, the largest foreign delegations came from Germany, Italy, and
France. The Bolsheviks ran into considerable resistance from foreigners
in seeking to implement their program, but in the end they nearly always
had their way. The mood of the Congress was euphoric because during
its sessions the Red Army approached Warsaw in a campaign that Communists saw as the opening stage of the conquest of Europe. In a state of
revolutionary delirium, Lenin on July 23, 1920, cabled a coded message
to Stalin in the Ukraine:

The situation in the Comintern superb. Zinoviev, Bukharin, and I, too, think that the revolution should be immediately exacerbated in Italy. My own view is that to this end one should sovietize Hungary and perhaps also Czechoslovakia and Romania.

This extraordinary message can be understood only in the context of a decision taken in early July 1920, in the midst of the war with Poland, to carry the revolution to Western and Southern Europe. In an address to a closed meeting of Communist leaders in September 1920, first made public in 1992, Lenin revealed that earlier that year the Politburo had decided to use the conflict with Poland as a pretext for advancing into the heart of the European continent.

The Polish-Soviet war was initiated by Poland. Pilsudski, who had adopted a neutral stance during the Russian Civil War in order to allow the Red Army to defeat Denikin, after the latter's fall made preparations for war with Soviet Russia. He did not intend to overthrow the Soviet government but to detach the Ukraine to serve as a buffer between Poland and Russia. He concluded a secret treaty with the Ukrainian nationalist leader Semën Petlura, and in late April a Polish-Ukrainian force crossed the border of the Soviet Ukraine, advancing on its capital, Kiev. On the face of it, the Poles were indisputably the aggressors. However, there is evidence from Soviet sources that the Red Army had been readying an attack on Poland before the Poles struck, for reasons which Lenin would spell out in his September 1920 speech.

The invaders made rapid progress against the Red Army. On May 7, the Poles occupied Kiev: it is said to have been the fifteenth change of regime in the Ukrainian capital since the breakdown of tsarism. But the fortunes of war soon changed. The expected uprising of Ukrainians never materialized. Instead there was an explosion of patriotic frenzy in Soviet Russia where even anti-Communists rallied behind the regime to defend what they perceived to be Russia's patrimony. In early June, Budënnyi's cavalry broke through Polish lines. Soon the invaders were in full flight, and the Red Army approached the ethnographic border of Poland. Worried that the Red Army would cross this border and advance into Poland proper, Lord Curzon, the British Foreign Minister, urged the Russians to make peace, warning that if they invaded Poland proper, Britain and France would intervene on her behalf.

The Politburo faced a historic decision. As Lenin explained it after the event, the crushing of the Whites had ended the "defensive" phase of the war against the Allies (for he viewed the Whites as Allied pawns):

And thus . . . we arrived at the conviction that the Allied military attack against us was over, that the defensive war against imperialism was over: we won it . . . (Please record less: this is not for publication) . . . We faced a new task. . . . We could and should take advantage of the military situation to begin an offensive war . . . This we formulated not in the official resolution recorded in the protocols of the Central Committee . . . [We learned] that somewhat near Warsaw lies not [only] the center of the Polish bourgeois government and the republic of capital, but the center of the whole contemporary system of international imperialism, and that circumstances enabled us to jolt that system, and to conduct politics not in Poland but in Germany and England.

These rather incoherent remarks indicate that Lenin actually believed that in the summer of 1920 Germany and England were in the throes of a revolution. He also thought Hungary and Czechoslovakia stood on the brink of an explosion. His conclusion was: "Had Poland become Soviet . . . the Versailles Treaty . . . and with it, the whole international system arising from the victories over Germany, would have been destroyed." As it turned out, this objective Hitler and Stalin would attain nineteen years later.

Overcoming the objections of Trotsky and the hesitations of the military command, Lenin persuaded his associates to disregard Curzon's warnings and order the Red Army march on Warsaw. On July 22, the Red Army received instructions to take the Polish capital by August 12. A five-man Polish Revolutionary Committee was set up to administer sovietized Poland.

It was in the midst of these events that the Second Congress of the Comintern opened its proceedings. A large map of the combat zone hung in the main hall, and the westward advance of the Red Army was marked daily to the cheers of the delegates.

At the Second Congress, Lenin pursued three objectives. First, to create in every country a Communist Party—either from scratch or by splitting off from existing socialist parties their most radical elements. These foreign affiliates, according to the Congress's resolutions, were to be subject to "iron military discipline" and display "the fullest comradely confidence" in the center—that is, Moscow. Second, unlike the Second or Socialist International, which was structured as a federation of independent and equal parties, the Comintern was to be centralized: in the words of Zinoviev, there had to be a "single Communist Party, with sections in different countries." The Comintern's Executive Committee was a department of the Central Committee of the Russian Communist

Party and carried out unflinchingly its commands. Third, foreign Communist parties were required to infiltrate and seize control of parliaments and trade unions in their respective countries. The ultimate objective of the Comintern was "armed insurrection" against all existing governments.

Some of Lenin's demands ran into opposition. Communists from the West objected particularly to Lenin's insistence that they take part in parliamentary elections and join trade unions, for they believed that such actions would only serve to reveal their weakness. But Lenin persisted in his strategy on the grounds that even small Communist nuclei in parliaments and trade unions could manipulate these institutions and influence public opinion. The existing "correlation of forces" so favored the "imperialists" that Communists had no choice but to follow a patient strategy of exploiting every disagreement in the enemy camp and forming temporary coalitions with every potential ally. He had Bukharin force through a resolution requiring Communist affiliates "to make use of bourgeois governing institutions for the purpose of destroying them." To ensure that foreign parties did not succumb to what Marx called "parliamentary cretinism," Communist legislators abroad were required to combine parliamentary work with illegal activity. According to a resolution of the Second Congress:

> Every Communist parliamentary deputy must bear in mind that he is not a legislator who strives for an understanding with other legislators, but a party agitator, sent to the enemy camp to carry out party decisions. The Communist deputy is accountable not to the amorphous body of voters but to his legal or illegal Communist party.

Before adjourning, the Second Congress adopted its most important document, listing twenty-one "Conditions" for admission to the Comintern. Lenin, its author, deliberately formulated the requirements for membership in an uncompromising manner to make them unacceptable to moderate, democratic socialists, whom he wanted excluded. The most important conditions were the following:

ARTICLE 2. All organization belonging to the Comintern
were to expel from their ranks "reformists and centrists."
ARTICLE 3. Communists had to create everywhere "parallel
illegal organizations" which, at the decisive moment,
would surface and take charge of the revolution.
ARTICLE 4. They were to carry out propaganda in the armed
forces to prevent them from being used for "counterrevolutionary" purposes.

ARTICLE 9. They were to seize control of trade unions.

ARTICLE 14. They were to help Soviet Russia repel the
counterrevolution.

ARTICLE 16. All decisions of the Comintern Congresses
and the Comintern Executive were binding on member
parties.*

When the Second Congress adjourned, the fall of Warsaw and the establishment of a Polish Soviet republic seemed imminent. The outnumbered Poles were falling back at a rate of fifteen kilometers a day. On July 28, the Red Army occupied Bialystok, the first purely Polish city, and two days later the self-styled Polish Revolutionary Committee announced that it was "laying the foundations of the future Polish Soviet Socialist Republic," declaring factories, landed estates, and forests national property.

The Red Army advanced into Poland on two fronts: in the north, the main army under Tukhachevskii; in the south, a smaller one under Egorov, with Stalin as political commissar. The Poles received no help from the West because British dock workers refused to load supplies destined for them, and Germany barred the transit across her territory of any military equipment bound for Poland. The French sent a military advisory body which the Poles ignored because it recommended a defensive strategy whereas they believed their best hope lay in a well-timed counteroffensive.

The precise cause of the Red Army's stunning defeat remains unclear to this day. Trotsky subsequently blamed Stalin for failing to carry out orders to have the Southern Army join Tukhachevskii. But the blame seems rather to rest with Lenin, who, taking victory for granted, directed the Red Army to pursue grander geopolitical objectives. Tukhachevskii, apparently on Moscow's orders, detached sizable forces besieging Warsaw and sent them to the Polish Corridor. The purpose of this operation was to occupy the Polish Corridor and turn it over to Germany, thereby reuniting East Prussia with Germany proper and gaining the support of German nationalists. Stalin apparently failed to move north to join Tukhachevskii not because he had chosen to disobey orders but because the mission of the Southern Army was to invade and sovietize Hungary and Czechoslovakia.

---

* Hitler, who emulated many of Lenin's methods, imposed a "25-point program" for admission to the Nazi Party in Germany and Austria.

In any event, as a result of these deployments, a fatal gap developed in the Soviet front, which Pilsudski brilliantly exploited. He surprised the Russians by launching a counteroffensive which imperiled their rear and forced them to retreat. Some Red divisions crossed into East Prussia, where they were disarmed and interned; nearly 100,000 men surrendered to the Polish army. Moscow had to sue for armistice; it was followed by a peace treaty signed in Riga in March 1921. By its provisions, Soviet Russia received much less advantageous borders than she could have obtained had she followed Lord Curzon's advice.

The debacle of his armies in Poland and the collapse of his ambitious plans for Western Europe had a crushing effect on Lenin. He had his first direct encounter with European nationalism and emerged the loser. Instead of meeting resistance only from "Polish White Guards," the would-be Russian liberators confronted a united Polish nation. "In the Red Army the Poles saw enemies, not brothers and liberators," Lenin complained to a German Communist:

> They felt, thought and acted not in a social, revolutionary way, but as nationalists, as imperialists. The revolution in Poland on which we counted did not take place. The workers and peasants . . . defended their class enemy, let our brave Red soldiers starve, ambushed them and beat them to death.

The experience cured Lenin of the fallacy that incitement to class antagonism, so successful in Russia, would always and everywhere override nationalist sentiment. It also made him very wary of ever again employing the Red Army outside Soviet borders. Trotsky told Chiang Kai-shek, who visited Moscow in 1923 as a representative of the Kuomintang, then an ally of the Communists, that after the war with Poland, Lenin had ordered that Soviet troops never be directly involved in campaigns against "imperialism" in order to avoid confrontation with nationalist forces.

As soon as the Second Congress of the Comintern adjourned, the Executive Committee proceeded to implement its resolutions. Western Europe now witnessed a repetition of the events that twenty years earlier had shattered the unity of Russian Social Democracy. In country after country, the radical wing of Social Democracy was split off to form a Communist Party; as a result, socialist parties everywhere emerged weaker.

The Italian Socialist Party (PSI) was the only major European socialist organization to attend the Second Congress. The majority, headed by

G. M. Serrati, voted to accept the Twenty-one Conditions and join the Comintern. A minority opposed this move but, for the sake of socialist unity, rather than break away submitted to it. The reformists remained in the PSI, instead of being expelled, as required by Article 2 of the Twenty-one Conditions. Lenin found this unacceptable. When Serrati refused to expel the minority, he became the object of a vicious slander campaign underwritten by the Comintern in which figured entirely unfounded charges of bribery. It ended with his expulsion from the Comintern. Serrati's followers eventually bowed to the Comintern's wishes. They broke away from the PSI to form the Italian Communist Party (PCI). In parliamentary elections held shortly afterward, the PCI received one-tenth of the votes cast for the socialists. The split weakened appreciably the Italian left and facilitated Mussolini's seizure of power in 1922.

The French Socialist Party voted in December 1920 by a plurality of three to one to join the Comintern. The majority declared itself the Communist Party; the defeated minority, as in Italy, retained the name of Socialist Party.

In Germany, the most radical elements concentrated in the Independent Social-Democratic Party (USPD), which favored a Soviet-type government. After prolonged vacillations, the USPD voted, in October 1920, to accept the Twenty-one Conditions and join the Comintern. German socialists then split three ways. One group, issued from the Spartacus League, became the United Communist Party of Germany (VKPD); another remained in the USPD; and the third remained loyal to the Socialist Party. The VKPD became the largest Communist Party outside Russia. As in Italy, the split facilitated the rise of nationalist extremists, who confronted not a united socialist front but three competing socialist parties.

Elsewhere in Europe, the Comintern set up splinter Communist parties which enjoyed little influence.

The second objective of the Comintern in order of importance, penetrating and assuming control over trade unions, was harder to attain, for workers proved far less attracted to Communist slogans than did intellectuals. Lenin, nevertheless, persisted in urging his followers to use any means, fair or foul, to gain a controlling influence over organized labor. We must, he wrote,

> in case of necessity . . . resort to every kind of trick, cunning, illegal expedient, concealment, suppression of truth, so as to penetrate the trade unions, to stay in them, to conduct in them, at whatever cost, Communist work.

The Comintern had the greatest success among workers in France, a country with strong syndicalist traditions. Even so, its attempts to take over organized European labor, mandated by Article 9 of the Twenty-one Conditions, ended in failure: "During the next fifteen years [1920–1935]," writes Franz Borkenau, "the communists in the West were unable to conquer a single union."

Puzzled and irritated by these failures, Lenin attributed them to the Europeans' inertia and lack of grit: "One must teach, teach and teach English Communists to work as the Bolsheviks worked," he admonished. The Russians, weaned on an ideology that saw in class conflict the only social reality, turned a deaf ear to warnings that Europe was different. But as experience would demonstrate time and again, European workers and farmers were neither anarchists nor strangers to the sentiment of patriotism. The reason communism fell on more fertile soil in Russia than in the West proved to be that imponderable factor scorned by Marxists: political culture.

Nor should it be left out of account that citizens of the more advanced European countries enjoyed welfare benefits that gave them a stake in the status quo: unemployment and sickness insurance as well as old age pensions. Workers who had such assistance from the state were not likely to want its overthrow, risking the benefits they had won from capitalism for the more generous but much less certain rewards of communism. The Bolsheviks failed to make allowance for this factor because pre-revolutionary Russia had had nothing of the kind.

Although it concentrated on industrial countries, the Comintern did not ignore the colonies. Lenin had become persuaded long before the Revolution by J. A. Hobson's *Imperialism* (1902) that advanced capitalism managed to survive only thanks to the raw materials, labor, and markets provided by the colonies. Depriving it of these profits would, in his judgment, deliver capitalism the coup de grâce.

The colonies, however, lacked a "proletariat" and hence the social base for a Communist revolution. To have them join in the struggle against "imperialism," it was necessary to find a surrogate for class war. This Lenin found in nationalism: reactionary in capitalist countries, it performed a progressive function in their dependencies. Lenin proposed to instigate in the colonies wars of "national liberation" in which the masses would join hands with the native "bourgeoisie" to expel the colonial masters. The Communists would promote and lead this struggle but maintain a distinct identity: once victorious, they would turn the masses against their erstwhile "bourgeois" allies.

The handful of Communists from the colonial areas who attended the Second Congress objected to this strategy on both moral and practical grounds. They did not want to form a common front with their class enemy, whom they regarded as no better than their colonial masters; and they did not wish to identify with reactionary nationalist sentiments. But Lenin stood his ground and prevailed. The Second Congress approved a resolution "actively to support liberation movements" in the colonies.

The experience of Turkey and China demonstrated the hazards of such a policy.

Kemal Atatürk, the Turkish head of state, turned to Moscow for help in ridding his country of Allied occupation forces. But willing as he was to use Soviet Russia against foreign powers, he had no intention of tolerating Communists on his own territory. He promptly liquidated the Turkish Communist Party and introduced a one-party dictatorship. Richard Loewenthal has called him the first nationalist dictator to embrace the Communist political model without embracing Communist ideology.*

In China in the 1920s, the Communist policy of supporting and at the same time infiltrating nationalist forces suffered an even worse debacle. Soviet Russia forged a common front with the Nationalist Party (Kuomintang) founded by Sun Yat-sen and headed by his successor, General Chiang Kai-shek, helping them to fight foreign powers on their territory. In return, the Kuomintang admitted Chinese Communists into its ranks. But in 1927, when he felt firmly in power, Chiang broke with the Communists, expelled them from the Kuomintang and suppressed their trade unions.

If in her foreign operations Soviet Russia had had to rely exclusively on Communists, her prospects would have been dismal, indeed: in the spring of 1919, when the Comintern came into being, there must have been more vegetarians in England and more nudists in Sweden than there were Communists in either country. By 1920–21, the number of supporters abroad had grown considerably, but even so they were too few either to carry out a revolution or to shape foreign governments' policies toward Moscow. Such successes abroad—especially in the West—as Moscow could lay claim to in the 1920s, it owed mainly to lib-

---

* Bolshevism's influence on Fascism and National-Socialism is discussed in Chapter 5 of my *Russia under the Bolshevik Regime*.

erals and "fellow travelers," individuals prepared to support the Soviet cause without turning Communist. Whereas liberals rejected both the theory and practice of communism and yet found certain areas of agreement with it, fellow travelers accepted communism as a positive phenomenon but did not wish to submit to its discipline. The two groups rendered Soviet Russia invaluable services.

The vast majority of liberals and fellow travelers consisted of intellectuals. For all its objectionable features, the Bolshevik regime attracted them as the first since the French Revolution to vest power in people of their own kind. In Soviet Russia, intellectuals who only a short time earlier had pounded the streets of Europe as penniless exiles, could expropriate the mightiest capitalists, execute political opponents, and muzzle "reactionary" ideas. Because they have little if any experience with the exercise of power, intellectuals tend wildly to overestimate what it can accomplish. Observing the Communists and fellow travelers who flocked to Moscow during the 1920s, the American journalist Eugene Lyons wrote:

> Fresh from the cities where they were despised and persecuted, they had never been so close to the honeypots of power and found the taste heady. Not, mind you, the make-believe power of leadership in an oppressed and underground revolutionary party, but the power that is spelled in armies, airplanes, police, unquestioned obedience from underlings, and a vision of ultimate world dominion. Relieved of the risks and responsibilities under which they labored at home, their yearning for position, career and privilege in many cases took on a jungle luxuriance . . . No one who has not been close to the revolutionary movement in his own country, can quite understand the palpitant anxiety with which a foreign radical approaches the realities of an established and functioning proletarian regime. Or the exaltation with which he finally confronts the signs and symbols of that regime. It is a species of self-fulfillment, a thrilling identification with Power. Phrases and pictures and colors, tunes and turns of thoughts connected in my mind with years of ardent desire and even a measure of sacrifice were now in evidence all around, in the places of honor, dominance, unlimited power!

Western liberals and socialists visiting Soviet Russia as guests of its government, as a rule, were not deceived by its pretenses at democracy. But they rationalized the seamy side of Soviet life in one of two ways: that it was either a legacy of tsarism and the consequence of Western hostility or an inevitable feature of the unprecedented attempt to build a truly free and egalitarian society.

Closely affiliated with such groups, but from entirely different motives, were Western reactionaries who liked Soviet Russia for no other reason than that their own governments, with which they were at odds, did not. In the words of *The New Republic*, they "loved Russia for her enemies." On these grounds some isolationist American senators defended Communist Russia. Similarly, the publisher William Randolph Hearst, for all his reputation as an ultrareactionary, extolled Lenin's regime as "the truest democracy in the world" because he despised Great Britain and Great Britain was anti-Soviet. In the 1930s, for the same reason, he would turn pro-Hitler.

Foreign fellow travelers were especially useful to Moscow because Communists lost credibility once it was realized abroad that they blindly followed orders from Moscow. Fellow travelers, on the other hand, perceived as obeying only the dictates of their conscience, gained a respectful audience. This appearance of independence was particularly effective in the case of prominent authors, whose literary reputation seemed to guarantee integrity. Pro-Soviet statements by such celebrated novelists as Romain Rolland, Anatole France, Arnold Zweig and Lion Feuchtwanger, or by scholars like Sidney and Beatrice Webb and Harold Laski, carried considerable weight with educated Westerners. Moscow assiduously cultivated sympathetic foreign intellectuals, treating them with a deference that exceeded anything to which they were accustomed at home.

In return, fellow travelers depicted Communist Russia to a curious but ignorant Western public as a country that endeavored, under the most difficult circumstances imaginable, to realize the highest ideals of Western culture. They passed over in silence the role of the Party and the security police, depicting Russia as a society governed by democratically elected soviets—the counterparts of American town meetings.

The motives of fellow travelers varied as much as did the personalities of those who made the pilgrimage to Moscow: in the words of Eugene Lyons, "anxiously heretical professors, atheists in search of a religion, old maids in search of revolutionary compensations, radicals in search of reinforcement for a wavering faith." Angelica Balabanoff, who as Secretary of the Comintern was in a position to know, says that on their arrival in Soviet Russia all visitors were placed in one of four categories: "superficial, naïve, ambitious, or venal." In practice, few fitted neatly into any single category. A "naïve" idealist found it easier to keep the faith if the reward was fame or money, while a "venal" visitor enjoyed his profits more if they could be justified with idealistic formulas, such as "trade promotes peace."

Material self-interest, and not only in the crude mercenary sense, turned many a foreigner into a Communist mouthpiece. Those willing to serve in this capacity enjoyed the patronage of a powerful Communist propaganda machine that took good care of its own. English fellow travelers had access to Victor Gollancz's Left Book Club, which at the height of its popularity in mid-1939 distributed pro-Soviet nonfiction to 50,000 subscribers. Books of a similar orientation under the Penguin imprint sold in the six figures. This happened at a time when *Darkness at Noon* by the disenchanted Communist Arthur Koestler, a book that in time would acquire the status of a classic, had in England an initial printing of 1,000 copies and total first-year sales of less than 4,000. Fourteen publishers rejected George Orwell's *Animal Farm* on the grounds that it was anti-Soviet. Western journalists accredited to Moscow could indulge in a style of life quite beyond the reach of their colleagues elsewhere—provided they wrote only what the authorities approved; the alternative was disaccreditation and expulsion. And, of course, for friendly businessmen there was money to be made from trade and concessions.

Most fellow travelers probably fitted in the "naïve" category. They believed what they were told about the Communist experiment because they desperately wished for a world free of war and want. Capitalism disgusted them because of the poverty it tolerated in the midst of affluence and because of its inner contradictions that they believed made for war. The aesthetes among them, revolted by the vulgarity of mass culture, were enchanted by Communist efforts to bring "high" culture to the people. They believed that man and society could be perfected; and since the world they knew fell far short of perfection, they readily accepted Communist ideals for Communist reality. In the process they learned to eject from their consciousness all contrary evidence. Koestler described how, living in Russia during the 1930s, a time of mass starvation and total extinction of human rights, he developed the habit of rationalizing whatever he saw and heard by treating Soviet reality as unreal—"a quivering membrane stretched between the past and the future." Having set up in his mind what he calls an "automatic sorting machine . . . I learned to classify automatically everything that shocked me as the 'heritage of the past' and everything I liked as 'seeds of the future.' " A mind thus conditioned could adjust to almost anything.

A classic example of an idealistic fellow traveler was the American journalist John Reed. The son of wealthy parents and a Harvard graduate, he went to Russia in 1917 without any knowledge either of that country and its language or of socialism. Having witnessed October

52. John Reed and Louise Bryant.

1917, he wrote an account of the Bolshevik coup, *Ten Days That Shook the World*, which came out in 1919 with an introduction by Lenin. Constructed like a movie script in which the Bolsheviks figure as the "good guys" and all their opponents as "bad guys," the book was widely perceived as an authentic account, even though it was little more than propaganda by an enthusiastic American in search of romantic excitement. Reed later joined the Comintern but soon quit, disenchanted with its authoritarian practices.*

The open hostility of Russia's Communist regime to capitalism as well as its denial of private property should have turned the Western business community into an uncompromising foe. In fact, many of the potbellied,

---

* Recently released Comintern documents reveal that in 1920 he had received from its Treasury 1 million rubles, equivalent to $1,000 or 50 ounces of gold.

top-hatted capitalists of Soviet propaganda posters behaved toward it in a remarkably friendly manner. No social group promoted collaboration with Soviet Russia more assiduously and more effectively than the American and European business communities. When the first Soviet trade missions arrived in Europe in the summer of 1920 in the quest of credits and equipment, big business welcomed them with open arms. Business circles believed that Russia—regarded by some as the greatest "empty" market in the world—offered boundless opportunities for trade and investment. Optimism about the future of the Soviet experiment rose high in early 1921, when Moscow adopted the New Economic Policy that sanctioned limited private enterprise and seemed to signal the abandonment of communism.

Businessmen eager to exploit Russia's natural resources as well as to sell her manufactured goods justified trading with a regime that had violated, at home and abroad, all norms of civilized behavior with the following arguments. First, every country was free to have a government of its choice. As Bernard Baruch put it in 1920: "The Russian people have a right, it seems to me, to set up any form of government they wish." Which sounded reasonable enough if, indeed, the Russian people had "set up" the Communist government.

Second, the argument ran, trade civilizes because it teaches common sense and discredits abstract doctrines. Lloyd George justified commercial relations with Moscow with such arguments: "We have failed to restore Russia to sanity by force. I believe we can do it and save her by trade. Commerce has a sobering effect in its operations. The simple sums of addition and subtraction which it inculcates soon dispose of wild theories." Henry Ford, who managed to combine rabid anticommunism and anti-Semitism with highly profitable commercial arrangements with the Soviet Union, also believed in the moral force of commercial reality. The more the Communists industrialized, he asserted, the more decently they would behave because "rightness in mechanics [and] rightness in morals is basically the same thing."

An additional motive behind this eagerness to come to terms with Soviet Russia was the tendency of businessmen to dismiss Communist theories as nothing but propaganda for the masses. They simply would not believe that anyone in his right mind could take seriously such wild ideas. Communists, therefore, either did not mean what they said—and this could be exposed by tempting them with material rewards—or they did, in which case they would soon yield to more realistic leaders. In either event, there was no harm in putting them to the test.

. . .

The Soviet regime encouraged these trends not only because it desperately needed Western capital but also because it calculated, rightly as events were to show, that trade would pave the way for diplomatic recognition.

By means of systematic propaganda, Moscow projected a favorable image of communism abroad. We shall treat the domestic propaganda activities of the Soviet regime in the following chapter and here confine ourselves to brief remarks about their international dimension. In their scope and intensity, these activities had no precedent: Lenin attached to propaganda the highest priority, attributing to it (along with the disunity of his opponents) his regime's ability to survive against overwhelming odds. Its prerequisite was complete control of all sources of information.

Moscow nationalized the wire services under an agency called ROSTA (The Russian Telegraphic Agency), which in 1925 was renamed TASS. The agency had a monopoly on wire news emanating from Soviet Russia.

In an age when the press served as the principal source of news, the best way to ensure that Soviet Russia received favorable coverage abroad was to accredit only those newspapers and journalists who gave evidence of a cooperative attitude. Since every major newspaper wanted a bureau in Moscow, most complied with the demand to assign there friendly correspondents. Journalists posted to Russia learned quickly to minimize, rationalize, or, if necessary, ignore adverse information, blur the distinction between Soviet intentions and Soviet realities, and deride the regime's critics. Once they acquired the habit, they engaged in self-censorship and sooner or later turned into purveyors of Soviet propaganda. Before cabling a dispatch, a correspondent had to secure approval of the Press Department of the Commissariat of Foreign Affairs. "One took them in," recalls the English correspondent and writer Malcolm Muggeridge, "to be censored, like taking an essay to one's tutor at Cambridge, watching anxiously as they were read for any frowns or hesitations, dreading to see a pencil picked to slash something out." One censor refused Muggeridge permission to file a story with the explanation, "You can't say that because it's true."

Papers that refused to play the game—the leading exemplar being the London *Times*—were denied permission to send a reporter. *The New York Times*, by contrast, had in Walter Duranty a highly compliant correspondent, who, in exchange for a luxurious lifestyle, which included the favors of a Russian mistress, turned into an outright apologist for the regime. His dispatches—which distorted Russian realities to the point of denying the Ukrainian famine of 1932–33 which claimed millions of lives—helped create in the United States a climate of opinion friendly to Stalin's Soviet Union, which in 1933 facilitated the granting of diplomatic recognition to that country.

Moscow also influenced Western opinion by financing foreign newspapers. One example was the *Daily Herald*, the organ of the radical wing of the British Labour party. In early 1920, this paper fell on hard times. Facing insolvency, its editor, George Lansbury, journeyed to Moscow in search of financial assistance. As soon as he had obtained subsidies, the *Daily Herald* adopted an unambivalently pro-Soviet position. Later that year, Krasin and Kamenev, who went to London to conclude a commercial agreement with Great Britain, carried with them precious stones and platinum worth £40,000; this sum, plus additional funds of £35,000, they turned over to Lansbury. Unfortunately for them, Scotland Yard had them under continual surveillance. When the facts were made public, Kamenev had to leave England and Lansbury was forced to return the money. The services Lansbury had rendered Moscow did not disqualify him from being elected in 1931 Chairman of the Labour Party.

By such means, the truth about Soviet Russia became concealed and a favorable climate was created for both economic collaboration and the normalization of diplomatic relations.

The issue of Russia's debts presented the main stumbling block to both expanded trade and diplomatic relations. When, in January 1918, the Soviet government repudiated all obligations of previous Russian governments (tsarist as well as Provisional), foreign governments and bond holders lost an estimated $6.59 billion—a sum that in purchasing power would be equal in the 1990s to ten times that figure. In addition, Soviet nationalization decrees inflicted heavy losses on foreign owners of Russian enterprises and securities; French investors alone lost $2.8 billion.

Moscow, well aware of this problem but both unwilling and unable to resolve it in a satisfactory manner, every now and then held out the lure of repayment: it would admit its obligation "in principle" but qualified it in such a manner as to render the principle meaningless. The main condition which it posed was that the West, in return for repayment of its losses, compensate Russia for the losses she had allegedly suffered as a result of Western intervention in the Civil War. An idea of what these losses were perceived to be can be obtained from a confidential report prepared by an official in the Commissariat of Finance. Billing the Allies for the direct costs of the Civil War, entirely charged to them, along with compensation for the deaths and injuries suffered by the Red Army, the official arrived at the sum of $8.25 billion. To this figure he added $15 billion owed for "losses caused by pogroms" and the "moral injury" inflicted on the Russian people. Adding the cost of epidemics, decline in education, and all the other ills that had afflicted Russia since October 1917, he arrived at the global sum of $92.9 billion, or some ten times what Russia owed the West.

The problem of dealing with a country that did not honor its debts was resolved, initially, by the fiction of entering into commercial relations with Russian cooperatives. Both the West and Moscow pretended that these were private associations, although they had in fact been nationalized. Next, in April 1921, Britain signed a trade accord with Soviet Russia. Other countries followed suit.

To the architects of Soviet Russia's foreign policy, four countries were of particular concern: France, the United States, Great Britain, and Germany. The highest priority they assigned to Germany.

France remained an implacable foe of Soviet Russia both because of the heavy financial losses she had suffered there and her fear of Russia's potential alliance with Germany. To prevent the latter, France built up a *cordon sanitaire* separating the two countries. France also conducted an intransigent policy toward Weimar Germany that had the effect of pushing German nationalists into Bolshevik arms. Moscow had little reason to expect anything from this quarter.

The United States, which did not involve itself in Continental rivalries and lost relatively little from Soviet expropriations and defaults, regarded Soviet Russia as an outlaw state and refused to have official dealings with her. In 1920, the U.S. Secretary of State explained that his country pursued such a policy because of the Soviet regime's violations of "every usage and convention underlying the whole structure of international law." Its leaders, he noted, "have frequently and openly boasted that they are willing to sign agreements and undertakings with foreign Powers while not having the slightest intention of observing such undertakings or carrying out such agreements." Furthermore, he continued, they declared that

the very existence of Bolshevism in Russia, the maintenance of their own rule, depends, and must continue to depend, upon the occurrence of revolutions in all other great civilized nations, including the United States. . . .

On these grounds, Washington refused to grant Soviet Russia diplomatic recognition, but it raised no objections to American citizens entering into commercial relations with her. These in the 1920s, were by no means negligible.

Britain made her peace with Soviet Russia. Churchill argued that the Bolsheviks were fanatics, that nothing would persuade them to abandon their cause: "Their view is that their system has not been successful because it has not been tried on a large enough scale, and that in order to secure success they must make it worldwide." But his anticommunism was widely regarded as a personal obsession, and he had no more success then than he would have later when he tried to raise the alarm about the Nazi threat.

Germany was the key to Soviet global ambitions: she was the most industrial country in Europe, with the largest working class; and she had been cast by the Allies in the role of an international pariah. Here, the main obstacles were not the nationalists and capitalists, both of whom were eager enough to make common cause with the Bolsheviks against the Allies, but the Social-Democrats. The intellectual leaders of the SPD, while approving of the October 1917 power seizure, criticized Russian Communists unsparingly for their suppression of political freedom, which they viewed as essential to socialism. Such criticism combined with the pro-Allied stance of the SPD made collaboration with it impossible and caused Moscow to turn to German nationalists of a conservative as well as radical persuasion.

These nationalists were obsessed with the Versailles Treaty and prepared to strike a bargain with anyone willing and able to help them cast it off. This meant, first and foremost, Russia. As soon as the terms of the Versailles Treaty were made public (May 1919), the Soviet Commissariat of Foreign Affairs denounced it in the strongest terms, while the Comintern released a proclamation under the headline "Down with the Versailles Treaty!" A year later (March 1920), during the abortive Kapp putsch organized by right-wing politicians and generals for the purpose of placing the country under a military dictatorship, the leaders of the German Communist Party, almost certainly on orders from Moscow, adopted a neutral stance, declaring that "the proletariat will not lift a finger for the democratic republic." If Moscow could not have a Communist Germany, it preferred a right-wing military dictatorship to a democracy governed by the Social-Democrats.

The most influential advocate of an alliance between Germany and Soviet Russia was General Hans von Seeckt, the Chief of the Army

Command and the country's highest-ranking military officer. Seeckt regarded the armed forces as the very soul of Germany: he viewed the Versailles Treaty, which had virtually disarmed Germany, as a death sentence on his nation. On being appointed in 1920 to head the Reichswehr, he drew up plans for the surreptitious rebuilding of German military capabilities in contravention of Versailles. This objective, he realized, could be attained only with the help of Soviet Russia. He wrote: "Only in firm cooperation with a Great Russia does Germany stand a chance of regaining her position as a world power." In pursuit of this aim, he initiated talks with Radek and other Soviet representatives on secret military cooperation to evade those provisions of the Treaty which denied Germany the sinews of modern warfare: military aviation, heavy artillery, tanks, and poison gas. The collaboration he initiated, which continued in greatest secrecy until the fall of 1933, was to prove of major importance to both the German and Soviet armies in preparing them for World War II.

When, in the summer of 1920, the Red Army approached the gates of Warsaw, Seeckt welcomed Russia's looming victory as tantamount to the liquidation of the Versailles settlement. For with Poland destroyed and Russia and Germany once again sharing a common frontier, the linchpin of the French *cordon sanitaire* would fall. "The future belongs to Russia," he wrote: she is inexhaustible and unconquerable. A Germany allied with Russia would earn the respect of the Allies; the alternative was for her to turn into a nation of "helots." He did not worry about the domestic repercussions of a pro-Communist course, believing that it would earn the German government the sympathies of radical elements. The results of the military collaboration which Seeckt initiated will be discussed in due course.

German business circles showed no less interest in collaborating with Soviet Russia. Before 1914, Russia had been Germany's major trading partner. The concern was that the "Anglo-Saxons" would take advantage of Germany's postwar weakness to step in and capture Russia's foreign trade. German business circles not only did not fear Communist subversion but believed that economic ties with Moscow would help stabilize their country by giving the Soviet regime an interest in preserving capitalist Germany. ("The Bolsheviks must save us from bolshevism" was a slogan launched by the Foreign Office.) After Germany had legalized trade with Soviet Russia (May 1920), the two countries experienced a rapid growth in economic relations. Financed with German credits, in the next decade Germany regained her traditional position as Russia's premier trading partner; by 1932, 47 percent of Soviet imports came from that country.

Thus, the groundwork for the German-Soviet rapprochement that the two powers would spring on an unsuspecting world in 1922 with the Rapallo Treaty was put in place.

In the final reckoning, the conventional efforts of Soviet diplomatic and economic agencies succeeded far better than the Comintern's efforts at subversion. The record of the Comintern, from its foundation in 1919 until its dissolution in 1943, is one of unrelieved failures. Probably the main cause was the Bolsheviks' ignorance of Europe. Their leaders had spent many years in the West: between 1900 and 1917, Lenin lived in Europe for all but two years, Trotsky all but seven, and Zinoviev all but five. But they had spent these years in narrow émigré circles, consorting only with the most radical elements of European socialism. They knew much but understood little. An insuperable mental barrier separated them from the West which they sought to revolutionize: The expression "iron curtain," was in use as early as 1920.

And they refused to be taught. "Is there nothing more to learn from the struggles, movements, and revolutions of other countries?" an exasperated British Comintern delegate asked Zinoviev. "Have the Russians come here not to learn, but only to teach?." Another British delegate to the Second Congress of the Comintern wrote on his return home:

> The utter incapacity of the Congress to legislate for the British movement was perhaps the most conspicuous fact here. Some of the tactics that were useful and successful in Russia would be grotesque failures if put into operation here. The difference between conditions in this highly organized, industrially-centralized, politically compact and insular country, and medieval, semi-barbaric, loosely-organized (politically) and politically-infantile Russia is almost inconceivable to those who have not been there to see.

Moscow would not only turn a deaf ear to such complaints but ruthlessly punish those who dared to criticize its policies. Thus a leading German Communist, Paul Levi, who had warned Moscow against staging putsches in his country, was in April 1921 declared a "traitor" and ousted. He was penalized not for being wrong, since even Lenin conceded that he had given sound advice, but for being insubordinate.

Given this attitude, Moscow increasingly came to rely on pliable and submissive individuals who inevitably turned out also to be unprincipled and corruptible. Angelica Balabanoff could not get over Lenin's readiness to spend whatever was necessary to buy followers and influence opinion. When she told him of her uneasiness, Lenin replied: "I beg you, don't economize. Spend millions, many, many millions." Funds were funneled through various routes: the archives of the Comintern record vast sums spent on foreign parties and publications as well as individuals. Such subsidies ensured Moscow's control over European Communists; at the same time they degraded their quality, repelling persons of conviction and attracting unscrupulous adventurers.

To these causes of the Comintern's failure may be added a third, one imponderable by its very nature. This had to do with the "Russianness" of Bolshevism. Russian radicalism had always been distinguished by an uncompromising extremism, an "all or nothing" and "go for broke" attitude that disdained compromise. The attitude derived from the fact that before seizing power Russian radicals, intellectuals with a tiny following, had nothing but ideas to give them identity. Such people could be found in the West, too, especially among the anarchists, but there they constituted an insignificant minority. Western radicals wanted to reshape rather than destroy the existing order, and so did their followers. The Russian radicals, by contrast, saw little in their country worthy of preservation. In their eyes, the Western Communists and sympathizers were not the real thing. "Bolshevism is a Russian word," wrote an anti-Communist émigré in 1919,

> but not only a word. Because in that guise, in that form and in those manifestations which have crystallized in Russia during nearly two years, bolshevism is a uniquely Russian phenomenon, with deep roots in the Russian soul. And when they speak of German bolshevism or of Hungarian bolshevism, I smile. Is that really bolshevism? Outwardly. Perhaps politically. But without its peculiar soul. Without the Russian soul. It is pseudo-bolshevism.

SPIRITUAL LIFE

F or Marxists, culture is a "superstructure" erected on the foundations of the economy and reflecting the interests and values of the class that dominates it. Religion is a primitive belief, a relic of the earliest stage of man's effort to understand the world around him; it is exploited by the economically dominant class to keep the laboring masses in subjection. The triumph of socialism will bring forth a new culture, one that expresses the interests and values of the proletariat, the new ruling class. Religion will disappear.

These propositions the Bolsheviks accepted as axiomatic. Once in power, they proceeded to implement them by seeking to create a new proletarian culture and launching a brutal assault on religious beliefs and practices. But within these general limits, the Bolsheviks disagreed a great deal on the best method of realizing their cultural and religious program, some calling for a ruthless liquidation of the heritage of the past, others preferring a subtler approach. Lenin, who in all matters had the last word, in the field of culture backed the more liberal trend but in that of religion favored persecution.

Culture as Propaganda

The Bolshevik leaders viewed culture in purely instrumental terms: it was a branch of government concerned with molding minds and promoting attitudes favorable to the construction of a socialist society. Essentially, its function was propaganda in the broadest sense of the word. This was the objective of literature, of the visual and performing arts, and, above all, of education.

The Bolsheviks, of course, did not invent propaganda. It had been practiced at least since the beginning of the seventeenth century, when the papacy established the Congregatio de Propaganda Fide to spread Catholicism. During World War I, all the belligerent powers engaged in it. The Bolshevik innovation consisted in assigning propaganda a central place in national life: previously employed to touch up or distort reality, in Communist Russia propaganda became a surrogate reality. Communist propaganda strove, and to a surprising extent succeeded, in creating a fictitious world side by side with that of everyday experience and in stark contradiction to it, in which Soviet citizens were required to believe or at least pretend to believe. To this end, the Communist Party asserted a monopoly over every source of information and opinion and, in time, severed all contacts of its subjects with the outside world. The effort was undertaken on such a vast scale, with such ingenuity and determination, that the imaginary universe it projected eclipsed for many Soviet citizens the living reality, inflicting on them something akin to intellectual schizophrenia.

Early Soviet cultural history reveals a striking duality: on one level, bold experimentation and unrestrained creative freedom; on another, relentless harnessing of culture to serve the political interests of the new ruling elite. While foreigners and historians focused on the whimsical creations of Bolshevik and fellow-traveler artists, the more significant phenomenon was the silent rise of a "cultural" bureaucracy for whom culture was only a form of propaganda, and propaganda the highest form of culture. In the 1930s, with Stalin firmly in control, the experimentation abruptly ceased and the bureaucracy took over.

The issue dividing the Bolsheviks over cultural policy in the early years of the new regime concerned the legacy of the past. One group, associated with the Proletarian Culture (Proletkult) movement, which had arisen before the Revolution, declared the creations of the "feudal"

53. Lunacharskii.

and "bourgeois" periods irrelevant to Communist society. They were best destroyed, or at least ignored, in order to unshackle the full creative powers of the working class. The leaders of the Proletkult, who enjoyed the powerful patronage of the Commissar of Enlightenment, Anatolii Lunacharskii, proceeded to translate their theories into action with great energy. They opened studios at which workers learned to draw and paint as well as "workshops" where they composed poetry.

On the content of the new culture, the theorists of Proletkult were vague, leaving its definition to the spontaneous creativity of the masses. On one thing, however, they agreed: they had no use for individual "inspiration," which they viewed as a "bourgeois" illusion. Culture grew out of economic relations among human beings and their never-ending struggle with nature. In a socialist society, based on the principle of collectivism, culture would necessarily assume a collective character. A prominent member of Proletkult, Aleksei Gastev, a metalworker turned poet and theorist, had visions of a future in which people would be reduced to automatons identified by ciphers instead of names, and divested of personal ideas and feelings:

> The psychology of the proletariat is strikingly standardized by the mechanization not only of motions, but also of everyday thinking. . . . This quality lends the proletarian psychology its striking anonymity, which makes it

possible to designate the separate proletarian entity as A, B, C, or as 325, 075, and 0, et cetera. . . . This signifies that in the proletarian psychology, from one end of the world to the other, there flow powerful psychological currents, for which, as it were, there exists no longer a million heads but a single global head. In the future, this tendency will, imperceptibly, render impossible individual thinking.

Some Proletkult theorists saw the daily newspaper as a model of collective creativity. They tried in "poetry workshops" to produce composite poems by having each participant contribute one line. At its best, Proletkult provided adult education for people who had never had any contact with art or literature; at its worst, it wasted time in dilettantish experiments that produced nothing of lasting value.

Its undoing was politics. Lenin viewed skeptically the whole notion of "proletarian culture." He had a very low opinion of the cultural level of the Russian masses and little faith in their creative potential. The task facing his government, as he perceived it, was to inculcate in the masses modern scientific and technical habits. He thought it absurd to discard the artistic and literary heritage of the past for the immature creations of amateur writers and artists recruited among workers. But he tolerated the activities of the Proletkult until he became aware of its political ambitions. Alexander Bogdanov, the founder and chief theorist of the movement, believed that cultural organizations should be independent of political institutions and coexist, on terms of equality, with party organizations. Owing to Lunacharskii's friendship, the network of Proletkult cells, which at their height enrolled 80,000 active members and 400,000 sympathizers, enjoyed exemption from supervision by the Commissariat of Enlightenment, which financed them. As soon as this fact was brought to his attention (this happened in the fall of 1920), Lenin ordered the Proletkult organizations to subordinate themselves to the Commissariat. Gradually the movement faded out of the picture.

The Communist regime under Lenin controlled cultural activities through two devices: censorship and strict monopoly on cultural organizations and activities.

Censorship was an old tradition in Russia. Until 1864, it had been practiced in its most onerous "preventive" form, long abandoned in the rest of Europe, which required every manuscript to be approved by a government censor prior to publication. In 1864, it was replaced by "punitive" censorship, under which authors and editors faced trial for the publication of material judged seditious. In 1906, censorship was abolished.

It is indicative of the importance which the Bolsheviks attached to controlling information and influencing opinion that the very first decree they issued on coming to power called for the suppression of all newspapers that did not recognize the legitimacy of their government (above, p. 155). The decree met with such resistance from all quarters, however, that it had to be suspended. In the meantime, the printed word was controlled by other means. The new government declared a state monopoly on newsprint and advertising. A special Revolutionary Tribunal of the Press tried editors who published information that was judged hostile to the authorities. Despite these impediments, a free press managed to survive; in the first half of 1918, several hundred independent newspapers appeared in Russia, 150 of them in Moscow alone. But they lived on borrowed time, since Lenin made no secret of the fact that he intended to shut down the entire free press as soon as conditions permitted.

The occasion presented itself in July 1918, following the Left SR uprising in the capital. Immediately after crushing the rebellion, the government closed all non-Bolshevik newspapers and periodicals, some of which had been founded in the eighteenth century. The unprecedented action eliminated, in one fell swoop, Russia's sources of independent information and opinion, throwing the country back to conditions that antedated Peter the Great, when news and opinion had been a monopoly of the state.

Like the tsarist regime, Lenin's government showed greater leniency toward books since they reached a relatively small audience. But in this field, too, it severely restricted freedom of expression by nationalizing printing presses and publishing houses. All books had to have the endorsement of the State Publishing House (Gosizdat).

Such piecemeal control of information and ideas by the state culminated in June 1922 with the establishment, under the Commissariat of Enlightenment, of a central censorship office innocuously called Main Administration for Literary Affairs and Publishing and popularly referred to by the abbreviation Glavlit. Except for materials emanating from the Communist Party and its affiliates, and the Academy of Sciences, all publications were henceforth subject to preventive censorship by Glavlit. Glavlit had a section that censored the performing arts. Russians quickly learned the art of self-censorship, submitting only material that experience had taught them might have a chance of obtaining a license. In the 1920s, Glavlit did not strictly enforce book censorship, but the apparatus was in place. In the 1930s, it would be used to eradicate every semblance of independent thought.

The new regime eagerly courted Russia's writers, but it encountered in this milieu almost unanimous antagonism. Apart from a few poets and novelists willing to collaborate, Russian authors reacted to the restrictions imposed on their craft in one of two ways: they either emigrated abroad or withdrew into their private world. Those who chose the latter path faced extreme material hardships, freezing in the winter and starving year-round. Submission to the new authorities alone guaranteed minimal living standards but, to their credit, few writers sold out.

Only one literary group, the Futurists, collaborated with the Bolsheviks from conviction. Futurism emerged in Italy on the eve of World War I; its adherents there later backed Mussolini. Italian as well as Russian Futurists loathed the bourgeoisie and all its works, yearning for a new culture attuned to modern technology and the rhythm of the machine age. Extolling barbarian brutality, they wanted museums and libraries swept from the face of the earth. The Futurists, who looked to "impulse" instead of reason for guidance, found fascism and communism attractive because the two movements shared their hatred of effete bourgeois civilization.

The poet laureate of the Bolshevik regime, the Futurist Vladimir Maiakovskii, in many ways personified the antithesis of the Communist ideal of the collective man. An obsessive egomaniac, he called his first play *Vladimir Maiakovskii*, his first volume of verse *I!*, and his autobiography *I Myself*. He made certain always to be at the center of attention, whether by staging scandalous plays, bellowing poems at public readings, or painting propaganda posters. Lenin despised his antics and thought his poems "arrant stupidity." But Maiakovskii prospered because he was the only poet of talent willing to sing the praises of the new regime: His innovative prosody as well as his scorn for traditional morality helped promote the Communist self-image as history's vanguard. In 1930, when the Stalinist authorities began to restrict his freedom, he committed suicide.

While honoring Maiakovskii, the authorities found much more to their taste the verses of Demian Bednyi, a poetaster who put in rhyme whatever slogans the regime thought appropriate at the moment. Trotsky praised him for writing not only in those rare moments when inspired by the muses, "but day in and day out, as events demand . . . and the Central Committee." His ditties are said to have given inspiration to wavering Red Army troops in combat.

Great poetry, lasting poetry, was written by poets who insulated themselves from their times. Anna Akhmatova and her husband, Nicholas Gumilëv, as well as Osip Mandelstam, Sergei Esenin, and Boris Pasternak, led quiet, private, unsubsidized, and unadvertised lives. For this they paid a price, however. Gumilëv was shot in 1921 for alleged membership in a counterrevolutionary organization: he is said to be the first Russian writer of note whose place of burial is unknown. Esenin killed himself in 1925. Mandelstam perished in 1939 in a Soviet camp. Akhmatova and Pasternak survived, but they had to bear humiliations that less stalwart souls would not have endured.

Alexander Blok presented a special case. A leading symbolist poet before World War I, he had shown no interest in politics before the Revolution. In 1917–18, however, carried away by the revolutionary turmoil, in a state of creative delirium he wrote what is widely recognized as the most outstanding poem to come out of the Revolution. "The Twelve" depicts armed Red Guards—murderous and pitiless—marching behind an invisible Christ to smash the "bourgeois" world. Blok's disenchantment began almost at once, the instant he saw the elemental forces whose praises he had sung extinguished by the iron hand of the state. He stopped publishing poetry and died in 1921, thoroughly disillusioned.

The novel fared badly in the early years of the new regime because writers of talent found it difficult to harness their art in the service of a political cause, a cause, moreover, that insisted on viewing the characters of a novel not as individuals but as specimens of their class. Most early Soviet fiction sought to depict the way the Revolution and the Civil War had shattered old values and manners. It stressed violence. A special genre was the anti-utopian novel represented by Zamiatin's *We*, which portrayed the nightmare world envisioned by Gastev. First published abroad, it inspired George Orwell's *1984*.

In a country in which much of the population could neither read nor write, the printed word reached few. Given their interest in influencing the masses, the Bolsheviks preferred other means of spreading their ideas. Of these, the most effective proved to be the theater and the cinema, art forms in which they encouraged experimentation. Alongside the traditional theater, the Communists relied on unconventional spectacles ranging from political cabarets and street presentations to outdoor reenactments of historical events.

54. Street theater.

Revolutionary drama was intended to generate support for the regime and, at the same time, instill contempt and hatred for its opponents. To this end, Soviet directors borrowed from Germany's and other Western countries' innovative techniques. They strove, above all, to abolish the barrier between actors and spectators by eliminating the formal stage and taking their plays to city streets, factories, and the front. Audiences were encouraged to interact with the performers. The line separating reality from fantasy was all but obliterated, which had the effect of obliterating also the distinction between reality and propaganda.

Agitational-propaganda, or "agit-prop," theater vulgarized the protagonists by reducing them to cardboard specimens of perfect virtue and unalloyed evil. The mental and psychic conflicts occurring within and among individuals which form the essence of genuine drama were ignored for the sake of primitive clashes between "good" and "bad" characters acting as their class status dictated.

Plays of this genre were often staged outdoors by professional actors disguised as casual bystanders to ridicule the old regime along with foreign "capitalists." They appealed to xenophobia and envy, fanning these feelings into open resentment and then idealizing them as expressions of class consciousness.

S. Tretiakov wrote a notable example of hate drama, the play *Do You Hear, Moscow?*, which Sergei Eisenstein, later to acquire fame as a movie director, staged in 1924 in Moscow. The action, which took place in contemporary Germany and depicted the struggle of Communist workers against the "Fascists," aroused the audience to a high pitch of excitement:

> The second and third acts created in the audience suitable tension which discharged itself in the fourth act in the scene showing [German] workers storming the Fascist platform. Spectators in the audience jumped from their seats. There were shouts: "Over there, over there! The count is escaping! Grab him!" A gigantic student from a worker's university, jumping to his feet, shouted in the direction of the cocotte: "Why are you fussing? Grab her," accompanying these words with a juicy curse. When the cocotte was killed on the stage and pushed down the stairs, he swore with satisfaction, adding, "She had it coming." This he said so forcefully that a lady in furs sitting next to him could no longer stand it. She leapt to her feet, blurting out in fright: "My Lord! What is going on? They will begin here, too," and ran for the exit. Every killed Fascist was drowned in applause and shouts. It was reported that a military man, sitting in the rear, pulled out his revolver and aimed it at the cocotte, but his neighbors brought him to his senses. The enthusiasm affected even the actors. Members of the stage crowd, students . . . placed there for decoration, unable to restrain themselves, joined in the assault on the installation. They had to be dragged back by their feet.

A kind of spectacle much favored in 1920 presented, under the open sky and with the participation of thousands of extras, reenactments of

55. Scene from Tretiakov's *Do You Hear, Moscow?*

historic events in a manner favorable to the Communists. The most celebrated of these was performed on the third anniversary of the October coup in the center of Petrograd, with 6,000 extras, under the title *The Capture of the Winter Palace*. Later made into a film by Eisenstein, it culminated in an assault of Red Guards on the Winter Palace, stills from which to this day appear as alleged depictions of an event that actually never took place.

Because such spectacles were prohibitively expensive, the government increasingly resorted to the cinema. The greatest influence on early Soviet cinema was that of the American D. W. Griffith. Russian filmmakers found especially attractive his techniques of close-ups and montage because they found them useful in stirring powerful emotions in audiences.

Artists, architects, and composers working for the new regime did not lag in adapting their skills to the country's revolutionary changes.

The most influential art movement of the 1920s, known as Constructivism, sought, like the early Communist theater, to break down the barriers between art and life. Inspired by the German Bauhaus, Russian Constructivists rejected formal art and attempted to inject aesthetics into the everyday. They worked in painting and architecture, industrial and typographic design, couture, and advertising. They aggressively rejected traditional "high art" in all its forms. Alexander Rodchenko turned out three "canvases" covered with nothing but the three primary colors, and declared painting to be dead.

Museums fell into disfavor as attention shifted to street art. Posters received much attention. During the Civil War they proclaimed the inevitable triumph of the Red Army over the enemy, who was depicted as repulsive vermin. Later, they served such didactic purposes as combating religion. In 1918 and 1919, artists in Soviet employ covered entire public buildings and residences as well as trains and streetcars with graffiti bearing propagandistic slogans.

Avant-garde architects believed that Communist structures had to be built of materials appropriate to the new era: declaring wood and stone "bourgeois," they opted for iron, glass, and concrete. The best-known example of early architectural design was Vladimir Tatlin's projected monument to the Third International. A leading Constructivist, Tatlin wanted "proletarian" architecture to be as mobile as the modern metropolis. Accordingly, he designed his monument as a structure in permanent motion. The building was to have three levels. The lowest rotated once a year, the middle once a month, and the highest once a day;

56. Workers toppling the statue of Alexander III in Moscow.

400 meters (1,200 feet) tall, it was designed to exceed the highest building in the world. It was never built. Tatlin also designed a man-powered
flying machine that never got off the ground.

Musical activity declined as Russia's best composers and performers
emigrated abroad. Those who remained concentrated on innovation.
They staged "musical orgies" in which the instruments were not the dis-
carded "bourgeois" winds and strings, but motors, turbines, and sirens.
An officially designated "Noisemaster" replaced the conductor. "Sym-
phonies of Factory Whistles," performed in Moscow, produced such
bizarre sounds that the audiences could not recognize even familiar
tunes. The new genre had its greatest triumph in the presentation in
Baku in 1922, on the fifth anniversary of the October coup, of a "con-

cert" performed by units of the Caspian Fleet—foghorns, factory sirens, two batteries of artillery, machine guns, and airplanes.

The creations of writers and artists subsidized by Lenin's government had next to nothing in common with the taste of the masses, their intended audience. The latter's culture remained rooted in religion. Studies of Russian reading habits indicate that both before and immediately after the Revolution, peasants and workers read mainly religious tracts; their tastes in secular reading ran to escapist literature. The experiments in novel and poetry, painting, architecture, and music reflected the European avant-garde, and as such catered not to popular tastes but to those of the cultural elite. Stalin understood this very well. On attaining absolute power, he cut short experimentation and imposed literary and aesthetic standards which—when they did not merely reproduce creations of the past, whether the literary classics or "Swan Lake"—in crude realism and didacticism surpassed the worst excesses of the Victorian era.

The Russian language has two words for education: *obrazovanie*, which means "instruction," and *vospitanie*, which means "upbringing." The first refers to the transmission of knowledge; the second to the molding of personality. The entire Soviet regime dedicated itself to *vospitanie* in the sense that all the institutions of the state, whether trade unions or the Red Army, had the mission of inculcating in the citizenry the spirit of communism and creating a new type of human being—so much so that

57. Agitational streetcar.

to some contemporaries Soviet Russia appeared like one gigantic school. This was "education" in the broad meaning of the word, as defined by Helvétius (above, p. 23). But the Bolsheviks also paid much attention to education in the narrower, more conventional sense. As with everything else in Communist Russia, classroom activities had to be conducted in a politically correct manner: Lenin dismissed out of hand the idea of an ideologically "neutral" education. Accordingly, the 1919 Party Program defined schools as "an instrument for the Communist transformation of society." This entailed "cleansing" pupils of "bourgeois" ideas, especially of religious beliefs. It also involved inculcating positive Communist values and a scientific, technological outlook.

Ideally, instruction as well as upbringing, seen as responsibilities of the state, were to begin the instant a child saw the light of day. Parents had no claim on their children. According to Evgenii Preobrazhenskii, an authoritative Communist spokesman in such matters:

> From the socialist point of view it is utterly senseless for an individual member of society to treat his body as inalienable personal property, because the individual is only one link in the evolution of the species from the past to the present. But ten times more senseless is a similar view of "one's" offspring.

Ambitious plans were drawn up to remove the children from parental care, but they came to naught for lack of funds. The proponents of such radical ideas had failed to take into account that whereas mothers take care of their children free of charge, others have to be paid for such work.

A decree of May 1918 nationalized all schools. A few months later, they were merged into a single system of Consolidated Labor Schools with standardized curricula on two levels: the lower for children ages eight to thirteen and the higher for those ages thirteen to seventeen. Attendance was obligatory for school-age children of both sexes, who were taught together.

The new schools severely restricted the authority of the teachers. Called "school workers," or *shkraby* for short, they could not discipline pupils, assign them homework, or grade them. School administration was vested in committees in which "school workers" shared authority with the older pupils as well as manual laborers from nearby factories. Lunacharskii, who admired John Dewey's educational philosophy, laid stress on "learning by doing." The most advanced educational ideas imported from the West were tried, but they succeeded only in a few model schools: in the others, the teachers' incomprehension of the new methods as well as a shortage of funds led to a general lowering of standards. Fiscal constraints were, indeed, very severe. In 1918–21, the share of the Commissariat of Enlightenment in the national budget stayed under 3 percent; in Lunacharskii's estimation, this money covered between 25 and 33 percent of its requirements. By 1925–26, according to him, Soviet per capita allocations for education were one-third lower than they had been in 1913. As had been the case in the final years of the tsarist regime, despite promises of universal education, only 45 percent of eligible children attended school.

Contemporary sources indicate that only those innovations struck root which lowered academic requirements and the authority of teachers. The following excerpt from a contemporary literary work, written in the form of a fifteen-year-old boy's diary, conveys something of the atmosphere prevailing in Soviet schoolrooms of the early 1920s:

October 5

Our whole group was outraged today. This is what happened. A new *shkrabikha* ["school worker"] came to teach natural science, Elena Nikitishna Kaurova, whom we nicknamed Elnikitka. She handed out our assignments and told the group:

"Children!"

Then I got up and said: "We are not children."

To which she: "Of course, you are children, and I won't address you in any other way."

I answered: "Please be more polite, or we may send you to the devil."

That was all. The whole group stood up for me.

Elnikitka turned red and said: "In that case be so good as to leave the classroom."

I answered: "In the first place, this is not a classroom but a laboratory, and we are not expelled from it."

To which she: "You are a boor."

And I: "You are more like a teacher of the old school. Only they had such rights."

That was all. The whole group stood up for me. Elnikitka ran off like she was scalded.

On the fourth anniversary of the October coup, Lunacharskii sadly conceded the failure of the government's ambitious plans to revolutionize education:

War Communism seemed to many the shortest road to Communism . . . For us, Communist pedagogues, the disappointment was especially keen. The difficulties of building a socialist system of popular education in an ignorant, illiterate country grew beyond all measure. We had no Communist teachers at all: the material means and the moneys were insufficient.

The melancholy truth was that for all the boasting about the advances in the quality and accessibility of education, many children not only lacked the benefit of formal schooling but lost through the Revolution and its aftermath the most elementary right assured to most animals—namely parental care. These were the *besprizornye*—orphans and abandoned children—who during the 1920s roamed Russia like prehistoric creatures. Contemporaries estimated their number at between 7 and 9 million, three-quarters of them under age thirteen and three-quarters of them children of workers and peasants. They lived in gangs, surviving by begging, scrounging, stealing, and prostitution. "Going about in packs, barely articulate and recognizably human, with pinched faces, tangled hair and empty eyes," recalled Malcolm Muggeridge. "I saw them in Moscow and Leningrad, clustered under bridges, lurking in railway stations, suddenly emerging like a pack of wild monkeys, and scattering and disappearing." The government placed some of them in state-run colonies, but they proved psychically broken and socially unassimilable. Stalin would draw from their ranks many loyal henchmen, young men without family or community roots, who had only him to look to for protection.

The Bolsheviks left higher education untouched for the first year, although they realized well enough that the majority of the professors,

58. *Besprizornye*.

many of them adherents of the liberal Constitutional-Democratic Party, opposed their regime and everything it stood for. Lenin attached immense importance to science as an instrument for modernizing Russia and was prepared to go to great lengths to secure the cooperation of academics. "A great scholar, a great specialist in this or that field," he told Lunacharskii, "must be spared to the most extreme limit, even if he is a reactionary." The verb "spare" (*shchadit'*) in this context suggests that such tolerance was meant to be conditional and temporary.

This policy benefited especially the country's leading scientific institution, the Academy of Sciences. An arrangement was worked out with it by virtue of which, in return for being allowed to retain its autonomy, the Academy concentrated on applied rather than pure science. Alone of Russia's cultural institutions, it enjoyed exemption from control by the Commissariat of Enlightenment and Glavlit.

The universities were less fortunate. Between 1918 and 1921, the Communists liquidated academic self-government, abolished, for all practical purposes, faculty tenure, and filled the universities with unqualified but politically promising students.

A decree of October 1, 1918, did away with the doctor's and master's degrees and dismissed professors who had taught at the same institution for ten or more years or held chairs anywhere for more than fifteen. Their posts were thrown open to a nationwide competition, applicants for which required no higher degree but only a suitable "reputation." Several new universities came into being, some of them specifically to instruct in Communist theory. In the winter of 1918–19, the authorities closed juridical faculties and departments of history, where they had encountered the strongest resistance, and replaced them with faculties of "social science" which taught Marxism-Leninism. In 1921, on Lenin's orders, all students at institutions of higher learning had to take obligatory indoctrination courses on historical materialism and the history of the Bolshevik Revolution.

The status of higher education was definitively regulated by the university statute of September 1921, which restored many provisions of the notoriously reactionary statute of 1884. University faculties lost the right to choose rectors and professors; the authority to do so was transferred to the Commissariat of Enlightenment. The government ignored academic protests and dismissed professors who took part in them; in some instances they were exiled abroad.

The Communists turned topsy-turvy the procedure of university admissions by the sensational decree of August 2, 1918, which empowered all citizens aged sixteen and older to enroll in an institution of higher learning of their choice without having to submit proof of previous schooling, undergoing entrance examinations, or paying tuition. Such "open admission," advocated by some American radicals in the 1960s and even adopted by some U.S. colleges, flooded Russian universities with students who had neither the proper preparation nor a serious commitment to studies. Most of them soon quit the unfamiliar milieu, and the universities in the 1920s remained a preserve of youths from the middle class and the intelligentsia.

Once they became aware of this fact, the authorities took remedial action in the form of "Worker Faculties." Attached to institutions of higher learning, the so-called Rabfaki offered crash courses to workers and peasants eager to acquire a higher education. They proved quite successful and enabled many otherwise unqualified students to enroll at universities.

Even so, the social makeup of the universities did not change much: in 1923–24, workers accounted for only one in seven students. Compared with the universities in the final years of tsarism, the proportion of workers and peasants actually declined, in no small measure because the hardships of everyday existence under communism made higher studies a luxury that few could afford.

One of the most ambitious cultural endeavors of the early Bolshevik regime was a nationwide program to eliminate illiteracy. While illiteracy was not as prevalent in Russia as commonly believed—in the final years of tsarism more than four out of ten citizens could read and write—the new government attached great importance to universal literacy in order to expose all citizens to its propaganda and teach them modern industrial skills. Accordingly, in December 1919 it decreed the "liquidation of illiteracy" for citizens ages eight to fifty. Citizens able to read and write, if so instructed, had to impart their skills to those who could not; illiterates who refused to learn faced criminal prosecution. Tens of thousands of "liquidation points" were set up in the cities and villages to offer crash courses that usually lasted for three months. Peasants stayed away in droves, however, because they associated Bolshevik schooling with the propagation of atheism. Between 1920 and 1926, some 5 million persons in European Russia went through literacy courses.

As with so much else that the Communists attempted in their early years without reckoning the difficulties and costs, convinced that every problem could be resolved by the application of sufficient energy and compulsion, no miraculous improvements occurred. Before the Revolu-

59. Nadezhda Krupskaia.

tion, 42.8 percent of the population had been literate; among men, the proportion of literates had been 57.6 percent. The drive against illiteracy raised these figures to 51.1 and 66.5 percent, respectively. The results thus showed no dramatic spurt but rather continuation of the progress attained under tsarism. In one respect no advance was recorded. Because Soviet schools could accommodate only half of the eligible children, children who mastered reading and writing were counterbalanced by an equal number of those who had no such opportunity and grew up illiterate. Lenin's wife, Nadezhda Krupskaia, who played an active role in this effort, conceded regretfully that it had merely "stabilized" illiteracy.

The Russian language, over the course of the Revolution and Civil War, underwent interesting changes. The most striking was the widespread use of telescoped words such as Sovnarkom and Proletkult. "Sir" (*gospodin*) gave way to "comrade" (*tovarishch*). A new orthography simplified spelling. "God" was henceforth to be written with a small *g*.

Such were the ways of the official caste and the urban inhabitants. Peasants, for their part, spoke as they had always done and reinterpreted the new vocabulary in their own way. Thus, according to surveys conducted in the 1920s, they defined "civil marriage" to mean "unmarried people living together," "kammunist" to be "someone who does not believe in God," and "billion" to refer to "paper money." When asked about Karl Marx, whom they called "Mars," they responded: "the same as Lenin."

The founders of socialism provided little guidance in matters of ethics save to declare all moral standards to be the by-product of class relations and hence relative and transient. In this view, every class produced its own ethics; the so-called eternal principles of right and wrong were sham. Even so, the Communists faced the task of defining the ethical norms of a socialist society. The two Communist theorists who occupied themselves with this question, Preobrazhenskii and Bukharin, declared that under communism the only criterion of morality was the good of the cause. According to Bukharin, " 'ethics' transforms itself for the proletariat, step by step, into simple and comprehensible rules of conduct necessary for communism." Such was the theory. But since "communism" is an abstraction that does not act, the implementation of this principle had to be left to its custodian, the Communist Party—or, more precisely, the party's leaders, who, being human, could be expected also to attend to their personal interests. It thus meant, in effect, equating ethical criteria with the interests of the government. When in the late 1930s both Preobrazhenskii and Bukharin were tried, tortured, and executed on Stalin's orders for crimes they had not committed, by their own standards they had no grounds for complaint: "communism" in this instance, too, acted as it deemed "necessary."

The Revolution was intended to bring fundamental changes in the status of women, which, according to Friedrich Engels, the socialists' authority on the subject, under the conditions of a class society amounted to domestic slavery. Under socialism, emancipated from household chores by communal kitchens and day-care centers, women would take jobs and become full-fledged members of society. One result of this change would be the flourishing of love because the marriage bond would no longer rest on a woman's economic dependence. An unhappy union could be dissolved by simple divorce procedures.

Faithful to these precepts, the Communists in December 1917 introduced a novel (for the time) divorce law that allowed either partner to terminate a marriage on grounds of incompatibility. They did not, as yet, legalize abortion, but they tolerated it and it was widely practiced. Gen-

60. Alexandra Kollontai.

erally carried out under unhygienic conditions by unqualified personnel, the procedure claimed numerous victims. To remedy the situation, in November 1920 the government legalized abortions performed under medical supervision. This law, authorizing abortion on demand, was also the first of its kind.

In Russia, as in other countries during World War I, sexual morals loosened considerably. The idea of free love—love based solely on sexual attraction—imported from Scandinavia and Germany, gained acceptance in avant-garde circles. Communists justified it along with their general repudiation of "bourgeois" values and conventions.

The apostle of free love in Soviet Russia was Alexandra Kollontai, the only woman to reach the higher councils of the Communist regime. The pampered daughter of an affluent general, she married and divorced early, and during the war joined the Bolsheviks. She both preached and practiced unconstrained sexual license as a precondition of emotional maturity and successful male-female relations. Her affairs scandalized some Bolsheviks and amused others, endowing her with a notoriety that obscures the fact that she was far from a typical Communist. Lenin rejected with disgust the philosophy of free love and the maxim, attributed to her, that having sex should be as matter-of-fact as drinking a glass of water. While the general turbulence of the period made for a great deal of casual sex, surveys of Russian student youth in the 1920s revealed that they did not share Kollontai's views on the matter. The majority of young women questioned yearned not for sex but for love and marriage.

Unrestrained sexual license did not prevail because it was not what most young people wanted, but also because it ran contrary to what the authorities, determined to mobilize society, had in mind. The trend pointed toward traditional mores. The reaction culminated in 1936 with the promulgation of a new family code that outlawed abortion. Under Stalin, the state sought to strengthen the family: free love fell into disfavor as unsocialist. As in contemporary Nazi Germany, stress was placed on raising sturdy lads for the army.

Lenin's relative tolerance of intellectuals came to an abrupt end in the spring of 1922. He turned against them with a fury rooted in the sense of failure that had haunted him since March 1921, when the collapse of the economy had forced him to allow free retail trade and postpone indefinitely the construction of a Communist society (see Chapter XV). But it also seems to have been caused by physical changes connected with repeated strokes, which found expression in paranoia and aggressive hostility even toward his closest associates. He found insufferable the glee with which liberal and socialist intellectuals greeted his failures.

In March 1922, he declared an open war on "bourgeois ideology." He told the GPU, the successor to the Cheka, that the ranks of the intelligentsia were filled with counterrevolutionaries, spies and "corrupters of youth," who had to be rendered harmless. The security police carried out his mandate, arresting 120 prominent academics, most of whom it deported to Germany. A decree issued at this time reinstated the tsarist practice of internal exile for troublemakers, who could be sentenced by administrative procedures for up to three years. Permanent exile abroad, however, instituted at this time, was a Bolshevik innovation.

Compared with his political and economic practices, Lenin's cultural policies displayed a relative liberalism. Although in the last year of his conscious life, before being rendered mute by a disabling stroke, he persecuted independent thought with a vengeance, his rejection of the Proletkult's hostility against the cultural heritage of the past ensured for successive generations of Soviet citizens access to the world's great literature, art, and music. This helped them to survive, intellectually and spiritually, unprecedented trials. At the same time, his instrumental approach to culture, his conception of culture as a branch of propaganda, perverted its function and contributed to the creative sterility that would characterize the Soviet period once the initial flush of experimentation had exhausted itself. Worse still, the Communist regime in Lenin's day had already methodically corrupted the "low" culture of the ordinary people by assailing their religion and traditional values. The result was a spiritual vacuum that eviscerated communism and contributed greatly to its ultimate self-destruction.

War on Religion

The culture of the vast majority of the peoples inhabiting what had been the Russian Empire centered on religious beliefs and observances, for it was religion that gave them a sense of dignity and imbued them with fortitude. The vast majority of Christians, Jews, and Muslims took no part in the "high culture," the preserve of secularized elites who were indifferent to religion if not openly hostile to it. For that reason, the seizure of power by a belligerently atheistic minority of that secular minority, bent on uprooting religion, had a devastating effect on the common people. Next to economic hardships, no action of Lenin's government inflicted greater suffering on the population at large than the profanation of its religious beliefs, the closing of the houses of worship, and the mistreatment of the clergy.

Bolshevik policy toward religion had two aspects—one cultural, the other political. In common with other socialists, the new rulers of Russia viewed religious belief as a superstition that impeded modernization. But they attached no less importance to organized religion, especially the dominant Orthodox Church, because of its institutional strength and conservative ideology.

As in other realms of cultural policy, the Bolsheviks disagreed on how best to advance their objectives. Some argued that religious faith was a primitive expression of a genuine spiritual need that had to be satisfied by being channeled into secular beliefs. Others favored a direct assault by means of persecution and ridicule. The two tactics coexisted for a while, but in the end the proponents of crude atheism won out.

61. Patriarch Tikhon.

In regard to organized religion, the new authorities took an uncompromising stand from the outset: it had no place in a Communist society. The campaign against it, centered on the Orthodox Church, assumed a variety of forms: depriving the clergy of a livelihood, despoiling the houses of worship and converting them to utilitarian uses, outlawing religious instruction and replacing religious holidays with Communist festivals.

Under tsarism, Orthodox Christianity was the established church. Singled out for favors and privileges, the church paid for its favored status with utter dependence on the monarchy. Since Peter the Great, who had abolished the Patriarchate, it was administered by a ministry of spiritual affairs, the so-called Holy Synod, headed by a layman. Reform-minded clergymen saw in this dependence on the monarchy a source of weakness and urged a more independent course, but they constituted a small minority of the predominantly conservative ecclesiastical hierarchy.

In 1917, the church convened in Moscow a Council, the first in 250 years. The conservatives easily outvoted the reformers who wanted the church to be administered by councils, and reestablished the Patriarchate. The choice fell on Tikhon, the Metropolitan of Moscow, a man of moderate views and deep faith but of a rather pliable personality. Tikhon wanted the church to stay out of politics and devote itself exclusively to providing spiritual succor at a time of unusual hardship. He ignored the measures which the new regime enacted to limit the activities of religious bodies, such as nationalizing the landed properties of churches and monasteries, legalizing civil marriages, and taking over church-run schools. But he found it impossible to remain silent in the face of the civil war which the Bolsheviks had unleashed. On January 19/February 1, 1918, he issued an encyclical against the "monsters of the human race" who sowed "in place of Christian love, the seeds of malice, hatred and fratricidal strife." He anathematized Christians who participated in such abominations.

The Bolsheviks responded to Tikhon's encyclical the very next day with a decree which spelled out the principles that would henceforth guide the activities of religious bodies in Russia. Misleadingly titled "On the Separation of Church and State," it did disestablish the Orthodox Church, but this was only one of its provisions. The decree struck at the economic foundations of the church by ordering the confiscation of all its assets, including church buildings and objects used in rituals, and, at the same time, forbidding the clergy to levy dues. Supplementary decrees outlawed the teaching of religion to minors. The authorities interpreted the principle of separation of church and state to mean that the church could not act as a body; they tolerated individual church chapters but no overarching church. Any cooperation or even consultation among the clergy of different parishes served as prima facie evidence of counterrevolution. Unwilling to risk popular wrath while the Civil War was in progress, the regime did not strictly enforce the provisions of this decree; but it laid down the rules which would be implemented as soon as it felt firmly in the saddle.

Throughout 1918 soldiers, sailors, and Red Guards broke into churches and monasteries, plundering objects of value. In some localities they lynched priests and attacked religious processions. According to Communist sources, between February and May 1918, 687 persons lost their lives while taking part in religious processions or defending church properties. The Communist government and the Orthodox Church found themselves in a state of war.

The war intensified in October 1918, when Tikhon publicly condemned the Red Terror, appealing to Communist leaders to stop their abominations: "Otherwise, all the righteous blood you shed will cry out against you (Luke 11:51) and with the sword shall perish you who have taken up the sword (Matthew 26:52)." For these words, he was placed under house arrest.

By 1921–22, the Orthodox Church had lost its privileges as well as its assets. Even so, it retained a unique status, being the only institution in Soviet Russia (apart from the minuscule Academy of Sciences) to remain outside the control of the Communist Party. Lenin found this situation intolerable. Although the church had accommodated itself to his regime and presented no direct threat to it, in his highly irritable state of mind, seeking scapegoats for his failures, he determined to bring it down. To this end he provoked an open conflict, using the tried tactics of a coordinated assault from within and without: from within, by exploiting dissent between conservative and reform-minded clergy; and from without by having the former arrested and tried on spurious charges of subversion. The antichurch campaign, launched in March 1922, was meant to destroy, once and for all, what remained of the autonomy of religious bodies—in other words, to carry "October" to organized religion, the last institutional vestige of the old order.

The casus belli was the church's alleged indifference to the plight of more than 30 million Soviet citizens suffering from the famine that struck the country in the spring of 1921 (see Chapter XV). The idea of using the famine as a pretext for crushing the church originated with Trotsky, who suggested that the church be required to surrender all objects of value, including the so-called consecrated vessels; these were to be sold and the proceeds used to help the starving. Once they made up their minds to follow this strategy, the authorities rejected every compromise offered by Tikhon, for they were less interested in helping the victims of famine than in destroying the church.

A decree issued on February 26, 1922, instructed soviets to remove from churches articles made of gold, silver, and precious stones. No exception was to be made for "consecrated" vessels used in rituals, the improper use of which the church considered to be sacrilegious. As expected, Tikhon refused to comply with the terms of this decree, threatening those who helped implement it with excommunication. For this defiance he was once again punished with house arrest.

As the forceful seizures got under way, crowds of faithful in many localities physically resisted the troops. Hundreds of incidents of such defiance were recorded and promptly attributed to the work of "counterrevolutionary" organizations allegedly acting on the orders of Russian

62. Soldiers removing valuables from Simonov
Monastery in Moscow, 1925.

émigrés. One such episode occurred at Shuia, a textile town northeast of
Moscow, where in early March unarmed civilians fought off a company
of soldiers equipped with machine guns. Alarmed by such defiance, the
Politburo resolved temporarily to suspend confiscations.

But Lenin, who was ill and did not participate in these deliberations,
overruled his colleagues. He decided that the famine offered a unique
opportunity to break the church by demonstrating to the mass of peasants its alleged un-Christian callousness in the face of mass suffering. In
a lengthy note to the Politburo written on March 19, 1922, but made

public only in 1970, he insisted on the campaign being pressed with full vigor:

> It is now and only now, when in regions afflicted by the famine there is cannibalism and the roads are littered with hundreds if not thousands of corpses, that·we can (and therefore must) pursue the acquisition of [church] valuables with the most ferocious and merciless energy, stopping at nothing in suppressing all resistance . . . Send to Shuia one of the most energetic, intelligent and efficient members of the All-Russian Central Executive Committee . . . with verbal instructions conveyed by a member of the Politburo. This instruction ought to call for the arrest in Shuia of as many as possible—no fewer than several dozen—representatives of the local clergy, local burghers, and local bourgeois on suspicion of direct or indirect involvement in the violent resistance . . . As soon as this is done, he ought to return to Moscow and make a report . . . On the basis of this report, the Politburo will issue detailed instruction to the judiciary author-ities, also verbal, that the trial of the Shuia rebels who oppose help to the starving should be conducted with the maximum swiftness and end with the execution of a very large number . . . and, insofar as possible, not only in that city, but also in Moscow and several other church centers . . . The greater the number of representatives of the reactionary bourgeoisie and reactionary clergy we will manage to execute in this affair, the better.

The Russian historian D. A. Volkogonov, who has enjoyed unrestricted access to Russia's archives, has seen in Lenin's papers an order from him demanding to be informed, on a daily basis, how many priests had been shot.

The "trials" began almost immediately. These were spectacles that had more in common with "agitational" theater than with judiciary pro-ceedings, for the cast of characters was carefully chosen and the outcome preordained by the authorities. In April 1922, fifty-four priests and lay-men were subjected to such procedures in Moscow; in June, similar pro-ceedings were staged in Petrograd. Some of the defendants received death sentences. An English journalist learned that the antichurch cam-paign of 1922 claimed the lives of 28 bishops and 1,215 priests. Recently released evidence indicates that more than 8,000 persons were executed or killed in the course of 1922 during the conflict over church treasures. The results of this campaign, in monetary terms, were meager; the churches had far less wealth than popular imagination attributed to them. As best as can be determined, the operation realized between $4 and $8 million, the lower figure apparently being closer to the truth. Very little if any of that money went for famine relief, funds for which came mostly from American and European sources.

. . .

The campaign against the church was accompanied by a drive against religious beliefs and rituals. In 1919, the authorities ordered the exposure of the relics of saints to which devout Russians attributed miraculous powers. They revealed that the tombs contained not perfectly preserved remains of saints, as the church asserted, but either skeletons or dummies. Whatever effect these exposures had on intellectuals, on ordinary people they produced the opposite of that intended. An old peasant explained to an American visitor: "Our holy saints disappeared to heaven and substituted rags and straw for their relics when they found that their tombs were to be desecrated by nonbelievers. It was a great miracle."

Undeterred, the atheist organizations, relying especially on the Communist youth organization called Komsomol, launched in late 1922 a campaign to discredit Christmas and the holidays of other faiths. Many cities witnessed mock religious celebrations, of which the so-called "Komsomol Christmas" acquired the greatest notoriety. Bands of youths were commanded to parade with effigies and to lampoon ceremonies under way in nearby churches. Performers dressed as priests and rabbis rode along the streets of Moscow, clowning and shouting blasphemies. Behind them marched young girls chanting:

> We need no rabbis, we need no priests,
> Beat the bourgeois, strangle the kulaks!

Similar carnivals took place in other cities. In the Belorussian town of Gomel, for example, which had an ethnically mixed population, a "trial" of Orthodox, Christian, and Jewish "gods" was staged at a local theater. The judges, seconded by the audience, condemned the "gods" to death, following which, on Christmas Day, they were ceremoniously burned in the city square.

Measures were taken to discredit in the eyes of children St. Nicholas, the Russian Santa Claus, and the angels, who were accused of being used to "enslave the child's mind." To counteract such decadent beliefs, the authorities organized on Christmas Eve theatrical performances which regaled their young audiences with "satires on the Lausanne Conference, the Kerensky regime, and bourgeois life abroad."

According to eyewitnesses, people reacted to such acts of sacrilege with dumb horror. That this was indeed the case is confirmed by a resolution by the Communist Party in 1923 to curtail activities of this kind on the grounds that they only intensified "religious fanaticism." Henceforth, the atheistic campaign was pursued in less ostentatious ways. The Society of the Godless, in its journal and other publications, exposed all religions to ridicule. In the case of Jewish subjects, they had recourse to anti-Semitic stereotypes that anticipated Nazi practices.

So much for the external assault on the church and religion. But, as noted above, this assault was accompanied by a campaign to split the church from within. This the regime accomplished by detaching the reformist elements of the Orthodox Church and forming them into a separate "Living Church." This body came into existence in March 1922, at the very time when the government initiated the campaign to confiscate church valuables. Managed by a special department of the GPU, it made use of renegade priests on its payroll.

In May 1922, several priest-collaborators visited Tikhon at the monastery near Moscow where he had been confined. They demanded that he convoke a Church Council and withdraw from all church affairs. The Patriarch yielded and was replaced by a new institution, managed by the government through the security police, called the Higher Church Administration, essentially a restored Holy Synod. A shrill public campaign followed, calling for the abolition of the Patriarchate; it frightened a number of bishops into joining the Living Church. Those who defied the illegitimate new hierarchy were arrested and replaced with more compliant clergymen. By August 1922, the Orthodox Church was split: of its 143 bishops, 37 gave allegiance to the Living Church, 36 opposed it, and the remaining 70 sat on the fence. Tikhon anathematized the Higher Church Administration and everyone connected with it. The Patriarchal Church, virtually outlawed, went underground.

The utter subservience of the Living Church to the new regime manifested itself in the resolutions of the Second Church Council, which it convened in April 1923 and packed with adherents. The assembly hailed the October 1917 coup as a "Christian deed," denied that the Communists persecuted the church, and voted gratitude to Lenin for his role as "world leader" and "tribune of social justice." The Soviet government, it declared, alone in the world strove to realize "the ideal of the Kingdom of God." The Patriarchate was abolished.

At this point Tikhon surrendered. Apparently frightened by the prospect of a permanent split in the church, in June 1923 he addressed a letter to the authorities recanting his "anti-Soviet" past and withdrawing the anathema on the Living Church. As a reward, the patriarchal churches were permitted to reopen. Tikhon died in April 1925: in a testament of questionable authenticity, he urged Christians to support the Soviet government. From that time onward, until the Communist regime's collapse in the early 1990s, the church gave it no more trouble.

Having served its purpose, the Living Church lost support in the Kremlin and gradually disappeared from view. In the early 1930s, most of its leaders were arrested.

Although many Christians felt that their persecution was the work of Jews, Jewish institutions also suffered from Bolshevik antireligious policies.* It has even been argued that in some respects Jews were more victimized than Christians because their religious institutions not only performed rituals and educated youth but served as centers of Jewish life. Nora Levin is one scholar who supports this view:

> The assault on Jewish religious life was particularly harsh and pervasive because a Jew's religious beliefs and observances infused every aspect of his daily life. . . . Family relations, work, prayer, study, recreation, and culture were all part of a seamless web, no element of which could be disturbed without disturbing the whole.

The persecution of Jewish religious observances was entrusted to the Bund, the party of Jewish Social-Democrats which in 1921 merged with the Communist Party. The Bundists shared the Bolshevik scorn for religion and hated with a particular passion Zionism, its much more successful contender for Jewish loyalties. Organized into "Jewish Sections" (*Evsektsii*), they carried out the usual antireligious activities, desecrating synagogues and transforming them into clubs or warehouses. They also abolished the traditional Jewish organs of self-government. It was the Jewish Sections that persuaded the Russian Communist Party to ban Hebrew as a "bourgeois" language (it favored Yiddish) and persecute Zionists.

Ultimately, the Evsektsii went the way of the Living Church, being liquidated in December 1929. Most of their functionaries were purged and some executed.

---

* One of the reasons for the widespread perception that Jews stood behind the persecution of the Orthodox Church was the Communist practice of deliberately using them in the antireligious campaign. Maxim Gorky, a novelist close to Lenin, wrote, in May 1922, to a Jewish publication in New York: "I know of cases of young Jewish Communists being purposely involved [in the persecution of the church] in order that the philistine and the peasant should see: it is the Jews that are ruining monasteries [and] mocking 'holy places.' It seems to me that this was done partly from fear and partly from a clear intent to compromise the Jewish people. It was done by anti-Semites of whom there are not a few among the Communists."

63. The antireligious play *Heder*. The letters on the actors' backsides spell "kosher."

The Catholic Church did not escape the onslaught either. In March 1923, the authorities opened a show trial of sixteen Catholic clergymen, most of whom were Poles. The church's highest dignitary in Russia was condemned to death but received a reprieve under strong foreign pressure. Another priest, however, was shot.

Of the three major faiths, Islam received the most tolerant treatment. This is explainable largely by Moscow's fear that persecution of the Muslim religion would have an adverse effect on the Islamic population in the Middle East, which it assiduously courted. Mullahs received the right to vote denied to priests and rabbis; they could also engage in religious instruction and keep clerical properties. These privileges the Muslim clergy retained until the end of the decade.

The effect which persecution had on the religious sentiments of the population is difficult to assess. The general impression one gains from eyewitness accounts is that while the Communists succeeded in weakening the Orthodox Church, their antireligious campaigns had the opposite effect, intensifying religious feelings. In the 1920s, churches filled with worshippers and immense crowds took part in church holidays. Some contemporaries believed that Communist persecution raised religious fervor to heights never before attained.

But ahead lay trials such as no religion had ever had to endure.

COMMUNISM IN CRISIS

*Nothing has been left that could obstruct
the central government; but, by the
same token, nothing could shore it up.*

—ALEXIS DE TOCQUEVILLE

NEP—The False Thermidor

Thermidor is the month of the French Revolutionary calendar when, in 1794, the Jacobin terror came to a sudden end and the country began the return to normalcy that twenty years later would culminate in a Bourbon restoration. To professional revolutionaries the word was anathema; the Bolsheviks were determined to stop at nothing to prevent a Thermidorian counterrevolution.

Yet despite their resolve, in the spring of 1921 the collapse of the national economy and the outbreak of nationwide rebellions forced the Bolsheviks to adopt measures subsumed under the name New Economic Policy (NEP), which many contemporaries interpreted as marking the end of the Jacobin phase of the Russian Revolution and the beginning of its "Thermidor." The analogy turned out to be false: the NEP was not a permanent departure from revolutionary violence but a breathing spell that a few years later would give way to even greater excesses.

The most obvious difference between the genuine French Thermidor of 1794 and the Russian pseudo-Thermidor of 1921 was that whereas the former led to the overthrow of the French Jacobins, in Russia the neo-Jacobins stayed in power and themselves initiated the reforms. They were, therefore, in a position to abandon them once the danger of a counterrevolution had disappeared. "I ask you, comrades, to be clear," Zinoviev said in December 1921, "that the New Economic Policy is only a temporary deviation, a tactical retreat, a clearing of the land for a new and decisive attack of labor against the front of international capitalism." Second, unlike the French Thermidor, the Russian retreat affected only economics; economic liberalization was counterbalanced by intensified repression and the tightening of political controls. Most contemporaries misunderstood the tactical nature and the limited scope of the retreat, viewing it as the beginning of the end of the Revolution.

War Communism had all but destroyed Russia's economy (above, p. 199). The end of the Civil War did not put an end to it: on the contrary, the year 1920 witnessed the wildest experiments in labor legislation and monetary policies. The government persevered with forcible confiscations of peasant food "surplus," which in many cases was not surplus at all but grain needed for sustenance and planting of next year's crop. Since the weather in 1920 was unfavorable to agriculture, the meager bread reserves dwindled still further and the countryside began to experience the first symptoms of famine.

Such mismanagement eroded what was left of Bolshevik support, turning followers into enemies and enemies into rebels. The "masses," who during the Civil War had been told by the regime that the Whites and their foreign backers bore responsibility for all their hardships, refused to accept such explanations once the war had ended. Communist workers, a small minority to begin with, began to turn in their membership cards; in 1920–21 only 2 or 3 percent of industrial labor still belonged to the Party. Peasants, their ranks swollen by demobilized Red Army soldiers, took to arms. In 1920 and early 1921, the Russian countryside from the Black Sea to the Pacific was the scene of peasant rebellions that in size and scope eclipsed all rural uprisings under tsarism. Involved on both sides were hundreds of thousands; the combat losses suffered in this civil conflict exceeded by a considerable margin those incurred in the conflict between Whites and Reds. The Bolsheviks in Lenin's own words were but a drop of water in the nation's sea—and the sea was raging.

The new regime survived this national revolt by a combination of repression and compromise: unrestrained brutality in quelling the rebellions and concessions in the shape of the New Economic Policy. Disposing of an immense army, incomparably better equipped and professionally led, it crushed the disunited peasants, who had neither a political program nor unified command, exactly as the tsars had done. But military force would not have sufficed: ultimately it was the abandon-

64. A "food detachment" about to depart for the village.

ment of food requisitioning that pacified the countryside and saved the Bolsheviks.

The most dangerous of these peasant revolts broke out in mid-1920 in the province of Tambov, 350 kilometers southeast of Moscow. A prosperous agrarian province, before the Revolution Tambov had produced up to 1 million tons of cereals annually, nearly one-third of which was exported abroad. War Communism eliminated the surplus and cut into grain reserves. According to Vladimir Antonov-Ovseenko, the Soviet official charged with quelling the Tambov rebellion, in the years immediately preceding World War I, the inhabitants of Tambov had consumed annually 293 kilograms of cereals per person and disposed, in addition, of 121 kilograms of animal fodder. In 1920–21, they had only 69 kilograms of cereals per person, minus seed grain but without allowance for fodder. After making compulsory deliveries to the state, the population was left with barely 25 kilograms per person, about one-eighth of what it needed to survive. Already by January 1921, according to Antonov-Ovseenko, half of the province's peasantry went hungry.

The Tambov rebellion broke out spontaneously, but it soon found a leader of exceptional talent and courage in Alexander Antonov (no relation to Antonov-Ovseenko), who put together a large guerrilla force to

65. Alexander Antonov.

wage partisan warfare against the regular Red Army and special Cheka detachments sent to liquidate it. By early 1921, Antonov had under his command somewhere between 20,000 and 50,000 partisans with whom he staged hit-and-run attacks on Communist military and administrative objectives. Following each such raid, the partisans melted in the villages. Moscow, declaring the rebels "bandits," sent reinforcements to Tambov, but success proved elusive because the Red Army lacked experience with guerrilla combat. It became apparent that the only way to quell the disorders was to isolate the rebels from their families and sympathizers. This required resort to terror: concentration camps, the seizure and execution of hostages, mass deportations. Antonov-Ovseenko requested and obtained from Moscow authorization to resort to such measures.

But famine stalked not only the countryside. During the winter of 1920–21, the food and fuel supply situation in the cities of European Russia recalled the eve of the February Revolution. In Petrograd, which again suffered the most because of its remoteness from food-producing areas, factories had to shut down: laid-off workers scouring the countryside for food ran the risk of being intercepted by "barring detachments," which confiscated their haul.

It was against this background of hunger and unemployment that in February 1921 the sailors of the nearby Kronstadt naval base, once extolled by Trotsky as "the pride and beauty" of the Revolution, raised the banner of revolt.

66. A typical street scene under War Communism.

The spark that ignited the mutiny was a government order reducing the already meager bread ration in Moscow and Petrograd by one-third. This measure provoked disturbances and strikes in both cities. At the end of February 1921, Petrograd workers threatened a general strike unless they were granted, in addition to the right to procure unhindered food from peasants, honest elections to soviets, freedom of speech, and an end to police terror. When news of the industrial disorders reached the naval base, the sailors adopted the workers' slogans and formed a Provisional Revolutionary Committee to take charge of the island's defenses against the anticipated assault from the mainland. The rebels had no illusion about their ability to withstand the might of the Red Army, but they counted on rallying the country and its armed forces to their cause.

In this expectation they were disappointed. Unlike Nicholas II, Lenin fought back. Together with Trotsky, he immediately blamed the Kronshtadt mutiny on White Guard generals allegedly manipulated by the Socialists-Revolutionaries and French intelligence services. Lenin dispatched Trotsky to Petrograd to take charge of the operation. Trotsky ordered the mutineers to surrender at once or face military retribution: with minor changes in wording, his ultimatum could have been issued by

67. "Help!" (1921 poster by Moor).

68. A common sight on the streets of Moscow and
Petrograd during the years 1918–21.

a tsarist governor-general. He further ordered the wives and children of
the mutinous sailors residing in Petrograd to be taken hostage.

On March 7 the Red Army, under Tukhachevskii's command, attacked
Kronshtadt over the frozen waters. In the rear of the attacking force
stood Cheka machine-gun detachments with orders to shoot retreating
soldiers. The assault turned into a rout as fire from the naval base cut
down the assailants. Some Red soldiers refused orders to charge; about
1,000 went over to the rebels. Trotsky ordered the execution of every
fifth soldier who had disobeyed orders.

The day after the first shots had been fired, the Provisional Revolutionary Committee of Kronshtadt issued a programmatic statement,
"What we are fighting for," that accused the Bolsheviks of betraying the
Revolution and instituting a tyranny far worse than tsarism. It called on
the nation to overthrow the "Communist autocracy" and put in its place
a democratic regime based on honestly elected soviets.

During the week that followed, while bolstering his army with reliable
reinforcements, Tukhachevskii kept the naval base off balance with
nightly raids. The country's failure to respond to their appeals disheartened the sailors, whose food supplies were running short. The final
assault by 50,000 Red troops against the 17,000 defenders began on the
night of March 16–17. The attacking force managed to creep close
before being noticed. Ferocious fighting ensued, much of it hand to
hand. By the morning of March 18, the Communists controlled the

island. They slaughtered several hundred prisoners. The rest of the defenders, save those who had managed to escape over the ice to Finland, were sent to concentration camps in the Far North, from which few returned. The campaign did nothing to enhance Trotsky's reputation; and although he loved to dwell on his military and political triumphs, in the memoirs he wrote while in exile he omitted any mention of his role in this tragic event.

While the mutiny in the north went down in defeat, the Tambov rebellion continued to rage. Lenin and Trotsky received periodic reports from the field staff of the Military-Revolutionary Committee there concerning operations against the "bandits" as if it were a regular war front. Although the staff claimed victory after victory, Moscow had to face the fact that the rebels, waging unconventional warfare, could not be subdued by conventional military means. Lenin therefore resolved to resort to unbridled terror. Entrusting the operation to Tukhachevskii, in command of an army of more than 100,000 men, he authorized him and Antonov-Ovseenko to take whatever measures they deemed necessary to deprive the partisans of popular support. Using lists of partisans supplied by paid informers, the Cheka incarcerated their families. Antonov-Ovseenko reported to Lenin that to break the silence of the civilian population, Red commanders employed the following procedures:

69. Red Army troops assaulting Kronshtadt.

A special "sentence" is pronounced on the villages in which their crimes against the laboring people are enumerated. The entire male population is placed under the jurisdiction of the Revolutionary Military Tribunal: all the families of the bandits are removed to a concentration camp to serve as *hostages* for the relative who belongs to a band. A period of two weeks is given the bandit to surrender, at the end of which the family is deported from the province and its property (until then sequestered provisionally) is confiscated for good.

For all their savagery, these measures still failed to produce the desired results, whereupon a new directive raised higher yet the level of terror:

1. Citizens who refuse to give their names are to be executed on the spot . . .
4. A family that has concealed a bandit is to be arrested and exiled from the province. Its property is to be confiscated, and its oldest member to be executed on the spot without a trial.
5. A family that offers shelter to members of a bandit's family or conceals the property of a bandit is to be treated as bandits; the oldest worker of such a family is to be executed on the spot, without a trial. . . .
7. This order will be carried out strictly and mercilessly. It is to be read to village assemblies.

Such terror, accompanied by a large-scale military operation that employed poison gas to smoke out the partisans hiding out in the woods, isolated the rebel peasant force. With the abolition of forced food exactions in March 1921 (below, p. 352), the main cause of rural rebellions in Tambov and elsewhere was removed and the countryside quickly calmed down.

The ability of Antonov to keep at bay a vastly superior regular army made a strong impression on the Communist military command. It ordered studies to be made of unconventional warfare and subsequently added partisan operations to its repertory; these it used to advantage in World War II. The invading Germans, for their part, would replicate the methods of terror against the civilian population that the Red Army had developed in 1920–21 in campaigns against peasant guerrillas.

The need to pacify the countryside with concessions became apparent to Lenin even before Kronstadt, but he was exceedingly loath to grant the peasants' main demand—the right freely to dispose of their produce—because it would strengthen a class which he considered to be implacably antisocialist. On one occasion he even declared that "we" would rather die than allow free commerce in grain. Kronshtadt finally forced his hand. On March 15, the day before Tukhachevskii launched his final assault on the naval base, the Politburo resolved to abolish the forced requisitioning of peasant surplus. Henceforth, the peasants would pay the government a fixed tax in produce. The remainder the government expected to obtain by bartering manufactured goods. But since manufactured goods were unavailable, nearly all the surplus found its way to the market, ending the state's monopoly on retail trade. Once this happened, the authorities had no choice but to open up the entire consumer economy to free enterprise. They retained, however, a tight grip on heavy industry, banking, wholesale trade and foreign trade, and transport—the economy's "commanding heights." This was the essence of the New Economic Policy.

Soon Moscow gave up the idea of abolishing money. Paper rubles, issued as rapidly as the printing presses would allow, had lost nearly all value. While continuing to flood the country with worthless paper, the government adopted a new monetary standard in the form of a gold-based currency called *chervonets*.

The benefits of NEP appeared first and foremost in agriculture. Encouraged by the new tax policy to increase cultivation, peasants began to grow more food; the cultivated acreage (though not the yield per acre) in 1925 matched that of 1913. But these improvements came too late to prevent a disastrous famine that in 1921–22 wiped out millions.

Industrial production recovered much more slowly due to lack of capital. Lenin counted heavily on foreign investments, but these failed to materialize because foreigners hesitated to invest in a country that had defaulted on its loans and nationalized private assets. In the final year of NEP (1928), the Soviet Union had only thirty-one foreign enterprises with capital (in 1925) of a mere $16 million. The majority of these enterprises engaged not in manufacture but in the exploitation of the country's natural resources, especially timber.

NEP precluded comprehensive economic planning, which had to be given up for the time being. Instead, Lenin concentrated on an ambitious program of electrification which he expected to lay the foundations of a modern industrial economy. These hopes did not materialize owing to the lack of funding, estimated at $500 million annually for ten to fifteen years.

In their totality, the economic measures introduced after March 1921 marked a severe setback for the prospects of communism in Russia. In

70. An open market under the NEP.

1921, Lenin admitted that War Communism had been a mistake (above, p. 193) and tacitly conceded that his critics before the Revolution had been right in arguing that Russia needed a long period of capitalist development before she would be ready for socialism, let alone communism. He did not spell out how long he believed the NEP would last; but he hinted that it would not be abandoned soon. When, in 1928–29, Stalin liquidated the NEP and went over to forced collectivization and industrialization, he acted in Lenin's spirit but moved much earlier and faster than Lenin would have done had he still been alive.

To the Bolsheviks, the loosening of economic controls, which allowed, however conditionally, the reemergence of private enterprise, spelled political danger. They made certain, therefore, to accompany the liberalization of the economy with a further tightening of political controls. "As the ruling party," Trotsky said in 1922, "we can allow the speculator in the economy, but we do not allow him in the realm of politics." The period that followed the introduction of the NEP thus combined economic liberalization with intensified political repression. The latter took the form of persecution of the Orthodox Church and rival socialist parties; increased harassment of the intelligentsia; stricter censorship; and harsher criminal laws against political dissidence.

The security police remained the principal instrument of political control, changing under the NEP from an agency of blind terror into an all-pervasive branch of the bureaucracy. The extent to which the security police penetrated every facet of Soviet life is indicated by the positions held by its head, Felix Dzerzhinskii, who served, at one time or another, as Commissar of the Interior, Commissar of Transport, and Chairman of the Supreme Council of the National Economy. The Cheka, which had acquired an odious name, was abolished in February 1922 and immediately replaced by an organization innocuously named State Political Administration, or GPU (two years later renamed OGPU). Like the tsarist Department of the Police, the GPU was part of the Ministry (Commissariat) of the Interior.

Theoretically, the GPU enjoyed narrower powers than did the Cheka in that ordinary crimes (i.e., crimes of a nonpolitical nature) were removed from its jurisdiction and transferred to the Commissariat of Justice. In reality, it had broad discretion to deal with economic offenses and "banditry" as well as suspicious individuals, and could not only exile citizens by administrative order but condemn them to death. It operated a network of concentration camps, the most notorious of which, the Northern Camps of Special Designation, located in the frozen wastes of the Far North, claimed many lives. With a civilian staff of more than 100,000 full-time employees and a sizable military force, it was quite free of external controls.

The principle of "revolutionary legality" was routinely violated under the NEP, as before, not only because of the judiciary powers granted the GPU but also because Lenin regarded law as an arm of politics and courts as agencies of the government. He spelled out his conception of legality in 1922 in connection with the drafting of Soviet Russia's first Criminal Code. Lenin took an active part in the preparation of this document, which under Stalin would serve to condemn millions of Soviet citizens to penal servitude and death. Dissatisfied with what he believed to be excessive leniency on the part of the jurists charged with the task, he defined political crimes to include "propaganda and agitation or participation in organizations or assistance to organizations that help (by means of propaganda and agitation)" the international "bourgeoisie." Such "crimes," which in effect embraced every form of independent political activity, carried the death penalty. Implementing Lenin's instructions, jurists drew up Articles 57 and 58 of the Criminal Code under which the victims of Stalin's terror would be convicted. That Lenin realized the implications of his instructions is evident from the guidance he gave the Commissar of Justice. The task of the judiciary, he wrote, was to "legitimize" terror (above, p. 220). For the first time in legal history, the function of judiciary proceedings was defined to be not dispensing justice but justifying indiscriminate state violence.

The whole thrust of legal theory and practice under Lenin was to eliminate all obstacles that stood in the way of punishing those whom the government for any reason found undesirable. Communist legal historians, referring to the practices of the 1920s, defined law as "a disciplining principle that helps strengthen the Soviet state and develop the socialist economy." Court procedures were streamlined to facilitate the task of the prosecution. Thus "guilt" did not require an actual breach of law but only a perceived "intent" to break it. Guilt could also be determined by the harmful consequences of an action for society, whether or not it violated any law. The rights of defendants were severely limited; defense attorneys, who had to be Party members, had to take their clients' guilt for granted and confine themselves to pleading extenuating circumstances. One prominent Soviet jurist argued in 1929, before Stalin's terror got under way, that Soviet law permitted a person to be condemned even in the absence of guilt. It was hardly possible to have gone further in the destruction of law and due process.

These principles were applied in the trials of Orthodox and Catholic churchmen, but also in a spectacular show trial of the leaders of the Socialist-Revolutionary Party staged concurrently in Moscow. (The Mensheviks, whom the regime had less reason to fear, received a reprieve until 1931, when they, too, were subjected to sham legal proceedings.) In all these cases, the authorities predetermined the choice of the defendants as well as their sentences, and the quasi-judiciary proceedings served to teach the population at large a political lesson. Lenin informed the judiciary authorities in charge that he wanted "exemplary, *educational* trials." Trotsky concurred: in a letter to the Politburo he called for a trial that would be "a polished political production."

The SR trial involved two groups of defendants: one, the intended victims; the other, "friendly" offenders willing to give state evidence for which they would be reprieved, providing the populace with an example of the rewards of collaboration. The SR leaders were denied proper counsel and suffered numerous indignities, including a staged demonstration of "workers," joined by Bukharin, one of the defense lawyers, who clamored for their death. The judges condemned eleven of the accused to capital punishment under Article 57, while pardoning those who turned in state evidence. To everyone's surprise, the death sentences were commuted. It is known from Trotsky's memoirs that he had convinced Lenin to spare the SRs for the time being from fear that their comrades would retaliate with a wave of anti-Bolshevik terrorism, of which the two of them, presumably, would be primary targets. It was announced, therefore, that the executions would not take place if the SR Party ceased to engage in terrorism and subversion against the Soviet regime. In the 1930s and 1940s, when the regime no longer feared them, they were systematically killed off. Only two active Socialists-Revolutionaries, both women, are known to have survived Stalin.

These political scores were settled against the background of a famine that in the number of victims had no precedent in European history.

Russia had experienced throughout her history periodic crop failures due to unfavorable weather. Experience had taught the peasant to cope with such natural disasters by setting aside sufficient reserves to carry him through one or even two years of bad harvests. But in 1920–21, the effects of drought were exacerbated by the Bolshevik agrarian policy. The ensuing debacle confirmed the peasant saying that "Bad crops are from God, but hunger comes from men." The drought that made itself felt in 1920 and continued into the following year accelerated a catastrophe that was bound to happen sooner or later as the result of Bolshevik food requisitions. The impounding of surplus that as often as not consisted of grain essential for the peasants' survival, ensured disaster. By 1920, in the judgment of the Commissariat of Supply, the peasant harvested just enough to feed himself and provide for seed. He had none of the reserves that in the past had cushioned him against adverse weather.

The drought of 1921 struck approximately half of the country's food-producing areas; 20 percent of them experienced total crop failures. At its height, the population afflicted by the famine in Russia and the Ukraine numbered 33.5 million. Worst affected was the Volga Black Earth region, in normal times a prime supplier of cereals; here in some provinces the 1921 harvest yielded less than 90 kilograms per person—half the quantity required for survival, with nothing to spare for seed grain.* In most of the rest of the country, the harvest yielded between 90 and 180 kilograms, which barely sufficed to feed the local population, with no surplus. Production in the twenty principal food-growing provinces in European Russia struck by the famine, which before the Revolution had yielded 20 million tons of cereals annually, in 1920 declined to 8.45 million tons, and in 1921 to 2.9 million, or, by 85 percent. In 1892, by contrast, when Russia last suffered a major famine, the harvest fell only 13 percent below normal. The difference has to be in large measure attributed to Bolshevik exactions, which caused the peasant to curtail his acreage and, in some cases, deprived him of seed grain.

In the spring of 1921, peasants in the areas struck by the famine resorted to eating grass, tree bark, and rodents. Enterprising Tatars sold a substance called "edible clay," which fetched as much as 500 rubles a pound. There were confirmed cases of cannibalism. Soon millions of wretched human beings abandoned their villages and headed for the nearest railroad station hoping to make their way to regions where, rumor had it, there was food. They clogged the railway depots, for they were refused transportation, because until July 1921 Moscow persisted in denying that a catastrophe had occurred. Here, in the words of a contemporary, they waited "for trains which never came, or for death, which was inevitable." Visitors to the stricken areas passed village after village with no sign of life, the inhabitants having either departed or lying prostrate in their cottages, too weak to move. In the cities, corpses littered the streets, where they were picked up, loaded on carts—often after having first been stripped naked—and dumped into unmarked mass graves.

The famine was accompanied by epidemics that ravaged bodies weakened by hunger. The main killer was typhus, but hundreds of thousands also fell victim to cholera, typhoid fever, and smallpox.

The Soviet government watched the spread of the famine in a state of paralysis, for, in the words of the French historian Michel Heller, it "confronted a problem which, for the first time, it could not solve with resort to force." Initially it pretended that there was nothing wrong. Then, when the catastrophe could no longer be denied, it blamed it on "White Guardists" and "imperialists." Finally, when the full extent of the

---

* Although the figures varied from region to region, a rough estimate held that a peasant needed annually a minimum of 163 kilograms of grain for sustenance, with an additional 40 to 80 kilograms for seed. Before 1914, the average annual consumption per capita had been 270 kilograms (seed grain included).

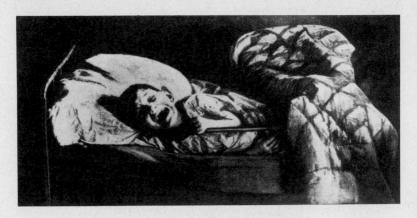

71. One victim of the 1921 famine.

72. Corpses of starved children.

tragedy became apparent, unwilling to ask for foreign help on its own behalf, it turned to prominent private persons. In July, Maxim Gorky issued, certainly with Lenin's approval, an appeal to foreign countries soliciting food and medicines. The government also authorized the formation of a nonpartisan committee, supervised by a Communist cell, to organize famine relief.

Ten days after Gorky's appeal, Herbert Hoover, then U.S. Secretary of Commerce, responded. He had organized the American Relief Administration (ARA) to help postwar Europe with food and other essentials, and now offered similar assistance to Russia. Lenin found it odious to accept help from the leading capitalist country, especially since Hoover demanded, as a precondition of aid, the release of all Americans from Soviet prisons and governmental noninterference with his relief program. "The baseness of America, Hoover, and the League of Nations is rare," Lenin told the Politburo. "One must punish Hoover, one must *publicly slap his face*, so that the *whole world sees*." But he had no choice in the matter and accepted Hoover's offer with its conditions.

In the summer of 1922, with its activities at their height, ARA fed some 11 million persons a day. Other foreign organizations nourished an

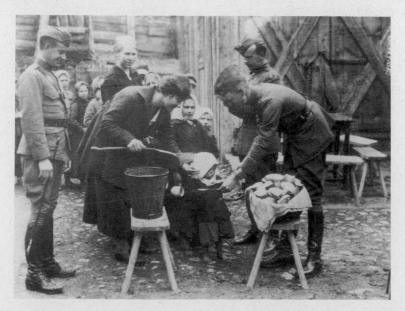

73. American Relief workers feeding Russian children during the 1921–22 famine.

additional 3 million. Foreign relief agencies also supplied medicines. In consequence of these activities, by early summer of 1922, deaths from starvation had virtually ceased. It is estimated that Hoover's philanthropic activities saved at least 9 million people from certain death. Even so, it is estimated that between 1920 and 1922, 5.1 million Soviet citizens perished from hunger and accompanying diseases. It was the greatest human disaster in European history, other than those caused by war, since the Black Death of the fourteenth century.

The activities of the ARA came to an end in June 1923, in part because its services were less needed and in part because it became known that while accepting charity from America, the Soviet government was offering grain for sale abroad to earn cash for purchases of industrial and agricultural equipment. The opening of Soviet archives in the 1990s brought to light the additional fact that at the height of the famine, Trotsky spent millions of dollars to buy rifles and machine guns in Germany.

The New Economic Policy affected also Soviet foreign policy, which, now that Soviet Russia had been recognized by the great powers, more explicitly than ever operated on two distinct levels: the conventional diplomatic-commercial and the unconventional subversive-revolutionary. Moscow eagerly pursued diplomatic normalization to encourage foreign trade and investments, which formed an integral part of the NEP. It gave up fomenting insurrections: apart from a hastily improvised and unsuccessful putsch in Germany in 1923, it made no further attempts to overthrow European governments. Instead, it implemented, through the Comintern, its long-term strategy of infiltrating Western institutions.

In the Comintern, as within Russia, the NEP led to a tightening of political controls by the Communist Party. The Twenty-one Conditions subordinated foreign Communist parties to Moscow, but they had preserved the illusion that the Comintern was a federation of equals. This illusion it dispelled in December 1922 at the Comintern's Fourth Congress. The resolutions of this congress stated explicitly that, first, foreign Communist parties had no right to independent opinions, and second, that whenever the two happened to come into conflict, the interests of the Soviet state—soon to be renamed the Soviet Union—invariably took precedence over those of its affiliates' home countries.

In preparation for the Fourth Comintern Congress, Moscow eliminated from its structure all traces of federalism. Bukharin, who took charge, interpreted Article 14 of the Twenty-one Conditions, requiring foreign Communists to help Soviet Russia repel the "counterrevolution," to mean they had the obligation at all times to support the foreign policy of the Soviet government. In effect, the Communist was to have only one fatherland, Soviet Russia, and one government, the Soviet government.

To prevent foreign parties from questioning or interfering with the resolutions of the Comintern's highest nominal authority, its congresses, it was now laid down that henceforth its member parties would convene only after the Comintern Congress had held its meetings. This clause ensured that foreign delegates could not move independent resolution on behalf of their national organizations. Indeed, they were explicitly forbidden to bring with them binding mandates. The national parties lost even the right to send representatives of their choice to the Comintern Executive; these were to be selected by the Congress. No resignations of Comintern officials were to be countenanced unless authorized by the Communist Executive, on the grounds that "every executive post in a Communist Party belongs not to the person holding it, but to the Communist International as a whole." Of the twenty-five members of the new Executive, fifteen were required to reside in Moscow.

The Fourth Congress adopted the new rules unanimously, the only dissenting voice being cast by the delegate from Brazil. In consequence, according to Julius Braunthal, the historian of the socialist internationals:

> The Communist International had now been transformed into a Bolshevik world party, rigidly centralized and with military-type discipline; ready, as the Congress had demonstrated, to accept Russian orders without question. And the Communist parties all over the world had now, in fact, become sections of the Russian Communist Party, ruled by the Politbureau which also ruled the Russian state. They had thus been reduced to agencies of the Russian government.

The new arrangement had the advantages that usually derive from tight organization and discipline. But it also tended to blind the Comintern Executive to the great variety of situations with which its foreign affiliates, or more precisely, branches, had to contend, imposing on them stereotypes based on Bolshevik experiences in Russia. Some foreigners acquiesced to these methods from respect for Bolshevik successes, others for career reasons. Those who refused to fall in step were purged, with the result that dissent was effectively silenced.

The European socialist parties, and the Second International, its coordinating body, the prime object of Communist hatred, reacted to these developments in an ambiguous manner. Like the Mensheviks, they condemned the Bolsheviks for their violent methods and the destruction of liberty. At the same time, again like the Mensheviks, they demanded a "hands off" policy in regard to Soviet Russia and her prompt diplomatic recognition. This they justified with the argument that bolshevism represented a transient aberration of a fundamentally progressive historic phenomenon, which, left in peace, would inevitably evolve toward democracy. Foreign intervention in internal Soviet affairs, stated a resolution adopted in May 1923 by a gathering of European socialist parties in Hamburg, would aim not at correcting the "errors of the current phase of the Russian Revolution"

> but at destroying the Revolution itself. Far from establishing a genuine democracy, it would merely set up a government of bloody counterrevolutionaries, to act as a vehicle for the exploitation of the Russian people.

Russia's foreign policy on the conventional level continued to center on Germany, a country that its leaders saw both as the most likely arena of the European revolution and as a potential ally against the "capitalist" superpowers, Great Britain and the United States. Moscow pursued concurrently the two objectives—subversion of Germany and collaboration with her—even though on the face of it they were irreconcilable.

The most consequential event in post–World War I global relations, second only to America's refusal to join the League of Nations, was the Rapallo Treaty, which Soviet Russia and the German government sprang on an unsuspecting world on April 26, 1922, in the course of an international conference at Genoa. The conference had been convened to settle the political and economic problems of Eastern and central Europe left unresolved at Versailles, and to reintegrate Russia and Germany into the international community. The invitations issued to these two countries were the first they had received since the end of the war. But behind the backs of the conference's organizers, Moscow and Berlin were plotting a separate treaty that was certain to break up the Genoa meeting and exacerbate the animosity between victors and losers in World War I, a development Moscow devoutly desired.

Germany had weighty reasons for coming to terms with Moscow. One of these was trade. Before 1914, Germany had been Russia's leading commercial partner, a position she now feared to lose to Britain and the United States. In 1921 and early 1922, Moscow held numerous talks with German entrepreneurs, in the course of which the two parties discussed far-reaching plans of German help in the reconstruction of Soviet

Russia's economy. Even more important loomed geopolitical considerations. Germany chafed under the terms of the Versailles Treaty, which reduced her to the status of a pariah nation, forbidden to maintain a significant army. Many Germans felt that their country could regain her status as a world power only in an alliance with Soviet Russia, another pariah state.

From Moscow's point of view, exacerbating relations between Germany and the Allies represented a primary objective of foreign policy. Moscow also wanted German capital, as well as German military equipment and know-how. The defeat in the war with Poland had made the Kremlin keenly aware of how backward its forces were; the Red Army, despite its victory in the Civil War, had proved no match even for a second-rate Western army. It required modernization, and this it could accomplish only with German help. It so happened that Russia's interest in German military assistance coincided with Germany's need for Russia's help in circumventing the provisions of the Versailles Treaty which forbade her to acquire tanks, military aviation, heavy artillery, and poison gas. General von Seeckt, the head of the German Reichswehr, was the driving force behind Russo-German military collaboration carried out in the greatest secrecy from 1919 onward, but especially so after March 1921. Continuing until September 1933, nine months after Hitler came to power, it helped to prepare both countries for World War II, which they desired and promoted.

For all the potential benefits of cooperation with Moscow, Germany shrank from concluding with it a formal treaty for fear of Allied reaction. Soviet diplomats helped them overcome their hesitations by resorting to a ploy that Stalin would use even more successfully in 1939—namely, dropping hints that they were about to conclude a separate treaty with the Allies. German diplomats swallowed the bait. In the midst of the Genoa Conference, the two countries signed, at nearby Rapallo, a bilateral accord that settled their differences. By its terms, the signatory powers granted each other diplomatic recognition and most-favored status, and renounced mutual financial claims arising from World War I and Soviet nationalization decrees. Rapallo wrecked the Genoa Conference, which had been convened to settle all outstanding matters by consensus of the interested parties and to eliminate the barriers separating Russia and Germany from the rest of the international community.

Rapallo led to the rapid growth of Soviet-German trade, at the expense of Soviet trade with Britain; in 1922–23, one-third of Russian imports came from Germany. Even more important, it unlocked the doors to vigorous military collaboration. The Germans opened in several Russian cities facilities for the manufacture and testing of weapons forbidden them by the Versailles Treaty. The most important of these was the aviation base at Lipetsk, where, flying airplanes smuggled in from Holland, German pilots trained in tactics the Wehrmacht would employ in World War II. A German participant in these activities claimed afterwards that they laid the "spiritual foundation" of Hitler's Luftwaffe. Many of Hitler's future generals and marshals took part in these exercises. In return, they invited Red Army officers to attend German military academies. In 1933, when this collaboration came to an end, Marshal Tukhachevskii, then Deputy Commissar of War, told the German chargé d'affaires in Moscow, that "it would never be forgotten that the Reichswehr had given decisive aid to the Red Army in its organization."

Thus the two powers responsible for World War II joined in a deadly game that would see them first as allies and then as enemies. The Western powers, which received more than one warning of these surreptitious activities, did nothing to stop them.

The Crisis of the New Regime

The political crisis that shook the Communist Party in 1921–22 was primarily due to the fact that the suppression of rival political groups and publications did not eliminate dissent but merely shifted it into the inner ranks of the Party. In the words of Trotsky: "Our party is now the only one in the country; all discontent goes exclusively through our party." This development violated the cardinal tenet of bolshevism, the key to its successes—namely, disciplined unity that required unquestioned compliance with decisions reached by the Party's directing organs. It confronted the Bolsheviks with a difficult choice: whether to sacrifice unity and all the advantages that flowed from it by tolerating open dissent within their ranks or to outlaw open dissent and risk both the ossification of the Party's directing organs and its estrangement from the rank and file. Lenin unhesitatingly opted for the second alternative. By this decision, he laid the groundwork for Stalin's personal dictatorship.

One of the major concerns of the Bolshevik leaders in the early 1920s, and especially of Lenin, was the seemingly unstoppable bureaucratization of their regime. They had the feeling—and the statistical evidence to support it—that the government was being weighed down by an overblown and parasitic class of functionaries who used their office for personal benefit. The more the bureaucracy expanded, the more of the budget it absorbed and the less got done. For Lenin, who had expected his revolution to reduce the civil service to a minimum and eventually eliminate it altogether, the bloated white-collar workforce turned into a source of obsessive anxiety.

That they should have been surprised by this development only provides further evidence that underneath the hard-bitten realism of the Bolsheviks lurked remarkable naïveté. They should have been able to foresee that the nationalization of the country's entire organized life, economic activity included, would necessarily expand the ranks of the civil service. But it apparently never occurred to them that "power" (*vlast'*), of which they never had enough, meant not only opportunity but also responsibility; that the fulfillment of that responsibility was a full-time occupation calling for correspondingly large cadres of professionals; and that these professionals were unlikely to be concerned exclusively or even primarily with public welfare but would also attend to their private needs. The bureaucratization of life that accompanied Communist rule opened up office careers to lower-middle-class elements previously excluded from them; they were its principal beneficiaries. And even bona fide workers, once they had left the factory floor for the office, ceased to be workers—they merged with the bureaucratic caste and acquired its habits.

The Bolsheviks had failed to anticipate such an evolution because their Marxist philosophy of history taught them to regard politics exclusively as a by-product of class conflicts, and government as nothing but an instrument of the ruling class—a view that precluded the state and its officialdom from having interests distinct from those of the class they were said to serve—in the Soviet case, the "proletariat." The same philosophy prevented them from understanding the nature of the problem once they had become aware of it. Like any tsarist conservative, Lenin could think of no other way of curbing the abuses of the bureaucracy than by piling one "control commission" on top of another, sending inspectors out into the field, and insisting that there was nothing wrong that "good men" could not set right. The systemic sources of the problem eluded him to the end.

Bureaucratization occurred in the apparatus of the Party as well as that of the state.

Although it had been structured from the beginning in a centralized fashion, the Bolshevik Party had traditionally observed within its ranks a certain degree of democracy. The Central Committee made collectively the day-to-day decisions, while the annual party congresses, composed of delegates chosen by local party organizations, determined the general party "line."

As the Communist Party assumed ever greater responsibilities for managing the country, its ranks expanded and so did its administrative apparatus. In March 1919, the Party had 314,000 members. At that time, the Central Committee created, alongside the Secretariat, which handled the paperwork, two new offices: the Politburo and the Orgburo (above, p. 153). The establishment of these organs initiated the process of concentrating authority in Party affairs at the top, in Moscow. By the end of the Civil War, the Communist Party had a sizable staff of officials occupied exclusively with party work; this personnel lost virtually all contact with the masses of workers whose interests they were supposed to represent. Nor did the process stop there, for from the body of white-collar personnel there emerged an elite employed in Moscow by the Party's central organs. In the summer of 1922, this group numbered more than 15,000. In the words of the Harvard political scientist Merle Fainsod:

> The bureaucratization of party life had inevitable consequences . . . The party official engaged exclusively on Party business was at an obvious advantage compared with the rank-and-file Party member who had a full-time job in a factory or in a government office. The sheer force of professional preoccupation with Party management rendered the officialdom the center of initiative, direction, and control. At every level of the Party hierarchy, a transfer of authority became visible, first from the congresses to conferences to the committees which they nominally elected, and then from the committees to the Party secretaries who ostensibly executed their will.

The Central Committee apparatus, step by step, spontaneously, and almost imperceptibly, supplanted the local organs of the Party, not only making most of the decisions on their behalf but also appointing their executive personnel. Provincial Party officials were no longer locally chosen but sent from the center. Similarly, Moscow appointed delegates to the Party's congresses, nominally its highest authority.

The process of centralization did not stop there, advancing with an inexorable logic. First the Communist Party took over all organized political life in Russia; then the Central Committee assumed direction of the Party; next, the Politburo began to make all the decisions for the Central Committee; then three men—Stalin, Kamenev, and Zinoviev—

took charge of the Politburo; until finally one man alone, Stalin, decided for the Politburo. Once the process culminated in a personal dictatorship, it had nowhere further to go, with the result that Stalin's death led to a gradual unraveling of the centralized structure and the disintegration of the Party's authority over the country, ending, ultimately, in the collapse of the Communist state.

The authority which Party members enjoyed in a society that deprived its citizenry of all rights inevitably led to corruption and other abuses. Lenin's lofty ideal of a selfless Communist cadre that set an example of hard work and modest wants never even came close to realization. In their official capacity, Party members, like tsarist officials, enjoyed virtual immunity from legal prosecution, which left them free to bully and exact tribute from ordinary citizens. To make matters worse still, the Party began to corrupt its own bureaucracy. Officials high up in the hierarchy received extra food rations as well as special housing and clothing allowances and medical care. They traveled in upholstered trains, while ordinary citizens had to fight for wooden seats. The very highest among them were entitled to lengthy stays in foreign sanatoria at government expense. The Party's leaders qualified for dachas. The first to acquire a country retreat was Lenin, who in October 1918 took over an estate at Gorki, thirty-five kilometers from Moscow, the property of a tsarist general. Trotsky appropriated one of the most luxurious landed estates in Russia, belonging to the Iusupovs, while Stalin made himself at home in the country house of an oil magnate.

So much for the Party bureaucracy.

The state bureaucracy expanded at an even more spectacular rate. Its growth resulted from two causes: the government assuming responsibilities previously exercised by private interests, and featherbedding encouraged by the prevailing lawlessness and shortages. An example of the former is the expansion of the Commissariat of Enlightenment, which assumed control over all schools, private and church-run, as well as all aspects of cultural life and censorship. As a result, by May 1919 it had on its payroll ten times as many employees as had had the corresponding tsarist ministry.

Russians on the government payroll gained many advantages: access to goods beyond the reach of ordinary citizens, as well as opportunities to pocket bribes and tips. They enrolled in droves. In the very first year of the Communist dictatorship, the ratio of white- to blue-collar workers was one-third higher than in 1913. Although railroad traffic declined fivefold and the number of railroad workers remained stationary, the bureaucratic personnel managing transport increased by 75 percent. Overall, between 1917 and the middle of 1921, the number of government employees grew nearly five times—from 576,000 to 2.4 million. By then, speaking in round figures, the country had twice as many bureaucrats as factory workers.

Because the Bolshevik ranks had few people with the requisite education and experience in management, the government had to engage large numbers of ex-tsarist officials, especially in the central ministries. A Russian historian has found that more than one-half of the officials in the central offices of the commissariats, and perhaps 90 percent of the officials in the upper echelons of the state bureaucracy, had held some administrative position before October 1917. The Australian scholar T. H. Rigby, studying the same evidence, has arrived at the startling conclusion that the changes in administrative personnel made by the Bolsheviks in the first five years of their rule could be compared with those that had occurred in Washington "in the heyday of the 'spoils system.' "

Lenin was exasperated by this development, which turned over commanding positions of the state to people he regarded as implacable enemies of his regime. But there was little he could do about this situation; it resulted from his insatiable appetite to own and run everything.

Lenin was not alone in expressing dismay at the bureaucratization of Soviet life and the critical role played in running the Russian state and economy by "bourgeois specialists." It also angered pro-Bolshevik workers, especially those of the Metallurgical Union headed by Alexander Shliapnikov, one of the very few genuine workers to attain high status in the Bolshevik Party. Of all the trades, the Metallurgists showed the greatest loyalty to the Bolsheviks both before and during the Revolution. They approved all the measures the new government enacted in order to silence the political opposition and restrict personal freedoms. When the Kronshtadt rebellion broke out, they were among the first to volunteer for the Red Army force sent to suppress it. But they became increasingly troubled that in a "proletarian dictatorship," the proletariat had little to say and power was concentrated in the hands of the intelligentsia. In their view, this development estranged the regime from labor.

Party apparatchiks dubbed members holding such views "Workers' Opposition." The movement surfaced at the Ninth Party Congress held in March 1920, which put an end to the collegiate management of the economy and the whole practice of "workers' control," entrusting managerial responsibility to professional personnel, who often had held similar positions before the Revolution. Trade unions henceforth were not to interfere with management or assert their members' rights but to concentrate on maintaining labor discipline. This policy, enforced for the sake of industrial efficiency, encountered strenuous resistance from unionized workers, who saw themselves subjected to the authority of the same "*burzhui*" who had bossed them under the old regime.

To arrest this development and gain for the workers their rightful place, the spokesmen for the Workers' Opposition introduced at the Tenth Congress two motions. The first called on the Party to purge itself of opportunists and increase worker participation in the apparatus; every Communist should be required to spend at least three months a year doing physical labor. The second called for the gradual transfer of control over the economy to the trade unions.

Lenin dismissed these proposals as a "syndicalist deviation" and warned of the dangers of "petty bourgeois spontaneity." To justify themselves, Lenin and some other Bolsheviks claimed that the "Workers' Opposition" did not represent true workers, most of whom had given their lives in the Civil War, but peasants who had taken their place. In response to Lenin's claim that the ranks of Russian labor were filled with "malingerers" and not true proletarians, Shliapnikov pointed out that sixteen of the forty-one delegates to the Tenth Congress supportive of the Workers' Opposition had joined the Bolshevik Party before 1905 and all had done so before 1914. Another counterargument held that the Workers' Opposition made a fetish of democracy. Trotsky stated that the Party could assert its dictatorship even if it "temporarily clashed with the transient mood of worker democracy."

The Party leadership thus found itself in a rather absurd position: it claimed to govern Soviet Russia on behalf of the "proletariat," which accounted perhaps for 1 percent of the country's population, and of that 1 percent only 2 or 3 percent belonged to the Party—and then, when pressed by its minuscule worker following to alter its course, denying that Soviet Russia even had a working class. By now the "proletariat" had become a pure abstraction, an ideal in the minds of Bolsheviks which existed only to the extent that it did as it was told.

In the voting, the resolutions of the Workers' Opposition went down in defeat. The group was ordered to dissolve; during the next several years its members were hounded out of the Party.

One important and long-lasting consequence of this conflict was the adoption by the Tenth Party Congress of a secret resolution outlawing the formation of "factions," defined as groupings organized around a platform different from that of the Party as a whole:

> In order to maintain strict discipline within the party and in all soviet activities, [in order] to attain the greatest unity by eliminating all factionalism, the Congress authorizes the Central Committee in instances of violations of discipline, or the revival or tolerance of factionalism, to apply all measures . . . up to exclusion from the party.

Some historians regard this resolution as a turning point in the history of the Communist Party and the Soviet state. Simply put, in Trotsky's words, it transferred the "political regime prevailing in the state to the inner life of the ruling party." Henceforth, the Party, too, was to be run as a dictatorship. Dissent would be tolerated only as long as it was individual—that is, unorganized. The resolution deprived Party members of the right to challenge the majority in control of the Central Committee, since individual dissent could always be brushed aside as unrepresentative, while organized dissent was illegal. It played a decisive role in Stalin's ascent to unlimited power.

It has recently become known from the recollections of Viacheslav Molotov that Lenin himself brazenly violated the ruling against the formations of factions by convening at the next, Eleventh Congress of the Party, a secret conclave of his loyal followers to draw up a list of candidates for elections to the Central Committee. When Stalin questioned this procedure, Lenin explained that it was necessary to ensure a satisfactory result.[10]

The earliest symptoms of Lenin's illness appeared in February 1921, when he began to complain of headaches and insomnia. The causes were partly physiological, partly psychological (the defeat in Poland and the concessions of NEP had shattered his customary self-confidence). In December the Politburo, believing that he was overworking himself, ordered him to take a six-week vacation, and forbade him to go to his Moscow office without the permission of the Secretariat. But these measures did not help. Lenin spent most of March 1922 in the country. He was gruff and irritable, his customary aggressiveness assuming ever more extreme and even abnormal forms; it was while in this state that he ordered the arrest, trial, and executions of the SRs and clergy. At the Eleventh Party Congress held that month he delivered two rambling speeches, replete with personal attacks on anyone who disagreed with him and subjecting even some of his closest associates to abuse. His physicians, among them experts brought from Germany, who had previously diagnosed his illness as "neurasthenia induced by exhaustion," now concluded that he suffered from a progressive paralysis that would inexorably end in incapacitation and death.

His associates had to consider his successor or successors. In the eyes of the world, Trotsky seemed the natural heir. But Trotsky's claim had more appearance than reality. He had joined the Party late, on the eve of the October coup, after having subjected Lenin and his followers for years to merciless criticism and derision. For this the Bolshevik Old Guard never forgave him. Unlike his principal rivals—Zinoviev, Stalin, and Kamenev—he held no executive post in the Party, which meant that he had no power of patronage. In elections for the Presidium of the Central Committee held at the Eighth Party Congress in March 1919, when he stood at the pinnacle of his fame, he came in ninth place, after Lenin as well as Stalin and Bukharin, who shared second place, and even after the relatively unknown M. Tomskii.[11] Two years later, at the Tenth Congress, he fared still worse, coming in tenth place, behind the self-effacing arch-bureaucrat Viacheslav Molotov. His personality did not help either, for he was viewed as arrogant and overly ambitious. Lenin had a low opinion of Trotsky as politician: in 1921, at a private meeting of Communists, he said that when it came to politics, Trotsky "didn't have a clue."[12]

Instead of Trotsky, Lenin relied increasingly in the day-to-day running of Party affairs on Stalin. The Georgian was an amiable team worker, a seeming moderate who knew how to get things done quietly and efficiently. Stalin took on himself all the drudgery of the paperwork that the other top Bolsheviks, preferring to bask in the limelight, did not want to handle. In April 1922, Lenin had him appointed General Secretary.[13] The post did not, at the time, appear to be of great importance, but combined with Stalin's membership in the Politburo and Orgburo—he alone belonged to all three of the Party's directing institutions—it provided him with a unique power base. Lenin relied on him to keep at bay dissenters like those in the Workers' Opposition. Stalin used his control over appointments to executive positions in the Party apparatus to nominate officials who were personally loyal to him. He took good care of them by offering them supplementary food rations and other perquisites. Once the decisive struggle for Lenin's succession got under way, he was in an unrivaled position to outmaneuver all competitors.

Surprisingly, Lenin did not anticipate that the system he had put in place bore the seeds of a personal dictatorship in the Party. When in the winter of 1918–19 a Menshevik historian urged him to assume dictatorial

74. The "troika," from left to right: Stalin (Rykov), Kamenev, Zinoviev.

powers in order to resolve the economic crisis, Lenin dismissed the idea as "utter nonsense"; the party apparatus had grown too gigantic to tolerate a dictator. He was worried by something quite different—namely a split in the party caused by personal rivalries, especially that between Stalin and Trotsky. But he had no idea how to prevent such animosities from breaking into the open and destroying the Party's monolithic structure.

At the end of May 1922, Lenin suffered his first stroke, which resulted in temporary paralysis of his right leg and arm and the loss of speech. For the next few months he would be out of commission. During this period, his responsibilities devolved on a troika, or triumvirate, of Kamenev, Zinoviev, and Stalin. Stalin met frequently with Lenin at Gorki, briefing him on developments and soliciting his counsel. According to Lenin's sister, Maria, who resided at Gorki, these were very friendly encounters. After securing Lenin's approval and settling matters among themselves, the triumvirate would submit to the Politburo and the Sovnarkom resolutions that these bodies routinely approved. Trotsky either voted with the majority or abstained. He had not a single ally in the Politburo.

Stalin played a brilliant game that deceived everyone, from Lenin down. He took a moderate position on every issue, sometimes arguing that Party unity took precedence over principle, and at other times that principles were paramount. He had no enemies, save perhaps Trotsky, and even him he sought to befriend until rebuffed: Trotsky, who described Stalin as the Party's "outstanding mediocrity," thought him too insignificant to bother with. At his country dacha, Stalin would gather the Party's leaders, sometimes with their wives and children, to discuss matters of substance but also to reminisce, sing, and dance. Nothing he did or said suggested that underneath that jovial exterior lurked murder. Like a predator mimicking harmless insects, he insinuated himself into the midst of his unsuspecting prey.

In September 1922, Lenin addressed a note to Stalin for the Politburo suggesting that it appoint Trotsky and Kamenev deputy chairmen, respectively, of the Council of Peoples' Commissars and the Council of Labor and Defense. Trotsky's admirers subsequently made much of this offer, some even claiming that Lenin had chosen Trotsky as his successor. He did nothing of the kind. In fact, Trotsky considered the offer so humiliating that in the minutes of the Politburo vote on Lenin's proposition he is recorded as "categorically refusing" the post. It was quite unprecedented for a high Communist official to refuse an assignment, and it did not enhance Trotsky's reputation with the Party.

Stalin returned to Gorki the very next day and apparently secured Lenin's consent to have Trotsky formally reprimanded. The Politburo, meeting in Trotsky's absence, expressed "regrets" that he had not seen fit to accept the proffered post. It was the first shot in the campaign to discredit him. Not long afterward, Kamenev, on behalf the triumvirate, in a personal communication to Lenin suggested expelling Trotsky from the Party. Lenin reacted furiously:

> To throw Trotsky overboard—this is what you are hinting at. It cannot be interpreted otherwise—the height of absurdity. Unless you think me hopelessly deceived, how can you think of it ???? Bloodied children before one's eyes . . .*

The political constellation, however, suddenly changed in Trotsky's favor. In the closing months of 1922, Lenin, in a state verging on clinical paranoia, came to feel that the triumvirate was weaving around him a web of intrigue that, in the guise of protecting his health, aimed at eliminating him from affairs of state. One item of evidence was the proce-

---

* The last line comes from Pushkin's *Boris Godunov* and refers to the hallucinations that Godunov experienced for (allegedly) murdering the young tsarevich in order to seize the throne.

dures followed at Politburo meetings that, with the doctor's permission, he began to attend in October 1922. Because he easily tired, Lenin sometimes had to leave these meetings early. The next day he would learn of critical decisions having been made in his absence. To put a stop to such practices he ruled on December 8, 1922, that Politburo meetings were to last no more than three hours, all unresolved matters being deferred to the next meeting. The agenda was to be distributed at least twenty-four hours in advance.

In his growing isolation Lenin drew near to Trotsky, another outcast. Their rapprochement began over a minor issue related to foreign trade. Unhappy that the Politburo intended to relax the state's monopoly on foreign trade, Lenin requested Trotsky to act as his proxy and beat down the proposal. A few days later (the night of December 15–16) he suffered a second stroke, following which physicians ordered him to refrain completely from political activity. Lenin, suspecting that the doctors took their orders from the triumvirate, refused to obey.

Trotsky succeeded in persuading the Politburo to accept Lenin's resolution on foreign trade. This event alarmed the triumvirate because it seemed to portend a looming alliance between Lenin and Trotsky. On the day Trotsky won his bureaucratic skirmish (December 18), Stalin and Kamenev secured from the Politburo a mandate giving Stalin supervision over Lenin's regimen. The critical clause read:

> To place on Comrade Stalin personal responsibility for the isolation of Vladimir Ilich [Lenin] both in respect to personal contacts with [Communist] workers and correspondence.

According to Stalin's instructions, Lenin was to work only at brief intervals by dictating to his secretaries, one of whom was Stalin's wife. He was to communicate with no one outside his household except the Politburo through the person of its General Secretary. Shortly afterwards, Lenin requested his secretary, Lydia Fotieva, to supply him with cyanide for use if he lost the capacity to speak.

On December 21, apparently distrusting his secretarial staff, Lenin dictated to Krupskaia a warm note to Trotsky, congratulating him on the Politburo victory. The contents of this note were at once communicated to Stalin, who now had confirmation of a looming Lenin-Trotsky coalition. The following day he telephoned Krupskaia, berating her crudely for having disobeyed the regimen he had established for Lenin and threatening her with an investigation by Party authorities. After hanging up, Krupskaia fell into hysterics, crying and rolling on the floor. Before she could communicate this news to her husband, Lenin suffered yet another stroke. On December 24, following the instructions of the Politburo (Bukharin, Kamenev, and Stalin), the doctors ordered Lenin to confine dictation to a maximum of ten minutes a day. His dictations were to be regarded as personal notes rather than communications requiring an answer; it was a subtle way of preventing him from intervening in affairs of state and corresponding with Trotsky. "Neither friends nor domestics," the instruction read, were "to inform Vladimir Ilich of anything about political life, so as not to give him material for reflections and excitement." Thus, under the pretext of safeguarding his health, Stalin and his associates in effect placed Lenin under house arrest.

Lenin's hostility toward Stalin, which was assuming obsessive forms, was aggravated by Stalin's high-handed methods of dealing with the ethnic minorities. Lenin wanted a highly centralized state in which all citizens, regardless of nationality, would be subject to the authority of Moscow. But he also wanted the minorities to be treated with utmost tact in order to overcome their suspicion of Russians bred by centuries of imperial domination. He believed that this end could be attained by granting the minorities pseudofederal status and limited cultural autonomy, while subjecting them to tight Party control. A complete stranger to nationalist sentiments, he despised and feared Great Russian chauvinism as a threat to the global Communist revolution.

Stalin, a Georgian who spoke Russian with a comic foreign accent, viewed the matter differently. He realized that the power base of communism lay among the Great Russian population. Of the 376,000 Party members registered in 1922, fully 270,000 (72 percent) were Russian, and a high proportion of the remainder were thoroughly Russified. Stalin early in his career identified with Great Russians: for a politician more interested in acquiring power at home than in overturning the world, Russian chauvinism spelled not danger but opportunity.

By 1922, the Communists had reconquered most of the borderlands populated by non-Russians. The Soviet state consisted of four republics: the Russian (RSFSR), the Ukrainian, the Belorussian, and the Transcaucasian. The last-named resulted from a forceful merger of the Azerbaijani, Armenian, and Georgian republics into a single federation. This was accomplished by the Communist Viceroy in the Caucasus, Sergo Ordzhonikidze, a close collaborator of Stalin's, over the strong objections of the Georgian Communists, who wanted their country to enter the union directly, as one of the constituent republics.

To regulate relations among the republics, Lenin asked Stalin in August 1922, when they were still on friendly terms, to chair a constitutional commission. Stalin came up with a proposal that was simplicity itself. The three republics would enter the RSFSR as autonomous entities, and the state organs of the Russian republic would assume all-Union functions. Under this arrangement, no distinction would be drawn between the Ukraine or Georgia, on the one hand, and the autonomous republics of the RSFSR, such as Bashkiriia, on the other. It was a highly centralist plan that reverted to the "Russian one and indivisible" principle of tsarist times.

This was not at all what Lenin had in mind. He wanted the major nationalities to enjoy the status of full-fledged union republics, with the whole panoply of commissariats. He did not fear that this arrangement would cause the country to fall apart, reasoning that any centrifugal trends the republics might evince would be paralyzed by the unitary Communist Party. He subjected Stalin's draft to a scathing critique. Rather than have the three republics dissolve in Russia, he wanted all four Soviet republics to form a new supranational entity called "Union of Soviet Socialist Republics of Europe and Asia," which foreign countries could join as they went Communist. Stalin had no choice but to accept Lenin's recommendations, even though he thought them "scholastic." In 1923–24, these proposals were incorporated into the constitution of the Soviet Union.

But Lenin's quarrel with Stalin did not end there. Information began to reach him that Stalin and Ordzhonikidze were running roughshod over the Georgian Communist opposition, which resisted incorporation into a Transcaucasian Federation. The more he learned about how Stalin and Ordzhonikidze treated the Georgians, the greater grew his anger. He thought that such behavior undermined communism's prospects in the colonial regions of the world. In the last months of his conscious life, the Georgian issue came to consume him. He let it be known that he was drafting a major policy speech for the forthcoming Twelfth Party Congress scheduled for March 1923 in which he would concentrate fire on Stalin and his nationality policies.

So deeply did he feel betrayed by his associates that during the thirteen months he had left to live, he categorically refused to see any of them. The chronicle of his activities indicates that during 1923 he saw neither Trotsky, nor Stalin, nor Zinoviev, Kamenev, or Rykov. All were kept out of sight on his explicit orders. He found himself in the same situation as Nicholas II in the last months of his reign, when he had cut off contact with even close relatives.

In late December 1922 and early January 1923, Lenin dictated in brief spurts several memoranda in which he gave expression to his deep concern over the destiny of Soviet Russia. The most important of these, subsequently labeled "Lenin's Testament," contained thumbnail characterizations of leading Bolsheviks as potential successors. Trotsky he described as the "most capable person in the current Central Committee" but overly self-confident and addicted to a noncollegial style of management. He recalled Zinoviev's and Kamenev's timidity in October 1917. Bukharin he identified as the Party's favorite yet not quite a Marxist. Stalin, he noted, had accumulated "unbounded power." "I am not convinced that he will always know how to use this power with sufficient circumspection." A few days later he added:

> Stalin is too coarse, and this shortcoming, fully tolerable within our midst and in our relations, as Communists, becomes intolerable in a General Secretary. For this reason I suggest that the comrades consider how to transfer Stalin from this post and replace him with someone who in all respects enjoys over Comrade Stalin only one advantage, namely greater patience, greater loyalty, greater courtesy and attentiveness to comrades, less capriciousness etc.

Lenin thus fathomed only Stalin's minor vices, flaws of conduct and temperament: his sadistic cruelty, his megalomania, his hatred of anyone superior to him in any respect, eluded him to the end, as it did everyone else.

The impression one gains from reading these rambling comments is that Lenin considered no one fit to succeed him. Fotieva immediately communicated these remarks to Stalin.

On March 5, 1923, Lenin overheard Krupskaia speaking on the telephone. Questioned, she told him of the incident with Stalin the previous December. Lenin sat down immediately and wrote a letter to Stalin in which he accused him of insulting his wife and indirectly, therefore, himself as well. If he did not want a breach in their relations, he had to retract what he had said and apologize. Stalin calmly responded that if Lenin wanted an apology he was prepared to give one, but he had no idea what he had done wrong.

Stalin faced political annihilation should Lenin, or Trotsky acting on Lenin's behalf, openly assail him at the forthcoming Twelfth Party Congress. He kept in constant contact with Lenin's physicians and learned that the prospects, from the patient's perspective, were not

75. Lenin at Gorki, 1923.

encouraging. Playing for time, Stalin announced unexpectedly on March 9 that the Congress was postponed for one month. The gamble paid off. The very next day (March 10), Lenin suffered a massive stroke that robbed him permanently of the power of speech. Until his death in January 1924, he could utter only monosyllables. In May he was moved for good to Gorki. For all practical purposes, he was now a living corpse. He displayed an uncharacteristic craving for praise and delighted in reading laudatory accounts of himself and his accomplishments.

With Lenin out of the picture, Trotsky found himself virtually isolated. He tried to save his position by placating Stalin and his followers. Thus he refused to carry out Lenin's request, made on March 5, to defend the Georgian case at the Party Congress. On the eve of the Congress, he assured Kamenev that he would support Stalin's reappointment as General Secretary. His behavior puzzled contemporaries and has puzzled historians since. The most likely explanation of his accommodating policy is the conviction that it was hopeless to challenge Stalin, especially for someone of Jewish nationality. Appeasement, however, proved unavailing. By now, the lines were sharply drawn and anyone who wanted to get on in the Party had to take a clear stand against him.

In October 1923, in desperate straits, Trotsky launched a counter-offensive. If insiders insisted on treating him as an outsider, then he would champion the cause of the outsiders. By this he meant those who, like himself, had joined the Party in 1917 or later and for this reason were denied access to premier posts monopolized by the Old Guard. First in a confidential letter to the Central Committee and then on the pages of *Pravda*, he charged that the Party had become intolerably bureaucratized and that the rank and file no longer dared to express their own opinions. These were the same arguments the Workers' Opposition had advanced but a short time before and that he himself had condemned.

The Party plenum voted 102 to 2 (with 10 abstentions) to reprimand him for "factionalism." The censure was justified by the fact that Trotsky had the support of the so-called Group of 46, which held similar views and with which he maintained contact.

The game was up for Trotsky; the rest was anticlimactic. He had no defense against the Party majority, for as he would himself concede in 1924: "None of us wants to be and none of us can be right against the Party. In the final analysis, our party is always right." In January 1925, he would be forced to resign as Commissar of War. There followed expulsion from the Party and exile, first to central Asia and then abroad; and, finally, assassination in Mexico by a Stalinist agent. The moves to oust him, orchestrated by Stalin, with the connivance of Zinoviev, Kamenev, Bukharin and the others, were carried out with the solid backing of the Party cadres, who believed they were preserving Party unity from a selfish schemer.

There are many instances in history when the loser earns posterity's sympathy because he is seen as morally superior to those who have vanquished him. It is difficult to muster such sympathy for Trotsky. Admittedly, he was more cultured than Stalin and his acolytes, intellectually more interesting, personally more courageous, and in dealings with fellow Communists, more honorable. But as in the case of Lenin, such

76. Stalin viewing Lenin's body.

virtues as he possessed manifested themselves exclusively within Party ranks. In relations with outsiders as well as those insiders who strove for greater democracy, he was at one with Lenin and Stalin—that is to say he believed that in their case normal ethical standards did not apply. Like the other Bolsheviks, he transferred to political life the standards of group loyalty prevalent in circles of organized crime, contributing to the criminalization of politics that characterized bolshevism and the totalitarian regimes that emulated it. He thus helped forge the weapons that destroyed him, for the instant he found himself in a dissenting minority, he became an outsider and therefore an enemy who had no claim to fair treatment. He suffered the same fate that was meted out, with his whole-hearted consent, to the opponents of Lenin's dictatorship: the Kadets, the Socialists-Revolutionaries, the Mensheviks; ex-tsarist officers who refused to fight for the Red Army; the Workers' Opposition; the Kronshtadt sailors; the Tambov peasants; the priesthood. He awoke to the dangers of totalitarianism only when it threatened him personally; his sudden conversion to party democracy was a means of self-defense, not a championship of principle.

Trotsky liked to depict himself as a proud lion brought down by a pack of jackals; and the more monstrous Stalin revealed himself to be, the more persuasive the image appeared to those in Russia and abroad who

wanted to salvage an idealized version of Leninism. But the record indicates that in his day he, too, was one of the pack. His defeat had nothing
ennobling about it. He lost because he was outsmarted in a sordid struggle for political power.

Lenin died on the evening of January 21, 1924. The top brass of the
Party rushed to Gorki to pay their last respects. Trotsky happened to be
in Tiflis en route to the Georgian resort of Sukhumi. Although he had
more than enough time to return for the funeral, he chose to proceed to
the Black Sea, where he basked in the warm sun while Lenin's body lay
in state in wintry Moscow attended by the Old Guard.

What was to be done with Lenin's remains? Lenin's widow wanted to
have him interred by his mother's side in Petrograd. But the Party's
leaders needed a physical Lenin to impress the peasants with his immortality, and so they decided to embalm him. A physician was found who
had carried out successful experiments with preserving indefinitely live
tissue by replacing the water in the cells with a chemical compound of
his own invention. This compound was said not to evaporate under normal temperature and humidity, to destroy fungi and bacteria, and to
neutralize fermentation. The embalming was completed in late July
1924, following which Lenin's body went on exhibit in a wooden mausoleum. In 1930, a mausoleum of stone replaced the temporary structure; it became an object of state-sponsored veneration. Twenty-two
scientists assigned to the mausoleum laboratory ensured that the
mummy did not decompose.

Thus the Bolsheviks, who five years earlier in a noisy campaign of
blasphemy and ridicule exposed as sham the relics of Orthodox saints,
created a holy relic of their own. Unlike the church's saints, whose
remains were revealed to be nothing but rags and bones, their god,
as befitted the age of science, was composed of alcohol, glycerin, and
formalin.

REFLECTIONS ON THE RUSSIAN REVOLUTION

he Russian Revolution of 1917 was not a single incident or even a process but a sequence of disruptive and violent acts that occurred more or less concurrently yet involved actors with differing and in some measure contradictory objectives. It began as a revolt of the most conservative elements in Russian society, disgusted by the Crown's familiarity with Rasputin and the mismanagement of the war effort. From the conservatives the revolt spread to the liberals, who challenged the monarchy from fear that if it remained in place, revolution would become inevitable. Initially, the assault on the monarchy was undertaken not, as widely believed, from fatigue with the war but from a desire to pursue the war more effectively: not to make revolution but to avert one. In February 1917, when the Petrograd garrison refused to fire on civilian crowds, the generals, in agreement with parliamentary politicians, hoping to prevent the mutiny from spreading to the front, convinced Tsar Nicholas II to abdicate. The abdication, made for the sake of military victory, brought down the whole edifice of Russian statehood.

Although initially neither social discontent nor the agitation of the radical intelligentsia played any significant role in these events, both moved to the forefront the instant imperial authority collapsed. In the spring and summer of 1917, peasants began to seize and distribute among themselves noncommunal properties. Next, the rebellion spread to frontline troops, who deserted in droves to share in the spoils; to workers, who took control of industrial enterprises; and to ethnic minorities, who aspired to greater self-rule. Each group pursued its own objectives, but the cumulative effect of their assault on the country's social and economic structure by the autumn of 1917 hurled Russia into a state of anarchy.

The events of 1917 demonstrated that for all its immense territory and claim to great power status, the Russian Empire was a fragile, artificial structure, held together not by organic bonds connecting rulers and ruled but by mechanical links provided by the bureaucracy, the police, and the army. Its 150 million inhabitants were bound neither by strong economic interests nor by a sense of national identity. Centuries of autocratic rule in a country with a predominantly natural economy had prevented the formation of strong lateral ties: Imperial Russia was mostly warp with little woof. This fact was noted at the time by one of Russia's leading historians and political figures, Paul Miliukov:

> To make you understand [the] special character of the Russian Revolution, I must draw your attention to [the] peculiar features, made our own by the whole process of Russia's history. To my mind, all these features converge into one. The fundamental difference which distinguishes Russia's social structure from that of other civilized countries, can be characterized as a certain weakness or lack of a strong cohesion or cementation of elements which form a social compound. You can observe that lack of consolidation in the Russian social aggregate in every aspect of civilized life: political, social, mental and national. From the political point of view, the Russian State institutions lacked cohesion and amalgamation with the popular masses over which they ruled. . . . As a consequence of their later appearance, the State institutions in Eastern Europe necessarily assumed certain forms which were different from those in the West. The State in the East had no time to originate from within, in a process of organic evolution. It was brought to the East from outside.

Once these factors are taken into consideration, it becomes apparent that the Marxist notion that revolution always results from social ("class") discontent cannot be sustained. Although such discontent did exist in Imperial Russia, as it does everywhere, the decisive and immediate factors making for the regime's fall and the resultant turmoil were overwhelmingly political.

Was the Revolution inevitable? It is natural to believe that whatever happens has to happen, and there are historians who rationalize this primitive faith with pseudoscientific arguments; they would be more convincing if they could predict the future as unerringly as they claim to predict the past. Paraphrasing a familiar legal maxim, one might say that psychologically speaking, occurrence provides nine-tenths of historical justification. Edmund Burke was in his day widely regarded as a madman for criticizing the French Revolution: seventy years later, according to Matthew Arnold, his ideas were still considered "superannuated and conquered by events"—so ingrained is the belief in the rationality, and therefore the inevitability, of historical events. The grander they are and the more weighty their consequences, the more they appear part of the natural order of things which it is quixotic to question.

The most that one can say is that a revolution in Russia was more likely than not, and this for several reasons. Of these, perhaps the most weighty was the steady decline of the prestige of tsardom in the eyes of a population accustomed to being ruled by an invincible authority—indeed, seeing in invincibility the criterion of legitimacy. After a century and a half of military victories and expansion, from the middle of the nineteenth century until 1917, Russia suffered one humiliation after another at the hands of foreigners: the defeat, on her own soil, in the Crimean War; the loss at the Congress of Berlin of the fruits of victory over the Turks; the debacle in the war with Japan; and the drubbing at the hands of the Germans in World War I. Such a succession of reverses would have damaged the reputation of any government. In Russia it proved fatal.

Tsarism's disgrace was compounded by the concurrent rise of a revolutionary movement that it was unable to quell despite resort to harsh repression. The halfhearted concessions made in 1905 to share power with society neither made tsarism more popular with the opposition nor raised its prestige in the eyes of the people at large, who simply could not understand how a true sovereign would allow himself to be abused from the forum of a government institution. The Confucian principle of T'ien-ming, or Mandate of Heaven, which in its original meaning linked the ruler's authority to righteous conduct, in Russia derived from forceful conduct; a weak ruler, a "loser," forfeited it. Nothing could be more misleading than to judge a Russian head of state by the standard of either morality or popularity. What mattered was that he inspire fear in friend and foe—that, like Ivan IV, he deserve the sobriquet of "Awesome." Nicholas II fell not because he was hated but because he was held in contempt.

Among the other factors making for revolution was the mentality of the Russian peasantry, a class that was never integrated into the political structure. Peasants made up 80 percent of Russia's population; and although they took hardly any active part in the conduct of state affairs, in a passive capacity, as an obstacle to change and, at the same time, a permanent threat to the status quo, they were a very unsettling element. It is commonplace to hear that under the old regime the Russian peasant was "oppressed," but it is far from clear just who was oppressing him. On the eve of the Revolution, he enjoyed full civil and legal rights; he also owned, either outright or communally, nine-tenths of the country's agricultural land and the same proportion of livestock. Poor by Western European or American standards, he was better off than his father and freer than his grandfather, who more likely than not had been a serf. Cultivating allotments assigned to him by fellow peasants, he certainly enjoyed greater security than did tenant farmers of Ireland, Spain, or Italy.

The problem with Russian peasants was not oppression but isolation. They were isolated from the country's political, economic, and cultural life, and therefore unaffected by the changes that had occurred since the time Peter the Great set Russia on the course of Westernization. Many contemporaries observed that the peasantry remained steeped in Muscovite culture: culturally, it had no more in common with the ruling elite or the intelligentsia than the native population of Britain's African colonies had with Victorian England. The majority of Russia's peasants descended from serfs, who were not even subjects, since the monarchy abandoned them to the whim of the landlord and the bureaucrat. As a result, for Russia's rural population the state remained even after emancipation an alien and malevolent force that took taxes and recruits but gave nothing in return. The peasant knew no loyalty outside his household and commune. He felt no patriotism and no attachment to the government save for a vague devotion to the distant tsar from whom he expected to receive the land he coveted. An instinctive anarchist, he was never integrated into national life and felt as much estranged from the conservative establishment as from the radical opposition. He looked down on the city and on men without beards. The French traveler Marquis de Custine heard it said as early as 1839 that someday Russia would see a revolt of the bearded against the shaven. The existence of this mass of alienated and potentially explosive peasants immobilized the government, which believed that it was docile only from fear and would interpret any political concessions as a signal to rebel.

The traditions of serfdom and the social institutions of rural Russia— the joint-family household and the almost universal system of communal landholding—prevented the peasantry from developing qualities required for modern citizenship. While serfdom was not slavery, the two institutions had this in common that like slaves, serfs had no legal rights and hence no sense of law. Michael Rostovtseff, Russia's leading historian of classical antiquity and an eyewitness of 1917, concluded that serfdom may have been worse than slavery in that a serf had never known freedom, which prevented him from acquiring the qualities of a true citizen; in his opinion, this was a principal cause of bolshevism. To serfs, authority was by its very nature arbitrary; and to defend themselves from it they relied not on appeals to legal or moral rights but on cunning. They could not conceive of government based on principle; life to them was a Hobbesian war of all against all. This attitude fostered despotism, for the absence of inner discipline and respect for law required order to be imposed from the outside. When despotism ceased to be viable, anarchy ensued; and once anarchy had run its course, it inevitably gave rise to a new despotism.

The peasant was revolutionary in one respect only: he did not acknowledge private ownership of land. Although on the eve of the Revolution he owned nine-tenths of the country's arable, he craved the remaining 10 percent held by landlords, merchants, and noncommunal peasants. No economic or legal arguments could change his mind; he felt he had a God-given right to that land and that someday it would be his. And by his he meant the commune's, which would allocate it justly to its members. The prevalence of communal landholding in European Russia was, along with the legacy of serfdom, a fundamental fact of Russian social history. It meant that along with a poorly developed sense of law, the peasant also had little respect for private property. Both tendencies were exploited and exacerbated by radical intellectuals for their own ends to incite the peasantry against the status quo.

Russia's industrial workers were potentially destabilizing not because they assimilated revolutionary ideologies—very few of them did, and even these few were excluded from leadership in the revolutionary parties. Rather, since most of them were one or at most two generations removed from the village and only superficially urbanized, they carried with them to the factory rural attitudes only slightly adjusted to industrial conditions. They were not socialists but syndicalists, believing that as their village relatives were entitled to all the land, so they had a right to the factories. Politics interested them no more than it did the peasants: in this sense, too, they were under the influence of primitive, nonideological anarchism. Furthermore, industrial labor in Russia was numerically too insignificant to play a major role in revolution; with at most 3 million workers (a high proportion of them seasonally employed peasants), they represented at best 2 percent of the population. Hordes of graduate students, steered by their professors, in the Soviet Union as well as the West, especially the United States, have assiduously combed historical sources in the hope of unearthing evidence of worker radicalism in prerevolutionary Russia. The results are weighty tomes, filled with mostly meaningless events and statistics that prove only that while history is always interesting, history books can be both vacuous and dull.

A major and arguably decisive factor making for revolution was the intelligentsia, which in Russia attained greater influence than anywhere else. The peculiar "ranking" system of the tsarist civil service excluded outsiders from the administration, estranging the best-educated elements and making them susceptible to fantastic schemes of social reform, invented but never tried in Western Europe. The absence until 1906 of representative institutions and a free press, combined with the spread of education, enabled the cultural elite to claim the right to speak on behalf of a mute people. There exists no evidence that the intelligentsia actually reflected the opinion of the "masses." On the contrary, the evidence indicates that both before and after the Revolution, peasants and workers deeply mistrusted intellectuals. This became apparent in 1917 and the years that followed. But since the true will of the people had no means of expression, at any rate, until the short-lived constitutional order introduced in 1906, the intelligentsia was able with some success to pose as its spokesman.

As in other countries where it lacked legitimate political outlets, the intelligentsia in Russia constituted itself into a caste; and since ideas were what gave it identity and cohesion, it developed extreme intellectual intolerance. Adopting the Enlightenment view of man as nothing but material substance shaped by the environment, and its corollary, that changes in the environment inevitably change human nature, it saw "revolution" not as the replacement of one government by another but as something incomparably more ambitious: a total transformation of the human condition for the purpose of creating a new breed of human beings—in Russia, of course, but also everywhere else. Its stress on the inequities of the status quo was merely a device to gain popular support; no rectification of these inequities would have persuaded radical intellectuals to give up their revolutionary aspirations. Such beliefs linked members of various left-wing parties: anarchists, Socialists-Revolutionaries, Mensheviks, and Bolsheviks. Although couched in scientific terms, their views were immune to contrary evidence and hence more akin to religious faith.

The intelligentsia, which we have defined as intellectuals craving power, stood in total and uncompromising hostility to the existing order; nothing the tsarist regime could do short of committing suicide would have satisfied it. They were revolutionaries not for the sake of improving the condition of the people but for the sake of gaining domination over the people and remaking them in their own image. They confronted the Imperial regime with a challenge that it had no way of repulsing short of employing the kind of methods introduced later by Lenin. Reforms, whether those of the 1860s or those of 1905–6, only whetted the appetite of the radicals and spurred them to still greater revolutionary excesses.

Buffeted by peasant demands and under direct assault from the radical intelligentsia, the monarchy had only one means of averting collapse, and that was to broaden the base of its authority by sharing power with conservative elements of society. Historic precedent indicates that successful democracies have initially limited power-sharing to the upper orders; these eventually came under pressure from the rest of the population, with the result that their privileges turned into common rights. Involving conservatives, who were far more numerous than the radicals, in both decision making and administration would have forged something of an organic bond between the government and society, assuring the Crown of support in the event of upheavals, and, at the same time, isolating the radicals. Such a course was urged on the monarchy by some farsighted officials and private individuals. It should have been adopted in the 1860s, at the time of the Great Reforms, but it was not. When finally compelled in 1905 by a nationwide rebellion to concede a parliament, the monarchy no longer had this option available, for the combined liberal and radical opposition forced it to concede something close to a democratic franchise. This resulted in the conservatives in the Duma being submerged by militant intellectuals and anarchist peasants.

World War I subjected every belligerent country to immense strains, which could be overcome only by close collaboration between government and citizenry in the name of patriotism. In Russia, such collaboration never materialized. As soon as military reverses dissipated the initial patriotic enthusiasm and the country had to brace for a war of attrition, the tsarist regime found itself unable to mobilize public support. Even its admirers agree that at the time of its collapse, the monarchy was hanging in the air.

The motivation of the tsarist regime in refusing to share political power with its supporters and, when finally forced to do so, sharing it grudgingly and deceitfully, was complex. Deep in their hearts, the Court, the bureaucracy, and the professional officer corps were permeated with a patrimonial spirit that viewed Russia as the Tsar's private domain. Although in the course of the eighteenth and nineteenth centuries Muscovite patrimonial institutions were gradually dismantled, the mentality survived. And not only in official circles: the peasantry, too, thought in patrimonial terms, believing in strong, undivided authority and regarding the land as tsarist property. Nicholas II took it for granted that he had to keep autocracy in trust for his heir; unlimited authority was to him the equivalent of a property title, which, in his capacity of trustee, he had no right to dilute. He never rid himself of the feeling of guilt that to save the throne in 1905 he had agreed to divide ownership with the nation's elected representatives.

The Tsar and his advisers also feared that sharing authority with even a small part of society would disorganize the bureaucratic apparatus and open the door to still greater demands for popular participation. In the latter event, the main beneficiary would be the intelligentsia, which Nicholas and his advisers considered utterly incompetent. There was the additional concern that the peasants would misinterpret such concessions and go on a rampage. And finally, there was the opposition to reforms by the bureaucracy, which, accountable only to the Tsar, administered the country at its discretion, deriving thereby numerous benefits.

Such factors explain but do not justify the monarchy's refusal to give conservatives a voice in the government, the more so that the variety and complexity of issues facing it deprived the bureaucracy of much effective authority in any event. The emergence in the second half of the nineteenth century of capitalist institutions shifted much of the control over the country's resources into private hands, undermining what was left of patrimonialism.

In sum, while the collapse of tsarism was not inevitable, it was made likely by deep-seated cultural and political flaws that prevented the tsarist regime from adjusting to the economic and cultural growth of the country, flaws that proved fatal under the pressures generated by World War I. If the possibility of such adjustment existed, it was aborted by the activities of a radical intelligentsia bent on toppling the government and using Russia as a springboard for world revolution. It was cultural and political shortcomings of this nature that brought about the collapse of tsarism, not "oppression" or "misery." We are dealing here with a national tragedy whose causes recede deep into the country's past. Economic and social difficulties did not contribute significantly to the revolutionary threat that hung over Russia before 1917. Whatever grievances they may have harbored—real and fancied—the "masses" neither needed nor desired a revolution; the only group interested in it was the intelligentsia. Stress on alleged popular discontent and class conflict derives more from ideological preconceptions than from the facts at hand—namely from the discredited Marxist theory that political developments are always and everywhere driven by class conflicts, that they are mere "foam" on the surface of currents that really determine human destiny.

The subordinate role played by social and economic factors in the Russian Revolution becomes apparent when one scrutinizes the events of February 1917. February was not a "workers' revolution"; industrial labor played in it the role of a chorus that reacted to and amplified the actions of the true protagonist, the army. The mutiny of the Petrograd garrison stimulated disorders among a civilian population disgruntled over inflation and shortages. The mutiny could have been contained had Nicholas chosen to quell it with the same brutality Lenin and Trotsky employed four years later when faced with the Kronstadt uprising and nationwide peasant rebellions. But Lenin's and Trotsky's sole concern was holding on to power, whereas Nicholas cared for Russia. When the generals and Duma politicians persuaded him that he had to go to save the army and avert a humiliating capitulation, he went. Had staying in power been his supreme objective, he could easily have concluded peace with Germany and turned the army loose against the mutineers. The record leaves no doubt that the myth of the Tsar being forced from the throne by the rebellious workers and peasants is just that. The Tsar yielded not to a rebellious populace but to generals and politicians, and he did so from a sense of patriotic duty.

The social revolution followed rather than preceded the act of abdication. The garrison soldiers, peasants, workers, and ethnic minorities, each group pursuing its own aims, made the country ungovernable. What chance there was of restoring order was frustrated by the insistence of the intelligentsia running the soviets that they and not the Provisional Government were the true source of legitimate authority. Kerensky's inept intrigues, coupled with his insistence that democracy had no enemies on the left, accelerated the government's downfall. The country at large—its political entities as well as its resources—became the subject of *duvan*, "the division of loot," which no one was strong enough to stop until it had run its course.

Lenin rode to power on that anarchy, which he did much to promote. He promised every discontented group what it wanted. He took over the

Socialist-Revolutionary program of "land socialization" to win over the peasants. Among the workers, he encouraged syndicalist trends of "worker control" of factories. To the men in uniform, he held out the prospect of peace. To the ethnic minorities he offered national self-determination. In fact, all these pledges ran contrary to his program and all were violated soon after they had served their purpose, which was to undermine the Provisional Government's efforts to stabilize the country.

Similar deception was applied to divest the Provisional Government of authority. Lenin and Trotsky concealed their bid for one-party dictatorship with slogans calling for the transfer of power to the soviets and the Constituent Assembly, and they formalized it by a fraudulently convened Congress of Soviets. No one except a handful of the leading figures in the Bolshevik Party knew the truth behind these promises and slogans; few, therefore, realized what had happened in Petrograd on the night of October 25, 1917. The so-called "October Revolution" was a classic coup d'état. The preparations for it were so clandestine that when Kamenev disclosed in a newspaper interview a week before the event was to take place, that the party intended to seize power, Lenin declared him a traitor and demanded his expulsion. Genuine revolutions, of course, are not scheduled and cannot be betrayed.

The ease with which the Bolsheviks toppled the Provisional Government—in Lenin's words, it was like "lifting a feather"—has persuaded many historians that the October coup was "inevitable." But it can appear as such only in retrospect. Lenin himself thought it an extremely chancy undertaking. In urgent letters to the Central Committee in September and October 1917 from his hideaway, he insisted that success depended entirely on the speed and resoluteness with which the armed insurrection was carried out. "To delay the uprising is death," he wrote on October 24, "everything hangs on a hair." These were not the sentiments of someone prepared to trust the forces of history. Trotsky later asserted—and who was in a better position to know?—that if "neither Lenin nor [he himself] had been in Petersburg, there would have been no October Revolution." Can one conceive of an "inevitable" historical event dependent on two individuals?

And if this evidence still fails to convince, one has only to look closely at the events of October 1917 in Petrograd to find the "masses" acting as spectators, ignoring Bolshevik appeals to storm the Winter Palace, where sat elderly ministers of the Provisional Government clad in overcoats, defended by youthful cadets, a battalion of women, and a platoon of invalids. We have it on the authority of Trotsky himself that the October "revolution" in Petrograd was accomplished by "at most" 25,000–30,000 persons—this in a country of 150 million and a city with 400,000 workers and a garrison of more than 200,000 soldiers.*

From the instant he seized dictatorial power, Lenin proceeded to uproot all existing institutions so as to clear the ground for a regime subsequently labeled "totalitarian." This term has fallen out of favor with Western sociologists and political scientists determined to avoid what they view as the language of the Cold War. It should be noted, however, that the word found favor in Russia the instant the censor's prohibitions against its use had been lifted. This kind of regime, unknown to previous history, imposed the authority of a private but omnipotent "party" on the state, claiming the right to subject to itself all organized life without exception, and enforcing its will by means of unbounded terror.

Seen in perspective, Lenin owes his historical prominence not to his statesmanship, which was of a rather inferior order, but to his generalship. He was one of history's great conquerors—a distinction not vitiated by the fact that the country he conquered was his own.† His innovation, the reason for his success, was militarizing politics. He was the first head of state to treat politics, domestic as well as foreign, as warfare in the literal sense of the word, the objective of which was not to compel the enemy to submit but to annihilate him. This innovation gave Lenin significant advantages over his opponents, for whom warfare was either the antithesis of politics or else politics pursued by other means. Militarizing politics and, as a corollary, politicizing warfare enabled him first to seize power and then to hold on to it. It did not help him build a viable social and political order. He grew so accustomed to storming on all "fronts" that even after asserting undisputed authority over Soviet Russia and her dependencies, he had to invent ever new enemies to fight and destroy: now the church, now the Socialists-Revolutionaries, now the intelligentsia. This belligerence became a fixed feature of the Communist regime, culminating in Stalin's notorious "theory" that the closer Communism approached final victory, the more intense grew social conflicts—a notion that justified a bloodbath of unprecedented ferocity. It

---

* How few people in Russia can determine the country's political destiny was demonstrated in Moscow in August 1991, when a military putsch intended to restore the Communist regime was aborted by a few thousand pro-democratic demonstrators in a city of 9 million and a country of nearly 300 million.

† Clausewitz had noted already in the early 1800s that it had become "impossible to obtain possession of a great country with a European civilization otherwise than by internal division." Carl von Clausewitz, *The Campaign of 1812 in Russia* (London, 1843), 184.

caused the Soviet Union in the sixty years that followed Lenin's death to exhaust itself in entirely unnecessary domestic and foreign conflicts that eviscerated her both physically and spiritually.

The failure of communism, which since 1991 is no longer in dispute, having been conceded even by the ex-leaders of the ex-Soviet Union, is often blamed on human beings' falling short of its allegedly lofty ideals. Even if the endeavor failed, apologists say, its aspirations were noble and the attempt worthwhile. In support of this claim, they could cite the Roman poet Propertius: "*In magnis et voluisse sat est*"—"In great endeavors, even to want is enough." But how great could such an endeavor be if it was so at odds with ordinary human desires that pursuing it required recourse to the most inhuman methods imaginable?

The Communist experiment is often labeled "utopian." The term, however, is applicable only in the limited sense in which Engels used it to criticize socialists who did not accept his and Marx's "scientific" doctrines, by making in their visions no allowance for historic and social realities. Lenin himself was forced to admit toward the end of his life that the Bolsheviks, too, were guilty of ignoring the cultural realities of Russia and her unpreparedness for the economic and social order that they tried to impose on her. The Bolsheviks ceased to be utopians when, once it had become obvious the ideal was unattainable, they persisted in the attempt by resorting to unrestrained violence. Although utopian fantasies, whether Plato's or Thomas More's or their modern imitators', did postulate regimentation and coercion, actual utopian communities always rested on the concurrence of their members in the task of creating a "cooperative commonwealth." The Bolsheviks, by contrast, not only did not care to obtain such concurrence but dismissed as "counter-revolutionary" every manifestation of individual or group initiative. They also displayed a constitutional inability to deal with opinions that were different from their own except by abuse and repression. For these reasons they should be regarded not as utopians but as fanatics. Since they refused to admit defeat even when it stared them in the face, they satisfied Santayana's definition of fanaticism as redoubling one's efforts after forgetting one's aim.

Marxism and bolshevism, its offspring, were products of an era in European intellectual life that was obsessed with violence. The Darwinian theory of natural selection was promptly translated into a social philosophy in which uncompromising conflict occupied a central place. "No one who has not waded through some sizable part of the literature of the period 1870–1914," writes Jacques Barzun, "has any conception of the extent to which it is one long call for blood, nor of the variety of parties, classes, nations, and races whose blood was separately and contradictorily clamored for by the enlightened citizens of the ancient civilization of Europe." No one embraced this philosophy more enthusiastically than the Bolsheviks: "merciless" violence, violence that strove for the destruction of every actual and potential opponent, was for Lenin not only the most effective but the only way of dealing with problems. And even if some of his associates shrank from such inhumanity, they could not escape the corrupting influence of their leader.

Russian nationalists depict communism as alien to Russian culture and tradition, as a kind of plague imported from the West. The notion of communism as a virus cannot withstand the slightest examination since, although an intellectual movement international in scope, it first took hold in Russia and among Russians: the Bolshevik Party both before and after the Revolution was overwhelmingly Russian in composition, acquiring its earliest base in European Russia and among Russian settlers in the borderlands. Indisputably, the theories underpinning bolshevism, notably those of Karl Marx, were of Western origin. But it is equally indisputable that Bolshevik practices were indigenous, for nowhere in the West has Marxism led to the totalitarian excesses of Leninism-Stalinism. In Russia, and subsequently in Third World countries with similar traditions, Marxism fell on a soil devoid of traditions of self-rule, observance of law, and respect for private property. A cause that yields different results in different circumstances can hardly serve as a sufficient explanation.

Marxism had libertarian as well as authoritarian strains, and which of the two prevailed depended on a country's political culture. In Russia, those elements in the Marxist doctrine gained an ascendancy that fitted the country's patrimonial heritage. The Russian political tradition since the Middle Ages was for the government—or, more precisely, the ruler—to be the subject and "the land" the object. This tradition fused readily with the Marxist concept of the "dictatorship of the proletariat," under which the ruling party claimed exclusive control over the country's inhabitants and resources. Marx's notion of such a "dictatorship" was sufficiently vague to be filled with the content nearest at hand, which in Russia was the historic legacy of patrimonialism. It was the grafting of Marxist ideology onto the sturdy stem of Russia's patrimonial heritage that produced totalitarianism. Totalitarianism cannot be explained solely with reference either to Marxist doctrine or to Russian history; it was the fruit of their union.

Important as ideology was, however, its role in the shaping of Communist Russia must not be exaggerated. If an individual or a group professes certain beliefs and relies on them as a guide to conduct, it may be said to act under the influence of ideas. When, however, ideas are used not so much to direct one's personal conduct as to justify one's domination over others, whether by persuasion or force, the issue becomes confused, because it is not possible to determine whether such persuasion or force serves ideas or, on the contrary, ideas serve to secure or legitimize such domination. In the case of the Bolsheviks, there are strong grounds for maintaining the latter to have been the case, because they distorted Marxism in every conceivable way—first to gain political power and then to hold on to it. If Marxism means anything, it means two propositions: that as capitalist society matures it is doomed to collapse from inner contradictions, and that this collapse ("revolution") is effected by industrial labor ("the proletariat"). A regime motivated by Marxist theory would at a minimum adhere to these two principles. What do we see in Soviet Russia? A "socialist revolution" carried out in an economically underdeveloped country in which capitalism was still in its infancy; and power taken by a party committed to the view that the working class, left to its own devices, is unrevolutionary. Subsequently, at every stage of its history, the Communist regime in Russia did whatever it had to do to beat off challengers, without regard to Marxist doctrine, even as it cloaked its actions in Marxist slogans. Lenin succeeded precisely because he was free of the Marxist scruples that inhibited the Mensheviks. In view of these facts, ideology has to be treated as a subsidiary factor—an inspiration and a mode of thinking of the new ruling class, perhaps, but not a set of principles that either determined its actions or explains them to posterity. As a rule, the less one knows about the actual course of the Russian Revolution, the more inclined one is to attribute a dominant influence to Marxist ideas.

For all their disagreements, contemporary Russian nationalists and many liberals are at one in denying links between tsarist and Communist Russia. The former refuse to acknowledge the connection because it would make Russia responsible for her own misfortunes, which they prefer to blame on foreigners—especially Jews. In this they resemble German conservatives, who depict Nazism as a general European phenomenon in order to deny that it had any antecedents in Germany's past, or that Germany bears any particular blame for it. Such an approach finds a ready audience among the people affected, since it shifts the responsibility for whatever went wrong onto others.

Liberal and radical intellectuals—not so much in Russia as abroad—similarly deny affinities between communism and tsarism because that would make the entire Revolution a costly and pointless blunder. They prefer to focus on the declared objectives of the Communists and compare them with the realities of tsarism. This procedure does produce a glaring contrast. The picture, of course, changes substantially as soon as one compares Communist and tsarist realities.

The affinities between the regime of Lenin and traditional Russia were noticed by more than one contemporary, among them the historian Paul Miliukov, the philosopher Nicholas Berdiaev, the veteran socialist Paul Akselrod, and the novelist Boris Pilniak. According to Miliukov, bolshevism had two aspects:

> One is international; the other is genuinely Russian. The international aspect of Bolshevism is due to its origin in a very advanced European theory. Its purely Russian aspect is chiefly concerned with its practice, which is deeply rooted in Russian reality and, far from breaking with the "ancien regime," reasserts Russia's past in the present. As geological upheavals bring the lower strata of the earth to the surface as evidence of the early ages of our planet, so Russian Bolshevism, by discarding the thin upper social layer, has laid bare the uncultured and unorganized substratum of Russian historical life.

Berdiaev, who viewed the Revolution primarily in spiritual terms, denied that Russia even had a Revolution: "All of the past is repeating itself and acts only behind new masks."

Even someone entirely ignorant of Russia should find it inconceivable that on a single day, October 25, 1917, in consequence of an armed putsch, the course of the thousand-year-old history of a vast and populous country could undergo complete transformation. The same people, inhabiting the same territory, speaking the same language, heirs to a common past, could hardly have been fashioned into different creatures by a sudden change of government. It takes great faith in the power of decrees, even decrees backed by physical force, to believe in the possibility of such drastic mutation, unknown to nature. Only by viewing human beings as inert matter entirely molded by the environment could such an absurdity even be entertained.

To analyze the continuities between the two systems, we shall have reference to the concept of patrimonialism, which underpinned the Muscovite government and in many ways survived in the institutions and political culture of Russia to the end of the old regime.

Tsarist patrimonialism rested on four pillars: (1) autocracy—that is, personal rule unconstrained by either constitution or representative bodies; (2) the autocrat's ownership of the country's resources, which is to say, the virtual absence of private property; (3) the autocrat's right to demand unlimited services from his subjects, resulting in the lack of either collective or individual rights; and (4) state control of information. A comparison of tsarist rule at its zenith with the Communist regime as it looked by the time of Lenin's death reveals unmistakable affinities.

To begin with, autocracy. Traditionally, the Russian monarch concentrated in his hands full legislative and executive powers and exercised them without interference from external bodies. He administered with the help of a service nobility and a bureaucracy that owed allegiance to his person rather than to the nation or the state. Lenin from his first day in office instinctively followed this model. Although as a concession to the ideal of democracy he gave the country a constitution and representative bodies, they performed purely ceremonial functions, since the constitution was not binding on the Communist Party, the country's true ruler, and the Soviet counterpart of a parliament was not elected but handpicked by the same party. In the performance of his duties, Lenin resembled the most autocratic of the tsars—Peter I and Nicholas I—in that he insisted on personally attending to the most trifling details of state affairs, as if the country were his private domain.

As had been the case with his Muscovite forerunners, the Soviet ruler claimed title to the country's productive and income-producing wealth. Beginning with decrees nationalizing land and industries, the government took over all assets except articles of purely personal use; and since the government was in the hands of one party, and that party, in turn, obeyed the will of its leader, Lenin was de facto owner of the country's material resources. (De jure ownership lay with the "people," defined as synonymous with the Communist Party.) Industries were run for the state by state-appointed managers. Their output, and, until March 1921, the product of the land, were disposed of as the Kremlin saw fit. Urban real estate was nationalized. With private commerce outlawed (until 1921 and again after 1928), the Soviet regime controlled all legitimate wholesale and retail trade. These measures went beyond the practices of Muscovy, but they perpetuated its principle that Russia's sovereign not only ruled the country but owned it.

He also owned the people. The Bolsheviks reinstituted obligatory state service, one of the distinguishing features of Muscovite absolutism.

In Muscovy, the subjects of the Tsar, with minor exceptions, had to work for him either directly, in the armed forces or the bureaucracy, or indirectly, by cultivating his land or that conditionally leased to his servitors. As a result, the entire population was bonded to the Crown. Its manumission began in 1762, when the gentry were given the right to retire into private life and concluded ninety-nine years later with the liberation of the serfs. The Bolsheviks promptly revived the Muscovite practice, unknown in any other country, of requiring every citizen to work for the state: the so-called "universal labor obligation" introduced in January 1918 and enforced, according to Lenin's instructions, by the threat of execution, would have been perfectly understandable to a seventeenth-century Russian. In regard to peasants, the Bolsheviks revived also the practice of *tiaglo*, or forced labor, such as lumbering and carting, for which they received no compensation. As in seventeenth-century Russia, no inhabitant was allowed to leave the country without permission.

The Communist bureaucracy, both that employed by the Party and that by the state, quite naturally slipped into the ways of its tsarist predecessor. A service class with duties and privileges but no inherent rights, it constituted a closed and minutely graded caste accountable exclusively to its superiors. Like the tsarist bureaucracy, it stood above the law. It also operated without *glasnost*—that is, outside public scrutiny, administering much of the time by means of secret circulars. Under tsarism, advancement to the topmost ranks of the bureaucratic hierarchy bestowed hereditary nobility. For Communist officials, advancement to the highest ranks was rewarded with inclusion in the rolls of the *nomenklatura*, which brought entitlements beyond the reach of ordinary servitors, not to speak of the common people—the Communist equivalent of a service nobility. The Soviet bureaucracy, like the tsarist, did not tolerate administrative bodies outside its control and made certain they were promptly "statified"—that is, integrated into its chain of command. This it did to the soviets, the new regime's putative legislative organs, and to the trade unions, agencies of its equally putative "ruling class."

That the Communist bureaucracy should so quickly adapt old ways is not surprising, given that the new regime in so many respects continued old habits. Continuity was facilitated by the fact that a high percentage of Soviet administrative posts were staffed by ex-tsarist functionaries, who brought with them and communicated to Communist newcomers habits acquired in the tsarist service.

The security police was another important organization that the Bolsheviks adopted from tsarism, since they had no other prototype for what became a central institution of totalitarianism. Tsarist Russia was unique in that she alone had two police formations, one to defend the state from its citizens, the other to protect citizens from one another. State crimes were very loosely defined, little distinction being drawn between intention and deed. The tsarist state police developed sophisticated methods of surveillance, infiltrating society through a network of paid informers and opposition parties with the help of professional agents. The tsarist Department of Police had the unique authority to impose administrative exile for crimes that were not crimes in any other European country, such as expressing a desire for change in the political system. Through a variety of prerogatives granted it in the aftermath of the assassination of Alexander II, the tsarist police between 1881 and 1905 virtually ruled Russia. Its methods were all too familiar to Russian revolutionaries who, on coming to power, adopted them and turned them against their enemies. The Cheka and its successors assimilated the practices of the tsarist state police to such an extent that as late as the 1980s, the KGB distributed to its staff manuals prepared by the Okhrana nearly a century earlier.

Finally, as concerns censorship. In the first half of the nineteenth century, Russia was the only European country to enforce preventive censorship. In the 1860s censorship was eased and in 1906 it was abolished. The Bolsheviks promptly revived the most oppressive tsarist practices, shutting down every publication that did not support their regime and subjecting all forms of intellectual and artistic expression to preventive censorship. They also nationalized all publishing enterprises. These procedures went back to the practices of Muscovy; they, too, had no European equivalent.

In all these instances the Bolsheviks found models not in the writings of Marx, Engels, or other Western socialists but in their own history; not so much the history described in books but that which they had experienced in their own persons while fighting tsarism under the regime of Reinforced and Extraordinary Safeguard instituted in the 1880s to deter the revolutionary intelligentsia. These practices they justified with arguments borrowed from socialist literature, which gave them a mandate to behave with a brutality and ruthlessness that far exceeded anything known under tsarism, for tsarism was inhibited by the desire to be viewed favorably by Europe whereas the Bolsheviks treated Europe as an enemy.

It is not that the Bolsheviks wanted to copy tsarist practices. On the contrary, they wanted to have nothing in common with them, to do the very opposite. They emulated them by force of circumstance. Once they rejected democracy—and this they did conclusively on January 5/18, 1918, by dispersing the Constituent Assembly—they had no choice but to govern autocratically. And to rule autocratically meant ruling the people in a manner to which they had been accustomed. The regime introduced by Lenin on coming to power had its immediate antecedents in the most reactionary reign of Imperial Russia, that of Alexander III, under which Lenin had grown up. It is uncanny how many of his measures replicated the "counterreforms" of the 1880s and 1890s even if the labels were different.

One of the most controversial issues arising from the Russian Revolution is the relationship of Leninism to Stalinism—in other words, Lenin's responsibility for Stalin. Western Communists, fellow travelers, and sympathizers deny any link between the two Communist leaders, insisting that Stalin not only did not continue Lenin's work but repudiated it. This view became mandatory in Soviet historiography after 1956, when Nikita Khrushchev delivered his secret address to the Twentieth Party Congress; it has served the purpose of disassociating the post-Stalinist regime from its despised predecessor. Curiously, the same people who depict Lenin's rise to power as inevitable abandon their philosophy of history when they come to Stalin, whom they represent as a historic aberration. They have been unable to explain how and why history should have taken a thirty-year detour from its otherwise predetermined and immutable course.

An examination of Stalin's career reveals that he did not seize power after Lenin's death but ascended to it, step by step, initially under Lenin's sponsorship. Lenin came to rely on Stalin in managing the party apparatus, especially after 1920, when the Party was torn by democratic heresies. The sources indicate that contrary to Trotsky's retrospective claims, Lenin depended not on him but on his rival to carry on much of the day-to-day business of government and to advise him on a great variety of issues of domestic and foreign policy. Thanks to this patronage, by 1922, when illness forced Lenin increasingly to withdraw from affairs of state, Stalin was the only person who belonged to all three of the ruling organs of the Central Committee: the Politburo, the Orgburo, and the Secretariat. In these capacities, he supervised the appointment of executive personnel to virtually all branches of the Party and state administration. Owing to the rules established by Lenin to forestall the rise of an organized opposition ("factionalism"), Stalin could repress criticism of his stewardship on the grounds that it was directed not at him but at the Party and therefore, by definition, served the cause of the counterrevolution. That in the last months of his active life Lenin developed doubts about Stalin and came close to breaking off personal relations with him should not obscure the fact that until that moment he had done everything in his power to promote Stalin's ascendancy. And even when Lenin became disappointed with his protégé, the shortcomings he attributed to him were not very serious—mainly rudeness and impatience—and related more to his managerial qualifications than to his personality. There is no indication that he ever saw Stalin as a traitor to his brand of communism.

But even the one difference separating the two men—that Lenin did not kill fellow Communists and Stalin did so on a massive scale—is not as significant as may appear at first sight. Toward outsiders, people not belonging to his order of the elect—and that included 99.7 percent of his compatriots—Lenin showed no human feelings whatever, sending them to their death by the tens of thousands, often to serve as an example to others. A high Cheka official, I. S. Unshlikht, in his sentimental recollections of Lenin written in 1934, stressed with unconcealed pride how Lenin "mercilessly made short shrift of philistine party members who complained of the mercilessness of the Cheka, how he laughed at and mocked the 'humanness' of the capitalist world." The difference between the two men lay in their conception of the "outsider." Lenin's insiders were to Stalin outsiders, people who owed loyalty not to him but to the Party's founder and who competed with him for power; and toward them he showed the same inhuman cruelty that Lenin had displayed against his enemies.*

Beyond the strong personal links binding the two men, Stalin was a true Leninist in that he faithfully followed his patron's political philosophy and practices. Every ingredient of what has come to be known as Stalinism save one—murdering fellow Communists—he had learned from Lenin, and that includes the two actions for which he is most severely condemned: collectivization and mass terror. Stalin's megalo-

---

* Indeed, Viacheslav Molotov, who had the longest career in the Communist Party apparatus of anyone and knew both Soviet leaders very well, declared that Lenin was certainly "more severe"— i.e., inhumane—than Stalin. F. Chuev, ed., *Sto sorok besed s Molotovym* (Moscow, 1991), 184.

mania, his vindictiveness, his morbid paranoia, and other odious personal qualities should not obscure the fact that his ideology and modus
operandi were Lenin's. A man of meager education, he had no other
model or source of ideas.

In theory, one can conceive a Trotsky, Bukharin, or Zinoviev grasping
the torch from the dying Lenin and leading the Soviet Union in a different direction than Stalin. What one cannot conceive is how they could
have been in a position to do so, given the realities of the power structure
at the time of Lenin's illness. By throttling democratic impulses in the
Party in order to protect his dictatorship, and by imposing on the Party
a top-heavy command structure, Lenin ensured that the man who controlled the central party apparatus controlled the Party and through it
the state. And that man was Stalin.

The Revolution inflicted on Russia staggering human losses. The statistics are so shocking that they inevitably give rise to doubts. But unless
someone can come up with alternate numbers, the historian is compelled
to accept them, the more so as they are shared alike by Communist and
non-Communist demographers.

The following table indicates the population of the Soviet Union
within the borders of 1926 (in millions):

Fall 1917: 147.6
Early 1920: 140.6
Early 1921: 136.8
Early 1922: 134.9

The decrease—12.7 million—was due to deaths from combat and epidemics (approximately 2 million each); emigration (about 2 million); and
famine (over 5 million).

But these figures tell only half the story, since obviously under normal
conditions the population would not have remained stationary but
grown. Projections by Russian statisticians indicate that in 1922 the population should have numbered more than 160 million rather than 135
million. If this figure is taken into account, and the number of émigrés is
deducted, the human casualties of the Revolution in Russia—actual and
due to the deficit in births—rise to 23 million; that is, nearly two and a
half times the fatalities suffered by all the belligerent countries in World
War I and a loss exceeding the combined populations at the time of the
four Scandinavian countries plus Belgium. The actual losses were heavi-

est in the age group sixteen to forty-nine, particularly in its male contingent, of which it had by August 1920—that is, before the famine had done its work—eradicated 29 percent.

Can one—should one—view such an unprecedented calamity with dispassion? So great is the prestige of science in our time that not a few contemporary scholars have adopted, along with scientific methods of investigation, the scientists' habit of moral and emotional detachment, the habit of treating all phenomena as "natural" and therefore ethically neutral. They are loath to allow for human volition in historical events because free will, being unpredictable, eludes scientific analysis. Historical "inevitability" is for them what the laws of nature are to the scientist. But it has long been known that the objects of science and the object of history are vastly different. We properly expect physicians to diagnose diseases and suggest remedies in a cool and dispassionate manner. An accountant analyzing the finances of a company, an engineer investigating the safety of equipment, an intelligence officer estimating enemy capabilities, obviously must remain emotionally uninvolved. This is so because their investigations have as their objective making it possible to arrive at sound decisions. But for the historian, the decisions have already been made by others, and detachment adds nothing to understanding. Indeed, it detracts from it; for how can one comprehend dispassionately events that have been produced in the heat of passion? "*Historiam puto scribendam esse et cum ira et cum studio*" ("I maintain that history should be written with anger and enthusiasm"), wrote a nineteenth-century German historian. Aristotle, who in all matters preached moderation, said that there were situations in which "inirascibility" was unacceptable: "For those who are not angry at things they should be angry at are deemed fools." The assembling of the relevant facts must certainly be carried out dispassionately, without either anger or enthusiasm; this aspect of the historian's craft is no different from the scientist's. But this is only the beginning of the historian's task, because the sorting of these facts—the decision as to which are "relevant"—requires judgment, and judgment rests on values. Facts as such are meaningless, since they furnish no guide to their selection, ordering, and emphasis: to "make sense" of the past, the historian must follow some principle. He usually does have it; even the most "scientific" historians, consciously or not, operate from preconceptions. As a rule, these are rooted in economic determinism because economic and social data lend themselves to statistical demonstration, which creates the illusion of impartiality. The refusal to pass judgment on historical events rests on moral values, too—namely, the silent premise that whatever occurs is natural and therefore right; it amounts to an apology of those who happen to win out.

Judged in terms of its own aspirations, the Communist regime was a monumental failure; it succeeded in one thing only—staying in power. But since for Bolsheviks power was not an end in itself but a means to an end, its mere retention does not qualify the experiment as a success. The Bolsheviks made no secret of their aims: toppling everywhere regimes based on private property and replacing them with a worldwide union of socialist societies. They succeeded nowhere outside the boundaries of what had been the Russian Empire in spreading their regime until the end of World War II, when the Red Army stepped into the vacuum created in Eastern Europe by the surrender of Germany, the Chinese Communists seized control of their country from the Japanese, and Communist dictatorships, aided by Moscow, established themselves in a number of recently emancipated colonial areas.

Once it had proven impossible to export communism, the Bolsheviks in the 1920s dedicated themselves to constructing a socialist society at home. This endeavor failed as well. Lenin had expected through a combination of expropriations and terror to transform his country in a matter of months into the world's leading economic power: instead, he ruined the economy he had inherited. He had expected the Communist Party to provide disciplined leadership to the nation: instead, he saw political dissent, which he had muzzled in the country at large, resurface within his own party. As the workers turned their backs on the Communists and the peasants rebelled, staying in power required unremitting resort to police measures. The regime's freedom of action was increasingly impeded by a bloated and corrupt bureaucracy. The voluntary union of nations turned into an oppressive empire. Lenin's speeches and writings of the last two years reveal, besides a striking paucity of constructive ideas, barely controlled rage at his political and economic impotence; even terror proved useless in overcoming the ingrained habits of an ancient nation. Mussolini, whose early political career closely resembled Lenin's and who even as Fascist dictator observed the Communist regime with sympathy, concluded already in July 1920 that bolshevism, a "vast, terrible experiment," had miscarried:

> Lenin is an artist who worked on humans as other artists work on marble or metal. But human beings are harder than granite and less malleable than

iron. No masterwork has emerged. The artist has failed. The task has proven beyond his powers.

Seven decades and tens of millions of victims later, Lenin's and Stalin's successor as head of Russia, Boris Yeltsin, conceded as much in an address to the American Congress:

> The world can sigh in relief. The idol of Communism which spread everywhere social strife, animosity, and unparalleled brutality, which instilled fear in humanity, has collapsed. It has collapsed, never to rise again.

Failure was inevitable and imbedded in the very premises of the Communist regime. Bolshevism was the most audacious attempt in history to subject the entire life of a country to a master plan, to rationalize everybody and everything. It sought to sweep aside as useless rubbish the wisdom that mankind had accumulated over millennia. In that sense, it was a unique effort to apply science to human affairs; and it was pursued with the zeal characteristic of that breed of intellectuals who regard resistance to their ideas as proof of their soundness. Communism failed because it proceeded from the erroneous doctrine of the Enlightenment, perhaps the most pernicious idea in the history of thought, that man is merely a material compound, devoid of either soul or innate ideas, and as such a passive product of an infinitely malleable social environment. This doctrine made it possible for people with personal frustrations to project them onto society and attempt to resolve them there rather than in themselves. As experience has confirmed time and again, man is not an inanimate object but a creature with his own aspirations and will—not a mechanical but a biological entity. Even if subjected to the fiercest dressage, he cannot pass on the lessons he has been forced to learn to his children, who come into this world ever fresh, asking questions that are supposed to have been answered once and for all. To demonstrate this commonsensical truth required tens of millions of dead, incalculable suffering for the survivors, and the ruin of a great nation.

The question of how such a flawed regime succeeded in maintaining itself in power for so long certainly cannot be met with the answer that, whatever we may think of it, it had the support of its own people. Anyone who explains the durability of a government not based on an explicit mandate of its citizens by its alleged popularity must apply the same rationale to every other enduring authoritarian regime, including tsarism—which survived not seven decades but seven centuries—and then still face the unenviable task of having to explain how tsarism, presumably so popular, collapsed in a matter of days.

. . .

In addition to demonstrating the inapplicability of scientific methods to the conduct of human affairs, the Russian Revolution has raised the profoundest moral questions about the nature of politics—namely the right of governments to try to remake human beings and refashion society without their mandate and even against their will: the legitimacy of the early Communist slogan, "We will drive mankind to happiness by force!" Gorky, who knew Lenin intimately, agreed with Mussolini that he regarded human beings as a metalworker regards ore. His was but an extreme expression of an attitude common to radical intellectuals everywhere. It runs contrary to the morally superior as well as more realistic principle of Kant's that man must never be used as merely a means for the ends of others but must always be regarded also as an end in himself. Seen from this vantage point, the excesses of the Bolsheviks, their readiness to sacrifice countless lives for their own purposes, were a monstrous violation of both ethics and common sense. They ignored that the means—the well-being and even the lives of people—are very real, whereas the ends are always nebulous and often unattainable. The moral principle that applies in this case has been formulated by Karl Popper: "Everyone has the right to sacrifice himself for a cause he deems deserving. No one has the right to sacrifice others or to incite others to sacrifice themselves for an ideal."

The French historian Hippolyte Taine drew from his monumental study of the French Revolution a lesson that he himself described as "puerile," namely that "human society, especially a modern society, is a vast and complicated thing." One is tempted to supplement this observation with a corollary—that precisely because modern society is so "vast and complicated" and therefore so difficult to grasp, it is neither proper nor feasible to impose on it patterns of conduct, let alone to try to remake it. What cannot be comprehended cannot be controlled. The tragic and sordid history of the Russian Revolution—such as it really was, not as it appears to the imagination of those foreign intellectuals for whom it was a noble attempt to elevate mankind—teaches that political authority must never be employed for ideological ends. It is best to let people be. In the words attributed by Oscar Wilde to a Chinese sage: There is such a thing as leaving mankind alone—but there never was such a thing as governing mankind.

Glossary

NOTE: Accents indicate the stressed syllables.
The letter "ë" is pronounced "yo" and stressed.

agit-próp	agitation and propaganda
agit-súd/y	agitational trial/s
besprizórnyi/e	abandoned child/children
bol'shák	head of peasant household
bunt	rebellion, mutiny
burzhúi	bourgeois
Cheká	Soviet secret police (1917–22)
chervónets/y	gold-based currency introduced in 1922
chin	official rank
chinóvnik/i	official/s; bureaucrat/s
derévnia/i	village/s
Dúma	lower house of the pre-Revolutionary Russian parliament
duván	division of loot
dvoevlástie	dyarchy
dvor	household; court
dvoriáne	gentry
dvoriánstvo	the gentry collectively, as a class
Fabzavkóm/y	Factory Committee/s (1917–20)
glásnost'	open government
glavk/i	subdivision/s of VSNKh
Glavlít	Central Censorship Bureau, created in 1922
Gosizdát	State Publishing House
GPU	Successor to the Cheka
gubkóm/y	Provincial Committee/s of Communist Party
inogoródnyi	peasant immigrant settled in Cossack region
intelligént/y	member/s of the intelligentsia
Ispolkóm	Executive Committee
iúnker	military cadet
Kavbiuró	Caucasian Bureau of Communist Party
kombédy	Committees of the (Village) Poor (1918)
Kompród	Commissariat of Supply

Komsomól	Communist Youth League
Komúch	Committee of the Constituent Assembly
kulák	prominent peasant, rural "exploiter"
Milrevkóm	Military-Revolutionary Committee
mir	peasant commune
muzhík/i	peasant/s
Narkomprós	Commissariat of Enlightenment
Naródnaia Vólia	People's Will
nomenklatúra/y	person/s in (or eligible for) high political or administrative positions
OGPU	successor to GPU
Okhrána	Imperial security police
peredýshka	breathing spell, respite
pogróm	beating and looting, usually of Jews
Proletkúlt	"Proletarian Culture" movement
pud	unit of weight equal to 16.38 kilograms
Rabfák/i	"Worker Faculty/ies"
Ráda	Ukrainian for "Soviet"
Revvoensovét	Revolutionary Military Council
soiúz	union; association
sovét/y	council/s
Sovnarkóm	Council of People's Commissars
STO	Council of Labor and Defense
tiáglo	in Muscovy, obligatory state labor
tsentr/y	same as *glavk/i*
ukáz	Imperial decree
vlast'	authority; government
vólia	freedom; license
vólost'	smallest rural administrative unit
VSNKh	Supreme Council of the National Economy
zémstvo/a	organ/s of provincial self-government

Chronology

This chronology lists the principal events dealt with in this book. Unless otherwise indicated, dates prior to February 1918 are given according to the Julian calendar ("Old Style"), which was twelve days behind the Western or Gregorian calendar in the nineteenth century and thirteen days behind in the twentieth. From February 1918 on, dates are given in "New Style," which corresponds to dates in the Gregorian calendar.

1899
February–March: strike of Russian university students

1902
Winter 1901–2: formation of Russian Socialist Revolutionary Party (PSR)

1903
Summer: formation of Russian Social-Democratic Labor Party (RSDRP); split into Menshevik and Bolshevik factions
July: Union of Liberation founded in Switzerland

1904
February: Japanese attack Port Arthur; beginning of Russo-Japanese war
November: Zemstvo Congress in St. Petersburg

1905
January 9: "Bloody Sunday" in St. Petersburg
September 5: peace between Russia and Japan signed at Portsmouth, N.H.
October: St. Petersburg Soviet formed; founding of Constitutional-Democratic (Kadet) Party
Mid-October: General Strike
October 17: October Manifesto

1906
April: Fundamental Laws (constitution) issued; convocation of Duma
July: Stolypin becomes Prime Minister

1907
June: new, restrictive electoral law for Duma

1911
September: Stolypin assassinated

1914
July 19/August 1: outbreak of war with Germany
August: Russians defeated in East Prussia

1915
Spring and summer: Germans invade and occupy Russian Poland
August: Nicholas II assumes command of Russian army and departs for the
        front; Progressive Bloc announces its program

1916
November: government under assault by Duma
December: murder of Rasputin

1917
February 23–27: demonstrations and mutinies in Petrograd
March 2: Provisional Government formed in agreement with Petrograd
        Soviet; Nicholas abdicates
April 3: Lenin arrives in Petrograd
April 21: first Bolshevik demonstrations in Petrograd and Moscow
May 4–5: Coalition Government formed
July 4: unsuccessful Bolshevik putsch in Petrograd; Lenin goes into hiding
July 11: Kerensky becomes Prime Minister
August 22–27: Kornilov affair
October 10–25: Bolsheviks seize power in Petrograd
October 26: Second Congress of Soviets, convened by the Bolsheviks, passes
        their Land Decree and other legislative acts; Bolshevik "Provisional
        Government" formed with Lenin as Chairman
November 21: Metropolitan Tikhon installed as Patriarch of Orthodox
        Church
November 12–30: elections to the Constituent Assembly
November 23/December 6: Russians, Germans, and Austrians agree on
        Armistice at Brest-Litovsk
December 6: Cheka established
December, late: formation of anti-Bolshevik White Army in the south

1918
January 5: Constituent Assembly meets and is dispersed that night
January 20: Communist decree on state-church relations
January 21: Soviet Russia repudiates foreign and domestic debts

January 28: Ukrainians proclaim independence
March 3: Soviet delegation signs German peace terms at Brest-Litovsk
Early March: Soviet government transfers capital from Petrograd to
    Moscow
May 1: inheritance abolished
May: Bolshevik offensive against the village begins
May 22: rebellion of Czechoslovak Legion breaks out
Summer: civil war in Russian countryside as peasants refuse to surrender
    grain
July 6: Left SR uprising in Moscow; following its suppression, non-
    Bolshevik newspapers and periodicals are shut down
Night of July 16–17: murder in Ekaterinoslav of Nicholas II, his family,
    family physician, and servants
July 29: Soviet Russia begins military conscription
August 27: Russo-German Supplementary Treaty signed with secret clauses
August 30: Fannie Kaplan shoots Lenin
September 4–5: Red Terror launched
November 17–18: Admiral Kolchak proclaimed Supreme Ruler of Russia in
    Omsk (Siberia)

1919
January: tax in kind imposed on peasants
March: creation of Politburo and Orgburo; Communist International
    founded
Summer: Denikin's White armies occupy the Ukraine
August–September: anti-Jewish pogroms in the Ukraine
October 13–14: Denikin's forces capture Orel
November: Red Army crushes Whites in the south and in Siberia

1920
February 7: Kolchak executed in Irkutsk
April 25: Poles and Ukrainians invade the Soviet Ukraine
May: Soviet delegation opens trade negotiations in London
July: Second congress of Communist International; Red Army invades
    Poland
August: outbreak of Antonov's rebellion in Tambov
Mid-August: Red Army defeated at gates of Warsaw and forced into full
    retreat
October 18: armistice with Poland
November: remnant of White armies evacuates the Crimea

1921
February: Red Army invades and conquers Georgia
February: mass strikes in Petrograd, followed by mutiny at Kronstadt naval
    base

March 15: Moscow abandons forcible requisitioning of food; beginning of
New Economic Policy
March 17: Red troops capture Kronshtadt
May: suppression of Tambov peasant rebellion
Summer-fall: catastrophic famine in much of Russia

1922
February–March: assault on church
April 3: Stalin appointed General Secretary
April–July: show trials of clergy in Moscow and Petrograd
April 16: Rapallo Treaty between Soviet Russia and Germany
May: Tikhon removed from Patriarchate
June 6: central censorship office created (Glavlit)
December: Lenin dictates his "Testament" and "Notes on the Nationality
Question"

1923
March 10: Lenin paralyzed

1924
January 21: Lenin's death

References

1. J. H. Elliott, *Imperial Spain, 1469–1716* (London, 1963), 73.
2. Richard Pipes, *Russia under the Old Regime* (London–New York, 1974), 303–4. Emphasis added.
3. A. A. Lopukhin, *Nastoiashchee i budushchee russkoi politsii* (Moscow, 1907), 32–33.
4. Alexander Herzen, *Sobranie sochinenii v tridtsati tomakh*, VII (Moscow, 1956), 74.
5. A. Herzen, *My Past and Thoughts*, III (London, 1968), 1215
6. The Russian Center for the Preservation and Study of Documents of Modern History (RTsKhIDNI), Fond 2, op.2, delo 492. The dating of this document is quite uncertain. It is possible that Lenin actually wrote it in early September 1918, after an unsuccessful attempt on his life.
7. RTsKhIDNI, Fond 2, op.1, delo 11800; written before November 21, 1919.
8. Zeev Sternhell, *The Birth of Fascist Ideology* (Princeton, 1994), p. 5.
9. F. Chuev, *Sto sorok besed s Molotovym* (Moscow, 1991), 176.
10. Ibid., 181.
11. RTsKhIDNI, Fond 41, op.1, delo 9, listy 79–80.
12. RTsKhIDNI, Fond 2, op.1, delo 24, 510.
13. Chuev, *Sto sorok besed*, 181.

Suggestions for Further Reading

Russia on the eve of the Revolution is depicted in Bernard Pares's *Russia and Reform* (London, 1907; reprint 1973) and *The Fall of the Russian Monarchy* (London, 1929; reprint 1988). A succinct account of the last years of tsarism is provided by Richard Charques, in *The Twilight of Imperial Russia* (Oxford, 1958; pb. 1965).

A general account of the Revolution, with emphasis on the political and military history of the period 1917–1920, is William Henry Chamberlin's two-volume *The Russian Revolution* (London-New York, 1935; reprint 1987). The so-called first revolution is recounted by Abraham Ascher in *The Revolution of 1905*, 2 vols. (Stanford, 1988–92).

Russia in World War I constitutes the subject of Norman Stone's *The Eastern Front, 1914–1917* (London-New York, 1975).

The standard history of the February Revolution is T. Hasegawa's *The February Revolution: Petrograd, 1917* (Seattle-London, 1981). The memoirs of Nicholas Sukhanov, translated and condensed by Joel Carmichael as *The Russian Revolution: A Personal Record* (Oxford, 1955; reprint 1984) are unmatched as a source. Alexander Kerensky's earliest recollections, *The Catastrophe* (New York-London, 1927; reprint 1971) give his version of events.

Leonard Schapiro's *History of the Communist Party of the Soviet Union* (New York, 1960; rev. ed., 1971) recounts authoritatively the activities of the Bolshevik Party from its foundation. Of the numerous biographies of the Bolshevik leader, David Shub's *Lenin* (New York, 1948) has special merit. Angelica Balabanoff's *Impressions of Lenin* (Ann Arbor, Mich., 1964) is very revealing. Boris Souvarine's *Stalin* (New York, 1939) has not been surpassed as an account of Stalin's early career.

Robert V. Daniels's *Red October* (New York, 1967) deals with the Bolshevik coup of 1917.

Leonard Schapiro in *The Origin of Communist Autocracy* (London-Cambridge, Mass., 1965, 1977) sheds light on the building of the one-party state in Russia.

The Red Terror is the subject of G. Leggett's *Cheka: Lenin's Political Police* (Oxford, 1981, 1986).

A succinct account of the Red-White struggle can be found in Evan Mawdsley's *The Russian Civil War* (London-Boston, 1987). The conflict between the Red Army and the peasantry at this time is treated by Vladimir Brovkin in *Behind the Front Lines of the Civil War* (Princeton, 1994).

The nationality question is discussed in Richard Pipes's *Formation of the Soviet Union: Communism and Nationalism, 1917–1923* (Cambridge, Mass., 1954; rev. ed. 1964).

Communist efforts to export revolution are recounted in Franz Borkenau's *The Communist International* (London, 1938; republished as *World Communism*, 1962).

Unfortunately, no books that are both reliable and comprehensive exist in English either on early Communist culture or on the treatment of religion.

Index

Since accenting in Russian follows no obvious rules, important and/or frequently cited proper names have been supplied with stress marks as appropriate; thus, "Miliukóv" should be accented on the last syllable. The letter "ë" is pronounced "yo" and stressed.

Page numbers in *italics* indicate illustrations.